DEVELOPMENT LAND
OVERAGE AND CLAWBACK

DEVELOPMENT LAND OVERAGE AND CLAWBACK

Christopher Jessel
Farrer & Co

JORDANS
2001

Published by
Jordan Publishing Limited
21 St Thomas Street, Bristol BS1 6JS

Copyright © Farrer & Co 2001
Reprinted May 2001
Reprinted November 2002
Reprinted May 2006

British Library Cataloguing-in-Publication Data
A catalogue record for this book is available from the British Library

ISBN 0 85308 669 9

Typeset by Mendip Communications Ltd, Frome, Somerset
Printed in England by Antony Rowe Ltd, Chippenham, Wiltshire

Contents

TABLE OF CASES   xiii
TABLE OF STATUTES   xxv
TABLE OF STATUTORY INSTRUMENTS   xxxi
TABLE OF EUROPEAN MATERIALS   xxxiii
TABLE OF ABBREVIATIONS   xxxv
INTRODUCTION   xxxvii

Chapter 1	**PURPOSE AND ORIGINS**	1
	1.1 Meaning and use	1
	1.2 Examples	2
	1.3 Terminology	3
	1.4 Development of the modern law	5
	1.5 Remote origins	6
	1.6 How overage works	7
	1.7 The forms of overage	8
	1.8 The outline of this book	9
	1.9 Practicalities and powers	9
	1.10 Development of the law	10

Chapter 2	**PROMISE TO PAY AND ASSIGNMENT**	11
	2.1 How promises work	11
	2.2 Position of the promisor	11
	2.3 Guarantees and undertakings	13
	2.4 Transfer of burden	14
	2.4.1 Proprietary methods	15
	2.4.2 Novation and release	16
	2.4.3 Benefit and burden	16
	2.5 Transfer of benefit	17
	2.5.1 Automatic transfer	17
	2.5.2 Untransferable overage	18
	2.5.3 Assignment – legal or equitable?	20
	2.5.4 Legal assignments	21
	2.5.5 Equitable assignment and trust	22
	2.5.6 Expectancies and future rights	22
	2.5.7 Agreement to assign	24
	2.5.8 Law of Property Act 1925, s 56	24
	2.5.9 Contracts (Rights of Third Parties) Act 1999	25

		2.5.10	Negotiable instruments	26
2.6	Perpetuity and limitation			27
2.7	Wagers			28
2.8	Penalty			29
2.9	Conclusion			30

Chapter 3   **POSITIVE COVENANTS**   33

3.1	General			33
	3.1.1	How positive covenants work		33
	3.1.2	Making positive covenants binding		34
	3.1.3	The original law of freeholds		37
	3.1.4	The modern law of freeholds		38
	3.1.5	Results of *Quia Emptores* 1290		39
3.2	Estate rentcharges			40
	3.2.1	How estate rentcharges work		40
	3.2.2	Nature of estate rentcharges		40
	3.2.3	Use of estate rentcharges apart from overage		41
	3.2.4	Use of estate rentcharges for overage		42
3.3	Rights of re-entry			44
	3.3.1	How rights of re-entry work		44
	3.3.2	Nature of re-entry		44
	3.3.3	Application of the rules		46
3.4	Restriction on the Register			47
	3.4.1	How restrictions on the Register work		47
	3.4.2	Fettering freedom of alienation		48
		(A)	The statutory context	48
		(B)	The *Oldham* case	49
		(C)	Charity land	50
		(D)	Trust land	50
		(E)	How far restrictions can be applied	51
		(F)	Land Registry Practice Leaflet 29	52
	3.4.3	Unregistered land		52
	3.4.4	A named person		53
	3.4.5	Expense		53
	3.4.6	Mortgages		53
	3.4.7	General		54
3.5	Conclusion			55

Chapter 4   **RESTRICTIVE COVENANTS**   57

4.1	Why restrictive covenants are used			57
4.2	How restrictive covenants work			58
4.3	Advantages			59
4.4	Conditions			59
4.5	Land of overage owner			60
	4.5.1	What if there is no land?		60
	4.5.2	What land?		61
	4.5.3	How much land?		62

4.6	Benefit of land not a bank account	63
4.7	Restrictive	66
4.8	The Lands Tribunal	68
4.9	Compensation ordered by the Tribunal	70
4.10	Equitable nature of covenant	70
4.11	Formalities of release	71
4.12	Conclusion	72

Chapter 5 **MORTGAGES AND CHARGES** — 75

5.1	How mortgages and charges work	75
5.2	Distinction between charges and mortgages	76
5.3	Legal or equitable?	76
5.4	Future payment	77
5.5	Clog on the equity	81
5.6	Priority	83
5.7	Continued involvement	85
5.8	Limitation and perpetuities	85
5.9	Charges and re-entry	87
5.10	Remedies	87
5.11	Trusts and charities	88
5.12	Conclusion	89

Chapter 6 **RANSOMS** — 91

6.1	How ransoms work		91
6.2	Ransom strip		92
	6.2.1	Location of the strip	92
	6.2.2	Occupation	93
	6.2.3	Rights of way – overage land as dominant	94
		Express grant	94
		Implied grant	95
		Physical capacity and improvement	96
6.3	Adjoining airspace and injunctions		98
6.4	Pipes, cables and other services		100
6.5	Air space over overage land		101
6.6	Subsoil and minerals		102
6.7	Light		104
6.8	Right of way where overage land is servient		105
6.9	Sporting and other profits		107
6.10	Statutory compensation		108
6.11	Conclusion		110

Chapter 7 **LANDLORD AND TENANT** — 111

7.1	How leases work		111
7.2	Leases and negative overage		112
	7.2.1	Statutory consent to improvements	114
		Business and farm business tenancies	114

		Landlord and Tenant Act 1927, s 19(2) and (3)	117
		Secure tenancies	117
		General	117
	7.2.2	Positive covenants in overage leases	118
	7.2.3	Break clauses	119
7.3		Leases and positive overage	119
	7.3.1	Capital payment	120
	7.3.2	Fines on assignment and renewal	120
	7.3.3	Overage receivable as income	123
	7.3.4	Turnover rents	125
		Mining leases	125
		Other turnover rents	127
7.4		Joining lease to freehold	128
	7.4.1	Enlargement	128
	7.4.2	Enfranchisement and first refusal	129
	7.4.3	Option to acquire the freehold	131
7.5		Leasehold structures to secure overage	132
	7.5.1	Intermediate leases	132
	7.5.2	Equitable leases	132
7.6		Conclusion	135
Chapter 8	**OPTIONS**		137
8.1		When options are used	137
8.2		Standard development option agreement	138
	8.2.1	Contents of agreement	138
	8.2.2	Overage in development agreements	139
8.3		Strict conditions	140
8.4		Reverse overage	140
8.5		How far options bind the land	141
8.6		Rights of pre-emption – how far they bind the land	143
8.7		Derivatives	145
8.8		Conclusion	146
Chapter 9	**VEHICLES**		147
9.1		How vehicles are used	147
9.2		Company	148
	9.2.1	How company overage works	148
	9.2.2	Powers of directors	149
	9.2.3	Class rights	150
9.3		Partnership	151
9.4		Joint venture	153
9.5		Limited Liability Partnership	153
9.6		Unincorporated association	153
9.7		Site reverters	154
9.8		Trust	154
	9.8.1	Use of trusts in overage	155
	9.8.2	Conditional and determinable interests	155

		9.8.3	Vested and contingent	158
	9.9		Use of express trusts in overage	160
		9.9.1	Documentation	160
		9.9.2	The trustees	160
		9.9.3	Trustees procedure and relations with beneficiaries	161
		9.9.4	Administrative powers	162
		9.9.5	Beneficial interest	163
	9.10		Tenancies in common	164
	9.11		Conclusions	165

Chapter 10   **GOVERNMENT CLAWBACK AND TAX**   167

	10.1		Government attitudes to development land disposals	167
	10.2		Clawback policy	170
		10.2.1	The Herstmonceux case	170
		10.2.2	Treasury guidelines	170
	10.3		Special rules	172
		10.3.1	Crown re-entry	173
		10.3.2	Restrictions on transfer and rents	173
		10.3.3	Privatised industries	174
		10.3.4	Local authorities	175
	10.4		Government claims to share in development value	175
	10.5		Planning gain	177
	10.6		Nationalisation of betterment for the community	178
		10.6.1	Planning	179
		10.6.2	Development charge in 1947	180
		10.6.3	Betterment levy in 1967	180
		10.6.4	Development gains tax in 1974	181
		10.6.5	Development land tax in 1976	182
		10.6.6	Vehicles	182
		10.6.7	The present position on development charges	183
	10.7		Current taxation	184
		10.7.1	Stamp duty	185
		10.7.2	Capital gains tax	186
		10.7.3	Income tax	189
		10.7.4	Valued added tax	190
		10.7.5	Inheritance tax	191
	10.8		Conclusions	191

Chapter 11   **NEGOTIATION AND DRAFTING**   193

	11.1		What needs to be considered	193
	11.2		The trigger event	193
		11.2.1	Uplift in value	194
		11.2.2	Start of development	196
		11.2.3	Realisation of value	196
		11.2.4	Choice of trigger	199

		11.3	Division of extra value	199
		11.3.1	Fixed price	199
		11.3.2	Gross or net?	200
		11.3.3	Ascertaining development value	201
		11.4	The relevant percentage	201
		11.4.1	General approach	202
		11.4.2	Illustrations from decided cases	203
		11.4.3	Successive tranches	206
		11.4.4	Development costs and expenditure	206
		11.5	Drafting issues	206
		11.5.1	Expression of overage intention	206
		11.5.2	Future changes in circumstances	208
		11.5.3	Maximising value	210
		11.6	Assignment	212
		11.7	Arrangements for payment	214
		11.8	Remedies	214

Chapter 12   **THE FUTURE**   217

12.1	How will overage develop?	217
12.2	Influences on the law	218
12.3	The attitude of the courts	218
12.4	Application of statutes	219
12.5	The nature of overage	220
12.5.1	Equitable nature of overage	221
12.5.2	Equitable nature of security	222
12.5.3	Completion of incomplete overage	223
	Equitable estoppel	224
	Constructive (or resulting) trusts	225
	Machinery	226
12.6	Treatment of overage rights	228
12.7	Sources of difficulties	229
12.8	Controlling overage	231
12.9	Reform	232
12.10	Social function	233

Appendix 1   **WORKED EXAMPLES**   235

Appendix 2   **PRECEDENTS AND DRAFTING**   243

1	PROMISE TO PAY AND POSITIVE COVENANT	244
Form 1.1	Positive covenant triggered by planning consent	244
Form 1.2(1)	Positive covenant by reference to disposal	249
Form 1.2(2)	Modification for allowable expenditure	255
Form 1.3	Restriction on the Register	257
Form 1.4	Deed of Covenant	257
Form 1.5	Valuation	259
Form 1.6	Re-entry	260

2	RESTRICTIVE COVENANT	260
Form 2	Restrictive covenant	260
3	CHARGE	261
Form 3	Deed of Charge	262
4	RANSOMS	263
Form 4.1	Airspace	263
Form 4.2	Top floor of office block	263
Form 4.3	Right of way	263
5	LEASEHOLD	264
Form 5.1	Negative overage lease at a premium	264
Form 5.2	Payment under lease	269
6	OPTIONS	270
Form 6.1	Option to acquire ransom, or freehold of lease or take release of right of way	270
Form 6.2	Reverse option	271
7	EXCESS PAYMENT ON SALE	272
Form 7.1	Excess payment	272
Form 7.2	Security	273
Form 7.2(1)	Equitable charge	274
Form 7.2(2)	Restriction on Register	274
Form 7.2(3)	Solicitor's undertaking	274
Form 7.2(4)	Costs	275
INDEX		277

Table of Cases

References are to paragraph numbers and Appendices.

AGB Research Ltd, Re [1995] BCC 1091, [1994] EGCS 73, [1994] NPC 56, ChD 3.3.3,
7.2.2
ANC Ltd v Clark Goldring and Page Ltd (2000) *The Times*, May 31 2.5.6
Ahmed v Kendrick (1987) 56 P&CR 120, [1988] 2 FLR 22, [1988] Fam Law 201,
CA 9.8.2
Air Jamaica Ltd v Charlton [1999] 1 WLR 1399, [1999] Pens LR 247, PC 2.6
Allnatt London Properties Ltd v Newton [1981] 2 All ER 290, (1980) 41 P&CR 11,
(1980) 257 EG 174 7.2.3
Alvis v Harrison (1990) 62 P&CR 10, HL 6.2.3
Amec Developments Ltd v Jury's Hotel Management Ltd [2000] NPC 125 11.4.2
Amsprop Trading Ltd v Harris Distribution Ltd [1997] 1 WLR 1025, [1997] 2 All
ER 990, [1996] NPC 154, ChD 2.5.9
Anchor Brewhouse Developments Ltd v Berkley House (Docklands) Developments)
Ltd [1987] 2 EGLR 173, (1987) 38 BLR 82, 284 EG 625 6.3
Ashworth Frazer Ltd v Gloucester City Council [1997] 1 EGLR 104, [1997] 26 EG
180, [1997] NPC 2, CA 7.3.3
Attorney-General v Blake [2000] 3 WLR 625, [2000] 4 All ER 385, [2000] 2 All ER
(Comm) 487, HL 4.5.1, 4.6, 4.7, 4.12, 11.5.1, 12.1, 12.5.3
Attwood v Bovis Homes Ltd (2000) *The Times*, April 18, ChD 6.4
Austerberry v Oldham Corporation (1885) 29 Ch D 750, 55 LJ Ch 633, 1 TLR 473,
CA 3.1.2

B&Q plc v Liverpool and Lancashire Properties Ltd [2000] All ER (D) 1059, (2000)
The Times, September 6 6.8
Bairstow Eves (Securities) Ltd v Ripley [1992] 2 EGLR 47, (1992) 65 P&CR 220,
[1992] NPC 78, CA 7.2.3
Bank of India v Transcontinental Commodity Merchants Ltd [1982] 1 Lloyd's Rep
586 5.4
Banner Homes Group plc v Luff Developments Ltd [2000] 2 WLR 772, [2000] 2 All
ER 117, (2000) *The Times*, February 17, CA 12.5.3
Bardsley v Baldwin. *See* Beardsley v Baldwin
Bass Holdings Ltd v Morton Music Ltd [1988] Ch 493, [1987] 3 WLR 453, [1987] 2
All ER 1001, CA 7.2.3
Batchelor v Kent County Council (1989) 59 P&CR 357, [1990] JPL 571, (1990) 154
LG Rev 493, CA 6.10, 11.4.2
Bater v Greenwich London Borough Council [1999] 4 All ER 944, [2000] L&TR 1;
sub nom Bater and Bater v Greenwich London Borough Council [1999] 2 FLR
993, CA 12.5
Baxendale v Instow Parish Council [1982] Ch 14, [1981] 2 WLR 1055, [1981] 2 All
ER 620 6.2
Beardsley v Baldwin (1741) 2 Stra 1151; *sub nom* Bardsley v Baldwin (1741) 7 Mod
Rep 417 2.5.10
Benito di Luca v Juraise (Springs) Ltd (1997) 79 P&CR 193 8.3
Beswick v Beswick [1968] AC 58, [1967] 3 WLR 932, [1967] 2 All ER 1197, HL 2.5.8

Bickford v Parson (1848) 5 CB 920, 17 LJCP 192, 12 Jur 377   3.1.2

Billson v Residential Apartments Ltd [1992] 1 AC 494, [1992] 2 WLR 15, [1992] 1
    All ER 141, HL   7.2

Bland v Ingram's Estates Ltd [1999] 2 EGLR 49, [1999] 25 EG 185, [1999] NPC 45,
    ChD; (2001) *The Times*, 18 January   5.9

Bleachers' Association's Leases, Re, Weinberg's Weatherproofs Ltd v Radcliffe
    Paper Mill Co Ltd. *See* Weinberg's Weatherproofs Ltd v Radcliffe Paper Mill
    Co Ltd

Bocardo SA v S and M Hotels Ltd [1980] 1 WLR 17, [1979] 3 All ER 737, (1979)
    39 P&CR 287, CA   7.2.3

Bowser v Maclean (1860) 2 De GF&J 415, 30 LJ Ch 273, 3 LT 456   6.6

Bracewell v Appleby [1975] 1 Ch 408, [1975] 2 WLR 282, [1975] 1 All ER 993   6.2.3,
    11.4.2, 12.3, 12.5.3

Brandt (William)'s Sons & Co v Dunlop Rubber Co Ltd [1905] AC 454, [1904–07]
    All ER Rep 345, 74 LJKB 898, HL   2.5.5

Briargate Development Ltd v Newprop Co Ltd; Same v Taylor Woodrow Property
    Co [1990] 1 EGLR 283, CA; [1989] 33 EG 42   2.5.2, 8.1, 11.2.3, 11.5.1, 12.1,
    App 2 form 1.2(1)

Brice v Bannister (1878) 3 QBD 569, 47 LJQB 722, 38 LT 739, CA   2.5.4

British Railways Board v Glass [1965] Ch 538, [1964] 3 WLR 913, [1964] 3 All ER
    418, CA   6.2.3

Brown v Heathlands Mental Health NHS Trust [1996] 1 All ER 133, (1996) 31
    BMLR 57, ChD   11.4.1

Brown & Root Technology Ltd v Sun Alliance and London Assurance Co Ltd [1997]
    EGLR 39, [1997] 18 EG 123, [1996] NPC 183, CA   3.4.2(*E*)

Buck v Robson (1878) 3 QBD 686, 48 LJQB 250, 39 LT 325   2.5.4

Bucknell v Vickery (1891) 64 LT 701, PC   5.4

Burrows & Burrows v Sharp (1991) 23 HLR 82, [1991] Fam Law 67, CA   12.5.3

Cambridge Credit Corporation Ltd v Lombard Australia Ltd (1977) 136 CLR 608   5.4

Campbell Connolly & Co Ltd v Noble [1963] 1 WLR 252, [1963] 1 All ER 237, 107
    SJ 135   2.5.6

Cannon v Villars (1878) 8 Ch D 415, [1874–80] All ER Rep 597, 47 LJ Ch 597   6.2.3

Cargill v Gotts [1981] 1 WLR 441, [1981] 1 All ER 682, (1980) 41 P&CR 300, CA   6.2.3

Carlill v Carbolic Smokeball Co [1893] 1 QB 256, 62 LJQB 257, 57 JP 325, CA   2.7

Catley Farms Ltd v ANZ Banking Group (NZ) Ltd [1982] 1 NZLR 430   5.4

Celtic Extraction Ltd (in Liquidation), Re; *sub nom* Official Receiver (as Liquidator
    of Celtic Extraction Ltd and Bluestone Chemicals Ltd) v Environment Agency;
    Bluestone Chemicals Ltd v Environment Agency [1999] 4 All ER 684, [1999] 2
    BCLC 555, [1999] 46 EG 187, CA   12.5

Chaloner (Inspector of Taxes) v Pellipar Investments Ltd [1996] STC 234, 68 TC
    238, [1996] NPC 23, ChD   10.7.2

Chambers v Randall [1923] 1 Ch 149, [1922] All ER Rep 565, 92 LJ Ch 227   4.5

Charrington v Simons & Co Ltd [1971] 1 WLR 598, [1971] 2 All ER 588, 22 P&CR
    558, CA   6.2.3

Chattock v Muller (1878) 8 Ch D 177   12.5.3

Childers Trustees v Anker (1997) 73 P&CR 458, [1996] 1 EGLR 1, [1995] NPC 113,
    CA   11.3.2

Christopher Moran Holdings v Bairstow. *See* Park Air Services plc, Re

Clarence Café Ltd v Comchester Properties Ltd (unreported)   3.3.3, 7.2.2

Cohen v Popular Restaurants Ltd [1917] 1 KB 480, [1916–17] All ER Rep 1113, 86
    LJKB 617   3.4.2(*E*)

Colehan v Cooke (1742) Willes 393   2.5.10
Co-operative Insurance Society Ltd v Argyll Stores (Holdings) Ltd [1998] AC 1,
   [1997] 2 WLR 898, [1997] 3 All ER 297, HL   7.2.2
Cooper v Stuart (1889) 14 App Cas 286, 58 LJPC 93, 60 LT 875   10.3.1
Cornick's Application, Re (1994) 68 P&CR 372, Lands Tribunal   4.2, 4.9, 11.4.2, 12.1,
   12.4, App 2 form 2
Cotton v Heyl [1930] 1 Ch 510, 99 LJ Ch 289, [1930] All ER Rep 375   2.5.6
Crabb v Arun District Council [1976] Ch 179, [1975] 3 WLR 847, [1975] 3 All ER
   865, CA   12.5.3
Crown Estate Commissioners v Dorset County Council [1990] 1 Ch 297, [1990] 2
   WLR 89, (1989) 60 P&CR 1   6.2.2
Crown Estate Commissioners v Possfund Custodian Trustees Ltd [1996] EGCS 172,
   ChD   2.8, 7.3.4
Croydon (Unique) Ltd v Wright [1999] 4 All ER 257, [1999] 3 EGLR 28, [1999] 40
   EG 189, CA   5.9

Da Costa, Re, Clarke v Church of England Collegiate School of St Peter [1912] 1 Ch
   337, 81 LJ Ch 293, 28 TLR 189   9.8.2
Daniells v Mendonca (1999) 78 P&CR 401, [1999] PLSCS 94, CA   6.3
Davenport (Inspector of Taxes) v Chilver [1983] Ch 293, [1983] 3 WLR 481, [1983]
   STC 426   2.5.6, 10.7.2
Deakins v Hookings [1994] 14 EG 133   6.7
Dean v Dean [1891] 3 Ch 150, 60 LJ Ch 553, 65 LT 65   9.8.2
Dillwyn v Llewellyn (1862) 4 De GF&J 517, [1861–73] All ER Rep 384, 31 LJ Ch
   658   12.5.3
Doe d Freeman v Bateman (1818) 2 B&A 168   3.2.2
Driscoll v Church Commissioners for England [1957] 1 QB 330, [1956] 3 WLR 996,
   [1956] 3 All ER 802, CA   4.6, 4.7, 7.2, 12.3
Duke of Beaufort v Patrick (1853) 17 Beav 60   12.5.3
Duke of Norfolk's Case, *sub nom* Howard v Duke of Norfolk (1681) 2 Swans 454, 2
   Rep Ch 229, 3 Cas in Ch 40   12.8
Dyke v Bishop of Bath and Wells (1715) 6 Bro PC 365   7.3.2

EMI Social Centre Ltd's Application, Re (1980) 39 P&CR 421, LT   4.6
Eardley v Granville (1876) 3 Ch D 826, 45 LJ Ch 669, 24 WR 528   6.3, 6.6, 12.3
Ebrahimi v Westbourne Galleries Ltd [1973] AC 360, [1972] 2 WLR 1289, [1972] 2
   All ER 492, HL   9.2, 11.5.2
Elsey v JG Collins Insurance Agencies Ltd (1978) 83 DLR (3d) 1, Sup Ct (Can)   2.8
Essex Furniture plc v NPI (unreported)   3.3.3, 7.2.2
Esso Petroleum Co Ltd v Kingswood Motors (Addlestone) Ltd [1974] QB 142,
   [1973] 3 WLR 780, [1973] 3 All ER 1057   3.4.2(*E*)
Exchange Travel Agency Ltd v Triton Property Trust plc [1991] BCLC 396, [1991]
   BCC 341   3.3.3, 7.2.2

Fairview New Homes plc v Government Row Residents Association Ltd [1998]
   EGCS 92, ChD   6.2.3
Farrage v North Wiltshire District Council. *See* Trustees of the Chippenham Golf
   Club v North Wiltshire District Council
Federated Homes v Mill Lodge Properties Ltd [1980] 1 WLR 594, [1980] 1 All ER
   371, (1979) 39 P&CR 576, CA   3.1.2, 4.3
Feist v Société Intercommunale d'Electricité Belge [1933] Ch 684   2.5.10

First National Securities Ltd v Hegerty [1985] 1 QB 850, [1984] 3 WLR 769, [1984]
    3 All ER 641, CA   9.8.2
Fisher & Gimson (Builders) Ltd's Application, Re (1992) 65 P&CR 312, [1993] JPL
    260, Lands Tribunal   11.4.2
Fleming v Self (1854) 3 De GM & G 997, 24 LJ Ch 29, 18 JP 772   2.2, 5.4
Fraser Pipestock Ltd v Gloucester City Council (1995) 71 P&CR 123, [1995] 2
    EGLR 90, [1995] NPC 26, ChD   7.3.3

Gadd's Land Transfer, Re, Cornmill Developments v Bridle Lane (Estates) [1966] Ch
    56, [1965] 3 WLR 325, [1965] 2 All ER 800   4.5.3
Gafford v Graham (1998) 77 P&CR 73, [1998] NPC 66, (1998) 142 SJLB 155, CA   4.6,
                                                                        4.8, 4.10, 11.5.1
Garner (Inspector of Taxes) v Pounds Shipowners & Shipbreakers Ltd [2000] 1 WLR
    1107, [2000] 3 All ER 218, [2000] STC 420, HL   2.7, 10.7.2
Gaynes Park Mansion Epping, Essex, Re. *See* Rainbow Estates Ltd v Tokenhold
General Credit and Discount Co v Glegg (1883) 22 Ch D 549   5.4
German v Chapman (1877) 7 Ch D 271, 47 LJ Ch 250, 42 JP 358, CA   4.7
Giles v County Building Constructors (Hertford) Ltd (1971) 22 P&CR 978   6.2.3
Gissing v Gissing [1971] AC 886, [1970] 3 WLR 255, [1970] 2 All ER 780, HL   12.5.3
Glegg v Bromley [1912] 3 KB 474, 81 LJKB 1081, [1911–13] All ER Rep 1138, CA
                                                                                      2.5.6
Goodson v Richardson (1873) LR 9 Ch App 221, 43 LJ Ch 790, 30 LT 142   6.3, 6.4
Governors of the Peabody Donation Fund v Higgins [1983] 1 WLR 1091, [1983] 3
    All ER 122, (1983) 127 SJ 596, CA   2.5.2
Graham v KD Morris & Sons Pty Ltd [1974] QD R 1   6.3
Greene v Church Commissioners for England [1974] Ch 467, [1974] 3 WLR 349,
    [1974] 3 All ER 609, CA   7.2.3
Greenwich Healthcare National Health Service Trust v London & Quadrant Housing
    Trust [1998] 1 WLR 1749, [1998] 3 All ER 437, (1999) 77 P&CR 133, ChD   6.8
Griffith v Pelton [1958] Ch 205, [1957] 3 WLR 522, [1957] 3 All ER 75, CA   3.1.2, 8.5

Halsall v Brizell [1957] Ch 169, [1957] 2 WLR 123, [1957] 1 All ER 371   2.4.3, 3.1.2
Hanning v Top Deck Travel Group Ltd (1993) 68 P&CR 14, [1993] EGCS 84,
    [1993] NPC 73, CA   6.2.2, 6.2.3
Hannon v 169 Queen's Gate Ltd [2000] 09 EG 179, (1999) *The Times*, November 23,
    ChD   7.1
Hare v Nichol. *See* Hare v Nicoll
Hare v Nicoll [1966] 2 QB 130, [1966] 2 WLR 441; *sub nom* Hare v Nichol [1966] 1
    All ER 285, CA   8.3
Harper v Burgh (1677) 2 Lev 206   3.1.2
Hemingway Securities Ltd v Dunraven Ltd [1995] 1 EGLR 61, (1996) 71 P&CR 30,
    [1995] 09 EG 322, ChD   3.4.2(*E*)
Herbert Smith v Honour (Inspector of Taxes) [1999] STC 173, [1999] BTC 44,
    [1999] NPC 24, ChD   10.7
Hertfordshire County Council v Ozanne [1991] 1 WLR 105, [1991] 1 All ER 769,
    (1991) 62 P&CR 1, HL   6.10, 11.4, 11.4.2
Hill v Booth [1930] 1 KB 381, [1929] All ER Rep 84, 99 LJKB 49, CA   3.1.2, 7.3.1
Holiday Inns Inc v Broadhead (1974) 232 EG 951; preliminary interlocutory
    application (1969) 19 December (unreported)   12.5.3
Holliday, Re [1922] 2 Ch 698, 92 LJ Ch 55, 127 LT 585   10.3.1

Hollis Hospital Trustees and Hague's Contract, Re [1899] 2 Ch 540, [1895–9] All ER
    Rep 643, 68 LJ Ch 673   12.8
Howard v Duke of Norfolk. *See* Duke of Norfolk's Case
Howard v Harris (1681) 1 Vern 33, 2 Ch Cas 147   5.5
Hughes v Pump House Hotel Co Ltd [1902] 2 KB 190, [1900–03] All ER Rep 480,
    71 LJKB 630, CA   2.5.4
Hunter's Lease, Re; Giles v Hutchings [1942] 1 Ch 124, [1942] 1 All ER 27, 111 LJ
    Ch 102   3.1.2
Hua Chaio Commercial Bank Ltd v Chiaphua Industries Ltd (formerly known as
    Chiap Hua Clocks & Watches) [1987] 1 AC 99, [1987] 2 WLR 179, [1985] 1
    All ER 110, PC   3.1.2

Inwards v Baker [1965] 2 QB 29, [1965] 2 WLR 212, [1965] 1 All ER 446, CA   12.5.3
Isenberg v East India House Estate Co Ltd (1863) 3 De GJ&S 263, 33 LJ Ch 392, 28
    JP 228   6.10
Island Holdings v Birchington Engineering Ltd (1981) July 7 (unreported)   12.5.3
Ives (ER) Investment Ltd v High [1967] 2 QB 379, [1967] 2 WLR 789, [1967] 1 All
    ER 504, CA   12.5.3

Jaggard v Sawyer [1995] 1 WLR 269, [1995] 2 All ER 189, [1994] EGCS 139, CA   4.6,
    4.10, 6.3, 6.8, 6.10, 7.2.2, 11.4, 11.4.2, 12.3, 12.5.3
Jelbert v Davis [1968] 1 WLR 589, [1968] 1 All ER 1182, 19 P&CR 383, CA   6.2.3
Jobson v Record (1998) 75 P&CR 375, [1998] 1 EGLR 113, [1998] 09 EG 148, CA   6.2.3
Joseph v Lyons (1884) 15 QBD 280, 54 LJQB 1, 51 LT 740, CA   2.5.3

Kelly v Barrett [1924] 2 Ch 379, [1924] All ER Rep 503, 94 LJ Ch 1, CA   4.5.3
Kelsen v Imperial Tobacco Co (of Great Britain and Ireland) Ltd [1957] 2 QB 334,
    [1957] 2 WLR 1007, [1957] 2 All ER 343   6.3
Kennet Properties Application, Re (1996) 72 P&CR 353, [1996] 45 EG 139, [1996] 2
    EGLR 163, Lands Tribunal   11.4.2
Kingston upon Thames Royal London Borough Council v Prince [1999] 1 FLR 593,
    (1999) 31 HLR 794, [1998] EGCS 179, CA   7.5.2
Kirby (Inspector of Taxes) v Thorne EMI plc [1988] 1 WLR 445, [1988] 2 All ER
    947, [1987] STC 621, CA   10.7.2
Knightsbridge Estates Trust Ltd v Byrne [1939] 1 Ch 441, [1938] 4 All ER 618, 108
    LJ Ch 105, CA   5.5, 5.8, 12.8
Kreglinger (G & C) v New Patagonia Meat and Cold Storage Co Ltd [1914] AC 25,
    83 LJ Ch 79, [1911–13] All ER Rep 970, HL   5.5

LM Tenancies 1 plc v Inland Revenue Commissioners [1998] 1 WLR 1269, [1998]
    STC 326, [1998] NPC 13, CA   10.7.1
Land Reclamation Co Ltd v Basildon District Council; Pitsea Access Road, Basildon
    [1979] 1 WLR 767, [1979] 2 All ER 993; *sub nom* Pitsea Access Road,
    Basildon, Essex, Re; Land Reclamation Co Ltd v Basildon District Council
    (1979) 38 P&CR 528, CA   6.2.3
Langevad v Chiswick Quay Freeholds Ltd; McAully v Chiswick Quay Freeholds Ltd
    (1998) 77 P&CR D39, (1999) 31 HLR 1009, [1999] 1 EGLR 61, CA   7.4.2
Leeming v Jones [1930] 1 KB 279, 99 LJKB 17, (1930) 15 TC 333, CA   10.7.3
Lester v Ridd [1990] 2 QB 430, [1989] 3 WLR 173, [1989] 1 All ER 1111, CA   7.4.2

Lim Teng Huan v Ang Swee Chuan [1992] 1 WLR 113, (1992) 64 P&CR 233,
    [1992] NPC 129, PC   12.5.3
Lind, Re [1915] 2 Ch 345   2.5.6
Linden Garden Trust Ltd v Lenesta Sludge Disposals Ltd; St Martin's Property Corp
    v Sir Robert McAlpine & Sons [1994] 1 AC 85, [1993] 3 WLR 408, [1993] 3
    All ER 417, HL   2.5.2
Loder v Gaden (1999) 78 P&CR 223, [1999] NPC 47, (1998) 78 P&CR D10, CA   6.2.3
Lomax Leisure Ltd, Re [1999] 3 WLR 652, [1999] 3 All ER 22, [1999] EGCS 61,
    ChD   3.3.3, 7.2.2
London and North Western Railway Co v Fobbing Levels Sewer Commissioners
    (1896) 66 LJQB 127, (1897) 75 LT 629, 41 Sol Jo 128   3.1.2
London and South Western Railway Co v Gomm (1882) 20 Ch D 562, [1881–5] All
    ER Rep 1190, 51 LJ Ch 530, CA   4.3, 4.7, 4.10, 8.5, 8.6, 12.5.1, 12.8
London County Council v Alan [1914] 3 KB 462, [1914–15] All ER Rep 1008, 12
    LGR 1003, CA   4.5.1
Lonsdale (Earl of) v Attorney-General [1982] 1 WLR 887, [1982] 3 All ER 579,
    (1983) 45 P&CR 1   6.6

McArdle, Re [1951] 1 Ch 669, [1951] 1 All ER 905, 95 SJ 284, CA   2.5.6, 2.5.7
McKay Securities plc v Surrey County Council [1998] EGCS 180, ChD   6.2.2, 6.2.3
Magdalen College, Cambridge (Masters and Fellows) Case (1616) 11 Co Rep 66b,
    [1558–1774] All ER Rep 236, *sub nom* Warren v Smith, Magdalen College
    Case 1 Roll Rep 151   10.3.1
Mainland v Upjohn (1889) 41 Ch D 126, 58 LJ Ch 361, 37 WR 411   5.4
Manchester Ship Canal Co v Manchester Racecourse Co [1901] 2 Ch 37, 70 LJ Ch
    468, 84 LT 436, CA   4.7, 8.6
Marren v Ingles [1980] 1 WLR 983, [1980] 3 All ER 95, [1980] STC 500, HL   10.7.2,
                                                                             12.5.1
Marson v Marriage [1980] STC 177, [1979] TR 499, (1979) 124 SJ 116   10.7.2
Marten v Flight Refuelling [1962] Ch 115, [1961] 2 WLR 1018, [1961] 2 All ER 696
                                                                             4.5.2
Mary Partington's Case (1613) 10 Co Rep 35b   9.8.2
Master v Hansard (1876) 4 Ch D 718, 46 LJ Ch 505, 36 LT 535, CA   4.5
Melville v Inland Revenue Commissioners [2000] STC 628   12.5
Metcalfe v Archbishop of York (1835) 1 My & Cr 547, 6 LJ Ch 65, 40 ER 485   5.4
Metropolitan Electric Supply Co Ltd v Ginder [1901] 2 Ch 799, 65 JP 519, 70 LJ Ch
    862   4.7
Mills v Blackwell [1999] NPC 88, (1999) 78 P&CR D43, (1999) 96(30) LSG 30, CA
                                                                             6.2.3
Mills v Silver [1991] Fam 271, [1991] 2 WLR 324, [1991] 1 All ER 449, CA   6.2.3
Milner's Safe Co Ltd v Great Northern and City Railway Co [1907] 1 Ch 208, 75 LJ
    Ch 807, 95 LT 321   6.2.3
Moran Holdings Ltd v Bairstow. *See* Park Air Services plc, Re
Mornington (Countess) v Keane (1858) 2 D&J 292, 27 LJ Ch 791, 4 Jur NS 981   5.4
Multiservice Bookbinding Ltd v Marden [1979] Ch 84, [1978] 2 WLR 535, [1978] 2
    All ER 489   5.4

Nationwide Building Society v Registry of Friendly Societies [1983] 1 WLR 1226,
    [1983] 3 All ER 296, (1984) 47 P&CR 221   5.4
National Provincial Bank Ltd v Ainsworth [1965] AC 1175, [1965] 3 WLR 1, [1965]
    2 All ER 472, HL   12.5

New Ideal Homes Ltd's Application, Re (1978) 36 P&CR 476, [1978] JPL 632,
    Lands Tribunal   11.4.2
Newbury District Council v Russell (1997) (unreported) (noted (1997) *Daily*
    Telegraph, March 8)   6.2.2
Newcomen v Coulson (1877) 5 Ch D 133, 46 LJ Ch 459, 36 LT 385, CA   6.2.3
Newis v Lark (1571) 2 Plowd 408, *sub nom* News v Lark Benl 196   9.8.2
News v Lark. *See* Newis v Lark
Nisbet & Potts Contract, Re [1906] 1 Ch 386, [1904–07] All ER Rep 865, 75 LJ Ch
    238, CA   11.2.2
Noakes & Co Ltd v Rice [1902] AC 24, 71 LJ Ch 139, 66 JP 147, HL   5.5
North Foreland Ltd v Ward (noted *Preston and Newsom on Restrictive Covenants*)   4.5.3
Northern Counties of England Fire Insurance Co, Re, Macfarlane's Claim (1880) 17
    Ch D 337, 50 LJ Ch 273, 44 LT 299   2.2

O'Brien v Bensons Hosiery (Holdings) Ltd [1980] AC 562, [1979] 3 WLR 572,
    [1979] 3 All ER 652, HL   12.5.1
Official Receiver (as Liquidator of Celtic Extraction Ltd and Bluestone Chemicals
    Ltd) v Environment Agency; Bluestone Chemicals Ltd v Environment Agency.
    See Celtic Extraction Ltd (in Liquidation), Re
Old Grovebury Manor Farm Ltd v W Seymour Plant Sales and Hire Ltd (No 2)
    [1979] 1 WLR 1397, [1979] 3 All ER 504, (1979) 39 P&CR 99, CA   2.5.2, 3.4.2(*E*)
Oldham Borough Council v Attorney General [1993] Ch 210, [1993] 2 WLR 224,
    [1993] 2 All ER 432, CA   3.1.4, 3.4.2(*B*)
Olympia and York Canary Wharf Ltd, Re; American Express Europe v Adamson
    [1993] BCLC 453, [1993] BCC 154, ChD   3.3.3, 7.2.2

P&A Swift Investments v Combined English Stores Group plc [1989] 1 AC 643,
    [1988] 3 WLR 313, [1988] 2 All ER 885, (1989) 57 P&CR 42, HL   3.1.2
Page (Inspector of Taxes) v Lowther [1983] STC 799, 57 TC 199, (1983) 127 SJ
    786, CA   5.11, 10.7.3
Pallant v Morgan [1953] Ch 43, [1952] 2 All ER 951, [1952] 2 TLR 813   12.5.3
Palmer v Carey [1926] AC 703, [1926] All ER Rep 650, 95 LJPC 146, PC   5.3
Paragon Finance plc v Thackerar & Co; Paragon Finance plc v Thimbleby & Co
    [1999] 1 All ER 400, (1998) 95(35) LSG 36, (1998) 142 SJLB 243, CA   12.5.3
Pardoe v Pennington; Vermuelen v Pennington (1998) 75 P&CR 264, CA   6.2.1
Park Air Services plc, Re; *sub nom* Christopher Moran Holdings Ltd v Bairstow;
    Moran Holdings Ltd v Bairstow [1999] 2 WLR 396, [1999] 1 All ER 673,
    [1999] 1 BCLC 155, HL   2.2, 3.3.3, 5.4, 7.2.2
Pascoe v Turner [1979] 1 WLR 431, [1979] 2 All ER 945, (1978) 123 SJ 164, CA   12.5.3
Patel v WH Smith (Eziot) Ltd [1987] 1 WLR 853, [1987] 2 All ER 569, (1987) 131
    SJ 888, CA   6.8
Pattison v Gifford (1874) LR 18 Eq 259, 43 LJ Ch 524, 22 WR 673   6.9
Peech v Best [1931] 1 KB 1, [1930] All ER Rep 68, 99 LJKB 537, CA   6.9
Penn v Miller (1927) 11 TC 610   10.7.3
Penn v Wilkins; Wilkins v Goldbourne (1975) 236 EG 203   6.4
Pennel v Payne [1995] QB 192, [1995] 2 WLR 261, [1995] 2 All ER 592, CA   7.2.3
Petrol Filling Station, Vauxhall Bridge Road, London, Re, Rosemex Service Station
    v Shellmex and BP (1968) 20 P&CR 1   5.5
Philips Hong Kong Ltd v Attorney-General of Hong Kong (1993) 61 BLR 41, (1993)
    9 Const LJ 202, (1993) *The Times*, February 15, PC   2.8

Pitsea Access Road, Basildon, Essex, Re; Land Reclamation Co Ltd v Basildon
    District Council. *See* Land Reclamation Co Ltd v Basildon District Council;
    Pitsea Access Road, Basildon
Plimmer v Mayor of Wellington (1884) 9 App Cas 699, 53 LJPC 105, 51 LT 475   12.5.3
Pole v Peake [1998] EGCS 125, [1998] NPC 121, (1998) *The Times*, July 22, CA   6.9
Ponsford v HMS Aerosols Ltd [1979] AC 63, [1978] 3 WLR 241, [1978] 2 All ER
    837, HL   7.3.3
Potter v Edwards (1857) 26 LJ Ch 468, 5 WR 407   5.4
Pritchard v Briggs [1980] 1 Ch 338, [1979] 3 WLR 868, [1980] 1 All ER 294, CA   8.6

R v Braintree District Council, ex parte Halls (2000) 80 P&CR 266, [2000] 36 EG
    164, [2000] EGCS 32, (2000) *The Times*, March 15, CA; [1999] EGCS 96,
    (1999) *The Times*, July 21, QBD   4.6, 7.4.3, 11.4.2, 12.4
R v Duchess of Buccleugh (1704) 6 Mod 150, 1 Salk 358   3.1.2
R v Plymouth City Council, J Sainsbury, Tesco Stores, ex parte Plymouth and South
    Devon Co-operative Society; *sub nom* R v Plymouth City Council, ex parte
    Plymouth and South Devon Co-operative Society (1993) 67 P&CR 78, [1993] 2
    PLR 75, [1993] 36 EG 135, CA   10.5
R v Worthing Borough Council and Secretary of State for the Environment, ex parte
    Burch (GH) (1983) 49 P&CR 53, [1984] JPL 261   10.2.2
R&A Millett (Shops) Ltd v Leon Allan International Fashions Ltd [1989] 1 EGLR
    138, [1989] 18 EG 107, CA   7.3.3
RCP Holdings Ltd v Rogers [1953] 1 All ER 1029   6.2.3
Raffaele v Raffaele [1962] WAR 238   12.5.3
Rainbow Estates Ltd v Tokenhold; *sub nom* Gaynes Park Mansion Epping, Essex, Re
    [1999] Ch 64, [1998] 3 WLR 980, [1998] 2 All ER 860, [1998] 2 EGLR 34,
    ChD   7.2.2
Ramsden v Dyson and Thornton (1866) LR 1 HL 129, 12 Jur NS 506, 14 WR 926   12.5.3
Razzaq v Pala [1997] 1 WLR 1336, [1997] 38 EG 157, [1997] BPIR 726, QBD   3.3.3, 7.2.2
Rhone v Stephens (Executrix) [1994] 2 AC 310, [1994] 2 WLR 429, [1994] EGCS
    50, HL   1.6, 2.4.3, 3.1.2, 4.1, 11.5.1, 12.5
Ridley v Taylor [1965] 1 WLR 611, [1965] 2 All ER 51, 16 P&CR 113, CA   12.5
Robinson, Re (1884) 27 Ch D 160, 53 LJ Ch 986, 51 LT 737, CA   2.5.2
Rochdale Canal Company v King (1876) 2 Sim NS 78   6.3
Rodick v Gandell (1852) 1 De GM & G 763   5.3
Rogers v Taylor (1858) 2 H&N 828   6.6
Rosling v Pinnegar; Pinnegar v Sewell and Norman (1986) 54 P&CR 124, (1987)
    137 NLJ 77, CA   6.2.3
Rudd & Son Ltd, Re; Fosters & Rudd, Re (1986) *The Times*, January 22, CA   5.4

S v UK (1984) (Application 10741/84) (1984) 41 DR 226, ECommHR   4.6
SJC Construction Co v Sutton London Borough Council (1975) 29 P&CR 322, CA;
    (1974) 28 P&CR 200, Lands Tribunal   4.6, 4.9, 11.4.2
Salvation Army Trustee Co Ltd v West Yorkshire Metropolitan County Council
    (1981) 41 P&CR 179   12.5.3
Santley v Wilde [1899] 2 Ch 474, 68 LJ Ch 681, 81 LT 393, CA   5.2, 5.5
Selby v Crystal Palace Gas Co (1862) 4 De GF & J 246   6.4
Sharp v Waterhouse (1857) 7 E&B 816, 27 LJQB 70, 3 Jur NS 1022   3.1.2
Sharpe, Re, ex parte Trustee of the Bankrupt's Property [1980] 1 WLR 219, (1979)
    39 P&CR 459, (1979) 124 SJ 147   12.5.3
Shaw (Tom) & Co v Moss Empires Ltd and Bastow (1908) 25 TLR 190   2.5.2

Shelfer v City of London Electric Lighting Co [1895] 1 Ch 287, [1891–4] All ER
    Rep 545, 64 LJ Ch 216, CA   6.3, 6.8, 12.3
Shiloh Spinners v Harding [1973] AC 691, [1973] 2 WLR 28, [1973] 1 All ER 90,
    HL   3.1.2, 3.3.2, 3.3.3, 12.5.2, App 1M
Sifton v Sifton [1938] AC 656, [1938] 3 All ER 435, 82 Sol Jo 680   9.8.2
Smith v River Douglas Catchment Board. *See* Smith and Snipes Hall Farm v River
    Douglas Catchment Board
Smith v Royce Properties Ltd [2000] EGCS 60, [2000] NPC 54   8.4
Smith and Snipes Hall Farm v River Douglas Catchment Board [1949] 2 KB 500;
    sub nom Smith v River Douglas Catchment Board [1949] 2 All ER 179, 113 JP
    388, CA   3.1.2
Snell & Prideaux Ltd v Dutton Mirrors Ltd [1994] EGCS 78, CA   6.8
Soltau v De Held (1851) 2 Sim NS 133, 21 LJ Ch 153, 16 Jur 326   6.8
South Eastern Railway v Cooper [1924] 1 Ch 211, [1923] All ER Rep 111, 93 LJ Ch
    292, CA   6.2.3
Spencer's Case (1583) 5 Co Rep 16a, [1558–1774] All ER Rep 68   3.1.2, 3.2.4, 7.3.1
Spiro v Glencrown Properties Ltd [1991] Ch 537, [1991] 2 WLR 931, [1991] 1 All
    ER 600   8.5
Stait v Fenner [1912] 2 Ch 504, [1911–13] All ER Rep 232, 81 LJ Ch 710   7.2.3
Standard Life Co Ltd v Greycoat Devonshire Square Ltd (2000) *The Times*, April 10,
    ChD   7.3.4
Stiles v Cowper (1748) 3 Atk 692   12.5.3
Stockport Metropolitan Borough Council v Alwiyah Developments (1983) 52 P&CR
    278, CA   4.6, 4.8, 4.9, 11.5.1
Stokes v Cambridge Corporation (1961) 13 P&CR 77, Lands Tribunal   6.10, 11.4, 11.4.2
Sudbrook Trading Estate Ltd v Eggleton [1983] 1 AC 444, [1982] 3 WLR 315,
    [1982] 3 All ER 1, HL   11.5.1, 12.5.3
Surrey County Council and Mole District Council v Bredero Homes Ltd [1993] 1
    WLR 1361, [1993] 3 All ER 705, [1993] NPC 63, CA; [1992] 3 All ER 302,
    (1991) 64 P&CR 57, [1991] NPC 125   4.5.1, 6.3, 8.2.2, 11.3.1, 11.5.1, 12.1, 12.5.3
Sutherland, Re, Winter v IRC. *See* Winter v IRC
Swift v Dairywise Farms Ltd [2000] 1 All ER 320, [1999] EGCS 137, [1999] NPC
    142, ChD   12.5
Swiss Bank Corporation v Lloyd's Bank Ltd [1982] AC 584, [1981] 2 WLR 893,
    [1981] 2 All ER 449, HL   5.2, 5.3, 12.5.2
Syndic in Bankruptcy of Salim Nasrallah Khoury v Khayat [1943] AC 507, [1943] 2
    All ER 406, PC   2.5.10
Syrett v Egerton [1957] 1 WLR 1130, [1957] 3 All ER 331, 101 SJ 869, DC   2.5.6

Tailby v Official Receiver (1888) 13 App Cas 523, [1886–90] All ER Rep 486, 58
    LJQB 75   2.5.6
Target Holdings Ltd v Priestly [1999] Lloyd's Rep Bank 175, (1999) 96(14) LSG 33,
    [1999] NPC 51, ChD   7.5.2
Tesco Stores Ltd v Secretary of State for the Environment and West Oxfordshire
    District Council [1995] 1 WLR 759, [1995] 2 All ER 636, (1995) 70 P&CR
    184, HL   10.5
Thamesmead Town Ltd v Allotey (1998) 30 HLR 1052, [1998] 3 EGLR 97, [1998]
    37 EG 161, CA   2.4.3
Time Products Ltd v Combined English Stores Ltd (1974) December 2 (unreported)   12.5.3
Tito v Waddell (No 2); Tito v Att-Gen [1977] Ch 106, [1977] 2 WLR 496, [1977] 3
    All ER 129   2.4.3

Trenberth (John) Ltd v National Westminster Bank Ltd (1979) 39 P&CR 104, (1979)
123 SJ 388, (1979) 253 EG 151   6.3
Trustees of the Chippenham Golf Club v North Wiltshire District Council; *sub nom*
Farrage v North Wiltshire District Council (1991) 64 P&CR 527, [1991] NPC
139, (1992) 156 LG Rev 863, CA   10.3.4
Tulk v Moxhay (1848) 2 Ph 774, [1843–60] All ER Rep 9, 18 LJ Ch 83 3.3.3, 4.1, 4.4, 4.7,
7.2, 12.4
Turquand's Case, Royal British Bank v Turquand (1856) 6 E&B 327, Exch Ch   9.2.2

United Land Company v Great Eastern Railway Company (1873) LR 17 Eq 158   6.2.3
United Scientific Holdings Ltd v Burnley Borough Council; Cheapside Land
Development Co v Messels Service Co [1978] AC 904, [1977] 2 WLR 806,
(1977) 33 P&CR 220, HL   8.3
Unity Joint Stock Mutual Banking Association v King (1858) 25 Beav 72, 27 LJ Ch
585, 6 WR 264   12.5.3

Vaux Group plc v Lilley [1990] 1 EGLR 60   7.3.2
Voyce v Voyce (1991) 62 P&CR 290, CA   12.5.3
Vyvian v Arthur (1823) 1 B&C 410   3.1.2

Walker v The Bradford Old Bank Ltd (1884) 12 QBD 511, 53 LJQB 280, 32 WR
644, DC   2.5.4
Walsh v Lonsdale (1882) 21 Ch D 9, 52 LJ Ch 2, 46 LT 858, CA   7.3.4, 7.5.2
Walsh v Secretary of State for India (1863) 10 HL Cas 367, 32 LJ Ch 585, 8 LT 839   2.6,
12.8
Wandsworth District Board of Works v United Telephone Co Ltd (1884) 13 QBD
904, 53 LJQB 449, 51 LT 148, CA   6.4
Ward v Kirkland [1967] Ch 194, [1966] 1 WLR 601, [1966] 1 All ER 609   12.5.3
Ward Construction (Medway) Ltd v Barclays Bank plc [1994] 2 EGLR 32   6.10
Warren v Smith, Magdalen College Case. *See* Magdalen College, Cambridge
(Masters and Fellows) Case
Weinberg's Weatherproofs Ltd v Radcliffe Paper Mill Co Ltd [1958] Ch 437, [1958]
2 WLR 1; *sub nom* Bleachers' Association's Leases, Re, Weinberg's
Weatherproofs Ltd v Radcliffe Paper Mill Co Ltd [1957] 3 All ER 633   7.2.3
Wellesley v Wellesley (1839) 4 Myl & Cr 561, 9 LJ Ch 21, 4 Jur 2   5.4
West v Sharp (1999) 78 P&CR D31, (1999) 96(19) LSG 29, CA   6.8
White v Richards (1993) 68 P&CR 105, [1993] RTR 318, [1993] NPC 41, CA   6.2.3
Williams v Earle (1868) LR 3 QB 739, 9 B&S 740, 37 LJQB 231   3.4.2(*E*)
Williams v James (1867) LR 2 CP 577, 36 LJCP 256, 16 LT 664   6.2.3
Wimbledon and Putney Commons Conservators v Dixon (1875) 1 Ch D 362,
[1874–80] All ER Rep 1218, 45 LJ Ch 353, CA   6.2.3
Winter v IRC [1963] AC 235, [1961] 3 WLR 1062, [1961] 3 All ER 855; *sub nom*
Sutherland, Re, Winter v IRC 105 SJ 929, HL   5.4, 12.6
Woollerton and Wilson Ltd v Richard Costain Ltd [1970] 1 WLR 411, 114 SJ 170   6.3
Wrotham Park Estate Co v Parkside Homes Ltd [1974] 1 WLR 798, [1974] 2 All ER
321, (1973) 27 P&CR 296   4.5.1, 4.6, 4.7, 4.10, 4.12, 6.3, 6.7, 6.8, 6.10, 7.2.2, 11.4,
11.4.2, 11.8
Wrotham Park Settled Estates v Hertsmere Borough Council [1993] 2 EGLR 15   11.4.1,
12.5.3

X v A (1999) 96(39) LSG 38, (1999) *The Times*, October 6, ChD   2.2

Yaxley v Gotts [1999] 3 WLR 1217, [2000] All ER 711, (1999) 79 P&CR 91, CA   12.5.3
Yenidje Tobacco Co Ltd, Re [1916] 2 Ch 426, [1916–17] All ER Rep 1050, 86 LJ
    Ch 1, CA   9.2, 11.5.2

Zetland (Marquess) v Driver [1939] Ch 1, [1938] 2 All ER 158, 107 LJ Ch 316, CA   4.5.2

Table of Statutes

References are to paragraph numbers and Appendices.

Access to Neighbouring Land Act
  1992 — 6.3
  s 1(2)(a) — 6.3
Administration of Estates Act 1925
  s 38 — 2.2
Agricultural Holdings Act 1986 — 7.2.1
  s 25(2)(b) — 7.2
  Sch 3, Case B — 7.2
Agricultural Tenancies Act 1995 — 7.2.1
  Pt III — 7.3.3
  s 1 — 7.2.1
  s 9(b) — 7.3.4
  s 13(3) — 7.3.3
    (5) — 7.3.3
  s 15 — 7.3.3
  s 21 — 12.5.3
  s 26 — 7.2.1

Bills of Exchange Act 1882 — 2.5.10
  s 9 — 2.5.10

Charitable Trusts Act 1853 — 3.4.2(*B*)
Charitable Trusts Amendment Act
  1855 — 3.4.2(*B*)
Charities Act 1960 — 3.4.2(*C*)
  s 29 — 3.4.2(*B*), 3.4.2(*C*)
Charities Act 1993
  s 36 — 3.4.2(*C*), App 1F
  s 38 — 5.11
Commons Registration Act 1965 — 6.9
Community Land Act 1975 — 10.6.5
Companies Act 1985
  s 35A — 9.2.2
    (1) — 9.2.2
    (2)(b) — 9.2.2
    (3)(b) — 9.2.2
    (4) — 9.2.2
  s 108(1) — 9.2.2
  s 125 — 9.2.3
  s 651 — 2.2
  s 653 — 2.2
  s 654 — 2.5.1

  s 654(1) — 2.5.1
Compulsory Purchase Act 1965
  s 7 — 11.4.1
  s 10 — 11.4.1
Contracts (Rights of Third Parties)
  Act 1999 — 2.5.3, 2.5.9, 7.5.1, App 2 form 4.3
  s 1(1) — 2.5.9
    (a), (b) — 2.5.9
    (2) — 2.5.9
    (3) — 2.5.9
Copyhold Acts 1841–1894 — 3.2.2
Countryside and Rights of Way Act
  2000 — 6.9
  s 68 — 6.2.2, 11.4.2
County Courts Act 1984
  s 138 — 5.9
Crown Estate Act 1961
  s 3(8) — 10.3.1

Development Land Tax Act 1976 — 10.6.5, 10.6.7
  s 1 — 10.6.5
  s 7(2) — 10.6.5

Ecclesiastical Leases Act 1571 — 3.4.2(*C*)
Electricity Act 1986
  Sch 3 — 6.4
Environmental Protection Act 1990 — App 1B

Finance Act 1965
  s 22(1) — 12.5.1
  Sch 6, para 23 — 10.6.4
Finance Act 1974 — 10.6.6
  s 38 — 10.6.4
  s 41 — 10.6.6, App 2 form 1.2(1)
  s 42 — 10.6.6, App 2 form 1.2(1)
Financial Services Act 1968
  s 75 — 9.9.3
Forfeiture Act 1870 — 3.3.2

Gaming Act 1845
  s 18   2.7
Gas Act 1986
  Sch 3   6.4
Grantees of Reversions Act 1540   3.1, 7.3.1
  s 1   3.2.4

Highways Act 1980
  s 278   10.1, 10.5
Housing Act 1985   1.3, 4.6
  Pt V   7.4.3
  s 97   7.2.1
  s 99A   7.2.1
  s 101   7.2.1, 7.3.3
  s 155   10.1
  Sch 6, para 5   12.4
         para 6   4.6, 12.4
Housing Act 1988   7.4.2
  s 13(1)(b)   7.3.3
  s 14(2)(b)   7.3.3
Housing Act 1996
  s 106   7.4.2
  Sch 9, para 1   7.4.2
Human Rights Act 1998   3.1.4, 6.4, 10.3.2
  s 6   10.3.2

Income and Corporation Taxes Act
  1988
  s 34   10.7.3
  s 776   10.7, 10.7.3
      (2)   10.7.3
          (a)   10.7.3
          (c)   10.7.3
Inheritance Tax Act 1984
  s 15(3)   10.7.5, 11.3.3
  s 104   10.7.5
  s 116   10.7.5
  s 212   7.5.2

Judicature Act 1875   7.5.2

Land Charges Act 1972
  s 2   4.11
      (5)(ii)   7.2
Land Commission Act 1967   10.6.3, 10.6.4,
                                               10.6.6
  s 27   10.6.3
  ss 27–35   10.6.3
  Schs 4, 5, 6   10.6.3

Land Compensation Act 1961
  Pt IV   10.2.2
  s 23   10.2.2
  s 26   10.2.2
Land Registration Act 1925   5.6
  s 28   11.6, App 2 form 3
      (2)   11.6
  s 50(1)   7.2
  s 58   2.4.1, 3.4.2(*A*), 3.4.7, 12.4
      (1)   3.4.2(*A*)
          (b)   3.4.4
      (2)   3.4.2(*A*)
  s 70   3.3.3, 3.4.3
      (1)(g)   7.5.2
  s 123   7.2.3
  Sch 2   3.4.2(*A*)
Landlord and Tenant Act 1730
  s 5   3.2.2
Landlord and Tenant Act 1927   7.2.1
  Pt I   7.2.1, 11.4.1
  s 1   7.2.1
  s 3(4)   7.2.1
  s 17   7.2.1
  s 19   7.2.1
      (1)   7.3.2
      (2), (3)   7.2.1, 7.3.2
      (4)   7.2.1
Landlord and Tenant Act 1954   6.2.2, 6.2.3,
                                        7.2.1, 7.3.3
  Pt I   7.4.2
  Pt II   App 2 form 6.2
  s 3   7.4.2
  s 34(1)(c)   7.3.3
      (2)   7.3.3
  s 38(1)   7.2.3
      (4)(b)   7.2.3, App 2 form 6.2
  s 63(2)   7.2.1
Landlord and Tenant Act 1987   11.2.3
  Pt I   7.4.2
  Pt III   7.4.2
Landlord and Tenant (Covenants)
    Act 1995   2.4.1, 3.1.2, 3.2.4, 7.3, 7.3.2,
                                        7.6, 11.6
  s 3   7.3.1
      (5)   7.5.1
  s 11   11.6
  s 16   11.6
  s 28(1)–(3)   7.3.1
Law of Property Act 1922
  s 145   7.3.2
  Sch 15, para 7(2)   7.3.2, 12.8
          para 12   7.3.2

Law of Property Act 1925   2.5.7, 3.4.2(*D*),
  9.8.2, 12.5.1
  s 1(2)(e)   3.3.3
  (6)   9.10
  s 2   9.8.2, 9.10, 11.5.3
  (2)   9.8.2
  (3)   5.4
  s 3   7.5.2
  (1)(b), (c)   5.4
  s 4   11.6
  (2)   2.5.2
  (3)   3.3.6
  s 5   7.5.2
  s 7   3.3.1, 3.3.2, 9.8.2
  (1), (2)   9.8.2
  s 26   3.4.2(*D*)
  s 27(2)   9.8.2
  s 28   5.4
  s 34   9.10
  s 50   5.5
  s 52   11.6, 12.5.1
  s 53   11.6
  (1)(b), (c)   2.5.5
  s 56   2.5.8, App 2 form 4.3
  (1)   2.5.8
  s 62   2.5.1, 3.1.2
  s 78   2.5.1, 4.3, 4.5, 4.5.2
  s 79   3.1.2, 4.5
  s 84   3.3.3, 4.2, 4.4, 4.6, 4.8, 7.2, 7.2.2,
  7.3.2, 7.4.1, 7.4.2, 11.5.1, 12.4,
  App 1L
  (1)   4.9, 11.4.2
  (i)   4.7, 4.9
  (ii)   4.2, 4.7, 4.9
  (12)   7.2
  s 85   5.2, 7.5.2
  s 94   5.6
  (1)   5.6
  (a)–(c)   5.6
  s 99   5.7
  s 101(1)(i)   5.10
  s 103   5.8
  s 104(2)   5.8
  s 114   2.4.1
  s 121   3.2.1, 3.2.3, 4.2.4
  (2), (3)   3.2.3
  (4)   3.2.3, 3.2.4
  s 136   2.5.4, 2.5.5, 11.6, 12.5.2
  (1)   2.5.4
  s 141   3.2.4, 7.3.1
  s 142   7.3.1
  s 144   7.3.2

s 146   3.3.2, 3.3.3, 7.2
s 149   12.8
  (3)   7.3.2, 7.5.2
s 153   3.1.2, 7.4.1, 7.6, App 2 form 5.1
  (8)   3.1.2, 7.4.1
s 186   8.6
s 205(1)(ix)   12.5.1
Law of Property (Amendment) Act
  1926   9.8.2
Law of Property (Miscellaneous
  Provisions) Act 1989   7.5.2, 8.5
  s 2   7.5.2, 8.5
  (1)   2.5.7
  (6)   2.5.7
Laws of Hammurabi 60–62   1.5
Leasehold Property (Repairs) Act
  1938   7.2
  s 1(5)(a)–(e)   7.2
  (6)   7.2
Leasehold Reform Act 1967   1.5, 7.4.2,
  11.2.3
  s 1AA   7.4.2
  (3)   7.4.2
  s 4   7.4.2
  s 10(4)   7.4.2
  (c)   7.4.2
  s 15(2)   12.4
  s 17   7.4.2
Leasehold Reform Housing and
  Urban Development Act 1993   11.2.3
  Pt I, Chs I, II   7.4.2
  s 34(9)(a)   7.4.2
  s 61   7.4.2
  Sch 6, para 4   11.3.2
  Sch 7, para 5   7.4.2
Limitation Act 1980   2.6, 3.2.3, 5.8
  s 20   5.8
  (3)   5.8
Limited Liability Partnerships Act
  2000   9.5
Local Government Act 1972
  s 123   10.3.4
  (1), (2)   10.3.4
Local Government and Housing Act
  1989
  Sch 10, para 3   7.4.2
Local Government (Miscellaneous
  Provisions) Act 1982
  s 33   3.1.2, 10.5
Local Government, Planning and
  Land Act 1980
  s 98   10.3.4

New Roads and Street Works Act
   1991   10.1
   ss 49, 50   6.4

Official Secrets Act 1911   12.5.3

Partnership Act 1890   9.3
   s 1(1)   9.3
Party Wall etc Act 1996   6.3
Perpetuities and Accumulations Act
   1964   3.3.3, 12.8
   s 1   2.6
   s 3   2.6
     (4), (5)   2.6
   s 9   8.4, 8.6, 12.8
     (1)   7.2.3, 7.4.3
     (2)   8.6
   s 10   2.6
   s 12   3.3.1
Planning (Consequential
   Provisions) Act 1990   App 2
                form 1.1(1)
Planning (Hazardous Substances)
   Act 1990   App 2 form 1.1(1)
Planning (Listed Buildings and
   Conservation Areas) Act 1990   App 2
                form 1.1(1)
Powers of Attorney Act 1971
   s 4   5.10
Prescription Act 1832   6.2.2, 6.2.3, 6.6

Quia Emptores 1290   3.1.2, 3.14, 3.1.5,
     3.2.2, 3.2.4, 3.4.2(*A*), 3.4.2(*B*),
     3.4.2(*C*), 3.4.2(*D*), 3.4.2(*E*),
     5.6, 9.9.4, 10.1, 10.3.1, 10.3.2,
              12.7

Rent Act 1968   7.4.2
Rent Act 1977   11.2.3
   s 70(3)(b)   7.3.3
Rentcharges Act 1977   3.1.5, 3.2.1, 3.2.4,
              3.5
   s 1(a)   10.3.2
   s 2(1)   3.2.4
     (3)(c)   3.2.1
     (4)   3.2.4
      (a), (b)   3.2.4
     (5)   3.2.3, 3.2.4
   s 14   10.3.2
Reverter of Sites Act 1977   9.7
Rights of Light Act 1959   6.7

School Sites Act 1841   9.7
Settled Land Act 1925   3.4.2(*A*), 3.4.2(*D*),
             5.4, 9.8.2
   s 13   9.8.2
   s 16   5.4
   s 29   3.4.2(*B*)
   s 47   12.4
   s 66   12.4
   ss 69–71   5.4
Social Security Administration Act
   1992
   s 187   2.5.2
Submission of the Clergy Act
   1534   3.4.2(*C*)
Superannuation Act 1972
   s 5(1)   2.5.2
Supreme Court Act 1981
   s 50   4.10, 11.4, 11.8

Taxation of Chargeable Gains Act
   1992
   s 21(1)   12.5.1
   s 99   9.9.3
Telecommunications Act 1974
   Sch 2   6.4
Tenures Abolition Act 1660   10.3.2
Town and Country Planning Act
   1947   10.6, 10.6.2, 10.6.6, 10.6.7
   Pt VI   10.6
   s 25   10.5
   s 61   10.6
   s 69   10.6.2
     (2)(a)   10.6.2
   s 70(2)   10.6.2
   Sch 3   10.6.2
Town and Country Planning Act
   1962
   s 37   10.5
   Sch 3   10.6.4
Town and Country Planning Act
   1971
   s 52   10.5
Town and Country Planning Act
   1990   App 2 forms 1.1(1), 5.1
   s 54A   10.6.1, 12.2
   s 55   10.6.1, App 2 forms 1.1(1), 5.1
     (2)   11.2.1
   s 57   App 2 form 1.1(1)
   s 59(2)(a)   App 2 form 1.1(1)
   s 65   11.5.3
   s 82   11.2.1
   s 106   4.5.1, 5.7, 8.2.1, 10.1, 10.5, 11.5.3,
              11.6, App 1L

Town and Country Planning Act
  1990 – *cont*
  s 171B 11.2.1
  s 299 7.2.1, 8.6, 10.2.2, 11.2.1, 11.5.3
Town and Country Planning
  (Crown Land) Act 1984 10.2.2
Trustee Act 1925 5.11, 9.8
  s 19 9.9.4
  s 26 2.2
  s 27 2.2
Trustee Act 2000 5.11, 9.9.3
  s 3(4) 5.11
  s 11 9.9.4
  s 28 9.9.3
  s 29 9.9.3
  s 34 9.9.4
  Sch 2 5.11
Trusts of Land and Appointment of
  Trustees Act 1996 3.4.2(*D*), 5.4, 9.8,
    9.8.2, 9.10, 11.5.3, 12.6
  Pt II 2.5.1
  s 6 5.4, 5.11, 9.9.4
    (6) 9.9.4
  s 7 9.9.5

s 8 9.9.4
  (2) 9.9.4
  (4) 9.9.4
s 9 9.9.3
  (8) 9.9.3
s 10 3.4.2(*D*)
s 11 9.9.3
s 13 App 1O
s 15(1)(d) 5.3

Value Added Tax Act 1983
  s 35A 10.1
  Sch 6A, para 1 10.1
Value Added Tax Act 1994
  s 35 10.7.4
  Sch 10, paras 1, 2 10.7.4

Water Industry Act 1991
  s 155 6.4
  s 156 10.3.3, 12.4
    (6) 10.3.3

Table of Statutory Instruments and Official Guidance

References are to paragraph numbers and Appendices.

Crichel Down Rules

10.2.2

D of E Circular 18/84   11.2.1, App 2 form 1.1(1)
D of E Circular 1 of 1997   10.5
D of E Planning Policy Guidance Note 6 (Town Centres and Retail Development),
    6 June 1996
    para 1.10

12.2

Foreign Compensation (Union of Soviet Socialist Republics) Order 1969,
    SI 1969/735

10.7.2

Government Accounting (Amendment No 8), Annex 32.1, March 1998   10.2.2

Insolvency Rules 1986, SI 1986/1925
    r 4.94
    r 6.114   2.2
    r 11.13   2.2
         2.2

Land Registration Rules 1925, SR&O 1925/1093   3.4.2(*A*), 3.4.2(*E*), 12.4
    r 235   9.9.4
    r 236   9.9.4
    r 306   9.9.1
    Sch 2, Forms 9–12D   12.5.2
Land Registration Rules 1996, SI 1996/2975   3.4.2(*A*)
Land Registry Practice Leaflet 29 (April 1999)   3.4.2(*F*)

References to Rating (Housing) Regulations 1990, SI 1990/434   7.4.2

Town and Country Planning (Environmental Impact Assessment) (England and
    Wales) Regulations 1999, SI 1999/293   12.2
Town and Country Planning (General Permitted Development) Order 1995,
    SI 1995/418
    art 4   8.6, 11.2.1
         10.6.1
Town and Country Planning (Use Classes) Order 1987, SI 1987/764   8.6 10.6.1, 11.2.1,
         App 2 form 1.1(1)

Table of European Materials

References are to paragraph numbers.

Convention for the Protection of Human Rights and Fundamental Freedoms (the
    European Convention)
    First Protocol   6.4
    Art 1   10.3.2
Council Directive 85/337 on Environmental Impact Assessment (OJ 1985
    L175/40)   12.2

Digest 19.13.24 (Ulpian)   1.5

Table of Abbreviations

ATA 1995	Agricultural Tenancies Act 1995
CA 1985/1989	Companies Act 1985/1989
C(RTP)A 1999	Contracts (Rights of Third Parties) Act 1999
HA 1985/1988/1996	Housing Act 1985/1988/1996
IR 1986	Insolvency Rules 1986
LLP	limited liability partnership
LPA 1922/1925	Law of Property Act 1922/1925
LP(MP)A 1989	Law of Property (Miscellaneous Provisions) Act 1989
LP(R)A 1938	Leasehold Property (Repairs) Act 1938
LRA 1925	Land Registration Act 1925
LRR 1925/1996	Land Registration Rules 1925/1996
LTA 1927/1954/1987	Landlord and Tenant Act 1927/1954/1987
LT(C)A 1995	Landlord and Tenant (Covenants) Act 1995
OFWAT	Office of Water Services
RA 1977	Rentcharges Act 1977
SLA 1925	Settled Land Act 1925
TA 1925	Trustee Act 1925
TLATA 1996	Trusts of Land and Appointment of Trustees Act 1996

Introduction

Your client is selling some land. The land has a present value for which a price is being paid but there is a chance that in a few years' time it may be worth more, perhaps because planning consent may be granted. There are good reasons to sell now but your client also wishes to have a share in the increase in value if and when it happens. How do you arrange it?

This book is about how a seller of land can both eat its cake, by having the proceeds of sale, and have it, by retaining future value. During the last 30 years or so, property lawyers have been developing methods of securing overage or clawback in this situation. Those methods have been evolving with practice and have been and are still being modified in the light of emerging problems. Therefore, this book is a report on law in the process of development, and at any moment a new court decision or a provision of an Act of Parliament could radically change the way the law is understood.

Because the law is evolving, lawyers do not always agree as to what the rules are. I expect that some readers of this book will not agree with the views I express. However, I hope that by setting out the main types of overage and the related rules passed down from previous centuries I can set out the outlines of the subject to encourage debate.

Overage is used by private landowners, by commercial companies, and by government. So far, few disputes about deliberately constructed arrangements for overage have reached the courts. There have, however, been many cases where land has become ripe for building and a former owner or a neighbour has tried to extract value from rights which were originally intended for purposes other than to secure future value.

There are different approaches to overage and different techniques to deal with it. Some are appropriate to one situation, some to another; there is no one method which applies to every set of facts. Any lawyer handling overage must be prepared to look at new approaches and adapt ideas to suit the special facts. This book will help those who negotiate overage and those who draft the provisions to understand the constraints on operation, and those who advise buyers or owners of land subject to overage, to understand the rights of their clients.

Chapter 1

PURPOSE AND ORIGINS

1.1   MEANING AND USE

The terms 'overage' and 'clawback' are used to describe the legal rights of a person who is not the owner of land to share in increased value usually arising from development.

The typical situation occurs where an owner of land needs to sell it. This could be in order to raise money (perhaps to pay off a loan), or because it is contaminated, or because of a policy to dispose of land which is surplus to operational needs. The land has long-term prospects for increase in value but these cannot be realised immediately. The land is therefore sold on the basis that if the value were to rise in the future the seller would be entitled to share. The rights of the seller then become an independent piece of property and can themselves be passed on to someone else.

Overage does not need to arise on a sale. Many of the cases concern the right of a neighbour to share in development value. Leases are a widespread method of reserving future value. Even where there is a sale, the overage can bind the land of the seller, not the buyer. There could be a grant of overage rights by a landowner in return for some benefit. For example, an owner could sell part of its land to a developer which is assembling a site from various landowners. The developer might include as part of the bargain a provision that if as a result of the construction of roads by the developer the owner's retained land rises in value the developer may share in that increased value. Furthermore, in theory, a landowner could sell overage rights over its own land for cash while retaining ownership of the land itself, although that would be a highly speculative investment for the buyer.

One important distinction is that between overage as such and the means of securing it. If a landowner wishes to have the right to a future share in added value of the land it is selling, it may instruct its lawyers to include an overage provision in the terms of sale. The owner is not directly concerned with the way that is done. The lawyers will have to prepare a scheme which will have the desired result. They may use a covenant or charge or lease or one of the other methods discussed in this book. That is a technical issue. The device used will be subject to its own, normally well-established, legal rules to be found in textbooks on covenants, mortgages or landlord and tenant. Little consideration may be given to separate rules about overage as such. Part of my purpose is to consider whether there are such rules and, if so, what they are. Overage may be understood as a contingent future interest,[1] and subject to the rules which apply to such interests. That may be different from the issue as to whether a covenant can be granted to secure a payment over freehold land, which is part of the law of covenants.

The typical overage arrangement is intended to cover development occurring between 10 and 30 years after the original sale. Overage can be used for shorter periods but, in that case, a development agreement of the type considered in Chapter 8 is more likely to be used (although such an agreement may contain overage provisions). If development is expected to be further in the future than, say, 30 years, the value of the right to share in future value, estimated at the date of the original sale, is likely to be worth less that the extra legal costs associated with the overage formalities.

1.2 EXAMPLES

It may be helpful to set out some typical situations where overage could be used. In Appendix 1 there are a number of examples and suggested solutions. The following are typical situations.

(1) A company has been occupying an industrial site which is now surplus to its needs. The site might be polluted and require remediation works but, even if not, planning consent could take several years. However, the company wants to dispose of the land now.

(2) A government department is selling off a surplus property such as an airfield or experimental farm. There is no immediate prospect of development but the department is required by Treasury Guidelines (see Chapter 10) to reserve what they call 'clawback'.

(3) A farming company is under pressure from a bank to reduce its borrowings. Its least productive land is on the edge of a village which has prospects of expanding but perhaps not for 20 years when a new road can be built and a new local plan agreed.

(4) A widow needs to sell her house and large garden to move into sheltered accommodation. Most of the nearby gardens have been built over but the local drainage system is inadequate for more use. The water company hopes to have a larger system in place in 10 years.

It will be evident from the range of cases discussed in this book that overage can arise in all sorts of situations. There can be straightforward commercial

---

1   See **9.8.3** and Chapter 12.

deals between property companies. There can be sales by local authorities who seek to control development and where overage is an incidental extra. Many cases are unforeseen, where land has been sold off and the seller or its successor tries to obtain a benefit from an unforeseen bargaining position. This book will consider the deliberate imposition of overage but the other cases can illustrate the legal principles involved.

1.3 TERMINOLOGY

The words 'overage' and 'clawback' are often used in the same sense. They are not legally defined terms of art but are words that have developed in recent years and are used by different people in different senses. In this book, overage will mean a payment in addition to the original price of land. It is commonly used in relation to additional rents under a lease where the lease might reserve a basic rent and then an additional payment dependent, for example, on turnover to be paid only if the tenant makes profits above a specified minimum.

The word 'overage' has been adapted from maritime law. Its meaning there is a payment for excess freight over the quantity intended to have been shipped or where more cargo is shipped than the quantities shown on the shipping document. In some cases, if a full cargo is not available for a vessel the shipping charterer will ask the owner to guarantee a minimum quantity of cargo and there will also be an option to lift the volume up to a full cargo known as overage. In such case, the freight for the extra cargo is usually paid for at a rate of half that of the basic charter party rate.

'Clawback' more usually refers to the situation where an initial payment has been forgone but may be required at a later stage. For example, when a public sector body such as a local authority is selling housing under the 'Right to Buy' under the Housing Act (HA) 1985, the buyer is entitled to pay a discounted figure but if he sells in the short term he will have to pay all or part of the discount back to the housing authority. The discount is 'clawed back'. The word 'clawback' is also used by the Treasury and politicians to mean what in this book is referred to as overage, possibly on the basis that the additional value in some sense really belongs to the government which is resuming its ownership, as contrasted with the private sector view that overage is an extra payment over and above the basic purchase price.

There is little accepted terminology in the law of overage. This book will use the following terms in a particular sense:

Overage   potential right to receive future payment in addition to original sale price to be paid when sold land later increases in value, for example on grant of planning permission or sale following development.

Overage land	land in respect of which overage may become payable.
Imposer	original seller who imposes overage.
Granter	original buyer who grants overage rights to imposer.
Overage owner	imposer or his successor having benefit of overage rights.
Landowner	granter or his successor as owner for the time being of overage land.
Recipient	overage owner or other person who receives overage payment when it becomes due.
Payer	landowner or other person liable to pay overage.
Trigger event	event, such as grant of planning consent or resale at value reflecting it or start of development which triggers overage payment.
Current use value	value from time to time of the overage land in its condition and use at the time of the original sale.
Development value	value of the overage land with the benefit of the uplift from the trigger event less the current use value at the date the trigger event occurs.
Market value	value of the overage land in the open market taking account of all factors known or reasonably expected, having regard to matters publicly available.
Hope value	element of value attributable to the possibility of a future uncertain event which could increase value.
Back land	land retained by the overage owner after sale of land adjoining a highway which does not itself have highway access and can be reached only through the developed land.
Vehicle	a legal structure such as a company or trust where the overage rights lie against the vehicle (or those such as trustees who control it) rather than against the land itself.
Positive overage	overage secured under an agreement which specifies how development value will be shared between the payer and recipient when the trigger event occurs.
Negative overage	overage arising from a situation where the overage owner has a veto on development of the overage land.

1.4 DEVELOPMENT OF THE MODERN LAW

The initiative for the imposition of overage derives from planning control. This in its modern form was introduced in 1948,[1] although its origins go back to the beginning of the twentieth century. Until the 1950s, transactions in all types of building land were fairly straightforward and typically involved a simple sale at a fixed figure. During the 1960s, planning permission became increasingly difficult to obtain and the value of land having the benefit of such permission increased dramatically so that land for housing could be worth a hundred times the value of the same land for agriculture. Furthermore, land prices could rise rapidly so that a farmer might sell land for 'a good price' at the time of sale only to find that the buyer resold after a few months at a handsome profit.

An early means of dealing with this for a landowner selling building land was by an option or conditional contract. Instead of selling the land outright for a single sum, the landowner would enter into an agreement with a developer under which the developer would obtain planning consent and then acquire the land for a price based on its new value. This suited the developer who depended on borrowed money and did not have to find that money until the value had increased but it did mean that the landowner might have to wait many years for payment. Landowners who needed money were therefore often prepared to sell the land at current value on the basis that if there was an uplift later they would be entitled to share. This was reinforced when a number of sites were sold on the basis of a particular planning consent and developers were subsequently able to obtain a more valuable one. Furthermore, in the case of large developments, it became the normal practice of local authorities to require land to be made available, for example for public open space. Many years later that space might be found to be no longer required and permission would be given for building on it. Particularly where the landowner continued to own land in the area, for example on sale of part of a family estate or a farm, the landowner saw no reason why he should not share in this uplift.

As a result, surveyors and solicitors increasingly advised their clients to include a provision for overage on any disposal. This is likely to have an effect on the initial price and it will always be a matter of judgment as to whether it is justified.

---

1   See **10.6.1**.

1.5 REMOTE ORIGINS

It is evident from what I have said above, that overage in its modern form depends on planning controls but the concept is very old indeed and a form of overage goes back to the very earliest laws of which we know, those of Ancient Babylon.

Babylon began as a small town of little importance but during the reign of its ruler, Hammurabi, from 1792 to 1750 BC, it became the centre of a great empire. Many people came to the city and the need arose to convert land to produce food. It appears that those having control of land were prepared to make agreements with farmers and gardeners for the land to be converted into a market garden on the basis that the gardener would get the initial benefit and, subsequently, the improved return should be shared equally. The law at the time was inadequate to provide remedies if someone entered into such an arrangement and broke it. Hammurabi enacted one of the first codes of law that has ever been known[1] to deal with this situation by providing remedies where the gardener had not carried out his part of the bargain and the land had not been improved to the benefit of the person who provided it. One cannot describe this relationship as a tenancy because this was over 1000 years before the invention of money but the principle is clear.

Going forward 2000 years, a different type of overage can be recognised under the Roman Empire. In the third century, the Empire was entering a period of crisis. Money was losing its value and there was growing pressure for wealthy people to invest all their money in land. Towards the end of that century, inflation got out of control but even in the earlier part it was beginning to have an effect. The Roman jurist Ulpian was an important legal adviser and was the praetorian prefect responsible for issuing and interpreting laws in Rome in the years around AD 220. He issued a formal opinion[2] stating that an arrangement under which a landowner sold land on the basis that if it was resold he or his heirs could share in any uplift in value was legally valid. It is evident from the reference to heirs that the arrangement he was considering was capable of lasting a long time.

Passing over the use of the power of medieval barons to charge for giving consent to sales, discussed at **3.3**, we come forward a further 1600 years to the period of the British Empire. There was a need for a good deal of substantial housing to be built in the middle years of the nineteenth century in England. Often the land was simply sold for this purpose but many landowners preferred to take a modest income from the land rather than receive a capital sum on the basis that they or their heirs would benefit later. The typical arrangement was to grant a lease for 99 years to a builder for an annual

---

1   Laws of Hammurabi 60 to 62.
2   Dig 19.13.24.

payment known as a ground rent which would be paid every year. The builder would then erect a house which was expected to last well over one hundred years and he would then sell the lease of the house to an occupier. The intention was that at the end of the 99 years the house would come back to the heirs of the original landowner who would then sell it for full value or charge a full rent. In 1954, Parliament intervened to give the occupiers of such houses the right to remain in occupation on payment of rent but this was not found sufficient and, in 1967, as a result of strong political pressure, Parliament passed the Leasehold Reform Act which allowed the owners of the house to buy out the owner of the land usually for a payment which was small by comparison with the value of the house.

These examples show the uses and restrictions of overage. It is used as in Ancient Babylon where resources are tight, as in Ancient Rome where values are changing and as in Victorian Britain where a landowner is prepared to take a long view. Its problems are shown as in Babylon that the person who agrees to make the improvement may in fact not do so, as in Rome that inflation may get out of control and simply affect the value of money as distinct from adding to the true value of land, and as in Victorian Britain that when the overage comes to be collected there may be strong objections on the part of the occupier. These are all problems which are faced by those who advise on overage.

1.6   HOW OVERAGE WORKS

There are two main types of overage – positive and negative.

Positive overage involves an agreement under which the imposer says to the granter 'if you wish you may realise additional value in the future and if you do you will make a payment to me'. In such a case, there needs to be a provision in the arrangement to calculate when the sum will be due and how much it will be.

This type of approach is used for unsecured promises, for positive covenants, for options in leases or with ransom strips, for mortgages and for special classes of shares in companies.

Negative overage on the contrary involves either a provision in the original disposal documents that the person acquiring and his successors will not develop or a mechanism, such as a ransom strip, under which the overage owner can prevent development. In such a case, there is no need for a provision for overage because the overage owner has control over the situation and can prevent development occurring and can therefore impose whatever terms it thinks fit.

This type of overage is used for restrictive covenants, for leasehold structures with tight covenants, for reverse options and for the normal ransom strip.

To some extent, the difference is similar to that between a condition precedent and a condition subsequent.[1] If a granter takes land on the basis of a restriction that it cannot be developed, that is a restriction going to the heart of what he acquires.[2] Just as under a condition precedent, the estate does not arise until the condition occurs, so the granter does not take title to the development value. By contrast, if he takes land with full development rights but is told that if he exercises some of his rights of ownership he must make a payment to the recipient, then that is like a condition subsequent. It is like saying that if an event occurs he will lose what he has. The law tends to uphold conditions precedent but discourage conditions subsequent and the same policy may be detected in overage.

1.7   THE FORMS OF OVERAGE

If overage were a mature legal topic, it would be possible to describe it according to different headings of substance such as the capacity of parties, the formalities for entering into overage, assignment of rights, termination of the arrangement and remedies.[3] But overage is not legally mature and is in an early stage of legal development.

Overage developed from many different sources of property law and, rather like the old forms of action, each type of overage has to be considered differently. Before the nineteenth century, litigation procedures were fragmented. Different rules applied to different types of proceeding such as the Writ of Right, Novel Disseisin, Writs of Entry, Trespass on the Case, Detinue, Account, Breach of Trust and other matters. Each type of proceeding had its own terminology, its own substantive rules, its own remedies and its own forms.

Much the same is true today of overage. Different rules apply to different types of overage and there is no unified set of rules that applies across the whole field.

The undeveloped state of the law is also indicated by the extent to which rights depend on whether or not a particular remedy, such as an injunction, is available or whether a claimant is limited to a remedy in damages. There can be different rules as to damages, depending on whether they are calculated according to common law rules or equitable rules and whether damages are awarded in their own right or as a substitute for an injunction. This emphasis

---

1   See **9.8.2**.
2   *Rhone v Stephens* [1994] 2 AC 310 at 317. See **4.1**.
3   Some issues are discussed in Chapter 12.

on remedies and procedure means that it can be difficult to give a coherent general account of the substantive law.

1.8 THE OUTLINE OF THIS BOOK

Following this chapter, each separate type of main overage system is described, setting out how each works and the main problems associated with it and some of the ways to get round those problems. There are then set out some of the special rules relating to public overage and then consideration of the practical issues of ascertaining the date of payment and the method of calculating the price. Finally, the broader issues and the likely attitudes of the courts to overage issues in general will be considered.

1.9 PRACTICALITIES AND POWERS

In what follows, it will normally be assumed that any imposer and granter are free to enter into any arrangement that can legally exist. For individuals and most companies that is true. However, many bodies such as trustees, local authorities and corporations either have limited powers or have special procedures and duties which may affect their ability to make these arrangements. There may, for example, be restrictions, either under statute or under a governing instrument, as to the length of time a lease or option can last. Consent may be needed from someone who is reluctant to give it. A limited power of investment may prevent the use of a charge. It will be for those advising or dealing with such bodies to check that the legal powers are available.

The perception of the market is also relevant. Even if a granter is prepared to enter into a particular arrangement, its funder may not be. If the overage method is a mortgage to secure future development value, the granter's bank may be unwilling to accept any form of second charge. A lender who will readily accept a re-entry clause in a lease may not do so on a freehold. Thus, certain devices may make land unable to be used as security and therefore unmarketable.

That point has to be faced at the outset. There is a generally held view that overage does not affect the price of land. That is not always true. Even if the prospect of future development is so remote that the duty to share it will not affect current values, the restrictions and paperwork associated with overage, or the need (eg in a restriction on the Register) to obtain the consent of the overage owner to a disposal, may mean that a buyer will offer less. That is a commercial reality to be considered when the intending imposer takes the decision to sell.

The key problem is one of security, and of competition for security. There is, in principle, no difficulty in taking a promise that if land becomes more valuable then that will trigger a payment to the recipient. As the land has extra value, that value can be used to fund the payment. Therefore, even if the payer has no spare cash apart from the land, the overage can eventually be paid.

But the granter may be an individual who has now died or become bankrupt, or a company which has been liquidated or dissolved and even if it still exists it may have sold on the overage land and have no present connection with it. Therefore, the recipient needs some recourse to the land itself, irrespective of changes in ownership.

Furthermore, there may be others with interests in the land. The current owner could have borrowed heavily from its bank, perhaps against the expectation that the land would rise in value. The bank will expect to be paid and will have taken a mortgage to protect its debt. How is the recipient to get ahead of the bank in the queue?

1.10 DEVELOPMENT OF THE LAW

The law of overage is developing fast and every few weeks there is a new case or important legal document. It follows that an account of the existing law can very quickly become out of date. Furthermore, many of the basic issues are unsettled and have never been tested in court or confirmed by Act of Parliament. Therefore, every statement in this book needs to be read with care. The views expressed are those of the author and others may well not agree either with the interpretation of the cases or with the underlying principles. Nevertheless, there is now a sufficient body of rules to be able to describe overage in general terms and to consider the way forward.

Chapter 2

PROMISE TO PAY AND ASSIGNMENT

2.1 HOW PROMISES WORK

This is the simplest form of overage. It operates as an arrangement directly between the original parties and has the minimum of formality. The original seller (the imposer) who intends to impose an overage payment on the buyer secures from the buyer (the granter) a grant of overage rights in the form of a promise that if the trigger event (such as the grant of planning permission) occurs the granter will pay the overage to the imposer. There is a simple contract debt payable at an unknown future time comprising an amount to be ascertained at that time. If the granter fails to pay then the imposer can sue for the money. The imposer then has all the normal remedies available to a judgment creditor. A promise does not, however, by itself carry any other rights in relation to the overage land.

This chapter describes contractual arrangements. Most of the rest of the book discusses overage as it affects property rights, but a right of property may, indeed usually does, involve a contractual or similar relationship, either at the outset as in a contract of sale, or throughout, as in a lease. Some of the issues raised in this chapter are therefore relevant to other chapters.

It is convenient to look also at the way in which such contractual rights can be assigned and, therefore, how similar rights (which may be seen as being closer to rights of property) can be transferred. The following chapters discuss different means of securing payment of overage by using types of interest in land which were evolved for other purposes. Overage rights themselves, apart from the method of securing them, can be capable of assignment, as discussed in this chapter.

2.2 POSITION OF THE PROMISOR

The granter will be personally liable to make the overage payment. If the granter is a company and goes into insolvent liquidation then the value of the imposer's claim will have to be ascertained as at the date of liquidation[1] and

---

1   Insolvency Rules 1986 (IR 1986), rr 4.94 and 11.13, but see *In re Northern Counties of England Fire Insurance Co* (1880) 17 Ch D 337 where the contingency occurs during the administration.

this will be determined having regard to the chances that the trigger event might occur and also giving a discount for the fact that payment is not due immediately.

If the liquidation is solvent and is on a company reorganisation or a similar basis then, once again, it would appear that the debt must be valued as at the date the company goes into liquidation.[1] It is, however, possible that the court may require some form of security to be given for the amount of the actual overage payment at the time it occurs but this should not be relied on in the present state of the authorities.[2] If the company does not go into liquidation but is simply struck off the register and dissolved, then as a potential creditor the imposer may have a claim within 20 years of the date of dissolution to have the company revived,[3] but this will be worth doing only if the company had assets which could be used and this is only likely to happen if the company still had an interest in land. In that case, the company would normally have to be revived for the purpose of dealing with the land in any event.

If the granter is an individual who goes bankrupt, the same provisions will apply as for the liquidation of an insolvent company.[4] If the individual dies then the liability is not by itself extinguished. The personal representatives will be liable if they distribute the individual's estate without advertising for creditors[5] and without providing for any liabilities of which they are aware. If the imposer draws the existence of the liability to their attention then the personal representatives will have to retain security unless the imposer is prepared to release them. If they advertise without knowledge of the potential claim and the imposer does not bring the matter to their attention, then they are not personally liable to the extent of any assets they have distributed,[6] but that does not extinguish the liability and the imposer would be able to pursue the claim against beneficiaries.[7]

If the granter comprises a body of trustees then, once again, the trustees cannot safely distribute trust assets to beneficiaries where there are any outstanding claims of which they are aware.[8] It is unlikely that trustees would enter into an unconditional commitment to make a payment at an unknown future time, but if they did they would need to make provision to cover it.

Therefore, it is clear that the value of the promise depends on the assets and continuing existence of the granter. In order to rely on this the imposer needs to be satisfied that the granter will need to be creditworthy. This must of

---

1   *Re Park Air Services plc* [1999] 1 All ER 673.
2   See *Fleming v Self* (1854) 3 De GM & G 997.
3   Companies Act 1985 (CA 1985), ss 651 and 653.
4   IR 1986, rr 6.114 and 11.13.
5   Trustee Act 1925 (TA 1925), s 27.
6   TA 1925, s 26.
7   Administration of Estates Act 1925, s 38.
8   TA 1925, s 26; *X v A* (1999) 96(38) LSG 38.

course apply at the time the trigger event occurs and the payment is due. For the reasons given above, it also needs to apply at periods before that because if the granter becomes insolvent then the overage obligation may effectively be extinguished by liquidation or bankruptcy even though the granter may have a realistic prospect of having assets at a later date.

For this reason, the promise to pay is suitable only in dealing with substantial bodies such as a national institution or a public limited company. It will be a matter for the judgment of the imposer as to whether this situation is likely to continue. Many of the larger institutions are established as charities and there may be a limit in their constitution to the extent to which they can give a commitment for a future uncertain payment. The same applies to the most creditworthy body of all, namely the Government. As explained in Chapter 10, the Government itself uses overage as imposer on a substantial scale and there may be a suggestion that if a private landowner is selling land to the Government overage could be used against it. This would not be acceptable to the Treasury. The Treasury will not authorise a government department to enter into a commitment to pay a sum of unknown size at an unknown future date.

Even where the granter is a body of substance such as a plc, it may be unwilling to give such commitment. The reason is that the obligation would need to be reflected in its accounts as a contingent future liability of uncertain size. So long as it can be certain that this will be relatively small in relation to the total assets of the company, it may not matter as the company will have undertaken various liabilities such as underleases and building contracts. Where, however, the overage commitment could be substantial in relation to the company's assets, this could lead to the insertion of a note on the accounts which might be unwelcome to investors.

2.3 GUARANTEES AND UNDERTAKINGS

If the granter does not itself have sufficient assets to be creditworthy, the imposer may ask for this to be supported by a guarantee. A guarantee is simply an undertaking by the guarantor that if the principal debtor does not meet its obligations then the guarantor will make good any loss. Where, for example, the overage land is sold to a subsidiary in a group of companies then the parent company may be asked to provide a guarantee and the same considerations as mentioned above apply to the value of the guarantee as they would apply to the original promise. It is normal in guarantees to provide that variations which do not materially affect the nature of the transaction, such as the giving of an extended period of time to pay, will not affect the liability of the guarantor.

Guarantees will most often be given by banks. A commercial bank will provide a guarantee in return for a fee. In the case of overage where the liability may be many years ahead, and the bank will charge a fee every year equal to a percentage of its potential maximum liability, the total cost to the granter may be substantial. Furthermore, a bank will not give an unlimited guarantee for an unknown sum. It will wish to limit its overall liability in cash terms and the fee will be charged by reference to the maximum exposure. In overage, therefore, a guarantee from a commercial bank may be unduly expensive.

In the case of very short-term overage, a solicitor's undertaking may sometimes be appropriate. If the original landowner sells land with the benefit of planning consent to a builder, the builder may be cautious about the price for which it can sell the completed houses. Equally, the landowner may consider that there is a possibility of gaining planning consent for more houses. It is therefore common practice to agree that if consent is obtained for an extra house then an additional sum will be payable. Similarly, it may be agreed that the immediate current sale price of the land has been calculated by reference to particular sale prices being achieved on particular houses built on various plots. It could then be agreed that if the builder was able to sell some of those houses for more than the estimated price, the uplift would be shared with the landowner. Such a sharing arrangement can in the short term be suitably managed on the basis of a solicitor's undertaking. The terms of the sale will provide that the builder authorises its solicitor to give an undertaking to pay the overage. The seller's solicitor will need to be satisfied not only that the builder will not withdraw instructions so that any sale money will pass through the builder's solicitor's hands but also that any bank or other interested party will agree to the sale money being dealt with in the same way. Provided that is done, the builder's solicitor will be able to give an undertaking to the seller's solicitor. This is suitable only for very short-term arrangements where the building and sale programme may take, perhaps, two years.

Where the granter has entered into a personal commitment, it may be able to accept an indemnity if it wishes to pass the responsibility on to a third party, perhaps on re-sale of the land. This will not reduce the liability of the granter to the imposer but the granter will itself have the benefit of an obligation on a third party to stand behind it. Once again, however, the same considerations apply as between the granter and the third party as mentioned above between the imposer and the granter.

2.4 TRANSFER OF BURDEN

Where the original granter is liable to go into liquidation or cease to exist or be lost to sight, the imposer will wish to be able to enforce its rights against the land as such, or the owner for the time being of the land. This involves the burden of the obligation to pay overage being passed on with the land when it changes hands. It also involves the obligation being made binding on any person with rights derived from the granter or its successor, such as a mortgagee or tenant.

The general rule is that the obligation to carry out duties under a contract cannot be imposed on a person who is not a party to that contract. If the position were as simple as that then this book would end with this chapter. The function of long-term overage is to set up an arrangement under which the obligation to make a payment when the value of the land increases is intended to be passed on from one owner of the overage land to the next. Such an obligation needs to be attached to a right of property.

In the case of devices other than a promise to pay, the provisions for enforcement are less direct. In principle, they lie not against the person who happens to be the owner of the land for the time being but constitute some form of charge on the land. Of course, land cannot itself pay money and the practical result is to oblige a future owner to make a payment or risk losing the land

2.4.1 Proprietary methods

(a) Charges
Charges are considered in Chapter 5. The benefit of a charge can be transferred by deed[1] but the charge itself is an incumbrance binding the land to whoever owns it for the time being. Section 58 of the Land Registration Act 1925 (LRA 1925) may be excluded so that the chargor is not personally liable but the charge will still be enforceable by selling the land.

(b) Leases
Leases are considered in Chapter 7. Where a lease is assigned from one tenant to another, it has long been established that the incoming tenant by virtue of taking the assignment accepts an obligation to perform the terms of the lease. The tenant will normally be subject to being personally sued on the terms of the express covenants[2] but there is an alternative remedy for the landlord to re-enter on the land and terminate the rights of the tenant. The tenant can rescue the position only by satisfying the obligation. The effect of the Landlord and Tenant (Covenants) Act 1995 (LT(C) 1995) is to reinforce this so that, even though the original tenant has entered into a personal obligation to pay money, that may not be enforceable after it has passed on the lease.

(c) Positive covenants
Positive covenants are considered in Chapter 3.

---

1   Law of Property Act 1925 (LPA 1925), s 114.
2   It is common practice in the case of leases to trustees, especially charitable trustees, to provide that a trustee will not be individually and personally liable beyond the assets under his control as trustee so that his personal fortune is not at risk because he has undertaken a trusteeship.

(d) Restrictive covenants

Restrictive covenants are considered in Chapter 4. In the case of restrictive covenants, there is no direct obligation to pay and the covenant itself may be drafted in such a form that it is not enforceable against the original covenantor after it has parted with its interest in the land, but the covenant remains enforceable against the land itself. The person entitled to the benefit would be able to claim an injunction against breach and if the landowner wished to be released from the obligation it would only be on terms acceptable to the recipient.

2.4.2 Novation and release

The main apparent exception to the rule that a contractual obligation cannot be passed on to a third party is in relation to novation and release. In the context of overage, this is most usually found in a term of the agreement which provides that if the owner for the time being wishes to sell at a time when the trigger event has not yet occurred then it will arrange for the new owner to enter into a direct covenant with the overage owner and it may also be provided that when that happens the former landowner is released from any obligation to pay overage. (The restriction on the Register discussed in Chapter 3[1] works in a similar way.) In the context of a simple promise to pay, novation works by an arrangement under which a new contract is created between the imposer and the new granter, and the former granter is then released from its liability. This is not a true exception to the rule that a burden cannot be passed on because it involves cancelling the previous contract and creating a new one.

2.4.3 Benefit and burden

There is a further apparent exception in relation to property law known as the rule in *Halsall v Brizell*,[2] sometimes known as the 'pure principle of benefit and burden'. Under this rule, if a person takes a benefit (typically a right of way to reach property) that benefit may be made conditional on the acceptance of a corresponding burden (such as an obligation to contribute to the cost of maintenance of the access). Although this is a well-established rule, and an exception to the principle that positive covenants cannot be made binding on successors in title, its application to overage is limited. It may of course be linked to a right such as to use an access, although that would more normally be covered by virtue of a ransom. In general, it is hard to see how a landowner whose land has substantially increased in value as the result of the grant of planning consent, could be considered bound to make an overage payment to a former owner of the land as a corresponding burden on which the benefit is conditional. In the typical overage case, a benefit such as planning consent

---

1   See **3.4.2**.

2   [1957] Ch 169. See *Thamesmead Town Ltd v Allotey* [1998] 37 EG 161, *Tito v Waddell (No 2)* [1977] Ch 106; *Rhone v Stephens* [1994] 2 AC 310.

attaches automatically to the land. Where, however, the increase in value arises from some other cause, or where for some good reason the ransom rules cannot be applied, then it may in special circumstances be possible to use the principle of benefit and burden but such occasions must be rare. Even if the bargain is of the type 'if you require a right of way for development purposes, you will pay a sum equal to one-third of the uplift in value', that is more like an option than a benefit and burden situation.

2.5   TRANSFER OF BENEFIT

The imposer will normally wish to be able to transfer the overage rights to a new overage owner. This could arise simply because they are likely to last for many years and the rights should be transmitted to the children of an individual or on a company reorganisation. More importantly, the rights can have value, especially as the prospect of development comes closer.

Until actual payment, the right to receive overage (as distinct from the means used to secure it) is a type of legal interest known as a chose (or thing) in action. In this, it is distinguished from a thing in possession, such as a piece of furniture in your house, or cash in your pocket. The right to such a thing cannot be enforced by having it, but by bringing an action for it and obtaining an order from the court, usually commanding payment of a sum of money in the form of payment of a debt or damages. The extent to which a person other than the original imposer can bring such proceedings is governed by the rules relating to the assignment of choses in action.

Certain types of overage such as a charge or an unsecured promise can be transferred by specific assignment. Rights can also be transferred automatically by operation of law.

2.5.1   Automatic transfer

On the death of an individual overage owner, the rights normally vest in his general personal representatives unless they terminate with his death. If the rights are jointly owned, title to them will normally pass to the survivor although if they were owned in common rather than jointly the survivor will hold them in trust for himself and the beneficiaries of the deceased overage owner's estate.

If the owner was an individual who has died, then this will mean his personal representatives. Normally, if there is a chain of executors then the executors of the last surviving executor of any previous executor will have legal title to sue and can be joined in the proceedings. If, however, the chain of executorship has been broken because a grant of letters of administration has been issued, then it would be necessary to obtain a grant of letters of administration *de bonis non*.

If the owner is a company then the rights will need to be dealt with by the company or, on liquidation, by its liquidator. If this is not done then, on dissolution of the company, the rights will vest in the Crown[1] under the CA 1985, s 654. However, the Crown will not normally be willing to join in an action to recover the property of a third party and, in that case, it will be necessary to restore the company to the Register.

If the overage owner was a dissolved company and the true analysis of the relationship between the imposer and the overage owner or recipient is one of trustee and beneficiary then the title will not vest in the Crown under s 654 at all (see subs (1)). A restoration will be unavoidable. As companies cannot be restored after 20 years (except in the context of a claim for damages for personal injury), this could present problems for long-term overage. In that case, the beneficiary of the trust may be able to appoint a new trustee under the Trusts of Land and Appointment of Trustees Act 1996 (TLATA 1996), Part II.

Some overage rights (as discussed in the following chapters) are annexed to land and cannot be separated from it. If the overage is by normal ransom strip then a transfer of the strip will transfer the overage. If it is by means of a right of way across the overage land then the right will pass on a transfer of the dominant tenement under the LPA 1925, s 62. If it is by restrictive covenant then it will pass with the benefited land under the LPA 1925, s 78. If it belongs to a landlord under a lease then assignment of the reversion assigns the overage right.

2.5.2   Untransferable overage

To the extent that a promise creates an interest in land then s 4(2) of the LPA 1925 provides that all rights and interests in land may be disposed of. That is simply defining the general rules. However, the parties may agree that an interest shall not be assigned and, of course, if the right in question is not an interest in land at all (and a simple promise would not be such an interest) then the section is not relevant.

Certain types of overage may be made personal so that they cannot be transferred at all. It is established that some rights are incapable of transfer as such.[2] These arise from public policy and transfer of overage would not normally be restrained for that reason.

There needs to be a specific provision for overage to be made personal. For example, Mr Smith sells some fields to Mr Green and imposes a provision that

---

1   Normally the Treasury Solicitor BV or, if the registered office was in Lancashire or Cornwall, in the Duchies.

2   For example, Social Security Administration Act 1992, s 187; Superannuation Act 1972, s 5(1); *Re Robinson* (1884) 27 Ch D 160. The fruits of an action may even so be assigned.

if Mr Green or his successors realise value from the fields they will pay overage. This may be personal to Mr Smith and last for his life only. Such overage rights would have a limited value (although in theory they could be assignable for an interest *pur autre vie*). Mr Smith may be able to realise the fruits of the overage[1] but probably not assign the overage itself.

Such an arrangement would be unusual in a commercial transaction. It could arise from the situation where Mr Smith lives next to the fields sold to Mr Green and to preserve his view and amenities he reserves a restrictive covenant against building so long as he continues to live in the house. If some years later he is considering moving into an expensive retirement home he might be attracted by a payment to release this personal right.

More often, it is found in a family situation, for example where a father owned several farms and on his death each child takes a different farm. If there are prospects of development, such an arrangement may be made for one generation only to achieve a short-term fairness. Thus if the father owned three farms and on his death George inherits Greenacre, Betty inherits Blackacre and Walter inherits Whiteacre, and Greenacre is on the edge of a village, George may agree with his siblings that if he gets planning consent for development, he will pay one-third to them personally, but not any other member of their family.

Rights which cannot be assigned should be distinguished from an agreement not to assign. The rights may not be of an inherently personal nature but the parties may agree as a term of the arrangement that the imposer will not transfer them. A transfer in breach of this term will be a valid transfer.[2] In *Linden Gardens Trust Ltd v Lenesta Sludge Disposals Ltd*,[3] Lord Browne-Wilkinson said:

> '[A] prohibition on assignment normally only invalidates the assignment as against the other party to the contract so as to prevent the transfer of the chose in action: In the absence of the clearest words it cannot operate to invalidate the contract as between the assignor and assignee and even then it may be ineffective on the grounds of public policy.'

---

1 See *Briargate Development Ltd v Newprop Co Ltd* [1989] 33 EG 42 at first instance. The subsequent Court of Appeal decision does not affect this general point although the particular decision of 'fruits' on the facts was reversed. In such a case, Mr Smith might declare a trust.

2 In *Tom Shaw & Co v Moss Empires Ltd* (1908) 25 TLR 190, Darling J said that a prohibition 'could no more operate to invalidate the assignment than it could interfere with the laws of gravitation'. Cases on landlord and tenant have held that an assignment of the premises demised by a lease will effectually transfer the premises to the assignee, but subject to a possible right of the landlord to re-enter for breach of covenant (*Old Grovebury Manor Farm Ltd v W Seymour Plant Sales and Hire Ltd (No 2)* [1979] 3 All ER 504; *Governors of the Peabody Donation Fund v Higgins* [1983] 3 All ER 122).

3 [1994] 1 AC 85 at 108.

but the breach may have no effect, or may invalidate the right to claim on the contract or may constitute such a breach as enables the granter to repudiate or rescind.

2.5.3 Assignment – legal or equitable?

The situation where the imposer wishes to ensure the benefit of the potential right to receive the overage payment can be claimed by a subsequent overage owner has been transformed by the Contracts (Rights of Third Parties) Act 1999 (C(RTP)A 1999) which can make assignment as such unnecessary by conferring a direct right on a future overage owner. The C(RTP)A 1999 relates only to transfer of benefit and does not change the rules on the transfer of burden but if the recipient is a different person from the imposer it will still be necessary to watch the details of the manner in which the title of the recipient to receive the overage payment can arise. Before considering the C(RTP)A 1999 (see **2.5.8**), we need to look at the preceding rule.

An assignment of overage rights can either be legal (in the sense of being governed by the rules developed by the old courts of common law) or equitable (in the sense of being governed by rules developed in the old Court of Chancery).[1] There are two main differences.

(1) The first is that a person claiming under an equitable assignment of a legal chose in action needs the assistance of the court. Formal title to the rights, in this context understood as a chose in action, will be vested in the imposer.

The recipient will need to satisfy the payer that it is entitled to collect, and give a good receipt for, the overage sum. In particular, if the payer refuses to pay, the recipient will need to persuade the court that it is entitled to bring a claim. The best, often the only, way is to join the imposer as a party and sue for the payment in the imposer's name, and satisfy the court that the recipient has a better title than the imposer, usually because it assigned the rights.

In the case of a legal assignment the recipient will be able to bring proceedings directly against the payer in the recipient's own name. If the chose in action is itself equitable then the recipient can claim in its own name without joining the imposer.

(2) The second difference is that on the face of it a person claiming the assistance of the equitable jurisdiction of the court is subject to that jurisdiction and the rules of equity. These include that the claimant must act properly and promptly and there are various equitable defences in the interests of justice that the payer may be able to invoke. In the case of a claim at common law then, in principle, provided the recipient can show

---

1 *Joseph v Lyons* (1884) 15 QBD 280.

that the sum is due, it is entitled to judgment. It may still be possible for the payer to claim the help of the equitable jurisdiction in appropriate cases, for example if the recipient has misled the payer about its intention to demand payment, but in such a case the task of the person resisting the claim is harder.

2.5.4 Legal assignments

As mentioned above, a legal right to receive an overage payment is a chose in action. It will not formally be a debt until the sum is ascertained and payable.[1] Under s 136 of the LPA 1925:

> '(1) Any absolute assignment by writing under the hand of the assignor (not purporting to be by way of charge only) of any debt or other legal thing in action, of which express notice in writing has been given to the debtor, trustee or other person from whom the assignor would have been entitled to claim such debt or thing in action, is effectual in law (subject to equities having priority over the right of the assignee) to pass and transfer from the date of such notice –
>
> (a) the legal right to such debt or thing in action;
>
> (b) all legal and other remedies for the same; and
>
> (c) the power to give a good discharge for the same without the concurrence of the assignor.'

It should be noted that it has to be in writing under the hand of the assignor although this would not prevent it being by deed.

The assignment has to be absolute. This has two aspects. First, it is not possible on this basis for the imposer to retain an interest in the overage payment. However, if the overage is assigned to persons who hold the legal chose as trustees for the assignor and assignee, then the assignment to them will be absolute even though they may hold in trust for other persons (who may include the assignor).

Secondly, it may be suggested that the very nature of overage may render this condition impossible to satisfy. Overage (as distinct from the method used to secure it) is a contingent future interest. It arises at an uncertain future time, such as when and if planning consent is granted, and the amount cannot be known until the development value is ascertained. This does not by itself prevent the original bargain being capable of being recognised at common law. The common law recognises future debts, contingent debts and unliquidated sums. In special cases, as where it is necessary to draw up accounts (which might apply on a joint venture), then the assistance of equity may be needed but in general the common law procedures are up to ascertaining overage.

---

1   A debt arising out of an existing contract but payable in the future is assignable under s 136 of LPA 1925. *Brice v Bannister* (1878) 3 QBD 569.

The issue is then whether an assignment of a contingent interest can be absolute. The answer must be that provided the imposer assigns all it has to assign, then that is absolute. The fact that what is being assigned is contingent does not affect the assignment. Thus in *Hughes v Pump House Hotel Co Ltd*,[1] a contractor engaged on building works assigned to a bank all moneys due from the building owner. This was held to be an absolute legal assignment even though payment depended on carrying out the contract. In *Walker v The Bradford Old Bank Ltd*,[2] a customer of a bank assigned a bank account to a trustee. At the date of assignment the balance was £48 and at the date of death £217. This was held to be a valid assignment of whatever was in the account from time to time.

2.5.5   Equitable assignment and trust

If the assignment cannot be legal within s 136 of the LPA 1925 then it has to be equitable. An assignment of a legal chose in action which does not satisfy the section, for example because notice is not given, or it is not absolute, will be equitable.[3] Any assignment of an equitable chose in action must be equitable, whatever formalities are used. Therefore, if the nature of overage is necessarily equitable then the assignment must be equitable.

The holder of a legal chose may declare itself to be a trustee for the new owner. Such a declaration does not need to be in writing.[4] However, an assignment of an equitable interest (and therefore chose) must be in writing under the LPA 1925, s 53(1)(c).

If it can be established that the imposer holds the overage payment as trustee for a subsequent overage owner then it may be possible under the TLATA 1996 for the beneficiary of the trust to have a new trustee appointed. In the ordinary case, however, there is no trust as such, there is simply an asset which is owned by one person and transferred to another.

2.5.6   Expectancies and future rights

In principle, an expectancy, such as an inheritance from a living person or a claim to damages in an action which has not yet gone to trial (as distinct from a disputed debt which is a chose) cannot itself actually be assigned as it is not an item of property. It can, however, be the subject of an agreement to assign. However, there are several cases in which the courts have upheld a present assignment of future rights.

---

1   [1902] 2 KB 190, see also *Buck v Robson* (1878) 3 QBD 686.
2   (1884) 12 QBD 511.
3   *William Brandt's Sons & Co v Dunlop Rubber Co Ltd* [1905] AC 454.
4   Under the LPA 1925, s 53(1)(b) it will have to be provable in writing.

Thus in *Tailby v Official Receiver*,[1] an assignment of future book debts was upheld. In *Cotton v Heyl*,[2] an assignment of future exploitation rights to an existing invention was a valid equitable assignment. In *Syrett v Egerton*,[3] an assignment of future royalties was a valid equitable assignment. In *Campbell Connolly & Co Ltd v Noble*,[4] there was an assignment of full copyright. At the time, English law provided for a single period of copyright but US law provided an initial period of 28 years, with a second 'renewal' period of a further 28 years contingent on the author being alive at the start of the renewal period. In this case the contingency occurred and the original assignment was held to extend to the renewal period.

In *Glegg v Bromley*,[5] there was an assignment of rights under an action in tort for false representation and it was held not to be an expectancy or a cause of action but an assignment of property, namely of the fruits of an action as and when recovered and therefore valid. Even more remarkably, in *Re Lind*,[6] a prospective beneficiary as next of kin of his mother assigned his expectant share to her personal estate. This was upheld as an assignment of property, not just a personal liability.[7]

If an agreement is made, then the contractual right will itself be a chose (separate from the expectancy which is the subject matter of the contract) and that chose is assignable. As the contract will be specifically enforceable, the contract will itself constitute an equitable assignment. However, in *Re McArdle*[8] there was a purported contract to assign an interest in an unadministered estate which was bad for lack of consideration. It was argued that it should take effect as an equitable assignment but the Court of Appeal held that as the contract itself was invalid, it could not be construed as an assignment.

Thus, there can be an assignment of the fruits of positive overage. A contract that 'if planning consent is granted, then you will pay' is an existing contractual right (even though contingent) and can be assigned. The fruits of negative overage, such as 'if an application is made to vary this restrictive covenant, then I will be in a position to charge overage', are a mere expectancy and therefore cannot be assigned. A contract that 'if I receive money from the release of a restrictive covenant then I will pay you half' is capable of being a valid contract (provided it complies with formalities such as consideration)

---

1 (1888) 13 App Cas 523.
2 [1930] 1 Ch 510.
3 [1957] 1 WLR 1130.
4 [1963] 1 WLR 252.
5 [1912] 3 KB 474.
6 [1915] 2 Ch 345.
7 But see the tax case of *Davenport v Chilver* [1983] STC 426.
8 [1951] 1 Ch 669.

and, if so, then the contractual right can be assigned, even though at the time there are no proposals or discussions for the covenant to be released.[1]

2.5.7   Agreement to assign

While an actual assignment can be gratuitous, an agreement to assign (unless by deed, in which case it will normally be an actual equitable assignment) needs consideration like any other contract. Section 2(1) of the Law of Property (Miscellaneous Provisions) Act 1989 (LP(MP)A 1989) provides that:

> 'a contract for the sale or other disposition of an interest in land can only be made in writing and only by incorporating all the terms which the parties have expressly agreed in one document or, where the contracts are exchanged, in each.'

For this purpose, 'interest in land' means any estate, interest or charge in or over land.[2]

The definition does not go further but, presumably, 'land' and 'interest' and 'estate' will be interpreted in the light of the LPA 1925. Overage by promise to pay cannot be an interest in land within the section.[3] Therefore, a contract to assign a promise to pay will not be subject to the LPA 1925, even though the payment itself may derive from land, and nor will an assignment of the fruits of overage. The means of securing it, such as a charge or lease or covenant will be an interest in land and therefore a contract to assign such a right will need to comply with the Act. However, an actual assignment is not a contract and therefore the transfer of such means will have to comply with the rules which relate to that assignment (usually requiring a deed, but sometimes going automatically with land) but not with the separate rules for a contract. If the specifically enforceable contract is itself the assignment in equity then it will have to comply because the equitable assignment can be enforced only to the extent that the contract which creates the equitable assignment is itself enforceable.[4]

2.5.8   Law of Property Act 1925, s 56

Under s 56(1) of the LPA 1925:

> 'A person may take an immediate or other interest in land or other property, or

---

1   An agreement to assign the fruits of a restrictive covenant or other overage which cannot be assigned by itself (because it is attached to land) can be compared with the distinction between an assignment of an action, which can be champertous and the fruits of an action, which is lawful (*ANC Ltd v Clark Goldring and Page Ltd* (2000) *The Times*, 31 May).

2   Section 2(6).

3   If it is a contingent future interest as suggested in Chapter 12, it may take effect as an equitable interest.

4   *Re McArdle* [1951] 1 Ch 669.

the benefit of any condition, right of entry, covenant or agreement over or respecting land or other property, although he may not be named as a party to the conveyance or other instrument.'

This section has been very restrictively interpreted by the courts. The efforts of Lord Denning and others to widen the application of the section to allow third parties to benefit under contracts in a number of cases were overruled by the House of Lords in *Beswick v Beswick*.[1] Subsequent attempts to use s 56 in a variety of circumstances have been resisted by the courts.[2] Although the person to take the benefit does not have to be named 'as a party', the person does have to be clearly and specifically identified and it has to be clear that the benefit is to the advantage of that person. The question of whether pure contractual right was 'property' for the purposes of the section was considered in *Beswick v Beswick*, and a contractual right can in certain circumstances constitute property but the purpose of the section is primarily land or an interest in land.

2.5.9 Contracts (Rights of Third Parties) Act 1999

The C(RTP)A 1999 provides in s 1 that:

'(1)   Subject to the provisions of this Act, a person who is not a party to a contract (a "third party") may in his own right enforce a term of the contract if –
   (a)   the contract expressly provides that he may, or
   (b)   subject to sub-section (2), the term purports to confer a benefit on him.'

Subsection (2) provides that subs (1)(b) does not apply if the parties did not intend the term to be so enforceable.

Under subs (3) the third party must be expressly identified in the contract by name, as a member of a class or as answering a particular description but need not be in existence when the contract is entered into.

The effect of this is that where a contract for overage is made between a granter and an imposer and if the contract so allows (and this might be impliedly by the use of words such as 'or its successor in title') then a person who falls within the contemplation of the contract can enforce the contract. It would appear that there is no need for a specific assignment of the contractual rights and the C(RTP)A 1999 makes it clear that the third party can sue in its own name. It is not intended to be a case of assignment, but a conferring of direct benefit.

In the overage context, a problem may arise in relation to identifying the third party. It is unlikely to be identified by name, or even as a member of a class (unless one can have a class of future landowners), and therefore it is necessary to refer to it as 'answering a particular description'. Certain types of

---

1   [1968] AC 58.
2   For example, *Amsprop Trading v Harris Distribution* [1997] 1 WLR 1025.

overage, such as the use of a restrictive covenant or a ransom strip, themselves depend on the overage owner having an interest in land which has benefited and it may well be that a reference to such an owner would be sufficient for this purpose. However, where there is a simple contract debt then it would normally not be appropriate to attach it to a particular land. In practice, therefore, if a complete stranger not in the direct contemplation of the parties at the time the overage contract was made is to have the benefit of this provision then the most suitable form of 'answering a particular description' is to provide that the third party must be a person to whom the benefit has been specifically assigned. If this is outside the scope of the contract, then it may have to be a person who can be ascertained by an objective test, such as a nomination procedure. If the overage is capable of being a legal thing in action then there is little advantage over the use of s 136 of the LPA 1925 except that it may be designed to assign the rights without giving notice to the landowner. If, however, overage is an equitable thing in action then use of this provision would be an advantage.

2.5.10   Negotiable instruments

Certain recognised types of legal transaction can be created by a document known as a negotiable instrument governed by the Bills of Exchange Act 1882. The best known example is a cheque. A bill of exchange is defined in s 1 as:

> 'An unconditional order in writing, addressed by one person to another, signed by the person giving it, requiring the person to whom it is addressed to pay on demand or at a fixed or determinable future time, a sum certain in money to, or to the order of a specified person, or to bearer.'

Most types of commercial negotiable instruments can be readily assigned without difficulty by a relatively informal procedure such as endorsement on the back.

There are problems with an overage payment being the subject of a Bill of Exchange. First, it must be unconditional. Overage depends on a future increase in value which may not occur. Therefore, it cannot be unconditional. A direction to pay at a future time that may never occur (eg 'when I marry'[1]) is not within the Act. A direction to pay at a time that must occur even though the date is not known (eg '10 days after the death of X'[2]) is valid and may cure the defect in some types of overage. However, most overage depends on a contingency that may never occur and therefore overage would be conditional for this purpose.

The payment must also be a sum certain in money. Section 9 of the 1882 Act allows that to be with interest, or by instalments, or by reference to a rate of

---

1   *Beardesly v Baldwin* (1741) 2 Stra 1151.
2   *Colehan v Cooke* (1742) Willes 393.

exchange. Thus there can be a payment by reference to another currency. In *Feist v Société Intercommunale d'Electricité Belge*,[1] judgment was given in such a sum in sterling as represented the gold value of a nominal sum in foreign currency in accordance with defined criteria. Again, however, a payment defined for example by reference to a proportion of the future value of land after planning permission had been granted would not be certain.

2.6 PERPETUITY AND LIMITATION

It is generally considered that the rule against perpetuities does not apply to simple contracts. The authority normally cited for this is *Walsh v Secretary of State for India*.[2] The East India Company entered into a covenant to repay to Lord Clive or his estate the money transferred by him to provide pensions for disabled officers and soldiers of the Company if the Company should ever discontinue its military force in India. In 1858, some 88 years later, following the Indian Mutiny, the government of India was transferred to the Crown. Lord Clive's representatives claimed the monies due from the Secretary of State and the claim was upheld.[3]

However, s 10 of the Perpetuities and Accumulations Act 1964 provides:

> 'Where a disposition inter vivos would fall to be treated as void for remoteness if the rights and duties thereunder were capable of transmission to persons other than the original parties and had been so transmitted, it shall be treated as void as between the person by whom it was made and the person to whom or in whose favour it was made or any successor of his, and no remedy shall lie in contract or otherwise for giving effect to it or making restitution for its lack of effect.'

Under s 3 of that Act there is a 'wait and see' rule under which, where apart from the Act disposition would be void for remoteness, then the disposition shall be treated as if it were not subject to the rule against perpetuities until such time (if any) that it becomes established that the vesting is too remote.

Section 10 applies to any disposition and must include a contract because of the reference in that section to a remedy in contract. It therefore has to be presumed for the purposes of the section that even if as a matter of law neither the benefit nor the burden could be transmitted to persons other than the original parties, nevertheless for the purpose of applying the test under s 10 it is assumed that benefit and burden could be transmitted and it is further assumed that such a transmission has occurred. If in that case the disposition

---

1   [1933] Ch 684; see also *Syndic in Bankruptcy of Salim Nasrallah Khoury v Khayat* [1943] AC 507.
2   (1863) 10 HL Cas 367.
3   See also *Air Jamaica Ltd v Charlton* [1999] 1 WLR 1399 on the application of the rule in the context of a contract of employment which gave rights under a pension scheme.

would be void for remoteness after the perpetuity period in question has passed then after that date the disposition will be void.

A simple contract debt is probably not within this provision because, following *Walsh v Secretary of State for India*, the rule does not apply to it. It is possible, as indicated later[1] in this book, that an agreement to make a payment to be ascertained from some unknown future date creates an equitable interest and that interest itself is likely to be subject to the rule against perpetuities. If, therefore, the contractual promise is for a normal type of overage payment then s 10 will apply to it and after the end of the perpetuity period the contract will be void.

The basic rule for the period in question is one which the 1964 Act takes over from the preceding law, namely a life in being plus 21 years. The lives in question are specified in s 3(5) and they include the person by whom the disposition was made and the person in whose favour it was made, that is, in this context, the imposer and the granter. In the case of individuals, that is straightforward so that if the overage payment falls to be made either by or to a human individual then the period in question will be the life of that individual (or the survivor of them) plus 21 years. Under s 3(4), where there are no lives then the period is a fixed one of 21 years. A company cannot be a life for this purpose and therefore in the normal situation of an overage payment by one company to another the period is fixed at 21 years. It is, however, possible under s 1 of the Act to specify a period not exceeding 80 years and if that is done then that will be substituted for a life plus 21 years, or for 21 years as the case may be. It would therefore be prudent to specify a perpetuity period even in the case of a simple promise to pay.

The Limitation Act 1980 will normally have no application to a promise to make a payment in the future. The usual limitation period in relation to simple contracts is 6 years, or 12 years if it is a specialty (that is typically a contract made by deed). However, the limitation period does not begin to run until a right of action has arisen and that right will not occur until a payment is due.

The Law Commission has proposed a major reform of the Rule against Perpetuities[2] which would abolish this restriction.

2.7 WAGERS

Wagering contracts are unenforceable and if overage constitutes a wager the payment cannot be recovered.[3]

---

1 See Chapter 12.
2 Law Com 251.
3 Gaming Act 1845, s 18.

It may reasonably be asked what is the distinction between 'If Blue Ribbon wins the 4.40 at Doncaster I will pay you £100' and 'If planning consent is granted for a housing development at Blackacre I will pay you £1m'. However, it is an essential feature of a wagering contract that both parties should be liable to lose. A wager arises only if two parties:

> 'professing to hold opposite views touching the issue of a future uncertain event, mutually agree that, dependent upon the determination of that event, one shall win from the other, and the other shall pay or hand over to him, a sum of money or other stake; neither of the contracting parties having any other interest in that contract than the sum or stake he will so win or lose, there being no other real consideration to the making of such contract by either of the parties. It is essential to a wagering contract that each party may under it either win or lose, whether he will win or lose being dependent on the issue of the event, and therefore, remaining uncertain until that issue is known. If either of the parties may win but cannot lose, or may lose but cannot win, it is not a wagering contract.'[1]

It follows from that definition that an overage contract will not normally be a wagering contract. First, in an overage contract, the imposer or recipient cannot lose. Secondly, the granter or landowner will normally have an interest in the contract or at least the land which has been subject to the contract.

However, if the contract is drawn in such a way that either party could lose, there might be a wager. *Garner v Pounds Shipowners & Shipbreakers Ltd*[2] concerned an option payment whereby the option sum was paid into a stakeholder account on the terms that the option money would be repayable if a restrictive covenant was not lifted. In this case the restrictive covenant was lifted and the case concerned the tax liability of the grantor but on different facts, an owner of land might agree to sell but on terms that if some condition was not satisfied it would repay what it had received. If what was due was no more than what had been originally paid, that is unlikely to be a wager (because there is no risk of loss). If the landowner had to pay back more than it received (perhaps because the buyer had incurred expense) there could be a situation amounting to a wager.

2.8 PENALTY

The equitable jurisdiction of the court gives relief against payment of unreasonable penalties.

Where the overage takes a form such as a restrictive covenant coupled with a provision that if the covenant is broken (as by the commencement of development) then a specified sum or a sum calculated in a specified way will be payable to the recipient, there might be a possible argument that if the sum

---

1   *Carlill v Carbolic Smokeball Co* [1893] 1 QB 256.
2   [2000] 1 WLR 1107.

exceeds the damages suffered by the recipient this might be void as a penalty. However, in *Philips Hong Kong Limited v Attorney-General of Hong Kong*,[1] the Privy Council cited with approval the view of Dickson J in the Supreme Court of Canada[2] that:

> 'the power to strike down a penalty clause is a blatant interference with freedom of contract and is designed for the sole purpose of providing relief against oppression for the party having to pay the stipulated sum. It has no place where there is no oppression.'

It follows from that that the power to strike down a penalty (which derives from the equitable jurisdiction of the court) will not be exercised in relation to a fair bargain between parties. Accordingly, it is not considered that the penalty jurisdiction has any application in relation to overage so long as that was negotiated as a commercial bargain.

In *Crown Estate Commissioners v Possfund Custodian Trustee Limited*,[3] the rent payable was 10 per cent of the tenant's rental income for an accounting year or a base rent of £135,000 per year whichever was the greater. If in any year the rents exceeded £38.50 per square foot then certain additional rents were payable. If the tenant failed to produce accounts then the landlord was entitled to assume that the tenant's income represented the open market rent currently payable. An issue arose as to whether the landlord's option to calculate rent by reference to the market if the tenant failed to produce accounts was a penalty. The court held that it was not. It was simply an alternative method of calculating the rent if the procedure specified in the lease had broken down because the tenant failed to produce appropriate figures. There was no suggestion that the overage rent as such was a penalty, merely that the assessment of rent if the tenant did not supply figures might be, but even that was not accepted by the court.[4]

2.9   CONCLUSION

The promise to pay as a simple contract is best used as a short-term arrangement. Although the benefit of the right to receive the overage payment may be made assignable, this may have to be done by way of equitable assignment with the associated need to seek the assistance of the court in enforcing any rights. The burden of it cannot normally be made assignable so that it can be used only against a payer which is likely to remain in existence and solvent and easily traced for the whole duration of the overage. Where it is

---

1   (1993) 61 BLR 41.
2   In *Elsey v JG Collins Insurance Agencies Ltd* (1978) 83 DLR (3d) 1, 15.
3   [1996] EGCS 172.
4   See **3.9** for the application of the penalty rules to estate rentcharges.

appropriate, as in the short-term arrangement for an immediate development which is likely to increase in value within a very few years, then it has the great advantage of simplicity without the need to involve the mechanisms discussed later in this book.

Chapter 3

POSITIVE COVENANTS

3.1 GENERAL

3.1.1 How positive covenants work

In Chapter 2 it was shown that a simple promise to pay has both the advantages and disadvantages which come from being a simple direct contract. It normally subsists only between the original parties and the legal structure is designed to be short term.

In order to provide a more durable arrangement, the parties can use a more solemn form of contract known as a covenant. A covenant is nothing more than a promise in the form of a deed. Its origins lie in the Middle Ages, when there was a special form of action on a covenant. While a contract must be supported by consideration, a properly executed covenant does not need to be. This is important in the overage context because, although there will be consideration on the original transaction, later relations between the parties may not involve consideration at all. The intention of using a covenant is to make the promise to pay binding between successors to the original parties.

This chapter considers the rules which apply to covenants generally, but it is specifically concerned with positive covenants. Because of the medieval origins, it would be helpful here to look at a few of the medieval rules. There are other special rules, developed in the nineteenth century,[1] which govern certain types of favoured restrictive covenants. The difference is money. A restrictive covenant restricts the use which a landowner can make of its land. For example, the covenant may provide that the land may not be used for building, or for any purpose other than as a single house and garden. A positive covenant requires money to be spent. It may require a building to be kept in repair. It may require a contribution to the shared cost of a common access way. It may, as with overage, involve the payment of a specific sum of money in defined circumstances. In the case of leases (discussed in Chapter 7), since the Grantees of Reversion Act 1540, Parliament has intervened to make positive covenants binding. In the case of freeholds, there has been no such intervention and the rules have to be derived from the remotest medieval

---

1   See Chapter 4.

origins of the common law. Many of the rules may seem strange to contemporary lawyers, so there follows some explanation of their purpose.

The granter covenants with the imposer in such a way as to bind successive owners of the overage land and to benefit successive overage owners that the overage will be paid on the trigger date.

3.1.2   Making positive covenants binding

As a general rule, the burden of covenants is not binding on successive owners.[1] As discussed in the next chapter, there is an exception for certain restrictive covenants. The rules in this chapter apply to all covenants and can be used equally well for those that are positive as for those that are restrictive but they are normally applied to positive covenants because many of the complications will not apply where a restrictive covenant satisfies the legal conditions.

As is explained below, the underlying rules for covenants affecting freehold land were originally similar to those affecting leaseholds. The leasehold rules have been considerably altered by statute over the centuries and we therefore need to consider the common law rules.

(1) The benefit of a covenant can be specifically assigned by itself as a chose in action as discussed in Chapter 2.

(2) If it can be said to 'touch and concern' land or 'relate to the subject matter' of a right affecting land then the benefit may pass automatically without express assignment.[2]

(3) As a general rule, the burden of a covenant cannot be assigned so that the covenantee (or his successor) cannot sue the successor of the original covenantor except for the special case of restrictive covenants.[3]

This last rule derives from the principle that a covenant (like a contract) cannot be enforced against a person who is not a party to it. As a covenant is a form of contract, the rules mentioned in Chapter 2 will apply but apart from that it is said that the burden of a covenant is not transmissible. This was established in the case of *Austerberry v Oldham Corporation*,[4] which was confirmed by the

---

1   LPA 1925, s 79 is purely drafting and does not by itself make binding any covenants which would not bind without it (*Rhone v Stephens* [1994] 2 AC 310).

2   At common law, the benefit of a positive covenant will run with the land for the benefit of which it was imposed (*Sharp v Waterhouse* (1857) 7 E&B 816; *Smith v River Douglas Catchment Board* [1949] 2 KB 500). The benefit of a positive covenant passes automatically with the land under s 62 of the LPA 1925 (*Griffith v Pelton* [1958] Ch 205; *Federated Homes v Mill Lodge Properties Ltd* [1980] 1 WLR 594).

3   *Austerberry v Oldham Corporation* (1885) 29 Ch D 750; *Rhone v Stephens* [1994] 2 AC 310.

4   (1885) 29 Ch D 750.

House of Lords in *Rhone v Stephens*[1]. Those cases concerned obligations on a landowner to maintain or contribute to the maintenance of property. The courts held that an obligation to make a payment either by spending money on your own land or by contributing to expenses on other land was a positive covenant and the burden could not bind the land of the covenantor so as to be enforceable against a successor in title.[2]

There are a number of specific exceptions to this.

(1) The rule in *Halsall v Brizell*[3] (the 'principle of pure benefit and burden') which provides that where a person has the benefit of some common service (such as a right of way) then the right can be made conditional on an obligation so that if the landowner does not contribute to maintenance when required then he will not be allowed to use the right of way. This is not suitable for use in overage cases.

(2) Covenants arising by reason of tenure. An obligation to repair a river wall may be enforced against successors[4] and so may an obligation to repair a bridge.[5]

(3) Where a long lease is enlarged under s 153 of the LPA 1925 then under s 153(8) the freehold will be subject to all the same covenants (including positive ones) and to all the same obligations of every kind as the term would have been subject to if it had not been enlarged.

(4) A local authority can impose positive covenants under s 33 of the Local Government (Miscellaneous Provisions) Act 1982.

(5) Rentcharges, discussed below.

(6) Rights of re-entry, discussed below.

(7) Entries on the Register, discussed below.

It is said that an obligation to pay money cannot touch and concern land (unlike, say, a covenant to repair) because the court cannot know what the

---

1 [1994] 2 AC 310.

2 The rule may be justified by the argument that it is one thing to bind land with a restriction, but quite another to oblige a stranger to a contract to make a payment to a person he does not know. That of course would undermine the basis of overage. The origin of the rule seems to be in the form of feoffment. On a freehold grant, the word *dedi* was used and consequently the assignee of the feoffee did not vouch to the feoffor. On a lease, the words used were *concessi* or *demisi* which implied a covenant by the landlord with an assignee of the term and therefore on the basis of reciprocity a covenant the other way would be enforced (*Spencer's Case* (1583) 5 Co Rep 16a).

3 [1957] Ch 169.

4 *London and North Western Railway Company v Fobbing Levels Sewer Commissioners* (1897) 75 LT 629.

5 *R v Duchess of Buccleugh* (1704) 6 Mod 150, 1 Salk 358 but this may be a special case arising from the Anglo-Saxon *trinoda necessitas*.

payment relates to. There is an obvious exception for rent, whether it issues out of a freehold or a leasehold.[1] Most of the cases[2] have concerned payment in leases. *Hill v Booth*[3] is a typical example. A lease contained a provision that the lessee would make payments of regular sums by instalments to the landlord. They were expressed to be by way of premium for the grant of the lease. The landlord's mortgagees sold the freehold to the tenant. The landlord claimed the unpaid instalments. The tenant claimed that the lease had ended when he acquired the freehold and the outstanding instalments ceased to be payable.

In the Court of Appeal, Scrutton LJ first held that the fact that the premium was said to have been 'reserved' out of the term was irrelevant. A reservation could relate only to well-established matters such as rent or an easement. The fact that the parties had referred to the payment as a reservation did not make it one.

Secondly, he held that it was a mere personal covenant which did not relate to the subject matter of the lease:

> 'I asked Mr Vaisey, [counsel for the tenant] who argued the case with his usual clearness, what would happen if the consideration for demising the premises had included a personal covenant by the lessee to buy his butcher's meat for ten years from a lessor who was a butcher. He said it was a difficult question. To me it does not seem difficult. Like a premium it would be a personal promise in consideration of the lease being granted.'

The result was that the covenant to pay did not relate to the land, that the former landlord could claim it as a personal debt from the former tenant, and that any successor to the former landlord, including the mortgagees, had no power to alter the rights. Equally, it follows that a successor in title to the tenant would not have to pay. In relation to leases, as discussed in Chapter 7, the rule has now been overturned by the Landlord and Tenant (Covenants) Act 1995 but the rule still applies to freeholds.

The obligation to pay overage, as a positive covenant, needs to be supported by some other legal device. The granter will therefore covenant with the imposer that he or his successors will pay overage and then the transfer will include one of the other provisions discussed below.

---

1   The leasehold authorities are: *Vyvian v Arthur* (1823) 1 B&C 410; *Bickford v Parson* (1848) 5 CB 920; and *Harper v Burgh* (1677) 2 Lev 206, which establish that only covenants to pay rent and covenants for services in the nature of rent ran with the reversion.

2   There are a great many. Relevant ones include: *Hill v Booth* [1930] 1 KB 381; *Re Hunter's Lease, Giles v Hutchings* [1942] 1 Ch 124; *Hua Chaio Commercial Bank Ltd v Chiaphua Industries Ltd* [1987] 1 AC 99; *P&A Swift Investments v Combined English Stores Group plc* [1989] 1 AC 632.

3   [1930] 1 KB 381.

A number of methods have been devised to try to make positive covenants and, in particular, the payment of overage binding on successors. There are three main approaches, these involve the use of a rentcharge, the use of a restriction on the register of title controlling transfers, and the use of a right of re-entry. They apply to freehold land but they correspond to methods which are regularly used in relation to leasehold overage land. Leases will be discussed in Chapter 7 but the three freehold methods broadly correspond to the leasehold devices of a variable rent, control over assignment, and the right of re-entry. The courts could not apply statutory rules where the statute refers only to leases. However, although the position is not clear beyond doubt, it is likely[1] that the courts would, in broad terms, apply to freehold land the common law rules which relate to leaseholds by analogy.

The reason for this is that there is no fundamental legal distinction between freehold and leasehold. A freehold is strictly a tenancy in fee simple. The main distinction between the two is that a freehold lasts for ever while a lease lasts for a defined term of years which can be, for example, 3000 years. The main distinctions arise from the historical development of the two types of estate and the consequences of the statute *Quia Emptores* 1290 and therefore it would be helpful to describe here something of the background to that Act and the rules contained in it which have given rise to some of the problems in relation to the law of freeholds.

In particular, one method used to make positive covenants enforceable – the restriction on the Register – works by restricting the alienation of a freehold. There has been a basic rule of English law since 1290 that fees simple are freely alienable. The following sections consider how this issue can be resolved.

3.1.3   The original law of freeholds

Following the Norman Conquest of 1066, a system of land law generally known as the feudal system was introduced into England. The phrase 'feudal system' was coined in a much later time and people living in the twelfth and thirteenth centuries would not have recognised feudal law as separate from general law. Under the feudal system, land would be granted by the king or some other lord to a knight or other person in return for services. These services might have originally been military such as the duty to serve in war but as time went by they were increasingly financial and, in particular, freehold land could be granted in return for an annual payment known as a chief rent.[2] This was a rent service in that it was payable to a superior in tenure.

---

1   *Shiloh Spinners v Harding* [1973] AC 691.
2   A chief rent was a rent payable to the chief lord or immediate tenurial superior. It includes a fee farm rent which has to be between one-quarter and one-half of the annual value. A chief rent could be nominal.

Because of the original military nature, the relation between a lord and a tenant of freehold land was considered to be personal and therefore the lord was entitled to control any assignment of the land.

If a tenant wished to sell his land, it was necessary for the buyer to take his place or be 'substituted' in the performance of the services. It will be readily understood that if the service was military the lord insisted on reserving the right to give or withhold consent. This is understandable where a knight's life could depend on the fighting ability of the man next to him in the cavalry charge. The rule came to be applied to other tenures. Thus the medieval lord could use this as a form of overage. If the freehold tenant wished to sell the land at a profit, the lord could impose, as a condition of giving consent, a requirement to pay over a share of that profit.

If the tenant remained in place but sublet the land (again as a subordinate freehold) to someone else, then the lord did not have the right to charge. So far as he was concerned, he still had the same tenant, owing the same services. The original process of grant by the Crown is known as infeudation and subordinate freehold tenancies were created by subinfeudation. This was in fact the preferred method of most landowners because it placed them in a position of landlord as against their buyer so that if, for example, the buyer died without heirs the seller could resume possession of the land sold. More seriously for the Crown whose revenue included various types of feudal dues (eg those payable following the death of the tenant), the system of subinfeudation was widely used as an artificial device to avoid the payment of money which would otherwise have been due to the Crown, a medieval form of tax avoidance.

As freeholds last forever, the effect of successive subinfeudations meant that titles became extremely complex. Under the modern law, there can be a chain of headlease, sub-lease, sub-underlease, tenancy, sub-tenancy and so on, but the chain will never become too complicated because any lease can last only for a limited period of time. In the case of freeholds, titles became extremely complicated and it was very difficult to know who had what rights in the land.

3.1.4 The modern law of freeholds

For these reasons, in 1290 Parliament passed the Act *Quia Emptores* which prohibited further subinfeudation. The Act did not apply to the Crown which could, of course, continue to infeudate and the special rules relating to the Crown and Crown overage will be considered in Chapter 10.[1]

The Act applied only to land in fee simple. At the time and until 1925 there could be legal freehold estates for life or under an entail and, as the law

---

1 Even though the statute does not apply, the Crown as a public authority may not be able to withhold consent to a transfer by virtue of the Human Rights Act 1998.

developed later, there could be other types of estate such as springing and shifting uses which became legal estates after 1536, and there could be conditional estates. These are relevant in the context of trusts discussed in Chapter 9. These continued to be held by subinfeudation as inferior freehold tenancies. Until 1925 they could subsist as legal estates. From 1925 to 1997 they could still be created as equitable interests but since then it has not been possible to create them even in equity although where they arise under arrangements in force in 1997 they will continue.

Quia Emptores 1290 did two things. The first was not only to prohibit future subinfeudation but to provide that, if any attempt was made to sell by subinfeudation, it would take effect as a substitution. However, the consequence of this, as interpreted by the courts, was that any rights that could have been created on the subinfeudation would continue in force as legal rights but would apply to the substituted estate rather than to the inferior estate. Where there was a burden on land and only part of the land was sold, the burden would be apportioned.

The second step which corresponded to this was to remove the right of the superior lord to give or withhold consent to a substitution either in whole or in part and therefore the right to make a charge if this happened.

This Act is the origin of the rule of English Law that land held in fee simple can be disposed of freely and without restriction. As will be discussed at **3.4.2(B)**, in the *Oldham Borough Council* case, the Court of Appeal speculated on the origin of this rule and considered that it might derive from some rule of common law but the basis of it is clearly enacted in a statute that is still in force.

3.1.5 Results of *Quia Emptores* 1290

The result of this Act in relation to the three relevant issues was as follows.

(1) Just as it was possible on subinfeudation to reserve a chief rent (in the same way as a normal rent could be reserved on a lease) so the right to a corresponding payment could now be reserved on a sale by substitution. As it was not payable to a superior in tenure, it could not be a rent service but had to be a rentcharge. The creation of new rentcharges was prohibited by the Rentcharges Act 1977 (RA 1977) subject to an exception for estate rentcharges mentioned at **3.2**.

(2) Any restriction on the right to assign a fee simple was removed and any provision requiring the consent of the seller became void. Modern statutory intervention has provided certain ways around this, initially in relation to trusts, and these will be discussed in relation to restrictions on the Register at **3.4**.

(3) Just as it was possible in the grant of an inferior freehold to reserve a right of re-entry exercisable in specified conditions, so this now became possible in relation to a disposal of freehold land. The modern law is discussed under rights of re-entry at **3.3**.

For the sake of completeness, a further approach may be mentioned which corresponds in some ways to the break clause in a lease. This is an option to repurchase. The rules for options for freeholds are discussed in Chapter 8.

As explained in **3.2.4**, rentcharges are (since 1977) unsuitable for overage. Rights of re-entry and options are subject to a time-limit known as 'the Rule against Perpetuities'. This rule was originally developed in the context of settlements and of trusts but it has a more general application. To the extent that a restriction on the Register subsists as a trust interest, the rule will apply there as well. The rule does not apply to rentcharges except in relation to certain types of rentcharge arising under trusts. It does not apply at all to covenants as such. The Law Commission has proposed a major reform of the rule and if that reform is enacted the rule will cease to apply to commercial interests of this sort. It will still apply, in a modified form, to trusts.

3.2   ESTATE RENTCHARGES

3.2.1   How estate rentcharges work

There are two approaches.

(1) Under s 2(3)(c) of the RA 1977, an estate rentcharge can be created for the purpose of making covenants to be performed by the owner of the land affected by the rentcharge enforceable by the rent owner against the owner for the time being of the land. The imposer reserves an estate rentcharge of a nominal amount and takes a positive covenant to pay the overage. When the trigger event occurs, the recipient can claim performance of that covenant and has the remedies under s 121 of the LPA 1925.

(2) As an alternative, the overage is secured by the rentcharge itself which originally secures a nominal payment but can become substantial if the trigger event occurs. However, as explained below, it appears that, under the RA 1977, a rentcharge can no longer be used or adapted to cover the size of payment needed for overage.

3.2.2   Nature of estate rentcharge

A rentcharge is a type of rent. There are two classes, namely rent services and rentcharges. A rent service is the typical type of rent between landlord and tenant and is payable to a tenurial superior. Under the modern law, that superior has to have an interest in the land.[1]

A rentcharge by contrast is payable to a person who does not have such an interest. Following *Quia Emptores* 1290, the seller of land was still permitted to continue to receive an annual payment (just as the superior freeholder had before) rather than being required to take a single sum of money but the payment was charged on the land rather than being payable by way of service for it.[2] The use of charges for overage will be considered in Chapter 5.

Originally, many rentcharges were rents seck, that is to say that while the rent owner had the right to pursue the owner for the time being of the land in debt, he did not have other remedies. It was common practice since long before 1290 for him to have a right of distraint and by s 5 of the Landlord and Tenant Act 1730 that right was extended to all such rents so that, strictly speaking, they no longer remained rents seck although the expression was still used. Furthermore, it became common practice to give the rent owner a right of re-entry. These rights are considered below at **3.3**.

A rent service has to be appurtenant to land.[3] A rentcharge by definition is not appurtenant to land and exists on its own as an incorporeal hereditament which can exist in gross. As such, it is a right of property and it can have other rights (such as distraint or re-entry) annexed to it.

3.2.3   Use of estate rentcharges apart from overage

Estate rentcharges are used widely for the performance of positive covenants which involve doing works or contributing to them. For example, on the sale of a housing estate with private roads, the developer may impose on each of the houses an estate rentcharge to contribute to the repair of the roads when needed. Initially, it will be of a nominal sum under s 2(5) of the RA 1977. A peppercorn would probably be best because even a payment as small as one penny might be lost under the Limitation Act 1980 if not collected every year. When repairs are needed to the common roads, the Residents' Association or other competent body serves notice on each of the house owners, requiring them to contribute their share. If they fail to pay, the Association can of course sue each house owner in debt, but that by itself may be of little help. If the Association obtains judgment it will of course have various remedies open to it but these will be no use if the house owner is bankrupt. However, under s 121 of the LPA 1925, the Association not only has a power of distress under s 121(2) but may also take possession of the house and let it under s 121(3) and even under s 121(4) may obtain a remedy equivalent to a mortgage which

---

1   Before 1290 the interest could be a lordship such as a manor. Under the Copyhold Acts 1841–1894, a lord could be granted a rentcharge on enfranchisement.

2   *Doe d Freeman v Bateman* (1818) 2 B&A 168 at 170.

3   Or some other similar interest in land such as a lordship.

allows the house to be sold, the cost of repairs to be paid out of the proceeds, and the surplus is payable to the house owner.

3.2.4   Use of the estate rentcharge for overage

The covenant to pay overage is a positive covenant and therefore falls within the RA 1977 but it is not within the direct contemplation of s 2(4). That defines 'estate rentcharge' as being:

> 'a rentcharge created for the purpose –
>
> (a)   of making covenants to be performed by the owner of the land affected by the rentcharge enforceable by the rent owner against the owner for the time being of the land; or
>
> (b)   of meeting, or contributing towards, the cost of performance by the rent owner of covenants for the provision of services, the carrying out of maintenance or repairs, the effecting of insurance or the making of any payment by him for the benefit of the land affected by the rentcharge or for the benefit of that and other land.'

Clearly, an overage payment does not fall under (b) and therefore it would need to be shown that the covenants referred to under (a) are capable of including overage covenants.

It is likely that such a covenant can be enforced only if in the old phrase it 'touches and concerns' the land. In relation to leases, the law has been materially changed by the LT(C)A 1995, but that Act extends only to leases and does not apply to covenants affecting freehold land. Such covenants must continue to relate to the subject matter of the grant.[1]

It is established that a simple covenant to pay money does not touch and concern land in this way at common law.[2] Such a covenant is simply an arrangement between the parties and the court will not enforce it between strangers. However, an overage payment is directly related to the value of the land. Its value entirely derives from a physical change in the land (or an intangible change such as a grant of planning consent) and may be linked to a covenant not to vary the use or a covenant not to develop as mentioned below under rights of re-entry at **3.3**.

Care must be taken that the overage payment is not capable of being expressed to be void as a penalty.[3] If there is a basic covenant not to change the use or not to build, but a provision that if this covenant is broken the landowner will pay the overage owner a sum representing a large proportion of the value of the

---

1   See *Spencer's Case* 5 Co Rep 16a for binding the leasehold. This was supplemented by statute from the Grantees of Reversion Act 1540, s 1 to the LPA 1925, s 141. See now LT(C)A 1995.

2   See notes to **3.2**.

3   See **2.8** for the position in contract.

land, then that might be construed by the court as being intended to represent damages for the breach of the covenant. If that is so then the covenant to pay will be enforceable only to the extent that it represents a genuine pre-estimate of the loss suffered by the covenantee. In that case, a substantial payment would not be treated as touching and concerning the land and would therefore not be enforceable. While there is nothing to prevent parties agreeing to make a payment in particular circumstances (apart from penalties under contracts), such a covenant is not directly related to the land.

It might be suggested that the amount of the overage could be covered by the rentcharge itself for the year in which the trigger event occurs. Thus the rentcharge will be a peppercorn for each year until the year in which the event occurred. For that year only the rentcharge would be a sum equal to the overage. After that the rentcharge would cease to be payable. However, s 2(5) of the RA 1977 states that a rentcharge of more than a nominal amount is not to be treated as an estate rentcharge unless it represents a payment for the performance by the rent owner of a covenant mentioned in subs (4)(b) which is reasonable in relation to that covenant. That subsection covers services, repairs, insurance and so forth but does not cover simple payments. Furthermore, the implication of s 121 of the LPA 1925 is that the payment covered by it is an annual sum (payable half-yearly or otherwise). The remedy confers on the rent owner a power of sale under s 121(4) but does not apply where the annual sum is not held for a legal estate. As will be discussed in Chapter 5 on mortgages, there is an argument that a charge for an amount that cannot be ascertained at the date of granting it may subsist only as an equitable charge and not a legal one, and that rule must apply to rentcharges just as much as it applies to charges for capital sums. It follows therefore that a rentcharge that is capable of being increased, say from a peppercorn to a sum which could be many hundreds of thousands of pounds, simply because planning consent has been granted, would not appear to be lawful under the provisions of the RA 1977. Therefore, the creation of such a 'rentcharge' would be prohibited under s 2(1).

The use of estate rentcharges for overage is untried. It is likely that a court would regard the estate rentcharge as designed specifically for services of the type set out in s 2(4)(b), even though the concept predates the RA 1977, and therefore is not suitable for overage. Even if the court was prepared to accept that an estate rentcharge of nominal amount could secure the performance of the separate positive covenant to pay overage, it is possible that as a matter of policy the court might consider that the intention of the RA 1977 was to abolish arrangements of this type. If so, the court would refuse to uphold them. As indicated above, it would be possible to take this approach on the ground that a covenant to pay money would not relate to the subject matter of the original grant, and therefore could not have been reserved under *Quia Emptores* and there have been no changes in the law which would make this type of payment enforceable.

3.3 RIGHTS OF RE-ENTRY

3.3.1 How rights of re-entry work

The disposition by the imposer contains an obligation on the granter to pay overage on the trigger date and contains a provision that, if he fails to do so, the imposer or his successors may re-enter on the land and terminate the rights of the granter or his successors. The covenant to pay (as a positive one) is not directly enforceable against the successor but if the successor fails to comply with it the right of re-entry arises. The payer will be entitled to relief against the exercise of this right on the terms that he complies with the original covenant.

A variation of this relating to negative overage applies to a restrictive covenant. The granter covenants not to carry out development or change of use and there will be a right of re-entry if the covenant is broken. The terms on which relief against the re-entry will be available are less clearly settled, although there may be a separate arrangement (incorporated in the disposition) that spells out the terms on which the parties accept that relief will be given.

A freehold subject to a right of re-entry is a legal estate in fee simple[1] although the re-entry must occur within the perpetuity period.[2] It is said to be a conditional fee, that is subject to re-entry on condition subsequent. It should be distinguished from a determinable interest, discussed at **9.8.2**, which subsists as an equitable interest under a trust of land.

3.3.2 Nature of re-entry

Re-entry must be distinguished from forfeiture, although the two are often confused and the same terminology is applied to both. A forfeiture arises under the general law and occurs when a tenant under a lease commits an act that is inconsistent with his status of being a tenant. The main surviving example is where the tenant denies the title of his landlord. This arises as a matter of law irrespective of any agreement. Originally, forfeiture was possible for freehold land although it became very rare except for forfeiture to the Crown for treason. That was abolished by the Forfeiture Act 1870.

Re-entry depends on the agreement of the parties. Most leases contain a provision that if the rent is not paid or any of the covenants are broken, and in some cases if other events occur such as the tenant becoming insolvent, then the landlord may re-enter and terminate the lease. For many centuries the courts have given relief against forfeiture and Parliament has also intervened, most importantly in s 146 of the LPA 1925, to place certain types of re-entry

---

1 LPA 1925, s 7.
2 Perpetuities and Accumulations Act 1964, s 12.

on a statutory basis. Those rules have been worked out in the context of the relationship between an original landlord and its successors on the one hand and an original tenant and its successors on the other.

The rules can apply as between parties who are not in that relationship. The leading case is *Shiloh Spinners v Harding*.[1] As it happens, the property there was leasehold but it is accepted that the same principles apply to freeholds.

Shiloh Spinners had a lease of a mill. Part of the land became surplus to their use but on that land were some buildings which supported other buildings on land they continued to occupy. They sold off the surplus land by an assignment of part of the land in the lease and included a positive covenant to repair the buildings that gave support. On the sale they reserved a right of re-entry if the supporting buildings fell into disrepair so that they could completely terminate the arrangement as if the assignment had never been made. The purchaser then re-sold to Mr Harding who was a demolition contractor. He demolished the buildings on the land he had bought which caused a breach of the obligations originally imposed by Shiloh.

The House of Lords considered various ancient authorities and the rules relating to rights of re-entry on freeholds. The reason for this was that although Shiloh actually held a leasehold interest they had sold not by sub-letting but by assignment which was equivalent to substitution. The House held that a right of re-entry was valid and could be exercised. It went on to hold that, in an appropriate case, the court had the power to give relief on suitable terms but in the present case they did not wish to interfere with the exercise of discretion by the trial judge who had decided that, because Mr Harding had deliberately broken covenants of which he was well aware, he should not be given relief. Although the court did not speculate on what might have happened, it can be assumed that if the destruction had been accidental and he had offered to put up some form of retaining wall then relief would quite likely have been granted.

Although s 146 of the LPA 1925, which governs the court's discretionary power to grant relief against re-entry (usually described as forfeiture), does not apply outside the relation of landlord and tenant, it embodies principles developed by the equitable jurisdiction of the court over the centuries and those principles can be applied equally to a right of re-entry on a freehold.

Re-entry for breach of condition should be distinguished from determination of a determinable interest which ends automatically. Determinable interests (save for a few specifically authorised by statute under s 7 of the LPA 1925) now subsist under trusts of land and are discussed in Chapter 9.

---

1   [1973] AC 691.

3.3.3   Application of the rules

The main issue both for the imposer and the granter is the extent to which relief against re-entry would be given either in the case of a positive covenant to pay overage or a restrictive covenant not to develop. From the point of view of the imposer, there is the problem mentioned above that a simple covenant to pay money in relation to freehold land may not be said to touch and concern the land. A right of re-entry by definition is exercisable against the land itself. However, it is reasonably clear that if (as will be the case) any buyer of the land is fully aware of the right of re-entry then, if the overage payment becomes due and it is not paid, it would seem fully acceptable on policy grounds that the parties be held to their bargain. It is clear from *Shiloh Spinners v Harding*[1] that such a right is not capable of protection in the case of unregistered land by a land charge so that it will be a question of actual notice. In the case of registered land, a right of re-entry is not an overriding interest under s 70 of the Land Registration Act 1925 and therefore it has to be protected by an entry on the Register. Although a right of re-entry is not itself security,[2] it is regarded by the courts for the purpose of relief as being similar to security. As a result of the origins of a right of re-entry in the pre-1290 law of the relation between lord and freehold tenant, it may be considered that an obligation to pay overage is as much a feature of the relation between the parties as an obligation to pay rent would be between a landlord and leasehold tenant. That being so, there seems no reason in principle why the right of re-entry should not be exercisable and equally, why, if the payer does indeed pay, relief should not be given.

In relation to negative overage where the covenant is in the form not to develop, the matter may be governed by the rules relating to restrictive covenants set out in Chapter 4. If the court considers that the purpose of the right of re-entry is simply to secure enforcement of the covenant then the same rules will be applied as under the rule in *Tulk v Moxhay*.[3] If, on the other hand, it is made clear that the purpose of the covenant is simply to protect overage and the right of re-entry is attached to that covenant then, once again, in principle there should be every reason to uphold the bargain. In the case of a restrictive covenant there will of course need to be protection either by registration of a land charge of Class D(ii) or by an entry on the Register of Title. Here the uncertainty arises from the point of view of the landowner. On

---

1   [1973] AC 691.
2   See **7.2.2** and cases cited, including *Exchange Travel Agency Ltd v Triton Property Trust plc* [1991] BCLC 396; *Re Olympia and York Canary Wharf Ltd* [1993] BCLC 453; *Re AGB Research Ltd* [1995] BCC 1091; *Razzaq v Pala* [1997] 38 EG 157; *Clarence Café Ltd v Comchester Properties Ltd* [1999] L&TR 303, ChD; *Essex Furniture plc v NPI* (unreported); *Re Lomax Leisure Ltd* [1999] EGCS 61; *Christopher Moran Holdings v Bairstow* [1999] 2 WLR 396.
3   (1848) 2 Ph 774.

the face of it, if development occurs then the right of re-entry will be exercisable. Although the court has jurisdiction to give relief, the court will need to be satisfied that this is in the contemplation of the parties. If the covenant is restrictive in substance then it is subject to variation under s 84 of the LPA 1925.

A further issue relates to the attitude of funders. Although financial institutions are familiar with re-entry clauses in leases and will accept a lease as a good security knowing that the right to relief against forfeiture is available, they are frequently not so familiar with the rules relating to relief on freehold land and, in consequence, may be less willing to lend money on the security of land subject to a potential right of re-entry. The statutory provisions for relief in s 146 of the LPA 1925 are limited to a right of re-entry in a proviso or stipulation in a lease.

Under s 4(3) of the LPA 1925, a right of entry affecting freehold land may be exercisable on condition broken or for any other reason but, unless it relates to a rentcharge held for a legal estate, it may be exercised only within the perpetuity period. Under the Perpetuities and Accumulations Act 1964, a 'wait and see' rule applies so that it is not necessary to know at the outset if the right could be exercisable outside that period. Under s 1(2)(e) of the LPA 1925, a right of entry annexed to a legal rentcharge is itself a legal interest but any other right of entry on freehold land must be equitable.

A right of re-entry is suitable for overage. It operates in relation to freehold land in a similar way to such a right for a lease. As leasehold rights can be used for overage, as discussed in Chapter 7, so can freehold re-entry.

3.4 RESTRICTION ON THE REGISTER

3.4.1 How restrictions on the Register work

The terms of sale provide in the normal way that the granter agrees to make the overage payment on the trigger event. The granter then agrees with the imposer that if it disposes of the land to another landowner then on the disposal any person acquiring will enter into a direct covenant with the overage owner to pay the overage and if the new landowner in turn resells there will be a similar covenant on that disposition and so on. The parties then apply to the Land Registry to enter on the Register of Title to the overage land a restriction that no disposition is to be registered without the consent of the overage owner. The imposer then agrees with the granter that if a deed of covenant in the agreed form is produced, the imposer will consent to the disposal.

In some cases, the parties try to short circuit the requirement for a formal consent by the overage owner. They seek to have the restriction registered in a form that no disposition is to be registered unless a transferee produces to the

Land Registry a deed of covenant in that form. However, this requires the Land Registry in effect to police the overage and it is understood that the Land Registry does not accept this burden.[1]

3.4.2   Fettering freedom of alienation

(A)   The statutory context
Overage by restriction on the Register works by controlling the power of the landowner to dispose of the land. It rests on the provisions of s 58(1) of the LRA 1925 which provides that:

> 'where the proprietor of any registered land ... desires to place restrictions on transferring ... the land or on disposing of or dealing with [it] ... in any manner in which he is by this Act authorised to dispose or deal with it ... the proprietor may apply to the Registrar to make an entry in the register that no transaction to which the application relates shall be effected unless ...'

one of certain things are done. The relevant ones are:

> '(b)   unless the consent of some person or persons, to be named by the proprietor, is given to the transaction;
> (c)   unless some such other matter or thing is done as may be required by the applicant and approved by the registrar.'

Under subs (2), if the registrar is satisfied with the right of the applicant to give the directions then he may enter the requisite restrictions on the Register but it is specifically provided that he has no duty to enter any restriction except on such terms as to payments of fees and otherwise as may be prescribed or to enter any restriction that he deems unreasonable or calculated to cause inconvenience.

This is supplemented by r 235 of the Land Registration Rules 1925 (LRR 1925[2]) (inserted by the Land Registration Rules 1996[3]) which allows an application under s 58 to be made by the proprietor or by any person with his consent. The application must be in Form 75 and state the particulars of the restriction required to be entered on the register and if the applicant is not the proprietor must be accompanied by a consent signed by him or his solicitor.

Schedule 2 includes various forms of restriction. Forms 9, 10 and 11 deal with the Settled Land Act 1925 (SLA 1925) and no new settlements can now be created under that Act.[4] Form 11A deals with the rights of beneficiaries under a trust of land.[5] Form 11B deals with the interest of beneficiaries in an estate

---

1   See **3.4.2(*F*)**.
2   SR&O 1925/1093.
3   SI 1996/2975.
4   See **3.4.2(*D*)**.
5   See **3.4.2(*D*)**.

and Forms 12, 12C and 12D deal with charities.[1] None of the specified forms specifically deals with overage, and the use for that purpose depends on a particular interpretation of the legislation.

It will be evident from the discussion of *Quia Emptores* 1290 that the intention of that Act was that the holder of land in fee simple should be free to sell land without any restriction. The words in the English translation are that it should be lawful for every freeman 'to sell at his own pleasure his lands and tenements or part of them'. Thus the superior lord could not in future control substitution. That Act is fundamental to English law of property and we therefore need to consider how it is possible for a restriction to be proposed.

(B) The Oldham case

The question of alienation arose in the case of *Oldham Borough Council v Attorney General*,[2] which related to a charity. As mentioned below, there are restrictions on disposals by charities and the particular question that arose in this case was whether or not some playing fields should be sold. In the course of his judgment Dillon LJ said:

> 'It is not in doubt, as a general proposition, that charitable trustees who hold land as part of the permanent endowment of a charity, or land which has been occupied for the purposes of a charity, have power to sell that land with the consent of the court, or of the Charity Commissioners.'

The judge went on to consider how the power of sale arose. It might have arisen under s 29 of the Charities Act 1960 or under s 29 of the SLA 1925 or:

> 'a general power at common law curtailed by section 29 of the Act of 1960, and previously by the Acts of 1853 and 1855,[3] which made the consent of the court or the Charity Commissioners necessary.'

The judge did not consider the extent to which this 'common law' power arose and, as indicated above, the power is indeed not a common law one at all but arises by virtue of statute, namely, *Quia Emptores* 1290. At common law, there could be (and before 1290 frequently was) a restriction on the power of sale.

The specific restrictions to which the judge refers relate to charity land and settled land and it is necessary to consider those because they are relevant to the restrictions as indicated above.

(C) Charity land

The restrictions for charity land derive from the old law of Mortmain which itself was relevant to *Quia Emptores* 1290. The general law that there could be

---

1   See **3.4.2(C)**.
2   [1993] Ch 210.
3   Charitable Trusts Act 1853; Charitable Trusts Amendment Act 1855.

no restriction on the sale of a fee simple applied to land belonging to the Church just as much as it applied to land belonging to other owners. However, there was a separate and parallel system of Church law which was not subject to regulation by Parliament and, ultimately, was subject to an appeal to the Pope in Rome. Under ecclesiastical law, land held for the Church could not be sold. Whatever the medieval law, at the latest under the Submission of the Clergy Act 1534,[1] ecclesiastical law became part of, and subject to, the general law of the land and thus Church land became saleable. This was found inconvenient and, under various statutes, initially the Ecclesiastical Leases Act 1571, restrictions were imposed on dealing with charitable land. Land held for institutions generally remained subject to the law of Mortmain (which prohibited land being transferred to a corporation without Royal licence) and if a licence in Mortmain was given the land could be made inalienable. During the nineteenth century, these rules were gradually rationalised and the Mortmain laws were finally abolished by the Charities Act 1960. As a result of the nineteenth-century legislation and s 29 of the Charities Act 1960 (now replaced by s 36 of the Charities Act 1993) there is a general rule that charity land cannot be sold but, in practice, a very wide power is conferred of sale with the consent of the Charity Commission and in the specific circumstances set out in s 36 of the 1993 Act charity trustees can sell even without that consent.

(D)   Trust land

A similar historical development applies to land held in trust. As mentioned above, *Quia Emptores* 1290 applied only to land held in fee simple and did not apply to other types of freehold land for life or in tail. These types of right were used particularly during the eighteenth century to render land belonging to a family inalienable for very long periods of time under the device known as the strict settlement. This was found inconvenient during the nineteenth century when the tenant for life was unable to sell, for example for a new railway or for the expansion of a town, and was unable to carry out other works such as digging coal or cutting down woods. As a result, Parliament intervened in a series of Settled Land Acts culminating in the SLA 1925. The legislation before 1925 retained the lesser freehold interests but conferred on the tenant for life a power of sale. Under the SLA 1925, the fee simple was vested in the tenant for life but he was given a power of sale exercisable only in certain circumstances and subject to the conditions laid down in that Act. That remains the case, although since the coming into force of the TLATA 1996 no new strict settlements can be created. Existing ones will continue until they run out under the perpetuity laws.

Parallel to the development of the strict settlement was originally the trust for sale. This was a device developed in the eighteenth and nineteenth centuries to hold land that was not intended as part of a family estate. Land used in

---

1   25 Henry VIII c 19 supplementing 24 Henry VIII c 12.

business such as a shop or factory or land held as an investment would be acquired for a family in the name of trustees. They were directed to hold this as an investment and therefore the intention was that it should be sold sooner or later. The doctrine of conversion was applied to such land so that where there was an obligation to sell (with a power to postpone the sale) the land was in law treated as if it were money and not land and the rules of inheritance that applied to it were the rules that applied to money.

This device was adopted and enlarged by the LPA 1925 which created a trust for sale in a wide variety of circumstances. As part of the machinery of the trust for sale, s 26 of the LPA 1925 provided for not more than two people to be able to consent to a sale (and therefore entitled to withhold their consent). It will be evident that because the land was treated for this purpose as being converted to money this was not in law a restriction on alienation of land. It was simply machinery in relation to the procedure for sale. In case those parties did not give their consent, the court was given power to override the refusal.

In the TLATA 1996 the doctrine of conversion was abolished and trusts for sale were changed into trusts of land. Nevertheless, that Act allowed for consent to be given to a sale under s 10. It should again be noted that this applies only in the trust context and any trust power must be operated for the benefit of the trust.

(E) How far restrictions can be applied

This background is, as indicated above, represented by the legislation. The forms of restrictions set out in the LRR 1925 relate to trusts and settlements and to charities. They do not relate to overage.

Therefore, there must be some doubt as to whether in having regard to the very wide terms of *Quia Emptores* 1290 there is power to impose a restriction on the sale of land in the interests of overage.

If there is a restriction and the landowner nevertheless disposes of the land, the overage owner may be in a difficult position. The conveyance or transfer will be effective to pass the freehold.[1] The transferee has a duty to lodge the transfer for registration within two months and if it does not do so the legal estate revests in the transferor,[2] but if the transferee does apply to the Land Registry and they simply do not register until the overage owner gives consent there may be a stalemate. If the new landowner refuses to give the covenant to pay overage then unless there is a right of re-entry the overage owner will have limited remedies. It is possible that the overage owner may be able to compel a

---

1   *Old Grovebury Manor Farm Ltd v W. Seymour Plant Sales and Hire Ltd (No 2)* [1979] 3 All ER 504.

2   *Brown & Root Technology Ltd v Sun Alliance and London Assurance Co Ltd* [1997] EGLR 39.

retransfer back to the seller,[1] but the authorities on that relate to leaseholds where there is no equivalent of *Quia Emptores*. The overage owner may have an action for damages,[2] since the previous landowner will remain liable on its own covenant but, if the sale has been by a liquidator or a bank enforcing its security, that is unlikely to be much help.

(F) Land Registry Practice Leaflet 29

The Land Registry has issued a Practice Leaflet on the subject, the current version dated April 1999. It is concerned with practical issues of drafting and does not go into the underlying legal issues. It does, however, make it clear that if the restriction is not limited to the lifetime of the restrictioner then it should make it clear who has the benefit thereafter, which indicates that the benefit is assignable in other circumstances. The Leaflet gives examples of restrictions in common use by developers of land, for example to ensure that buyers of house plots join the management company and contribute to the costs of common services, but the Leaflet also makes it clear that 'The examples below are for illustration only. Please do not take them as implying that we endorse the use of any particular form of restriction for this purpose'. The Leaflet does not discuss overage restrictions as such.

3.4.3 Unregistered land

The restriction can be placed on a register only if there is a register to place it on. Where the title to land is not registered, it is not possible to impose a restriction of this sort. Where land is held on trust, it is possible to provide that the trustees can sell only with the consent of a specified person but most cases of overage will not relate to trust land. In practice, it is unlikely now that overage land will be unregistered. It is compulsory to register title on every sale, on every lease for over 21 years and on many other types of change of ownership. There may be cases where land does not change hands and the original owner continues to hold the unregistered title but that land is to be subject to overage. Where that occurs, however, the covenant not to sell will be a personal covenant that will remain enforceable against the original granter. If the granter disposes of the land then, by definition, the disposition will give rise to an obligation to register and it will then be possible to place a restriction on the register. In such a case, the imposer can lodge a caution against first registration and it will be notified when the overage land changes hands. It can then require the restriction to be placed on the title.

However, it remains the case that this method cannot be used to secure overage on unregistered land. In principle, the rules for the two types of land

---

1   *Esso Petroleum Co Ltd v Kingswood Motors (Addlestone) Ltd* [1974] QB 142; *Hemingway Securities Ltd v Dunraven Ltd* [1995] 1 EGLR 61.
2   *Williams v Earle* (1868) LR 3 QB 739; *Cohen v Popular Restaurants Ltd* [1917] 1 KB 480.

should be the same although the courts recognise some inevitable differences.[1]

3.4.4 A named person

Section 58(1)(b) of the LRA 1925 provides that the consent to be given to the disposition must be the consent of some person or persons 'to be named by the proprietor'. Of course, it is possible to alter the person having the benefit of the restriction and in trust circumstances this is often done. It is worth noting that if there is a transmission of the overage rights then it will be necessary to change the restriction on the Register so that it refers to the new overage owner. This cannot be done ahead of time by the form of the original restriction because the name must be known. Apart from anything else, this is essential for the administration of the land registration system so that the Land Registry will know whose consent needs to be obtained.

3.4.5 Expense

There is a practical issue relating to the transmission of overage land. On each occasion, it will be necessary for the new owner to enter into a deed of covenant with the overage owner and for the overage owner to give consent to the disposition. This will involve extra work and therefore expense. By itself this is no argument against it but it is a continuing cost for the overage owner unless that cost can be thrown onto the landowner. The expense needs to be foreseen at the time the overage arrangements are made so that the parties know who will have to meet it.

3.4.6 Mortgages

The restriction will be in the form that no disposition is to be registered without the consent of the overage owner or the registrar or the court. Experience shows that banks and other institutions lending money to landowners find such overage devices as charges, leases and rights of re-entry unacceptable as potentially prejudicing their security. However, banks and others are apparently very ready to accept a restriction on the Register.

This is surprising in view of the potential problems that could arise on a sale. The landowner is in a direct contractual relation with the overage owner. If the landowner applies for consent to the sale and produces a deed of covenant by the buyer undertaking to pay overage or impose this obligation if it resells, then the overage owner is contractually bound to give consent to the sale. A mortgagee will normally not be in direct contractual relation with the overage owner and unless the mortgagee can take the benefit of the third party contract

---

1 As for overriding interests under s 70 of the LRA 1925, which have no direct equivalent in unregistered land.

rights it may find itself in a difficult position if it has to enforce its security over the overage land. It can of course require its purchaser to enter into a deed of covenant with the overage owner but the overage owner is not under a legal obligation to the bank in the same way as it would be to the landowner. This may be overcome by a direct covenant between the overage owner and the bank, although this adds to the expense of the mortgage.

It may well be that, in practice, if the problem arose a court or the registrar would order that on production of a suitable deed of covenant any objection of the overage owner should be overridden.

To a limited extent this problem could arise on other transmissions by act of law, for example on inheritance on death, but it is likely that the personal representatives would be treated as bound by and having the benefit of the contract in place of the deceased land owner.

3.4.7 General

The restriction on the Register is in wide use and is generally acceptable in the legal profession. Nevertheless, there are a number of issues which have not yet been decided. It has not been tested and doubts must remain as to whether it would be upheld by a court. A court is likely to be guided in this as in other issues by having regard to questions of public policy and the extent to which a deliberate overage bargain should be seen as overriding the general principle that land should be made freely alienable.

There must be many thousands of restrictions entered on registers of title around the country in this form. The Land Registry considers that it is obliged to enter such a restriction on request. In practice, it is likely that the court would give a wide interpretation to s 58 of the LRA 1925 if only because of the very large number of overage arrangements which have been made in reliance on and the interpretation given to that section. It is likely that, in view of the fact that many transactions have been carried out on the face of what the advisers to the parties considered to be a settled view of the law, the courts would accept this practice but the point is not beyond argument.

To the extent that overage by its nature creates a contingent future interest as discussed at **9.8.3** and **12.6** then it can only take effect behind a trust of land and therefore a restriction on the Register, which can be used to protect interests under trusts, is appropriate. If overage is not automatically a trust interest, and to the extent that it can be seen as an incumbrance on land or a fetter on ownership, the use of a restriction could still be held to be unlawful.

3.5 CONCLUSION

Positive covenants to pay are, in principle, suitable for overage but the law needs to be clarified before they can be seen to be entirely safe. Estate rentcharges, although designed to make positive covenants enforceable against future owners of land, are not appropriate for overage. Whatever their original function, the RA 1977 deals with them in the context of management and the provision of services and a court would be likely to limit their use to such circumstances.

Rights of re-entry should be suitable for overage provided that similar arrangements work on leaseholds but there must be a risk of the court granting relief on unpredictable terms.

Restrictions on the Register are widely used for overage and if the courts were to strike them down then many bargains made in good faith would be upset. There are problems of principle in using them, and restrictions were designed for trusts and charities. However, it is unlikely that a modern judge would find a widespread modern commercial arrangement unlawful because it offends against a statute passed in the thirteenth century to prevent barons exploiting their freehold subtenants.

The main difficulty with positive covenants is that they cannot stand alone but need another legal structure to support them. For that reason, many imposers and their advisers prefer to use restrictive covenants.

Chapter 4

RESTRICTIVE COVENANTS

4.1 WHY RESTRICTIVE COVENANTS ARE USED

It was seen in Chapter 3 that positive covenants do not bind the overage land and therefore cannot be directly enforced against purchasers from the granter. Thus, whilst a positive covenant can be enforced against the original granter, it cannot be enforced against a subsequent landowner without a special device being used. A number of methods of passing the burden on to successive owners have been considered, but each of these has problems.

For that reason, many imposers have wished to use restrictive covenants. As they are a type of covenant, the normal rules set out in Chapter 3 apply to them, including the general rule that at common law the burden cannot be enforced against successive owners. However, since *Tulk v Moxhay*[1] in 1848, it has been established that provided a restrictive covenant satisfies certain conditions, then an injunction (an equitable remedy) will be granted to restrain action in breach of the covenant by a later owner. This was explained by Lord Templeman in *Rhone v Stephens*[2] by saying that:

> 'the conveyance may however impose restrictions which, in favour of the covenantee, deprive the purchaser of some of the rights inherent in the ownership of unrestricted land . . . equity does not contradict the common law by enforcing a restrictive covenant against a successor in title of the covenantor but prevents the successor from exercising a right which he never acquired.'

In relation to overage, therefore, the analysis of land burdened by a restrictive covenant designed to protect overage is that the purchaser acquired land only to be used for its current use. The development value (or a portion of it) was never acquired and therefore continues to belong to the imposer.

Restrictive covenants are the most widely used overage device. Instructions to a solicitor from a selling agent will very often assume that this method is the one to be used and that it works. In this chapter doubts will be cast on that assumption. However, covenants remain a simple and straightforward method and, in practice, will usually perform as intended.

---

1   (1848) 2 Ph 774.
2   [1994] 2 AC 310 at 317.

As explained below,[1] the courts have indicated that restrictive covenants should not be used to secure a financial benefit. However, those remarks have been made in cases where the covenantee is trying to make money out of a covenant that was originally imposed for amenity purposes and therefore is trying to exploit an unplanned bargaining position.

4.2 HOW RESTRICTIVE COVENANTS WORK

A restrictive covenant used for overage is normally in the form of a provision such as 'not to use the land for any purpose other than agriculture (*or* a private garden *or* for some other current specified use)' or 'not to erect on the land any buildings or structures' or 'not to apply for or implement any planning consent on the land' or even simply 'not to carry out on the land any development' (*or* 'development for which planning consent is required').

The intention of the parties is that if the landowner wishes to develop the land or change the use to a more profitable one, it goes to the overage owner to negotiate a release or relaxation of the covenant in return for a payment.

This is not normally made explicit as the special benefit of a restrictive covenant, namely, to bind successors does not apply where it is not taken for the benefit of land.[2] Evidence that the overage owner is prepared to negotiate for a relaxation in return for cash may, before the Lands Tribunal, be fatal to his case.[3] Furthermore, the Lands Tribunal has discretion to vary or release restrictive covenants on certain grounds mentioned below.[4]

Accordingly, by analogy with s 84(1)(ii) of the LPA 1925, a statement will be included in the covenant stating that the land is being sold at a reduced price because of the existence of a covenant. On the basis of the Lands Tribunal decision in *Re Cornick's Application*,[5] this approach seems acceptable. Therefore, the form of covenant will go on to provide that the covenantee (the overage owner) reserves the right (on request from the landowner) to modify or release the covenant. However, it should be noted that s 84(1)(ii) refers only to reduction in value at the time of sale and *Re Cornick* was a case in 1994 concerning a covenant made in 1988. Land values may not have moved much in these years. Accordingly, this arrangement may not be suitable for the situation where an overage payment may be called for 20 or 30 years after the covenant was imposed.

---

1   See **4.6**.
2   See **4.5**.
3   See **4.9**.
4   See **4.8**.
5   (1994) 68 P&CR 372.

As a restrictive covenant is a type of covenant it can, of course, be supported by the methods used in the case of positive covenants such as a restriction on the Register. Nineteenth-century conveyances sometimes include a right of re-entry in the event of condition broken.[1] However, the powers of the Lands Tribunal under s 84 of the LPA 1925 apply to any restrictive covenant while they do not apply to positive covenants.

4.3 ADVANTAGES

Restrictive covenants have the advantages of being simple to draft and flexible enough to cover a wide range of circumstances. They are well and widely understood. Even if specific words are not used to annex the benefit to the land of the covenantee, and even if there is no assignment of the benefit of the covenant, the benefit will automatically run under s 78 of the LPA 1925[2] and as mentioned above the burden of the covenant automatically binds the land of the landowner. Furthermore, there is no perpetuity problem.[3]

4.4 CONDITIONS

As with other types of overage, there are problems arising from the conditions and rules associated with the use of restrictive covenants. Such covenants are designed for amenity and were originally developed in the nineteenth century as a private means of carrying out certain purposes which are now managed in the public interest by planning control. In the century between 1848 when *Tulk v Moxhay*[4] was decided and 1948 when a comprehensive system of town and country planning was introduced by Parliament, restrictive covenants were often the only means of preserving the amenity of an area against speculative building or undesired changes of use and they still have many of the features for which they were designed.

The restrictive covenant must benefit the land of the covenantee and not his pocket. It must be restrictive in substance and therefore cannot include an obligation to pay money. As it is equitable and the primary remedy to enforce it is an injunction, it is subject to the discretion of the court. Furthermore,

---

1   See **10.3.1** for use by the Crown.
2   *Federated Homes Ltd v Mill Lodge Properties Ltd* [1980] 1 WLR 594.
3   In *London and South Western Railway Company v Gomm* (1882) 20 Ch D 562 at 583, Jessel MR said that the freedom of restrictive covenants from the perpetuity rules was another exception like easements and charities. The Law Commission in a report on restrictive covenants recommended that they should cease to have effect after a given period of time unless a specific application was made to keep them in force, but this is unlikely to be implemented. See *Report on Obsolete Covenants* (1991) Law Com No 201.
4   (1845) 2 Ph 774.

because it operates in a similar way to a planning restriction, there is now a public law system under s 84 of the LPA 1925 for the discharge or variation of covenants. Each of these problems will now be considered.

4.5 LAND OF OVERAGE OWNER

At common law the benefit of a covenant (positive or restrictive) can either exist in gross, that is to say separately from land (such as a personal covenant to pay), or appurtenant to ('annexed to' or 'touch and concern' or 'relate to') and run with specified benefited land. The special rules discussed in this chapter relate to restrictive covenants which are annexed to and benefit land.[1]

4.5.1 What if there is no land?

Restrictive covenants obtain the benefit of running with and binding land only if they exist for the benefit of other land. This basic rule was laid down in 1914 in *London County Council v Alan*.[2] Mr Alan had entered into covenants with the London County Council restricting the use of some land that belonged to him. He sold part of the land and kept part of it. Breaches of the covenants occurred. The London County Council was able to succeed against him personally in relation to the land that he continued to own but could not do so against a purchaser from him because the Council had no land to be protected. In relation to the particular case of local authorities, the decision has been overcome by giving certain powers, notably under s 106 of the Town and Country Planning Act 1990, which allow them to enforce covenants even where they do not have any land capable of benefiting, but the general rule of law continues to apply in the case of private persons.

In 1993, in *Surrey County Council v Bredero Homes Ltd*[3] the Council sold some land to Bredero and on the sale imposed a covenant which in effect restricted development to the terms of an original planning consent for construction of 72 houses. Bredero later obtained a further planning consent which allowed them to build 77 houses. The Council claimed damages for breach of the covenant. The judge recognised that there was a direct covenant between the parties (in this case there was no question of following the burden because Bredero had entered into the covenant), but awarded nominal damages of £2. The Council appealed and the Court of Appeal found in favour

---

1   Before 1926 it was possible for a restrictive covenant taken for the benefit of land nevertheless to be a personal covenant the benefit of which did not pass with land, see *Master v Hansard* (1876) 4 Ch D 718 at 724; but the court would normally not permit the benefit of the covenant to pass, see *Chambers v Randall* [1923] 1 Ch 149. Since the enactment of the LPA 1925, ss 78 and 79, that may have changed.

2   [1914] 3 KB 642.

3   [1993] 1 WLR 1361.

of the developer. The Council would have been able to claim substantial damages under the principles laid down in the *Wrotham Park*[1] case only if the equitable jurisdiction of the court was available. That would apply only where the covenant was being enforced in equity and where the Council was able to claim an injunction. The Council could not make such a claim in this case because it had no land to benefit and so could not claim an injunction. Therefore, the court could not award damages. An injunction on its own would not lie at common law for the straight breach of the covenant itself and the Council therefore would be limited to the damage calculated on ordinary contractual principles. As the Council suffered no pecuniary loss, the damages were nominal.

This particular case was argued on the basis of normal restrictive covenant rules. It now appears from the decision of the House of Lords in *Attorney-General v Blake*[2] that if the covenant had been deliberately and expressly imposed for overage, and if the Council could have shown that on a sale of land for 77 houses it would have got a higher price than on a sale for 72, the result would have been different because the original parties were still involved. In a simple contract the claimant for breach can recover damages for loss of profit or loss of the right to bargain for a future payment. In *Attorney-General v Blake*, Lord Nicholls of Birkenhead pointed out that 'had the covenant been worded differently, there could have been provision for payment of an increased price if further planning permission were forthcoming'. Although their Lordships criticised *Bredero*, they did not overrule it.

4.5.2 What land?

The normal form of amenity restrictive covenant will be drafted to benefit 'the retained land of the seller and each part of it capable of benefiting' or 'the remainder of the land comprised in title number'. Sometimes the nature of the benefited land will be obvious. For example, if the owner of a seaside bungalow imposes an amenity covenant to protect his view when he sells part of his garden and the buyer constructs a large house that obstructs the view, it will be obvious that the purpose of the covenant was indeed to protect the view from a particular house.

Where land is sold off a large farm or a landed estate, the wording may need to be interpreted. As a general rule, the courts will be prepared to hold that the covenant is in principle capable of benefiting any land owned by the covenantee at the time of the sale even if that is several miles away.[3] The Lands Tribunal on an application to vary or release the covenant will not

---

1 See **4.6**.
2 [2000] 3 WLR 625.
3 See *Marten v Flight Refuelling* [1962] Ch 115, but this can be rebutted by appropriate evidence.

necessarily take that view. In its report on Land Obligations[1] the Law Commission recommended that any restrictions imposed in the future would have to be by reference to a particular area defined, for example, on a plan, but that report has not been implemented.

Where a restrictive covenant is used for overage, the overage owner needs to ensure that the benefit of the overage rights will not be shared with people who may later buy parts of his land. If a covenant is taken for and benefits a large area, unless there is wording to the contrary either (preferably) in the document which imposes the covenant on the original sale or (as a second best) in the subsequent sale document, then (under s 78 of the LPA 1925) the benefit will relate to all of it. Therefore, if the covenantee sells even a small part of his land, he will (unless something is said to the contrary) also sell part of the benefit of the covenant. It follows that the buyer of the part will have the right to enforce the covenant and, thus, to share in overage. Consequently, it is normal practice to annexe the benefit of the covenant to 'such part of the seller's land as shall not have been conveyed or transferred on sale or as shall have been so conveyed or transferred with the express benefit of this covenant'. It was held in *Zetland v Driver*[2] that such a restriction is effective. The effect of such wording is that where the benefited land passes by gift or inheritance then the benefit of the covenant will automatically pass with it, but if it is sold then a deliberate decision must be taken as to whether the overage rights pass to the buyer or not.

Alternatively, the covenant may be specifically annexed to a fairly small defined piece of land which will always belong to the overage owner.

Where there are such words and the overage owner wishes to sell part of its land, it may include either a reservation of the benefit of the covenant, or an agreement and declaration that no part of the benefit passes to the sold land, or a covenant on the buyer not to claim that benefit, or perhaps all three. These devices have not been tested in court.

4.5.3   How much land?

In general, the courts will presume that any piece of land is capable of benefiting from a covenant. Sometimes a restrictive covenant is combined with a ransom strip[3] and a covenant may be taken for the benefit of a very small piece of land. It will then be a matter of the particular circumstances as to whether or not the covenant really does benefit that land. In *Kelly v Barrett*,[4] the benefit of the covenant was stated to go with the road known as Fitzjohn's Avenue in Hampstead. The land subject to the covenant was next to that road.

---

1   *The Law of Positive and Restrictive Covenants* (1984) Law Com No 127.
2   [1939] Ch 1.
3   See Chapter 6.
4   [1924] 2 Ch 379.

At the date of the covenant the road was already a highway, but it was not then maintained by the local authority (although this did occur by the time the case came to court). The covenant restricted the land in question to a private house and the case concerned a doctor who wanted to use it professionally. The judge held that the covenant could not be enforced because the plaintiff only had the subsoil, and the surface of the land now belonged to the Highway Authority. This decision was approved by the Court of Appeal. The subsoil did not benefit from the covenant.

In *Re Gadds Land Transfer*,[1] there was another covenant restricting property adjoining a road to the use of a single house. In that case, the road had not been taken over by the Highway Authority and the covenant was upheld apparently on the basis that the owner of the road was entitled to improve it and if the covenant was broken it was possible there would be more wear on the road and therefore making it up would be more expensive.

There is some indication, however, that roads are not a satisfactory support. The case of *North Foreland Ltd v Ward*[2] concerned a compromised case where there were roads which had not been taken over by the county council and the judge expressed doubts as to whether they would be sufficient to support the covenant.

4.6 BENEFIT OF LAND NOT A BANK ACCOUNT

As mentioned above, restrictive covenants have been designed for amenity and the courts have expressed the view that they should not be used for the benefit of a cash claim. In many cases, the person seeking to uphold the covenant has simply tried to exploit a bargaining position which has arisen from a normal covenant intended for amenity not overage. This issue has arisen particularly in relation to decisions of the Lands Tribunal or in appeals from such decisions.

In 1956, in *Driscoll v Church Commissioners*,[3] which concerned covenants in a lease, the Church Commissioners were in fact seeking to enforce the covenant itself and were not seeking money. In the course of his judgment, however, Denning LJ said that the covenantee could enforce the covenant if it served a useful purpose:

'And in considering whether it still serves a useful purpose, I think it very important to see the way in which the landlord, or whoever is entitled to the benefit of the covenant, has used it in the past and seeks to use it in the present. If he uses it reasonably, not in his own selfish interests but in the interests of the

---

1   [1966] Ch 56.
2   Unreported, but noted in *Preston and Newsom on Restrictive Covenants*.
3   [1957] 1 QB 330.

people of the neighbourhood generally – as for instance when he gives his consent for any reasonable change of user – then it will serve a useful purpose. I should have thought that if he uses it unreasonably – for instance, to extract a premium as a condition of his consent ... it would no longer serve a useful purpose.'

In *Wrotham Park Estate Co v Parkside Homes Ltd*[1] in 1973 the land was sold off the Wrotham Park Estate in 1935 subject to a covenant not to develop except in accordance with a layout plan approved by the seller. At all material times the estate continued to own land in the neighbourhood. In 1971 Parkside started building works on the sold land without having a plan approved. In 1972 the estate issued a writ claiming an injunction to restrain building on the land and asking for the demolition of buildings erected in breach of the covenant. The court decided that it would not order the buildings to be demolished (it would be a waste at a time when housing was needed), but in exercise of its jurisdiction it would award damages and these should be such a sum as the estate might reasonably have demanded for relaxing the covenants. In all the circumstances of that particular case the estate was given 5 per cent of the likely profit of the housebuilder. The decision was approved by the House of Lords in *Attorney-General v Blake*.[2]

In 1974, in *Re S J C Construction Company Ltd's Application*,[3] the Lands Tribunal followed *Wrotham Park* and awarded the substantial sum of £9,500 and when that case was referred to the Court of Appeal in 1975 the court said that it would not interfere with the way in which the Tribunal had exercised its discretion. In that case, the proportion was 50 per cent of the profit and the case is considered a remarkably high award.

However, in 1979, in *Re EMI Social Centres Ltd's Application*,[4] there was a covenant in a lease restricting the use of the premises to the sale of alcohol. The person entitled to the covenant recognised that the application to the Tribunal was bound to succeed and the issue was what compensation should be paid. The claim was for £3,000 for loss of bargaining power, but the Tribunal held that there was no principle that such loss could be recovered and awarded £150.

The case of *Stockport Metropolitan Borough Council v Alwiyah Developments*[5] was decided by the Court of Appeal in 1983. The Council had originally owned two adjoining areas of land. It continued to own one of them as a housing estate. The other was sold in 1960 subject to a covenant that required it not to be used except for agriculture. Alwiyah Developments

---

1   [1974] 1 WLR 798.
2   [2000] 3 WLR 625.
3   (1974) P&CR 200 (LT), (1975) 29 P&CR 322.
4   (1980) 39 P&CR 421.
5   (1983) 52 P&CR 278.

applied to the Lands Tribunal for the restriction to be modified to enable it to build 42 houses. The Tribunal granted the application and awarded compensation calculated by reference to the diminution in value of the price that 11 of the houses on the council estate would suffer if they were sold because they previously had a view over open farmland and they would now look over a housing estate. The compensation was reduced because the tenants of the houses had a statutory right to buy at a low figure and the total compensation was assessed at £2,250. The Court of Appeal upheld the decision of the Tribunal and specifically considered the argument that the Council might be entitled to compensation for the loss of bargaining power. The Court held that the bargaining power had been rendered valueless by the provisions of s 84 of the LPA 1925. It said:

> 'A loss which is the consequence of an event is usually something which would not have ensued had that event not happened. If the discharge or modification had not been granted the bargaining power would have remained.'

It followed therefore that because Parliament had conferred power on the Lands Tribunal to modify the covenant, the Council could rely not on the original form of the covenant but only on the modified version.[1]

In 1994, in *Jaggard v Sawyer*,[2] the owner of adjoining land was entitled to the benefit of a covenant which prevented building on a private garden. A house was built and the owner in fact wished to have the building demolished because she resented the interference with her privacy and objected to extra traffic over a private roadway. The court refused to order that the house be demolished and awarded damages instead amounting to £694.44 representing a share of the total sum that might have been reasonably asked under the *Wrotham Park* rules for giving relief from the covenant.

In *R v Braintree District Council, ex parte Halls*,[3] a local authority which had sold a council house under the 'Right to Buy' legislation subject to a covenant to use as a single private dwelling-house sought to charge a sum as high as 90 per cent of the proceeds when the buyer wished to sell part of the garden for the building of a bungalow. The case came to court on judicial review of the Council's decision not to give consent under para 6 of Sch 6 to the HA 1985

---

1   In *S v UK* (1984) Appl 10741/84, [1984] 41 DR 226, a claimant from Northern Ireland argued that where restrictive covenants of which she had the benefit were extinguished, the compensation of £350 awarded was too low and a breach of her human right to the enjoyment of her possessions. The Commission of Human Rights in Strasbourg did not accept the argument that the compensation should reflect what would have been agreed between covenantor and covenantee in the absence of the legislation. The Commission concluded that the very purpose of the legislation was to prevent owners claiming large sums for the release of obsolete restrictions and therefore the claimant's private interests were properly subordinated to the public good.
2   [1995] 1 WLR 269, see also **6.3**.
3   (2000) 80 P&CR 266.

which prohibits the Council from charging for a consent. At first instance the judge found in favour of the Council. The Court of Appeal held that the Council was not entitled to charge because the overage purpose of the covenant was not authorised by the HA 1985 and its demand was unlawful.

It is important that the covenantee should seek to enforce the covenant itself and not make it clear that he was willing to accept a sum instead. In 1998, in *Gafford v Graham*,[1] negotiations had taken place between the parties and the covenantee indicated that he would be prepared to release the covenant in return for a payment. On that basis, he deliberately did not seek to enforce it. The Court of Appeal held that someone who knows he has rights and deliberately does not enforce them should not be given an injunction. His willingness to settle on payment of a cash sum could be reflected and taken into account in the award of damages, as should any diminution in the value of the land he retained.

It follows that where there is a covenant it can be dangerous for the covenantee to negotiate for a release for cash in case the negotiations break down and the correspondence is produced in evidence to the Tribunal or the court. It may be worth making any such negotiations 'without prejudice'. However, where there is a specific concluded bargain, the courts will give effect to the agreement irrespective of whether the Tribunal might have released the covenant.

4.7 RESTRICTIVE

In order to qualify for the special benefits of a restrictive covenant, it must be restrictive in substance. The form may be less important. A covenant to use land for agriculture may be construed as being restrictive in nature, namely not to use for any other purpose rather than to impose an obligation to carry on farming. In *Tulk v Moxhay* itself,[2] the covenant was actually positive in form and, indeed, provided that the covenantor should spend money by providing that he and his successors would:

> 'At all times thereafter at his and their own costs and charges, keep and maintain the same piece of ground and square garden, and the iron railing round the same in its then form, and in sufficient and proper repair as a square garden and pleasure ground, in an open state, uncovered with any buildings, in neat and ornamental order.'

---

1 (1998) 77 P&CR 73.
2 (1848) 2 Ph 774.

The covenant was nevertheless construed as a restrictive one.[1] On the other hand, a covenant not to allow a structure to fall into disrepair will be construed as positive because it imposes an obligation to spend money or carry out building works.

A covenant not to sell without offering the land to a specified person could be treated as positive.[2] In addition it would now be regarded as being in substance not a covenant at all but a right of pre-emption[3] and subject to the perpetuity rules.

It follows therefore that an obligation to make an overage payment must be a positive covenant. Sometimes an attempt is made to overcome this problem by including a restrictive covenant in normal form such as not to erect any buildings and then adding a provision to the document that if the landowner wishes to erect buildings, he will be entitled to approach the overage owner and require a release of the covenant in return for a payment.

One problem with this approach is that the form of the deed as a whole, taking all the provisions together at the time of the original sale, is that the overage owner is prepared to release the covenant for money and this runs up against the problems set out above. There can be no objection to a payment that actually compensates the person having the benefit of the covenant for ascertained loss.[4] Equally, there can be no objection to a payment for the sum equal to the difference between the unencumbered and encumbered values of the land at the time of sale.[5] Furthermore, the courts are obviously prepared to accept that a covenant can be released on payment of a suitable sum that might be charged if the covenantee is approached.[6] However, in view of the remarks of Lord Denning in *Driscoll v Church Commissioners*,[7] it will not be acceptable for an overage owner to exploit his position. One point that has not been determined is the position if this is not exploitation but the fulfilment of

---

1 See *Metropolitan Electric Supply Co Ltd v Ginder* [1901] 2 Ch 799 per Buckley J at 809: 'The contract really is a contract, the whole of which is in substance the negative part of it, that he will take the whole from them, involving that he will not take any from anybody else. I therefore think that the fact that the contract is affirmative in form and not negative in form is no ground for refusing an injunction'. See also *London and South Western Railway Company v Gomm* (1882) 20 Ch D 562 at 583; *German v Chapman* (1877) 7 Ch D 271.

2 *Manchester Ship Canal Co v Manchester Racecourse Co* [1901] 2 Ch 37. The court recognised this was a right of first refusal but the contract which contained the right was scheduled to an Act of Parliament and as such was capable of overriding general rules of law.

3 See Chapter 8, also *London and South Western Railway Company v Gomm* (1882) 20 Ch D 562.

4 LPA 1925, s 84(1)(i).

5 LPA 1925, s 84(1)(ii).

6 *Wrotham Park Estate Company v Parkside Homes Ltd* [1974] 1 WLR 798.

7 [1957] 1 QB 330.

an explicit overage bargain. In view of *Attorney-General v Blake*,[1] it appears that the courts will take the view that such a bargain entered into at the outset of the original sale is something that should be enforced.

A second and more fundamental problem is that the courts may consider the substance of the obligation to be positive, not restrictive. Although the documents appear to say 'not to build but if you do then to make a payment', the true position is 'to pay if you build'. The essential feature of the bargain is the payment not the prohibition against building. That being so, it is possible and indeed likely that the courts would hold that restrictive covenants developed since *Tulk v Moxhay*[2] are not designed or suitable for securing payment in this way. It is also possible that the rules relating to conditions subsequent and precedent may have a bearing on the way the courts would interpret such a provision.

4.8   THE LANDS TRIBUNAL

The position of the Lands Tribunal has been indicated above because a number of the cases involving payment have come to the courts on appeal from the Tribunal. Section 84 of the LPA 1925 confers on the Lands Tribunal (without prejudice to any concurrent jurisdiction of the court) power on the application of any person interested in any freehold land affected by a restriction (or leasehold land where the lease is for more than 40 years and 25 years has passed) arising as to the use of the land or building on the land to discharge or modify the restriction provided the Tribunal is satisfied on various matters. The jurisdiction relates to restrictions and does not extend to positive covenants. The scope of the Tribunal's powers and the way in which its discretion is to be exercised have themselves been the subject of considerable litigation, but they are not directly relevant to the question of overage.

– Ground (a) is that by reason of changes in the character of the property or the neighbourhood or other circumstances the restriction ought to be deemed obsolete.

For example, it could be a suitable ground where at the time of the original sale the overage land is open country. The seller may foresee the possibility that building might develop in the area and indeed wish to claim overage for that reason. If in fact the land then becomes surrounded by developed land, the neighbourhood would have changed and the landowner might be able to succeed in an application for removal of the covenant. In such a case, the principle in *Stockport Metropolitan*

---

1   [2000] 3 WLR 625.
2   (1848) 2 Ph 774.

Borough Council v Alwiyah Developments[1] would apply, so that once the covenant was varied, the rights of the covenantee would relate only to the new position not the position before variation. Thus, the change in the neighbourhood, namely the very thing that allowed development to occur, so giving overage value to the covenant, could itself undermine the basis for securing the overage.

– Ground (aa) is that where the restriction impedes reasonable use of the land and the restriction does not secure to the persons entitled to the benefit of it any practical benefits of substantial value or the restriction is contrary to public interest and that money would be an adequate compensation for the loss or disadvantage which a person will suffer.

   In such a case, if the continued existence of the covenant would impede some reasonable use of the land or would do so unless modified, the Tribunal may release or modify the restriction. By definition in an overage case the overage owner is only interested in money and from the wording of the section it seems that by definition money would not be a 'practical' benefit. Once again therefore it follows that the Tribunal would have jurisdiction to release the covenant and any basis of claiming compensation on the covenant would, on the same principles as above, be restricted to the form of the covenant as varied, thus again undermining the overage.

– Ground (b) is that the persons of full age and capacity for the time being entitled to the benefit of the restriction in respect of the land to which the benefit of the restriction is annexed have agreed either expressly or by implication to the covenant being discharged or modified.

   Once again, if the whole basis of an overage transaction is that the covenant can be released or modified in return for payment this must bring the restriction within the paragraph. Indeed, that was the underlying ground for the decision in *Gafford v Graham*.[2] Although there was nothing written into the original covenant, the covenantee had in fact been prepared to negotiate a release in return for cash and both in the county court and the Court of Appeal the existence of those negotiations was considered to be relevant. Even though the negotiations may be on the basis of a particular figure, the court is not bound to award that figure and may well award something less. Therefore, even if the parties have built a formula into their original negotiations, the court is not bound by it, although it may be a matter to take into account.

– Ground (c) is that the proposed discharge or modification will not injure the persons entitled to the benefit of the restriction.

   The section goes on to say (in relation to all four cases) that an order may direct the applicant to pay to any person entitled to the benefit of a

1   (1983) 52 P&CR 278.
2   (1998) 77 P&CR 73.

restriction a sum of money. It must follow that the loss of the right to receive an overage payment of money is not an injury for this purpose. Accordingly, the same principles will apply as set out above.

4.9 COMPENSATION ORDERED BY THE TRIBUNAL

Section 84(1) of the LPA 1925 provides that if the Tribunal discharges or modifies a restriction, it:

> 'may direct the applicant to pay to any person entitled to the benefit of the restriction such sum by way of consideration as the Tribunal may think it just to award under one, but not both, of the following heads, that is to say, either –
>
> (i)   a sum to make up for any loss or disadvantage suffered by that person in consequence of the discharge or modification; or
>
> (ii)   a sum to make up for any effect which the restriction had, at the time when it was imposed, in reducing the consideration then received for the land affected by it.'

Section 84(1)(ii) is unlikely to be of much assistance to an overage owner, except perhaps in the short term where there was a clear difference in value of the land with and without the covenant at the time of imposition and values have not moved.[1] It is just possible that 'make up for any effect' might allow a recalculation of values in the light of changed circumstances but 'then received' must refer back to the cash figures at the date of imposition.

Section 84(1)(i) is more useful and is the basis of substantial awards as in *SJC Construction Co v Sutton London Borough Council*.[2] However, as *Stockport Metropolitan Borough Council v Alwiyah Developments*[3] shows, the loss or disadvantage is that suffered after variation because the covenant under discussion is itself subject to release or variation. Therefore, in most cases compensation under this provision will not make up for the loss of overage rights.

4.10 EQUITABLE NATURE OF COVENANT

As we have seen at common law, the burden of a covenant cannot bind successors in title. Therefore, the covenant can only operate in equity. All equitable remedies are at the discretion of the court. Of course, the court must exercise that discretion in accordance with established legal principles. Section 50 of the Supreme Court Act 1981 provides that where the court has jurisdiction to entertain an application for an injunction or specific perform-

---

1   See *Re Cornick's Application* (1994) 68 P&CR 372.
2   (1974) 28 P&CR 200 (LT), (1975) 29 P&CR 322.
3   (1983) 52 P&CR 278.

ance, it may award damages as well or instead. *Jaggard v Sawyer*[1] is a good example of the court exercising its discretion not to give a specific enforcement of a covenant but awarding damages instead and awarding as damages such sum as the court thought appropriate. To the extent therefore that the rights of the covenantee to overage depend on a clear ascertainable sum, those rights are liable to be set aside by the court exercising its equitable jurisdiction. It may well be that the court would consider it fair to give effect to the original bargain between the parties, but in the present state of the law this cannot be relied on.

Furthermore, the right to enforce the covenant is subject to the equitable doctrine of *laches* or delay. If a breach of covenant occurs (eg the start of building works) and the overage owner knows of the breach and takes no action to enforce his rights, he will lose the chance to do so and will not later be able to claim the assistance of the courts.[2] Therefore, it can be dangerous to negotiate for too long.

Restrictive covenants are said not to be subject to the rules against perpetuities,[3] but a normal covenant is vested at once. A covenant to take effect in the future or to secure a contingent future interest may be subject to the rule, so long as it continues to apply.

4.11 FORMALITIES OF RELEASE

Even where the landowner does not succeed in having the covenant set aside or the payment reduced, there is a technical problem in relation to the title. While not of great importance, this adds a minor complication to the use of restrictive covenants. In the increasingly rare cases where the title of the covenantor is unregistered, the covenantee will need to protect his interests by registering a D(ii) land charge under s 2 of the Land Charges Act 1972 against the estate owner. In practice, most changes of ownership of land will give rise to a requirement for first registration so this is now unusual. It could still be relevant in the case of a reverse overage where the sale includes a commitment by the seller that if its retained land increases in value it will pay a share of the increased value to the buyer. In that case, it is the seller who continues to own the overage land with unregistered title. Where this does apply, the Land Charges Registry will normally not cancel a land charge of this class because it cannot be satisfied as to who has the full benefit of it. Although, in theory, where the covenant relates only to land which continues in the ownership of the covenantee, this can be demonstrated, in practice it can be difficult to

---

1 [1995] 1 WLR 269.
2 *Gafford v Graham* (1998) 77 P&CR 73. For this reason, in *Wrotham Park* the estate had to act promptly.
3 *London and South Western Railway Company v Gomm* (1882) 20 Ch D 562.

persuade the Land Registry to cancel the entry. The entry will therefore remain on the title and will be there to be investigated by any subsequent purchaser. As indicated above, this is no longer such a common problem.

In practice, more important is the attitude of the Land Registry in relation to covenants entered on the Register of Title. They also will not cancel a notice of restrictive covenant although they are prepared to enter a note against it that a deed between certain parties is expressed to modify it. Therefore, it is necessary for any future owner of the land affected to obtain a copy of the deed and investigate the circumstances in which the overage owner claimed to be entitled to release the burden of the covenant. In a straightforward case this should not be a problem, but if there have been any difficulties (eg a long chain of transmissions on the part either of the landowner or the overage owner) then this can add to the costs of transferring title and may make the overage land less marketable in the future.

4.12 CONCLUSION

The use of restrictive covenants for overage is widespread. The attempt to use them (irrespective of the purpose for which they were originally imposed) to extract money from landowners has led to a number of disputes in the courts. Therefore, there is more law on this aspect of overage than others. The general trend of the decisions does not support the use of this device for overage. While there appears to be no specific decided case on a planned and premeditated overage structure involving a restrictive covenant expressly used for that purpose, the general tendency of the courts has not been favourable to those who wish to extract money from the release of a restrictive covenant. However, the courts do recognise that covenants have a value and landowners are prepared to pay to be released from them, and since *Wrotham Park* this trend has become well established. It remains to be seen how the House of Lords' decision in *Attorney-General v Blake*[1] will affect this. That case concerned damages for breach of an existing covenant and not a deliberate overage device.

It has to be said, however, that only in special circumstances will a restrictive covenant be suitable. A major difficulty for many imposers is that the overage owner must retain land nearby which is capable of benefiting. Where land is sold from a large farm or estate this may be practicable, but in many cases the sale will be of all the land belonging to the imposer in the neighbourhood. It is unsettled whether a covenant of this nature can be attached to a ransom strip or roadway but it must be doubtful.

---

1   [2000] 3 WLR 625.

Furthermore, a covenant is vulnerable to release or variation by the Land Tribunal. The Tribunal has a discretion and it may not exercise that discretion where the covenant was deliberately made for overage purposes, but this point has not been tested. Having regard to the origins of covenants in preserving amenity and protecting a neighbourhood, the Tribunal might consider that they should not be used for financial gain.

Undoubtedly, covenants have a nuisance value. There will be many cases, particularly where the overage sums are not large and where there could be long delays in taking a case first to the Tribunal and then on appeal to the courts, where the landowner considers it preferable to buy off the covenant by paying a sum of money. In practice, therefore, covenants will continue to be used on a wide scale. However, particularly in the case of potential large sums of overage, where the landowner is prepared to take several years and spend the necessary money to see a case through the Land Tribunal and the courts, it is not a method to be recommended. Equally, a landowner may simply disregard the covenant and develop in breach of it. If the overage owner does not take prompt proceedings, he will lose his rights.

Chapter 5

MORTGAGES AND CHARGES

5.1 HOW MORTGAGES AND CHARGES WORK

The basis of overage is a commitment to make a payment of money at some stage in the future and that commitment is supported by giving the recipient rights over the land from which the overage derives. The most usual method by which a future payment secured on land is arranged is a charge or mortgage.

A mortgage is treated for some purposes as being itself land and for other purposes as being an interest in land. A mortgagee whose mortgage is created by deed has certain powers over the land if the mortgage debt is not paid, including a power to sell the land and pay itself out of the proceeds. Under certain types of charge, the chargee does not immediately have these remedies as of right. It may, however, apply to the court for an order for sale of the exercise of other remedies. The order is to a considerable extent discretionary although the court's discretion has to be exercised in accordance with the legal rules.

The mortgage or charge is appropriate for use in overage. It is well understood and there are millions of mortgages in place around the country. The remedies are well known and there is a great deal of experience in operating them. Nevertheless, the mortgage itself was not designed for overage and issues arise in adapting it for that purpose.

The overage mortgage works by the granter giving the imposer a mortgage or charge to secure the amount of the overage payment when it arises. It secures nothing until the trigger event (such as planning consent) occurs. When that happens, the charge automatically secures the overage payment. If the payer does not pay, the recipient can sell the overage land (with the benefit of the planning consent just granted) and take payment out of the proceeds.

Charges can also be used to secure an income instead of a capital payment. The charge secures a proportion of the development value when that accrues, as on grant of planning consent, but nothing then becomes payable. On first occupation of developed property, interest begins to run. In this way, a charge can work in a similar way to an improvement lease.[1]

---

1   See **7.3.3**.

5.2 DISTINCTION BETWEEN CHARGES AND MORTGAGES

There are distinctions in law between charges and mortgages, but for most purposes they can be considered the same, and since 1925 the rules relating to the two have been assimilated to a considerable extent.

A mortgage is 'a conveyance of land or an assignment of chattels as a security for the payment of a debt or the discharge of some other obligation for which it is given'.[1] Before 1926, mortgages of freehold land were made by conveying the land to the mortgagee subject to a right to a reconveyance on redemption. Since 1926 that has been prohibited and under the LPA 1925, s 85, a mortgage of a freehold is made by either a demise for a term of years or by a charge by deed expressed to be by way of legal mortgage. Mortgages by demise are now rare.

A charge involves the appropriation of a separate fund out of which the sum due to the chargee is to be paid.[2] That might be considered suitable for overage as the trigger event creates extra value which should be sufficient to comprise a fund to support a charge. However, at present the development value does not create a legally separate fund capable of being independently charged. Therefore, the usual method is to create a mortgage.

5.3 LEGAL OR EQUITABLE?

There are distinctions between equitable mortgages and charges and legal mortgages and charges which are relevant to overage.

The normal type of mortgage on a house, farm or factory is a legal mortgage. There can be more than one legal mortgage on the same property. This raises issues of priority.[3] A legal mortgage is normally created by deed to secure a debt owing to a lender.

Equitable mortgages and charges arise in a number of ways. Where the mortgagor has only an equitable interest in the property, for example as beneficiary under a trust or as tenant in common, then the mortgage itself can only be equitable. The power of the mortgagee in that case may not extend to the property itself, but only to the interest of the mortgagor. However, where a mortgage is held under a trust of land, the mortgagee may be able to apply to the court for an order for a sale of the land itself even though the mortgagor may not have had the entire interest in the land and the court will decide in accordance with the principles referred to in s 15(1)(d) of the TLATA 1996.

---

1   *Santley v Wilde* [1899] 2 Ch 474 per Lindley MR.

2   See *Swiss Bank Corporation v Lloyds Bank Ltd* [1982] AC 584 at 594.

3   See **5.6**.

Therefore, even in the case of an equitable charge over a legal estate, one of the methods of conferring on the chargee a power of sale through an equitable mortgage of a legal estate is to make the chargee trustee (with power to appoint an additional trustee to give a receipt for capital money) with power of sale.

An equitable mortgage may also arise where there is some formal defect in the completion of the mortgage document. It would also arise where the mortgage is not created by deed but in some other way, such as by an agreement.

An agreement to grant a mortgage in the future will always be equitable.

'An equitable charge may, it is said, take the form either of an equitable mortgage or of an equitable charge not by way of mortgage. An equitable mortgage is created when the legal owner of the property constituting the security enters into some instrument or does some act which, though insufficient to confer a legal estate or title in the subject-matter upon the mortgagee, nevertheless demonstrates a binding intention to create a security in favour of the mortgagee, or, in other words, evidences a contract to do so: see *Fisher and Lightwood's Law of Mortgage* (9th edition, 1977), p 13. An equitable charge which is not an equitable mortgage is said to be created when property is expressly or constructively made liable, or specially appropriated, to the discharge of a debt or some other judicial obligation, and confers on the chargee a right of realisation by judicial process, that is to say by the appointment of a receiver or an order for sale: see *Fisher and Lightwood*, p 14.'[1]

5.4 FUTURE PAYMENT

The nature of overage is that it cannot be ascertained at the time the arrangements are made. It relates to a future uncertain payment.

This by itself is not a problem. In *Multiservice Bookbinding Ltd v Marden*,[2] the amount repayable was to be ascertained by reference to the value of the Swiss franc. The court held this was a valid mortgage even though the amount could not be known at the date the mortgage was taken out. In *Nationwide Building Society v Registry of Friendly Societies*,[3] the mortgage was index-linked according to the retail prices index. This was a 'friendly' case rather than one being hotly resisted by a mortgagor in default and, therefore, the decision must be regarded with some caution, but the court considered the issues and accepted that such a repayment was valid.

---

1 *Swiss Bank Corporation v Lloyds Bank Ltd* [1982] AC 584 at 594; see also citation of *Palmer v Carey* [1926] AC 703 and *Rodick v Gandell* (1852) 1 De GM & G 763 at 613 of *Swiss Bank Corporation*.

2 [1979] Ch 84.

3 [1983] 3 All ER 296.

There will then be other sums payable in addition to the principal. These could include a premium or a commission.[1] In addition, all mortgages will allow the lender to recover any outstanding interest and the costs associated with enforcing the security and those of course cannot be ascertained at the date the charge is taken out.

Of course, mortgages for 'all monies due' to a bank have been familiar for many years and under such mortgages the sum secured can vary from day to day and is not predictable at the outset, even if there is a maximum drawing limit.

The 1854 case of *Fleming v Self*[2] concerned security for a continuing subscription to a building society, the duration of which was uncertain. Lord Cranworth LC said:

> 'Now, generally speaking, a security of this nature is not redeemable. Where a mortgage is made to secure an annuity for the life of another, or to indemnify against contingent charges, or for any other object not capable of immediate pecuniary valuation, redemption is impossible.'

In that particular case, the mortgagor had a contractual right to redeem under the rules of the society, and the issue concerned the calculation of the sum due. That particular conclusion has been overruled by later authority,[3] but the principle above is still valid.

Such charges, however, all relate to the repayment of money paid either to the mortgagor or on behalf of the mortgagor to a third person under a guarantee, indemnity or surety. The situation of overage is different because at the date of the mortgage there is no debt to give rise to the liability.

More difficulty arises in relation to contingent future liabilities but the courts have not allowed conceptual problems to frustrate commercial reality. In the case of *In re Rudd & Son Ltd*,[4] a development company undertook with a local authority to construct some roads on its building site. The council was concerned that if the company became insolvent the roads would not be completed and therefore asked it to provide performance bonds to secure that the funds would be available. The company arranged for its bank to give the bonds and the bank in return took a mortgage on the land of the company. The company went into insolvent liquidation. At the time, nothing was due to the local authority, and possibly nothing might ever be due if in some way the roads could be completed without cost to the authority. The liquidator of the company asked the bank to vacate the mortgages. The Court of Appeal held

---

1   *General Credit and Discount Co v Glegg* (1883) 22 Ch D 549; *Bucknell v Vickery* (1891) 64 LT 701; *Potter v Edwards* (1857) 26 LJ Ch 468; and *Mainland v Upjohn* (1889) 41 Ch D 126.
2   (1854) 3 De G M & G 997.
3   *Re Park Air Services plc* [1999] 1 All ER 673.
4   (1986) *The Times*, 22 January.

that the bank was entitled to refuse to do so because there were still certain contingent liabilities outstanding under the suretyship for the bonds. As the bank had given an undertaking to the local authority that if the company failed to pay the bonds if they became due to the local authority then the bank would pay in their place, the bank was still exposed and the court held that the bank was entitled to retain its security until its liability was ascertained. This case reinforces some cases in other common law jurisdictions along the same lines.[1]

Wellesley v Wellesley[2] concerned a separation settlement. The husband agreed to pay the wife a sum of money including an annuity to be secured on land. At the time he was only tenant for life of some land, but subsequently he became entitled to a greater interest and the land itself became held by trustees subject to the husband's power to charge sums on the land. The husband refused to pay the annuity and the wife sued the trustees. The court held that the action succeeded. The court had power to enforce the promise to charge the land and that promise could be enforced against the trustees whose title derived through the husband.

In *Wellesley v Wellesley* there was an existing liability, although it did not arise from an earlier advance of cash. There was a present debt to *pay*, although not to *repay*. However, there is a well-established type of charge which does not even require that. Under various family arrangements in the eighteenth and nineteenth centuries, it was common practice for the family estate to pass to the eldest son. Other members of the family, including daughters and younger sons, would receive a money payment and that payment would be charged on the family estates and it would be the responsibility of the eldest son to make arrangements for payment. The charge was frequently held by trustees or it might be given to the person who had the benefit. Such a charge would not only arise in favour of the person who might be named in the original settlement or the will of the person setting up the arrangements, but power might be given to some future inheritor of the estate to make similar provisions for his own children. These would all be done by way of charge and the charge did not represent any money that had already been paid to the head of the family. It was a completely new sum payable out of the family estates to the junior members. Such charges have been valid for many centuries and in principle there seems no reason why the same rules should not apply to overage.

Since the coming into force of the SLA 1925 family charges of this sort have only arisen under settlements, and since the TLATA 1996 they can only arise

---

1   *Catley Farms Ltd v ANZ Banking Group (NZ) Ltd* [1982] 1 NZLR 430; *Cambridge Credit Corporation Ltd v Lombard Australia Ltd* (1977) 136 CLR 608; and *Bank of India v Transcontinental Commodity Merchants Ltd* [1982] 1 Lloyd's Rep 506.
2   (1839) 4 Myl & Cr 561.

under trusts of land. In these cases they subsist 'behind the curtain' in that they do not directly affect other persons dealing with the land, they operate only in equity. If the family sells the land, the rights which were originally to a charge on it are converted into rights against the proceeds of sale and are not binding on the purchaser.

There are provisions in ss 16 and 69–71 of the SLA 1925 for such a charge to be satisfied by a legal mortgage on the land itself and that would be binding on the purchaser. Such powers applied not only to settled land but also, under s 28 of the LPA 1925, to trusts for sale. It appears that the present power is s 6 of the TLATA 1996, but that section is primarily aimed at management and it is open to a court to hold that such an equitable charge cannot now be converted into a legal charge. Before the TLATA 1996, s 3(1)(b) of the LPA 1925 authorised the creation of a charge in such a case. Those provisions were repealed by the TLATA 1996, but s 3(1)(c) still remains – requiring an estate owner to give effect to equitable interests. Under s 2(3), certain equitable interests are excepted from the normal effect of overreaching where land is sold by trustees. It may be a difficult issue as to whether a particular form of overage falls within s 2(3), but a registered equitable charge will do so as will an estate contract to create a legal estate.

As the nature of overage is that it can only arise in the future, it may be argued that a charge to secure overage can only be equitable. At the time the charge is granted, it does not secure any liability at all. Therefore, it may be interpreted as an agreement to create a charge in the future or an agreement that on the occurrence of certain future events such as the grant of planning consent, a mortgage will then automatically arise. Although the matter has not yet been decided, it is possible that such an interest may be regarded as being equitable.

However, there is no doubt that the existence of a contingent future charge can have a present value. *In re Sutherland*[1] was an estate duty case where the value of shares in a company depended on its potential liability for a tax charge which might not arise and therefore was a contingent liability. The case was governed by English law, but the House of Lords drew on Scottish authorities to decide that a contingent liability is:

> 'a liability which, by reason of something done by the person bound, will necessarily arise or come into being if one or more of certain events occur or do not occur. If English law is different – as to which I express no opinion – the difference is probably more in terminology than in substance.'[2]

In *Mornington v Keane*,[3] Lord Mornington covenanted to secure an annuity by either a charge on freeholds, or an investment in stocks or by the best means in his power. The covenant was held to be enforceable as such, but it did not

---

1   [1963] AC 235.
2   Per Lord Reid at 249.
3   (1858) 2 D&J 292.

create any lien on Lord Mornington's property. In *Metcalfe v Archbishop of York*,[1] an incumbent agreed that if he were to be preferred to another benefice he would charge it. In 1814 he was preferred to another living and in 1817 charges of that sort were prohibited. No charge was executed. The court held that the covenant created an equitable charge independently of the covenant to execute a legal charge.

5.5　CLOG ON THE EQUITY

It is essential that whatever the form of the charge for overage, the landowner should not be entitled to 'redeem' or discharge it before the sum becomes due and, in particular, should not do so at a time when the trigger event has not occurred.

As a general rule, a mortgage cannot be made irredeemable. This is fundamental to the background basis of a mortgage. Originally, mortgages were created by the transfer of the freehold to the lender on the terms that if the debt was paid by a specified date (typically 6 months after the loan) known as 'the legal redemption date', then the lender would transfer the freehold back to the borrower. Strict time-limits were imposed on this and even if the borrower was a day late after the legal redemption date in tendering his payment, he would lose his land. This was considered harsh and from the Middle Ages the Courts of Equity intervened to protect borrowers and allow them to redeem in a wide variety of circumstances.[2] In modern conditions, the remedy of foreclosure (which would allow the mortgagee to become the owner of the land) is very restricted and the mortgagor has a long period of time in which to claim relief from the court. Even where that is not desired and the mortgagee simply wishes to sell the land, there are a number of ways in which a mortgagor can apply for relief.

It follows that the concept of an irredeemable mortgage is one that is not acceptable to the law. However, there was a good deal of litigation on this at the beginning of this century, as a result of which it has become clear that a postponement of a mortgage as part of a good and sensible bargain provided it is for a limited time is something that can be validly agreed and the courts will respect that agreement.

The rules can, for the purposes of application to overage, be summarised as follows.

(1)　If the legal redemption date has passed, the landowner can redeem the charge even though there may be an agreement to let the charge run on.[3]

1　(1835) 1 My & Cr 547.
2　See the account of Viscount Haldane in *G & C Kreglinger v New Patagonia Meat and Cold Storage Co Ltd* [1914] AC 25 at 35.
3　*Knightsbridge Estates Trust Ltd v Byrne* [1939] 1 Ch 441 at 456.

(2) The parties can agree that the charge will not be redeemed for a fixed period, but they cannot create an irredeemable charge (as distinct from a debenture).[1]

(3) There must be mutuality of bargaining power.[2]

(4) In particular, if the deal is one-sided, harsh or oppressive, the landowner will be entitled to redeem and have the estate back unfettered.[3]

(5) The chargee cannot normally stipulate for a collateral advantage which nullifies the rules set out above, but this rule (originally established to prevent lenders getting round the usury laws, which laid down maximum rates of interest) will not be applied to upset a fair bargain.[4]

(6) Equally, if the landowner wishes to redeem, the courts will hold him to his bargain and not allow this if it upsets the deal.[5] An example is *Santley v Wilde*, which concerned a form of overage. A lady had a lease of a theatre with 10 years to run. She needed to borrow for the business which involved subletting the theatre. The lender agreed to lend on the terms that she would pay one-third of the net profits from underleases. The borrower later wished to redeem without paying the profits. The court held her to her bargain. She could redeem, but only on the terms that she accounted for the profit rent. As Lord Parker said in *G & C Kreglinger v New Patagonia Meat and Cold Storage Co Ltd*,[6] 'But except in the case of mortgages to secure moneys advanced by way of loan, I can find no trace in the authorities of any equitable right to redeem without giving effect as far as possible to the terms of the bargain'.

(7) Although the true rule is 'once a mortgage, always a mortgage', if the true bargain is not a mortgage at all but something else (eg a family settlement dressed up as a mortgage), the court (at least in its equitable jurisdiction) will have regard to the substance and not the form and in that exceptionable case will permit an irredeemable mortgage.[7] Similarly, a commercial sales agreement taking the form of a mortgage will be interpreted on its true nature.[8]

Applying these rules to overage, the position will be that if the deal is freely negotiated between parties of similar bargaining strength and is part of an arrangement, such as the sale of land, which is a proper transaction on its own,

1   *G & C Kreglinger v New Patagonia Meat and Cold Storage Co Ltd* [1914] AC 25 at 38.
2   *Knightsbridge Estates Trust Ltd v Byrne* [1939] 1 Ch 441 at 454, 461.
3   *Noakes & Co Ltd v Rice* [1902] AC 24, confirming the long-established rules of equity.
4   *G & C Kreglinger v New Patagonia Meat and Cold Storage Co Ltd* [1914] AC 25 at 37; and *Knightsbridge Estates Trust Ltd v Byrne* [1939] 1 Ch 441 at 455.
5   *Santley v Wilde* [1899] 2 Ch 474.
6   *G & C Kreglinger v New Patagonia Meat and Cold Storage Co Ltd* [1914] AC 25 at 49.
7   *Howard v Harris* (1681) 1 Vern 33, 2 Ch Cas 147 as explained in *G & C Kreglinger v New Patagonia Meat and Cold Storage Co Ltd* [1914] AC 25 at 36.
8   *Re Petrol Filling Station, Vauxhall Bridge Road* (1968) 20 P&CR 1.

the courts will hold the parties to their bargain. The legal redemption date should be the trigger date[1] and, if so, then the mortgage cannot be unilaterally redeemed early by the landowner by offering something less than the overage sum. It does not matter how many years the arrangement is capable of lasting, so long as there is some prospect that at some time in the future the landowner can have the charge released, but that can properly be postponed until after the trigger date.

In any event, the court has a discretionary power under s 50 of the LPA 1925 to discharge land from any incumbrance and declare the land free of it on any sale or exchange. This is subject to the condition of the section that a sum of money has to be paid into court to meet 'the contingency of further costs, expenses and interests, and any other contingency, except depreciation of investments, not exceeding one-tenth part of the original sum paid in, unless the court for special reason thinks fit to require a larger additional amount'. This is a wide power, but where overage is deliberately used by parties and the rights of the overage owner can be protected only by a continuing interest in land by a charge, it is unlikely to be exercised.

5.6 PRIORITY

The main issue in overage is to provide security so that the overage owner has an asset that will apply notwithstanding other calls on the proceeds of the land. This can involve the recipient in competition with a bank which has lent money on the security of the overage land. The issue of priorities is a frequent one in mortgages and there is a great deal of law on the subject as competing lenders each try to gain an advantage where the borrower has become bankrupt or gone into liquidation and the land is not of sufficient value to discharge all the debts.

In theory, this should not be a problem. If the landowner wishes to borrow from a bank, he will do so on the security of the current use value while overage is secured on the development value. In practice, however, a bank is not prepared to limit its security in this way and there are issues of definition[2] which mean that the two separate values cannot be distinguished as separate assets.

The general rule on priority is set out in s 94 of the LPA 1925. Previous distinctions between legal and equitable mortgages have largely been displaced by priority being governed in the order of registration. Assuming all competing charges are properly registered and have been made by deed, under s 94(1):

---

1   This also has advantages for limitation. See **5.8**.
2   See Chapter 12.

'a prior mortgagee shall have the right to make further advances to rank in priority to subsequent mortgages (whether legal or equitable) –

    (a) if an arrangement has been made to that effect with the subsequent mortgagees; or

    (b) if he had no notice of such subsequent mortgages at the time when the further advance was made by him; or

    (c) whether or not he had such notice as aforesaid, where the mortgage imposes an obligation on him to make such further advances.'

It will be noted that the section assumes an advance and that is an initial objection to securing the overage debt in this way. The overage payment is not advanced. It is something that will arise automatically by virtue of a future event such as the grant of planning consent and under the arrangement between the parties the overage automatically accrues to the recipient. At the date of the initial charge the mortgage will secure nothing or a nominal sum. If the landowner then makes a normal charge in favour of the bank, that will take priority because it cannot be said that the overage owner has an obligation to make an advance of the overage sum.

The obvious way around this is by deed of priority by arrangement under paragraph (a). In principle, there is no reason why a bank should not agree that if the trigger event occurs then its charge should be postponed to the overage charge. Such an agreement if contained in the bank's mortgage deed would be binding on a successor to the bank as owner of the bank mortgage because it would operate as a restriction within the mortgage itself. Clearly, a bank would not be prepared to do this without some good reason and, therefore, the overage charge needs to contain a restriction on the Register to protect it.

Although a restriction to protect the interest of a prior chargee is not one of those specifically mentioned in the LRA 1925, there is an established practice that many mortgages will contain such a restriction and the Land Registry has considerable experience in entering them. Even though they do not have statutory justification, their widespread use means that they are now unlikely to be struck down as an unlawful fetter on the freehold. However, the point remains open and it is still possible to argue that such a restriction is contrary to *Quia Emptores* 1290.[1]

Another practical issue is often encountered. Lending institutions prefer where possible to have a first legal charge. If a prior charge is taken to protect overage, then the bank's mortgage can only be a second or subsequent charge. Although there are many lenders that specialise in second mortgages, they do so by accepting a higher risk and charging a higher rate of interest, and this is not normally acceptable to solvent borrowers. The main reason is that although of course land can be sold subject to a subsisting first charge, few buyers are prepared to take the land on that basis.

---

1   See **3.14**.

There is little experience of dealing with this in the context of overage. The overage mortgages most often used are in arrangements with bodies that are likely to keep land for a long time and do not need to borrow on the security of it such as local authorities. In the case of land that is intended to be readily marketable and particularly land with potential development value which may be passed from one developer to another, the existence of the first charge may in practice be found to limit the mortgageability and therefore marketability of the land. In theory this need not be so, as the charges will be secured on separate values, but at present the law does not recognise those values as distinct and would see the charges in competition.

5.7   CONTINUED INVOLVEMENT

As the mortgage is a present interest even though for a nominal sum, the overage owner in his capacity as chargee will be involved in various dealings with the land. For example, if in order to obtain planning consent the landowner is required to enter into an agreement under s 106 of the Town and Country Planning Act 1990, any mortgagee on the land will have to join in the agreement. Similarly, if unlawful development takes place, the local authority will serve notice on any mortgagee which may be under legal duty (however theoretical its practical enforcement) to rectify the breach of planning control. This may be seen as an advantage as it means that the overage owner will be involved in the development process, but it will also involve expense.

Under s 99 of the LPA 1925, a mortgagor in possession of land has a power of leasing, including a building lease for up to 999 years at the best rent that can reasonably be obtained without taking a fine. For building leases, see Chapter 7. All commercial leases exclude this power of the mortgagor under s 99 as a matter of course. The purpose of overage is to sell the land as unfettered as possible so that the overage owner does not interfere with normal management. Therefore, in overage by charge the powers in s 99 will need to be modified but not excluded altogether.

5.8   LIMITATION AND PERPETUITIES

In *Knightsbridge Estates Trust Ltd v Byrne*,[1] it was held as part of the ratio that the rule against perpetuities does not apply to mortgages. In relation to overage, this could present a problem. The context of the decision was an actual loan of money that had been received and would have to be repaid at some time. The court did not consider the situation of a charge to secure a

---

1   [1939] 1 Ch 441 at 463. In that case, the deal was to last 40 years.

contingent future interest such as overage and the case cannot be taken as authority that the rule cannot apply in any circumstances. If the Law Commission proposals on perpetuities are enacted, this will cease to be an issue.

Under s 20 of the Limitation Act 1980, no action may be brought to recover mortgage money or the proceeds of the sale of land after 12 years from the date on which the right to receive the money accrued. Under s 20(3), the right to receive a principal sum of money is not to be treated as accruing so long as the property comprises a future interest. In the case of a normal mortgage to secure money actually advanced, the traditional practice[1] was to provide for the mortgage debt itself to be made due and payable 6 months after the date of the mortgage. Under s 103 of the LPA 1925 there are provisions for notice to be served requiring payment of the mortgage money. Modern practice is to provide for the power of sale to arise automatically, usually immediately on the grant of the mortgage. Sometimes it may be accompanied by an agreement that it will not be exercised unless an instalment is overdue, but that does not alter the fact that it becomes payable immediately. In the case of a normal mortgage where there are regular payments of interest or other acknowledg-ments, the fact that the mortgage money has become due is not the problem even though the mortgage itself may run for a great many years because payment by the mortgagor acknowledges the continued existence of the debt. In the case of overage, however, there will be no payment until the trigger event occurs. That being so, it is sensible to provide in the mortgage deed that the legal redemption date will not occur (and therefore the power of sale will not arise) until the trigger event occurs.[2] This will protect the landowner against an unexpected sale by the overage owner and will protect the overage owner against the operation of the Limitation Act 1980. If overage is to be treated as a future interest, this may be covered by the provisions referred to above, but in the present state of the law it would not be wise to rely on it.

The effect of including such a provision in the Deed of Charge is that if the recipient is seeking to recover the overage by enforcing the power of sale and the mortgage the buyer will need to investigate if the trigger event has actually occurred. Under s 104(2) of the LPA 1925, where a conveyance is made in exercise of the power of sale conferred by the Act, the purchaser's title is not impeachable on the ground that no case had arisen to authorise the sale and the purchaser is not concerned to see or inquire whether a case has arisen to authorise the sale. In practice, therefore, a purchaser should be fully protected and in any event it will not be difficult to determine whether the trigger event has occurred.

---

1   See **5.5**.
2   This is also relevant to clogs, see **5.5**.

5.9 CHARGES AND RE-ENTRY

If overage is protected by a charge, then it should not be coupled with the reservation of a right of re-entry. As indicated above,[1] the courts have intervened for many centuries to protect mortgagors against foreclosure, namely losing the land simply because the mortgage debt is not paid. Furthermore, this has been enlarged into a rule against collateral advantages where the mortgagee will be prevented from using his stronger financial position as lender to obtain for himself an advantage which is not strictly related to the commercial transaction of the loan. The rules in this regard have been modified so that a proper commercial arrangement, such as tying the brand of drinks sold in a particular pub to the output of a brewer who is also a lender, is recognised and legitimate but they are watched carefully so that the position of the lender is not abused. Nevertheless, the lender will not be able so to fulfil its position that it can simply take over ownership of the property as this will be seen as a disguised form of foreclosure and foreclosure can only be exercised in accordance with the rules which include elaborate provisions to protect the interests of the borrower. If a charge is coupled with the right of re-entry, there is a risk that the overage owner may exercise that right in order to repossess the land. As discussed above, it is likely that relief would be given against re-entry on terms that the overage sum is paid. Nevertheless, there must be a risk that coupling a charge with its remedies with re-entry and its remedies may be considered to be an oppressive burden on the overage land.

If there is double overage, where the granter has originally given a right of re-entry to one imposer and subsequently has given a charge to another imposer, and if a charge to secure overage does fall to be treated as equitable, the second overage owner will not be entitled directly to claim relief against re-entry.[2]

5.10 REMEDIES

If the overage sum is not paid when it is due, the recipient normally would exercise a power of sale and this can be done under s 101(1)(i) of the LPA 1925 where the mortgage, whether legal or equitable, is made by deed. There are other remedies, such as putting in a receiver to let the land and take rents, which may be appropriate in particular cases, but normally the recipient is interested in a capital payment.

---

1   See **5.5**.

2   *Bland v Ingram's Estate Trustees* [1999] 25 EG 185. The apparent decision to the contrary in *Croydon Unique Ltd v Wright* [1999] 40 EG 189 turned on the construction of s 138 of the County Courts Act 1984 and did not affect the common law position. See the dissenting judgment of Pill J in *Croydon*.

If an overage charge must be treated as an equitable mortgage because it is interpreted as an agreement to pay in the future, provided it is made by deed the power of sale is still available. Previously there was a common practice of requiring the borrower to 'attorn tenant' to the lender by acknowledging that he was the lender's tenant. The principal reason for this was to enable the lender to exercise the power of distraint on the land and is now of little value. Equitable mortgages are also frequently accompanied with a power of attorney that would itself give the lender a power of sale which would not otherwise be implied in an equitable charge not by deed. Under s 4 of the Powers of Attorney Act 1971, where a power of attorney is given by way of security it is irrevocable. Nevertheless, such a power is a personal arrangement and will only bind the grantor and not any later landowner and, therefore, it is unlikely to be of much help in the normal overage context.

5.11 TRUSTS AND CHARITIES

In the unlikely event of a charity giving an overage charge, the consent of the Charity Commission will be needed under Charities Act 1993, s 38, because it is not a charge to secure repayment of money borrowed.

In general, trustees (whether charitable or not) cannot charge land in the trust except for the benefit of the trust. As mentioned above, a special type of family charge to secure a future payment is authorised by the statute, but apart from that trustees must take special care in giving any charge. They have power to do so under the TLATA 1996, s 6, but the power must still be exercised for the benefit of the trust, not an outside imposer.

If trustees take a charge as imposers (and it was suggested in *Page v Lowther*[1] that in an appropriate case they might be under a duty to obtain overage), they need to ensure they have the power. Section 3(4) of the Trustee Act 2000 confers on trustees a limited power of investing in loans secured on land, but does not by itself authorise an overage mortgage. It seems from the context that it is permissible to leave part of the sale price outstanding on a mortgage. This was permitted under the provisions of the Trustee Act 1925 repealed by the Trustee Act 2000 and is expressly preserved by amendments in Sch 2 applying to settled land. Trustees who do not have exceptionally wide express powers may still be able to rely on s 6 of the TLATA 1996, but they will need to check those powers. The express power in s 3(4) of the Trustee Act 2000 extends only to a contract under which one person provides another with 'credit' and that is not apt to describe an overage mortgage.

---

1   [1983] STC 799, 57 TC 199. The case actually concerned a leasehold structure but the logic would apply to a charge.

5.12 CONCLUSION

Mortgages and charges can be useful in overage. The technical arguments sometimes raised against them, such as clogs and uncertain sums, are not persuasive. However, they are not suitable where the landowner wishes to use the land as security for borrowing. First, banks will not normally be willing to see any prior charge on the title. Secondly, even if they are, the overage charge will not secure any debt and therefore a later incumbrancer will obtain priority. If a landowner does not need to borrow, overage mortgages can be useful.

If it were possible to draw a legal distinction between the (present) current use value and the (prospective future) development value, then the future value could be designated as a separate fund on which a charge (as distinct from a mortgage) could be secured, but the law has not yet developed to that stage.

Chapter 6

RANSOMS

6.1 HOW RANSOMS WORK

A ransom is an area or volume adjoining the overage land or a right or interest in land affecting the overage land and, as a result of the position of the ransom land or the nature of the right, development cannot take place on the overage land without the consent of the owner of the ransom. It is strictly a form of negative overage, although it may be combined with a device, such as an option to purchase the ransom, which converts it to positive.

The most common form of ransom is the ransom strip and where there is such a strip the respective positions of the parties will be clear. The landowner will not like being ransomed, but it will accept an unavoidable situation. Many of the decided cases therefore concern the use of other ransoms such as rights of way, or airspace or sporting rights. They are a less certain way of obtaining overage and a number of the decided cases concern unsuccessful attempts to use such rights for overage.

The imposer retains ownership of the ransom subject only to such rights as will enable the granter to make proper use of the overage land for current purposes. When the trigger event occurs, the payer will need the co-operation of the recipient in order to exploit the development value and the payer may grant or release rights or sell land to enable development to take place.

The rights of the overage owner depend on its remedies. Unlike other forms of overage, the courts have not laid down consistent rules as to the ability to obtain an injunction as distinct from merely having a remedy in damages. There is also a distinction between damages at common law and in equity. This aspect is considered at **6.3**.

Ransoms have been the most litigated aspect of overage. The cases go back to the nineteenth century and so, well before modern expressions such as clawback and overage had been invented, Victorian lawyers were arguing over the same issues. As a result of this history of disputes, many fine distinctions have emerged in the legal rules.

6.2 RANSOM STRIP

The use of the ransom strip depends on the geographical situation of the overage land. In a typical case, the imposer will retain a strip of land between the overage land and the highway. If access is obtained over a private track, then the imposer remains the owner of that track. The granter is given a right of way for a limited purpose such as agriculture. The right of way may be further restricted, for example by its width being defined so that it is just wide enough for current purposes but is not wide enough for any likely future development.

The strip does not have to be a piece of undeveloped land. It may be a river, part of a garden or, as many cases illustrate, a private roadway. Railtrack plc is very aware of the value in the right to have a bridge built over the railway line to connect building land on one side to a highway on the other.

One issue relates to 'ransoming the ransom'. Suppose A Ltd owns a field adjoining a highway. It sells to B Ltd and retains ownership of a strip of land 6 feet wide alongside the highway and gives B Ltd an agricultural right of way over the strip. If B Ltd obtains planning consent to develop, then A Ltd will be well placed to demand a share, perhaps one-third, of the development value in return for a right of way for all purposes. Suppose, however, B Ltd resells to C Ltd. B Ltd then retains another strip 6 feet wide between A Ltd's strip and the land sold to C Ltd. If C Ltd gets planning consent, it will only be willing to pay one total figure for ransom. B Ltd has by a simple device halved the value of A Ltd's ransom.

Sometimes it is suggested that this problem can be overcome by a movable freehold. These are rare. The most common ones are foreshore, which moves as the coast advances and recedes, and lot meadows, where the particular area to be grazed by an owner in any year is determined by lot cast each year.[1] Both of these arise from ancient provisions of the common law and it is not considered possible to have new types of movable freehold now.

6.2.1 Location of the strip

It follows that the strip must be in a position which will effectively prevent development. It will do the imposer no good to retain a strip between the overage land and the highway if the landowner is able to do a deal with another neighbour to obtain access from a different direction. For this reason, some imposers wish to retain a strip of land all the way around the edge of the overage land. This can be difficult to administer and it may materially affect the value of the land.

---

1   See *Baxendale v Instow Parish Council* [1981] 2 All ER 620.

The strip itself may constitute a track across the overage land. In *Pardoe v Pennington*,[1] a farm was divided among members of a family and it turned out that, although it is possible that the parties were not aware of it at the time, one member retained ownership of a track. The land on each side of the track passed to another member. There is a normal presumption that the owner of land adjoining a track also owns the subsoil up to the middle line or *medium filum*. In this case, that presumption did not, on the facts, apply and therefore the owner of the soil of the track was in a strong bargaining position when access was needed over the track.

6.2.2 Occupation

The ransom strip needs to be managed during the period up to the trigger event which could be many years. If it is simply abandoned, it will degenerate and become covered in scrub. In that case, it will be liable to occupation by a squatter. The squatter could be a complete stranger who would thereby succeed to the rights of the overage owner. More likely, it will be the landowner of the overage land who simply takes over use of the strip, perhaps because the original fence or hedge is at the outer edge of the strip and there is no physical boundary between the strip and the overage land. In that case, also after 12 years the landowner will acquire title by adverse possession. The normal way of avoiding this is to give the landowner either a licence to occupy the strip or a lease of it which can be terminated when the trigger event occurs. Leases are discussed in Chapter 7, but it needs to be pointed out here that there can be problems in terminating them. If the overage land and the strip are used for agriculture, the lease of the strip will be a farm business tenancy and that can normally be terminated (by notice to quit or break clause) without difficulty. If it is used for some other form of business, it will be necessary to contract the lease out of the Landlord and Tenant Act 1954 (LTA 1954) or obtain court approval to a surrender. However, the landowner may need to acquire ownership (eg to dedicate the access as a highway) so that retention of simple ownership can be enough to reserve overage.

Where the overage owner retains land in the neighbourhood, it may of course be possible for it to continue to occupy the land or to lease it to some other person who will occupy it.

One special type of ransom derives from the right of a lord of the manor to what is known as 'manorial waste'. This can be common land,[2] a village green[3]

---

1 (1998) 75 P&CR 264.
2 *McKay Securities plc v Surrey County Council* [1998] EGCS 180, *Newbury District Council v Russell* unreported, but account in *Daily Telegraph*, 8 March 1997.
3 *Hanning v Top Deck Travel Group Ltd* (1993) 68 P&CR 14.

or a strip of roadside verge.[1] The lord as owner of what is otherwise a valueless piece of waste land can claim all the rights of a landowner, including the right to stop a neighbour crossing the land to gain access to his house. A developer is often prepared to pay a substantial sum for an unqualified right of access. This is a special form of overage in that the lord will usually not have owned the overage land in the recent past. As Rattee J said in *Newbury District Council v Russell*:[2]

> 'There is no doubt that the right of the landowner to object to trespassers upon the land, in particular by placing objects upon it or driving vehicles over it, is a valuable right. The defendants and their predecessors have in the past derived substantial sums from the grant of wayleaves and easements over the Common.'

The existence of this bargaining position gave rise to problems in a particular class of cases. In many parts of the country the owners of houses adjoining a common have used an access for well over 20 years. If the land had not been common they would have obtained a right of way under the Prescription Act 1832 but because it was unlawful to drive a motor vehicle across common land the Act did not apply.[3] Owners of common land were therefore able to charge large sums as ransoms. This was thought undesirable and s 68 of the Countryside and Rights of Way Act 2000 provides a procedure for the compulsory acquisition of a right of way in those circumstances. The owner of the common land is entitled to a payment in accordance with a scale to be laid down in regulations.

6.2.3   Rights of way – overage land as dominant

If the ransom land cuts off access to the highway from the overage land then the landowner will need access over it for the current use but the overage owner will resist that access being used for development purposes.

Express grant

The general rule is that where there is an express grant of a right of way for a specified and limited purpose or method of use, as for agriculture only or on foot only, then the servient owner can prevent use for a purpose or in a manner other than the one specifically authorised. Thus, in *Cannon v Villars*[4] (which concerned the scope of an implied right of way), Jessel MR said:

> 'Of course where you find restrictive words in the grant, that is to say, where it is only for the use of foot-passengers, stated in express terms, or for foot-passengers and horsemen, and so forth, there is nothing to argue.'

---

1   See *Crown Estate Commissioners v Dorset County Council* [1990] 1 Ch 297, where the claim did not succeed.
2   Unreported, but account in *Daily Telegraph* 8 March 1997.
3   *Hanning v Top Deck Travel Group Ltd* (1993) 68 P&CR 14.
4   (1878) 8 Ch D 415 at 421.

If the express grant is in general terms, as 'for all purposes', then on the face of it it means what it says, but there may be circumstances (eg the physical structure of the track or the number of other lawful users) that limit the use to a particular one. The test is whether a change or intensification of use by one landowner excessively burdens the route so as to inconvenience others.

Therefore, in drafting the terms of an express right of way in an overage context, it is important for the parties to be clear about what is intended and to use appropriate wording.

Implied grant

A risk is that the landowner may obtain a right of way over the strip by prescription.[1] The imposer will normally grant to the granter either a permanent right of way for current use purposes such as agriculture or it might give a licence or a lease of a right of way terminable on the trigger event (such a lease would not attract the protection of the LTA 1954 because a right of way is not 'premises'[2]) and so long as the use remains within that defined description there will be no problem. If, however, the landowner uses the access for some purpose not covered by the express grant, then a right of way may come into existence after 20 years under the Prescription Act 1832. As that prescriptive right of way would arise by virtue of the law rather than an express grant, there will be an issue as to the precise scope of the right so enjoyed. Thus, it may be open to a court to consider that a right of way has been acquired for all purposes.

If the right arises by prescription or implication of law, the normal rule is that use can only be for the purpose for which it was acquired by the use that gave rise to the acquisition.[3] This is subject to exceptions, such as where a right arises under a statutory provision.[4]

In *Williams v James*,[5] Bovill CJ said:

> 'In all cases of this kind which depend upon user the right acquired must be measured by the extent of the enjoyment which is proved. When a right of way to a piece of land is proved, then that is, unless something appears to the contrary, a

---

1   In *Hanning v Top Deck Travel Group Ltd* (1993) 68 P&CR 14, the overage owner was able to defeat this by showing that the access had been enjoyed illegally and therefore did not give rise to a prescriptive right.

2   *Land Reclamation Co Ltd v Basildon District Council* [1979] 1 WLR 767.

3   *Loder v Gaden* (1999) 78 P&CR 223.

4   See *Newcomen v Coulson* (1877) 5 Ch D 133 (inclosure award: agricultural use enlarged to villa residence); *United Land Company v Great Eastern Railway Company* (1873) LR 17 Eq 158 (railway: agricultural use enlarged to building) *South Eastern Railway v Cooper* [1924] 1 Ch 211 (railway: agricultural use enlarged to sand quarry); and *British Railways Board v Glass* [1965] Ch 538 (railway: agricultural use enlarged to caravan site).

5   (1867) LR 2 CP 577.

right of way for all purposes according to the ordinary and reasonable use to which that land might be applied at the time of the supposed grant. Such a right cannot be increased so as to affect the servient tenement by imposing upon it any additional burthen.'

Physical capacity and improvement

In *Jelbert v Davis*[1] there was an express right of way 'for all purposes ... in common with all other persons'. The original use was in fact agricultural. The dominant owner wished to use it for 200 camping units (caravans or tents). The court held that although there was a vehicular right, the proposed use would be excessive and interfere with the rights of the 'other persons'. In *Rosling v Pinnegar*,[2] there was a right of way in common with all other persons entitled thereto over a narrow winding lane to a fine Georgian mansion. The owner of the mansion wanted to open it to the public. The way also led to a village of 25 dwellings. The court held that while use for the public visiting the mansion was not itself a breach of the terms of the grant, the heavy use interfered with reasonable use by other persons entitled to it. In *White v Richards*,[3] there was an express right over a small track. The right extended to motor vehicles, but the dominant owner wished to use it for up to 16 heavy lorries per day. The court held that the nature of the construction of the track involved a necessary limitation to smaller vehicles, otherwise the surface would become damaged. In *Charrington v Simons & Co Ltd*,[4] a farmer sold some land to a company including a track over which the farmer reserved a right of way. The company had covenanted not to resurface the track so as to raise its level above the farmer's adjoining land. It did so despite the farmer's protests and then suggested it could ameliorate the breach by constructing shoulders onto the farmer's land. Buckley J found that the road as reconstructed interfered with the farming, awarded nominal damages and gave an injunction to restore the position, but deferred 3 years to enable ameliorating works to be done. The farmer's agreement would be necessary to the work and the judge indicated that if he did not co-operate, the injunction might be lifted. The farmer's appeal was allowed on the grounds that the suggested works would be a trespass and a greater interference with the farming and the suspension of the injunction was not a proper exercise of judicial discretion. Presumably, the same principles would apply if the farmer had retained ownership of the track and granted the company a right of way over it.

In *Wimbledon and Putney Commons Conservators v Dixon*[5] the use was predominantly for farming. The dominant owner claimed to use it for building

---

1   [1968] 1 WLR 589.
2   (1986) 54 P&CR 124.
3   (1993) 68 P&CR 105.
4   [1971] 1 WLR 598.
5   (1875) 1 Ch D 362.

a new house and the court refused to allow the burden on the servient tenement to be increased. In *RCP Holdings Ltd v Rogers*,[1] there was an established agricultural right of way by prescription. The attempt to use the track for a caravan site failed. In *Milner's Safe Co Ltd v Great Northern and City Railway*,[2] there was an implied grant of a right of way for a house. The owner pulled down the house and constructed a railway station. It was held that use by railway passengers was excessive. In *Giles v County Building Construc-tors (Hertford) Ltd*,[3] on the other hand, where there was a prescriptive right of way for two houses and they were to be demolished and replaced by a three-storey block of flats, there was no radical change in the character of the right and no excessive use. In *Fairview New Homes plc v Government Row Residents Association Ltd*,[4] there was a right of way for land used as an arms factory. The factory was closed and the owner claimed to use a very small portion of the land where it adjoined another road in connection with a residential development. The court refused an interim injunction for obstruc-tions to be removed. The issue was not decided, but the new use might have been excessive.

If the access is used for a purpose other than that permitted by the express grant, then until a new prescriptive right comes into existence the use will be vulnerable to challenge.[5] In *Bracewell v Appleby*,[6] the owner of a plot of land had a right of way 'of the fullest description' over a private roadway to a specified plot. He purchased a plot next door which did not have any right and claimed to be entitled to use the road to reach the new plot. The court held that the objectors, who also had rights over the private road, could have obtained an injunction if they had acted promptly. As they did not, and delayed until the house on the new plot was almost complete, they would not have an injunction but would have damages and were awarded £400 each.

The right to improve the surface of a track may depend on similar considerations. In *Mills v Silver*,[7] there was a track across a hill farm which was impassable in rough weather. The dominant owner was held not entitled to improve it by putting down several hundred tons of stone because to do so would increase the burden on the servient tenement. By contrast, in *Alvis v Harrison*,[8] the dominant owner built a long road on his own land but as part of the work he constructed a tarmac bellmouth on the verge. The House of Lords

---

1   [1953] 1 All ER 1029.
2   [1907] 1 Ch 208.
3   (1971) 22 P&CR 978.
4   [1998] EGCS 92.
5   It may also be challenged on the grounds of illegality: *Cargill v Gotts* [1981] 1 WLR 441; and *Hanning v Top Deck Travel Group Ltd* (1993) 68 P&CR 14.
6   [1975] 1 Ch 408; see also *Jobson v Record* [1998] 09 EG 148.
7   [1991] Fam 271.
8   (1990) 62 P&CR 10.

held that he was entitled to do so provided there was no heavy burden on the servient tenement and the work did not prejudice it regarded as a whole. This was a Scottish case, but the rule may be the same in England. However, in *McKay Securities plc v Surrey County Council*,[1] there was a right of way for all purposes. The dominant owner originally used its land for a warehouse, but then applied for planning permission for residential development. The wider use was upheld, but the plaintiff failed to establish that it had the right to cut vegetation on visibility splays in order to comply with the residential planning consent.

In *Mills v Blackwell*,[2] there was a right of way through a narrow gap in a wall. The dominant owner claimed the right to demolish part of the wall to create a more suitable access for his vehicles. The court held that even though the area over which the right of way was exercisable was shown on a plan as wider than the physical access, the owner had no right to make alterations to the land. Where an express right of way is being drafted for overage purposes, it will be sensible to cover the point expressly.

6.3 ADJOINING AIRSPACE AND INJUNCTIONS

Overage rights do not need to relate to the permanent occupation of the overage land. They can involve temporary access for works or to reach a building. The 'oversailing cases' discussed below illustrate that if the overage owner can prevent a new building being constructed in the first place, it could be a sufficient lever to secure a payment. They derive from the need to construct high buildings in the centre of modern cities. These are normally on their own plots or 'footprints' with full access from the street and normal services. However, in order to build to the height required for a modern city centre building to be profitable a special crane is needed. This has a long jib which swings round and will normally have to swing over the airspace of neighbouring plots. The owner of such a plot may wish to charge for permission for the crane to oversail its property.

The starting point is in two nineteenth-century cases. In *Eardley v Granville*[3] discussed at **6.6** (which related to the site of worked-out minerals underground), in 1876 Sir George Jessel MR said:

> 'He is a mere trespasser and he being a trespasser comes within the well-established doctrine of *Goodson v Richardson*[4] and *Rochdale Canal Company v King*[5] where damages would be no compensation for a right to

1   [1998] EGCS 180.
2   [1999] NPC 88.
3   (1876) 3 Ch D 826; see **6.6**. See also *Daniells v Mendonca* [1999] PLSCS 94.
4   (1873) LR 9 Ch App 221.
5   (1876) 2 Sim NS 78.

property, and the plaintiffs are entitled to prohibit him by injunction. There may be little or no injury to the estate, but if they restrain him he will be glad to pay a way-leave.'

In *Shelfer v City of London Electric Lighting Co*,[1] works done by the electricity company damaged a house and caused a nuisance. In the event, the injunction was granted on appeal because it was not sufficient that the wrongdoer was able to pay damages. However, in the course of his judgment, A.L. Smith LJ, whilst accepting that a wrongdoer cannot compulsorily purchase a right simply by being prepared to pay damages, emphasised that the award of an injunction is discretionary. The court's discretion will be exercised along established lines. First:

'if the plaintiff by his acts or laches [delay] has disentitled himself to an injunction the court may award damages in its place.'

Secondly, even though the case for an injunction may be made out, the court may award damages.

'In my opinion, it may be stated as a good working rule that –
(1) If the injury to the plaintiff's legal rights is small,
(2) And is one which is capable of being estimated in money,
(3) And is one which can be compensated by a small money payment,
(4) And the case is one in which it would be oppressive to the defendant to grant an injunction:-
then damages in substitution for an injunction may be given.'

The development of the modern law starts with *Kelsen v Imperial Tobacco Co (of Great Britain and Ireland) Ltd*,[2] where an advertising sign projected over a single-storey shop. An injunction was awarded as a matter of course. In *Woollerton and Wilson Ltd v Richard Costain Ltd*[3] trespass by an oversailing crane was admitted. The issue was whether an immediate injunction should be granted. Stamp J considered that he had no option but to grant an injunction, but that he had discretion to delay the operation of the injunction until the building works were completed. He was influenced by an offer of money by the developer to the landowner. The effect of this decision was to undermine the bargaining position of the owner of the ransom plot.

John Trenberth Ltd v National Westminster Bank Ltd[4] did not relate to airspace. The bank had a building in need of repair. In order to do so it had to go onto the plaintiff's land. The plaintiff refused consent. The court found that there was no case to refuse an injunction, however urgent the repairs and however little damage the plaintiff might suffer. Walton J considered the delay of the operation of the injunction in *Woollerton* could not be justified.

---

1   [1895] 1 Ch 287.
2   [1957] 2 QB 334. See also *Graham v K.D. Morris & Sons Pty Ltd* [1974] QD R 1.
3   [1970] 1 WLR 411.
4   (1979) 39 P&CR 104.

Anchor Brewhouse Developments Ltd v Berkley House (Docklands Developments) Ltd[1] was another oversailing case. In this case, too, *Woollerton* was not followed and an immediate injunction was granted.

Finally, the whole state of the authorities was reviewed in *Jaggard v Sawyer*.[2] This concerned a private road leading to some plots on which a small housing estate was built. The soil of the roadway was owned by the adjoining houses, subject to rights of way for the other owners. One owner built an extra house on his plot and the owner of part of the road claimed an injunction to prevent access. The Court of Appeal refused it and confirmed the trial judge's award of damages of £694.44 instead. The court based itself on *Shelfer*. It considered that *Woollerton* was wrong in holding that there was no jurisdiction to award damages, and *Anchor Brewhouse* was also wrong in considering that an immediate injunction must be granted. The court held, following *Surrey County Council v Bredero Homes Ltd*,[3] that where an injunction could have been granted in equity, then damages could be awarded instead, and, following *Wrotham Park Estate Co Ltd v Parkside Homes Ltd*,[4] it should not be a ransom price, but such a sum as might reasonably be required.

On the face of it, *Jaggard v Sawyer* undermines the basis of ransom strips altogether. In practice, they are still important. Where there is an invasion, either of land or of airspace, the claimant is on the face of it entitled to an injunction. The court has a discretion to substitute damages instead and will have regard to the *Shelfer* factors, including the conduct of the parties. However, where commercial landowners have taken up positions based on a regard for rights of property and the law of trespass, the courts should respect that. That must still be the basis of *Anchor Brewhouse* and that approach still governs arrangements for neighbours to redevelop their property. In the particular circumstances of *Trenberth*, Parliament has now intervened in the Access to Neighbouring Land Act 1992, but that applies to matters such as support and repair ('works reasonably necessary for the preservation of the whole or any part of the dominant land': s 1(2)(a)) and not to redevelopment. The Party Wall etc Act 1996 does allow some compulsory access for redevelopment, but does not extend to oversailing cranes.

6.4 PIPES, CABLES AND OTHER SERVICES

A right of way across the ransom strip may not be sufficient on its own. Most forms of development need other services such as water, sewerage, cables, electricity and similar rights. Clearly, however long a landowner has used an

---

1   [1987] 2 EGLR 173.
2   [1995] 1 WLR 269.
3   [1993] 1 WLR 1361. See **4.5.1**.
4   [1974] 1 WLR 798. See **4.6**.

access to get to a field of wheat, that will not give any right to lay a sewer for domestic purposes. In *Goodson v Richardson*,[1] a developer laid a water pipe in the subsoil of a highway without the consent of the owner of the subsoil. The owner was entitled to an injunction to have the pipe removed, even though the subsoil was of no value to him and even though the laying of the pipe did not affect his enjoyment of his land. In *Penn v Wilkins*,[2] it was held that an easement of way does not by itself give the right to pass sewage through pipes laid along the route of the way. In *Selby v Crystal Palace Gas Co*,[3] a dominant owner had a right to use roads 'as fully as if they were public roads' and that did give a right to authorise a gas company to lay pipes; however, that turned on the wide wording which was unusual. In *Wandsworth District Board of Works v United Telephone Co Ltd*,[4] a telephone line above a street was considered capable of being a trespass against the highway authority.[5]

The statutory undertakers that are responsible for providing services such as water, drainage, gas, electricity and telecommunications have statutory powers[6] to use a compulsory procedure (which varies from case to case) to put their services through the land of a third party and this could enable them to override an objection by the overage owner. Such powers are subject to compensation[7] for the compulsory acquisition of rights and even if this were not laid down in the specific codes in each relevant statute, it would be implied under the Human Rights Act 1998 and the First Protocol to the European Convention on Human Rights. The basis of compensation is discussed at **6.10**.

6.5 AIR SPACE OVER OVERAGE LAND

As an alternative to retaining a piece of the Earth's surface as a ransom strip, the imposer may retain ownership of the air space lying over all or part of the overage land. This might be used in a sale for agricultural purposes, for

1 (1873) LR 9 Ch App 221.
2 (1975) 236 EG 203.
3 (1862) 4 De GF&J 246.
4 (1884) 13 QBD 904.
5 In *Attwood v Bovis Homes Ltd* (2000) *The Times*, 18 April, there were existing drainage rights across the claimant's farmland. The claim that a developer had no drainage rights for a housing development failed on the ground that the volume of water being discharged was not increased.
6 Telecommunications Act 1974, Sch 2; Gas Act 1986, Sch 3; Electricity Act 1989, Sch 3; Water Industry Act 1991, s 155.
7 They are normally subject to compensation, but see New Roads and Street Works Act 1991, ss 49 and 50, which allow a 'street manager' who is not the owner of a private road to consent to the laying of pipes and other things. However, if this involves an individual being deprived of his possessions without compensation, there could be a breach of the First Protocol to the European Convention on Human Rights. Even if the deprivation can be justified in the public interest, compensation is still due.

example by selling the surface of the field and perhaps a volume of air extending 3 or 4 metres above the surface. As some agricultural machinery (eg combine harvesters) can be very large, the landowner should be given the right to use the air space which is retained in the ownership of the imposer for the passage of agricultural machinery. There may also need to be some form of agreement if, for example, an electricity company wishes to erect pylons, part of which will be in the ground space belonging to the landowner and the upper part of which will be in the air space belonging to the overage owner.

The method is more often used in relation to a sale of an existing building where the site may be redeveloped in the future. The imposer simply sells the building itself and perhaps a small amount of air space above to allow for aerials, satellite dishes, fire escape access and so on, and retains title to the space above so that the height of the building cannot be raised without the consent of the overage owner.

The precise limits of the sale need to be defined with great care. Although sometimes it will be sufficient to define the sale by reference to an existing building, and the Land Registry will accept such a description, this will be of little help if the building itself is destroyed either deliberately for redevelopment or by an accident such as a fire. Therefore, it is better to attach a vertical elevation drawing to the transfer, and if the site is irregular, perhaps several of them. The precise upper and lower limits need to be defined. This could be by reference to the existing ground level, but that is liable to change and, thus, it is better to have a surveyed drawing with heights surveyed by reference to Ordnance Datum Newlyn (above the benchmark sea level).

6.6 SUBSOIL AND MINERALS

In the same way as with airspace, the imposer may retain ownership of the subsoil. This is unlikely to be of much help unless the development will involve the excavation of basements or the need to lay services underground or provide deep foundations. Cases on this have usually turned on a specific reservation of minerals where the reservation is interpreted as comprising a specific volume of the earth underneath the land sold.[1] Under the rule against derogation from grant, a seller of land cannot at one and the same time sell land for value and deprive the buyer of the value for which it has paid. Therefore, any reservation of minerals will be treated as being subject to a natural right to the support of the surface. It is possible for the parties by contract to agree that the mineral owner will be entitled to break the surface in order to work the minerals, but that must be subject to the payment of

---

1 *Bowser v Maclean* (1860) 2 De GF&J 420; and *Eardley v Granville* (1876) 3 Ch D 826.

compensation, and it will normally only be temporary and subject to an obligation to restore.

Although the normal form of reservation of minerals takes effect as retaining ownership of a volume of air space, in some cases on a strict interpretation, the reservation is simply of mineral substances. This follows the old cases on copyhold land where a distinction was drawn between the property of the Lord of the Manor in the minerals and the right of the copyholder to possession of the land in which those minerals subsisted. In *Eardley v Granville*,[1] this operated as a form of overage by ransom. The Lord of the Manor and the lord's licensee of the minerals, Lord Granville, were entitled to work the minerals within the Manor of Newcastle. Between the access shaft and some coal that was to be worked lay the land of Mr Eardley. Under earlier workings, the coal had been removed under his land by the licensee of the Lord of the Manor leaving a void. Lord Granville claimed the right to pass through that void in order to work the minerals beyond. The court held that Mr Eardley had possession of the void left by the removal of the minerals and, therefore, was entitled to charge a wayleave. In a comparable case, therefore, if the true interpretation of the reservation of minerals is that the air space belongs to the landowner not to the overage owner, this may negative any ransom benefit from a mineral reservation. In practice, of course, minerals are normally reserved but not worked in such cases.

Where the minerals can be reached by underground working, there will always be an obligation for natural support of the surface and this exists independent of the agreement of the parties.

This natural right of support subsists only for the soil in its state as it existed at the date of the grant or reservation of the minerals. However, where buildings are erected on land, after 20 years they will have acquired a right to support under the Prescription Act 1832.[2]

Furthermore, in practice, if planning consent is granted for the erection of buildings, then planning consent will not also be granted for the working of the minerals or for any other action which could remove support. Thus, a reservation of minerals is of little use for overage purposes.

This is a point that arises frequently in practice where a development company buys land which is subject to a reservation of minerals perhaps made 100 years ago in favour of a local estate. Although some developers are concerned at the implications of this, in practice most do not consider it important. Sometimes they will be prepared to acquire the mineral rights from the owners for a small sum, but it is not useful as a substantial ransom.

---

1   (1876) 3 Ch D 826.
2   *Rogers v Taylor* (1858) 2 H&N 828.

Often mineral rights will be reserved as a matter of practice to retain ownership of known mineral deposits. That by itself is not overage. However, in recent years, orthodox and other medical practitioners have become interested in natural chemicals derived from limestone and other rocks in the cure of various ailments. An imposer may wish to reserve minerals to cover some unexpected future increase in value. (Much the same could apply to mineral waters in rocks.) However, in *Lonsdale (Earl of) v Attorney-General*,[1] there was a grant of mineral rights in general terms under part of the North Sea to the Earl's ancestor. At the time of the grant, the valuable mineral was coal. Associated with the coal was a dangerous and unwanted substance known as 'fire-damp'. By the time of the case, this had become recognised as a valuable asset known as 'natural gas'. The Earl claimed the right to exploit it. The court held that at the time of the grant no commercial or professional person involved with minerals would have reckoned fire-damp as an asset and, therefore, it was not included in the grant. It could follow that a mineral reservation would not cover substances not recognised as minerals at the time of the reservation, but the parties could overcome this by expressly referring to the possibility of as yet unknown substances becoming valuable.

6.7 LIGHT

The use of 'ancient lights' to obstruct development on adjoining land is well established. Express rights of light are rare, but they can arise by implication on division of a property on sale or by prescription. The details of whether a right arises in a particular situation depend on the facts and the extent to which the dominant tenement has enjoyed and needs light of a particular quality. In city centres, however, this can be a valuable bargaining factor. In order to prevent a right being acquired by buildings adjoining sites which may lie undeveloped for a long time, the Rights of Light Act 1959 allows a potential servient owner to register an imaginary obstruction.

In *Deakins v Hookings*,[2] the plaintiff had a right of light at the rear of her property. The defendant obtained planning consent for a rear extension. The plaintiff objected, but the defendant built it. The judge awarded a mandatory injunction to demolish it, but said that if his decision was overturned by the Court of Appeal he would award damages of £4,500 based on *Wrotham Park* principles but at 15 per cent of the enhancement value of the extension of £30,000 to the defendant's property.

---

1   [1982] 1 WLR 887.
2   [1994] 14 EG 133.

6.8 RIGHT OF WAY WHERE OVERAGE LAND IS SERVIENT

The imposer may retain rights across the overage land. Thus, a right of way may be retained, perhaps between back land and the highway, in such a position that it is likely to interfere with any foreseeable development on the overage land. Any easement in law must be subject to certain binding constraints. Amongst these are that the right must exist for the benefit of a definable dominant tenement and it must in fact accommodate that dominant tenement.

First, therefore, the overage owner must have land in the vicinity and the owner of that land must be capable of using the right of way. It does not have to be immediately adjacent, but it should be nearby. Thus, a right of way can be used in conjunction with a ransom strip, but is not appropriate if the overage owner has no land in the area.

Secondly, if a right of way is reserved for overage purposes only and does not actually benefit the land to which it is nominally attached, a court may not grant an injunction to protect it but leave the dominant owner to its remedy in damages. In *Greenwich Healthcare National Health Service Trust v London and Quadrant Housing Trust,*[1] Greenwich owned a private road, Baker Road, subject to rights of way. It was redeveloping its land and the proposals involved a new road junction. None of the persons known to have rights of way over Baker Road objected to the improvements, but there was no time to obtain formal deeds of release and in any case unknown persons entitled to rights could have appeared later. The judge noted that there could be no reasonable objection to the improvement, the known users had been given notice and a chance to object (London and Quadrant Housing Trust was concerned to protect its compensation rights) and the realignment was necessary to achieve an important public object. Therefore, he was prepared to make an order that the landowner would not be subject to an injunction against interference with the physical right of way. Where similar facts apply, the overage owner will still be entitled to obtain for damages under the principles in *Jaggard v Sawyer,*[2] but, as discussed below, these will be modest if there is no actual damage to the property for the benefit of which the right of way was reserved. However, the judge was cautious in granting the declaration. A determined overage owner who is aware of the proposals may be able to resist them. It remains to be seen if the courts will accept that a right of way can be used not for passing over land but also to protect overage rights.

---

1   [1998] 1 WLR 1749.
2   [1995] 1 WLR 269.

By analogy with the restrictive covenant cases,[1] the court might be able to hold that a right of way cannot be so used, but there is an important distinction that a restrictive covenant operates in equity and subject to equitable principles (such as that equity looks at the intent rather than the form) while a right of way subsists at common law. A court of equitable jurisdiction may still be able to restrain abuse of a common law right and that may be a justification for the decision in *Jaggard v Sawyer*. However, as a general rule, where a claimant has a right at common law, either to restrain a trespass[2] or a nuisance[3] (and interference with a right of way is a nuisance), then the claimant has an automatic right to the injunction, subject to the usual equitable rules and to *Shelfer*.[4] In *West v Sharp*,[5] a landowner granted a right of way over a large area of land. In fact, it was exercised over a narrow metalled strip. When the landowner planted trees and put up concrete obstructions, the people entitled to the right of way claimed an injunction. The Court of Appeal refused it on the ground that the users of the way could only object to something that substantially interfered with their ability to make proper use of their access and, therefore, they had not suffered damage. In that case, they wanted a wide turning area but the same logic would apply to the use of an excessively widely drawn right of way for overage.

In *Snell & Prideaux Ltd v Dutton Mirrors Ltd*,[6] the plaintiff had an express grant of a right of way over land belonging to the defendant. The defendant built a factory, part of which extended onto the way. From the 1960s the plaintiff had not used, and had showed no intention of using, the way for vehicles or otherwise than on foot. The way was still passable for that purpose. The Court of Appeal held that mere non-use of a right of way did not give rise to abandonment, and where it was likely to be useful in the future abandonment was not easily inferred. Here there had been a serious interference with the right, but the court would not issue a mandatory injunction to remove the factory and awarded damages based on the difference in value of the plaintiff's premises with full rights of access and with the now limited access. The case shows that simply reserving a right of way which might be useful in the future will be protected by the courts, but if the way is obstructed the damages will be based not on a ransom basis but on loss of value. However, if the overage owner is sufficiently vigilant to stop the building before it starts, there should be a good chance of an injunction or at least damages assessed on *Wrotham Park* principles.

1　See **4.6**.
2　*Patel v W.H. Smith (Eziot) Ltd* [1987] 1 WLR 853.
3　*Soltau v De Held* (1851) 2 Sim NS 133.
4　*Shelfer v City of London Electric Lighting Co* [1895] 1 Ch 287. See **6.3**.
5　(1999) 78 P&CR D31. See also *B&Q plc v Liverpool and Lancashire Properties Ltd* [2000] All ER (D) 1059.
6　[1994] EGCS 78.

6.9 SPORTING AND OTHER PROFITS

There are a variety of other rights which can subsist over land and which can be used for ransom purposes. The imposer may retain sporting rights and, so long as those rights have any value, he will be entitled to an injunction to prevent any work on the land which would adversely affect the enjoyment of those rights. However, if the nature of the area is changing in such a way that surrounding land is built on, it may well be that there will be little if any game on the overage land which is capable of being taken and, therefore, if the sporting rights become valueless the court would not be prepared to protect them simply on the grounds of overage. Once again, the court would be prepared to issue a declaration that no injunction will be given and the owner of the sporting rights would be left to a limited remedy in damages.

Sporting rights have been used to prevent development, although the courts examine whether the proposals will really impinge on the rights. In *Pattisson v Gifford*,[1] a landlord granted a right of shooting over an estate. He later issued particulars of sale in lots, stating that the land was suitable for villas and that residences might be erected on part of it but stating that the right of shooting existed. The shooting tenant applied for an injunction to restrain the owner from issuing the particulars. The application was refused. Jessel MR said, 'No cautious man who understood the particulars would buy that land for immediate building purposes'. He did indicate that he might have granted the injunction if the defendant had been going to grub up the plantations, but he would not necessarily grant it even if a few villas were to be constructed if that would not materially injure the shooting. That case was considered in *Peech v Best*,[2] where the owner of a farm of 700 acres granted a sporting lease and later sold some 12 acres to a buyer who intended to build training stables for race horses. The sporting tenant was granted an injunction because, as Scrutton LJ said, 'I should doubt myself, when the stables for 36 horses and the six stable boys are in occupation whether a game bird would be left within a quarter of a mile of the stables'. In *Pole v Peake*,[3] there was a dispute between a farmer and the owners of the sporting rights. Buxton LJ said that the sporting owners could not restrain normal farming practices, such as conversion of scrub land to use for farming, but the farmer could not 'adopt farming practices that interfere with the exercise of the respondents' shooting and rearing rights'. The conclusion is that a reservation of sporting rights is not suitable for overage as such. The court will inquire as to the effect of the proposed change in use, or development, on the actual sporting practice and will give an injunction only if there is in practice likely to be an interference. The sporting owner may have a claim in damages.

---

1   (1874) LR 18 Eq 259.
2   [1931] 1 KB 1.
3   [1998] EGCS 125.

It may be possible to use a right of common, although this must be considered risky. Common rights are largely ancient and most of them had to be registered under the Commons Registration Act 1965 by the end of 1970. However, it is possible for new rights of common to come into existence and, if they do, those rights can be registered and the land over which they are exercisable becomes common land. It thereby becomes unlawful to enclose it and it is subject to certain supervisory rights of the local authority and it may become subject to a public right to roam. The Act and the rules made under it make provision for the case where land ceases to be common land. A possible form of overage therefore may be for the imposer to retain, say, a right of estovers (the right to take wood) or a right of grazing for one pony, on the basis that if the land becomes capable of development then that right can be given up and the land will cease to be common and will have to be taken off the register. However, in view of the likely forms of protection for common land, this method of overage is not normally recommended. It is understood that the grant of a right of estovers has been used in Norfolk to create a modern common where the landowner wished to benefit the public and subject the land to statutory protection,[1] but that is very different from using such rights for overage and the courts are unlikely to be sympathetic to such a scheme.[2]

6.10 STATUTORY COMPENSATION

If the court is prepared to award an outright injunction preventing any infringement on the ransom area, that is an end of the matter and the landowner is delivered over 'bound hand and foot'[3] to the overage owner. If, however, the court is not prepared to give an injunction, it is necessary to determine the amount of compensation which is paid for infringement on the ransom.

The courts have experienced considerable difficulty with this (as discussed at **6.3** and **11.4.2**), but the present approach[4] is to award such a sum as might reasonably be required by a reasonable ransom owner treated as being a person willing to negotiate. The resulting payment may be very small and the principles discussed at **4.6** in relation to restrictive covenants are relevant.

Another relevant factor is the sum chargeable on compulsory acquisition. The majority of the cases on this that have reached the courts have concluded that this is a matter for the decision of a valuer and the courts will normally not

---

1   Sara Birtles 'The Impact of Commons Registration: a Norfolk Study' (1998) 20 *Landscape History* 83 at 95 Norfolk CL 443.

2   The Countryside and Rights of Way Act 2000 confers on the public a right of access over registered common land which could prevent the use of such a scheme.

3   *Isenberg v East India House Estate Co Ltd* (1863) 3 De GJ&S 263.

4   Exemplified in *Wrotham Park Estate Co v Parkside Homes Ltd* [1974] 1 WLR 411 and *Jaggard v Sawyer* [1995] 1 WLR 269.

interfere with a decision reached on valuation principles typically by the Lands Tribunal where these matters fall to be decided. Tribunal awards can be very substantial. The most quoted case is *Stokes v Cambridge Corporation*.[1] In that case, Cambridge Corporation owned some land between the highway and land belonging to Mr Stokes. That land could have become a ransom strip in different circumstances. The Corporation needed to acquire Mr Stokes' land under compulsory powers. It was accepted that, but for the acquisition, he would have obtained planning permission to develop his land. In his claim for compensation he argued that there should be no discount because of the ransom. The Tribunal did not accept that argument. Because of the nature of Mr Stokes' argument, his valuer had not put forward any figures to suggest what the ransom might be and, therefore, the Tribunal simply accepted the evidence given on behalf of the Corporation that a proper discount would be one-third of the development value of the land. That case is often quoted as authority for the proposition that a ransom payment should be one-third, but it will be evident that it does not support that proposition. In the case of *Hertfordshire County Council v Ozanne*,[2] a ransom payment of half the development value was accepted. In that case, however, the court specifically refused to interfere with the decision of the Tribunal and did not lay down any legal principles for determining the compensation.

It has to be recognised that there is a circular argument here. Many negotiations between private landowners take place against the background of the decisions on compulsory purchase. Those decisions have been made by the Lands Tribunal seeking to determine what price might reasonably be negotiated between persons who were not subject to the compulsory powers and in a situation where the actual scheme for the compulsory acquisition did not occur. Thus, the private sector is taking account of decisions affecting the public sector which reflect what the Tribunal responsible for assessing the amount of compensation payable by the public sector thinks would have been reached in the private sector in circumstances different from those which actually exist. In such cases as *Wrotham Park Estate Company v Parkside Homes Limited* and *Jaggard v Sawyer* the courts have adopted their own approach. On the other hand, in the compulsory purchase cases they are exercising a supervisory jurisdiction and deciding not to interfere with the decision of the Lands Tribunal. It is hardly surprising that there is continued confusion on the level of compensation. No doubt, the law will develop further on this aspect.

---

1   (1961) 13 P&CR 77.
2   (1991) 62 P&CR 1. See also *Batchelor v Kent County Council* (1989) 59 P&CR 357; and *Ward Construction (Medway) Ltd v Barclays Bank plc* [1994] 2 EGLR 32.

6.11 CONCLUSION

Ransoms can be an effective form of overage where physical circumstances allow but the courts are careful to strike a balance between the rights of neighbours and use the equitable and discretionary jurisdiction of injunctions to achieve this. In particular, the courts will not allow an accident of geography to give one neighbour a stranglehold over another. It is different in such cases as oversailing where there is a great deal of value and both parties are sophisticated commercial operators in a city centre. It may be different where the ransom is deliberately and expressly adopted as an overage device, and that is clear on the face of the documents. In the absence of such express statements (and perhaps, because it has not been tested, even in their presence), ransoms cannot be relied on as a certain means of overage.

Chapter 7

LANDLORD AND TENANT

7.1 HOW LEASES WORK

Overage can be used in relation to leases in the same way as freeholds. Thus, there can be covenants (both restrictive and positive), charges and ransoms. Covenants are considered below. For an example of a ransom, an imposer who owns an ageing office block may sell it and take back from the granter a lease of the top floor. The landowner will not be able to demolish and rebuild the block without the overage owner's agreement.[1] Options can be used as discussed at **7.2.3** and **7.4.3** in the context of a tenant's option to buy out the landlord or a landlord's right to break the lease.

There are, however, many specific rules relating to leases, particularly for positive covenants which provide more flexibility than freeholds can give. In addition, Parliament has intervened in the law of landlord and tenant in order to protect groups seen to be in a disadvantageous position and the statutory rules can complicate bargains never intended to be caught.

Leases can be used for both negative and positive overage. The negative leasehold overage works by the imposer selling to the granter a long lease typically for 250 years at a peppercorn rent subject to covenants limiting the use of the land and restricting development. There will be a normal leasehold right of re-entry which may be exercisable either on a breach of covenant or condition or on certain other events such as the grant of planning consent.

Leases for positive overage will usually be shorter, for perhaps 99 years or 120 years, and may reserve a basic ground rent either with or without a capital payment. There will often be an obligation on the tenant to make improvements such as the erection of buildings and when that occurs either a capital sum may be payable to the landlord or there may be a rent related to the increased value. These have evolved from an earlier type of 'improvement' lease well known in Victorian times, where the owner of a large estate would grant leases of plots of land at a ground rent often of a pound or two for 99 years with an obligation to build, on the basis that at the end of the term the

---

1   Much may turn on the construction of the lease. See *Hannon v 169 Queen's Gate Ltd* [2000] 09 EG 179.

house would revert to the landlord's heirs. As explained below,[1] that type of lease is no longer in use for houses, but it has led to modern versions which are still used.

7.2 LEASES AND NEGATIVE OVERAGE

This works in much the same way as a restrictive covenant. The lease will contain a restriction against new building or against making alterations or improvements to an existing building and a restriction against changing the use of the demised premises. In general, these leasehold covenants will be interpreted in the same way and according to the same rules as freehold restrictive covenants,[2] but they are more flexible and, in particular, the relation of landlord and tenant itself gives the landlord a sufficient interest to enforce the covenant so that there is no need for the landlord to have other land in the vicinity that benefits from the restrictive covenants. Unless the covenant is specifically taken for the benefit of other land, it will not be treated as benefiting any other property (whether belonging to the landlord or not) and, therefore, the landlord and the tenant will be free to vary the terms of the lease as they wish. For that reason, restrictive covenants in leases are not subject to registration either on the Land Charges Register[3] or on the Register of Title[4] as they are no direct concern of any other person.

The jurisdiction of the Lands Tribunal to vary or release restrictive covenants extends to covenants in leases under s 84(12) of the LPA 1925 where a term of more than 40 years has been granted and at least 25 years of the lease have elapsed but this does not apply to mining leases which have their own special rules for overage mentioned below. As discussed in Chapter 4, it is possible that the Tribunal might not vary a covenant specifically imposed for overage, but that cannot be relied on.[5]

As a result of this jurisdiction of the Lands Tribunal, leasehold overage provisions are sometimes deliberately limited to the first 25 years. A landlord who wishes overage rights to extend beyond that will need to include positive covenants in the lease. These can be difficult to draft where the intention is simply to impose negative overage. Thus, a covenant to maintain a part of a farm as agricultural land or amenity land as a garden could be interpreted as being restrictive in substance.[6] Furthermore, positive covenants cannot easily

---

1   See **7.4.1**.
2   See Chapter 4.
3   Land Charges Act 1972, s 2(5)(ii).
4   LRA 1925 s 50(1).
5   See the remarks of Denning LJ in *Driscoll v Church Commissioners for England* [1957] 1 QB 330 at 341, cited at **4.6**. That case concerned leasehold covenants.
6   See **4.7** and the discussion of *Tulk v Moxhay* (1848) 2 Ph 774.

be enforced as the courts will normally not grant an injunction.[1] In any event, an injunction is a discretionary remedy for the courts and the principles set out at **6.3** will apply. Where there is a breach of any covenant (whether positive or restrictive), the court has jurisdiction to give relief against exercise of the right of re-entry. This relief is normally given under s 146 of the LPA 1925.[2] The jurisdiction is discretionary and will be exercised in accordance with normal rules of law.

Where the overage land comprises existing buildings (or there are buildings to be erected immediately, even though the site may be redeveloped later) then a covenant to repair the buildings can more easily be taken to have a genuine positive nature and, therefore, is more readily recognised as a positive covenant. However, under the Leasehold Property (Repairs) Act 1938 (LP(R)A 1938) where there are at least 3 years left to run the tenant can claim the benefit of that Act. Where it does, the landlord needs the leave of the court to bring proceedings for re-entry, and leave will not be given unless the landlord establishes one of five grounds set out in s 1(5)(a)–(e). Most of those relate to the cost of works or diminution in value of the investment which is unlikely to be relevant to a normal overage situation. The fifth ground (e) is that special circumstances exist which in the opinion of the court render it just and equitable that leave should be given. It is possible that an agreement between the parties that overage should be payable in certain circumstances may constitute special circumstances, but this should not be assumed in the absence of a decision. However, the court is permitted under s 1(6), whether it grants or refuses leave, to impose such terms and conditions either on the landlord or on the tenant as it thinks fit. Therefore, it might be possible for a landlord to apply for consent, be refused, but nevertheless be given a charge to secure any overage that may be in prospect. This is particularly the case where a landlord has let a building which is now out of date and of no use and the tenant intends to redevelop. In this case, the court may allow the landlord to share the redevelopment value. Although this jurisdiction appears to exist under s 1(6), it has not yet been tested.

The covenant may be coupled with a break clause. This might be incorporated in the right of re-entry itself which could be exercisable not only on a breach by the tenant of a covenant or condition (which would give rise to the jurisdiction under s 146 of the LPA 1925 and, therefore, under the LP(R)A 1938), but it may be exercisable in circumstances which are not the tenant's fault (eg the grant of planning consent). Even if there is a covenant on the tenant not to apply for planning consent which has not been released under s 84 of the LPA 1925 (so that consent granted on the tenant's application

---

1 See **7.2.2**.
2 A limited equitable jurisdiction still exists: *Billson v Residential Appartments Ltd* [1992] 1 AC 494.

would give rise to a breach), the planning consent might have been granted on the application of some totally unconnected person or even on the application of the landlord itself (so there would be no tenant's breach). The right to re-enter could still occur irrespective of a tenant's default if the re-entry clause were worded appropriately. Equally, however, a separate break clause may be inserted in the lease under which the landlord can serve notice to terminate the lease if some event occurs such as the redevelopment of adjoining land.[1] Presumably, a tenant would require as a pre-condition of the exercise of such a break that the tenant's current use value should be compensated by the landlord.

7.2.1 Statutory consent to improvements

Parliament has intervened in certain leases to give tenants the right to make improvements irrespective of the wishes of the landlord. This has been done primarily to help business tenants who need or wish to improve their premises in order to further their businesses. Different rules apply to farming businesses[2] and to other types of business. In relation to residential tenancies, different rules again apply to secure tenancies, that is residential tenancies held from public sector landlords. These rules operate by conferring on the tenant a right, sometimes subject to obtaining consent from an independent body or arbitrator, to make improvements which qualify for compensation at the end of the tenancy. The landlord cannot veto the tenant's proposals (although it may be able to argue against them before the consent is given) and, therefore, it cannot charge overage on them as a condition of giving consent.

Where these statutory provisions apply, there is a risk that the landlord will be deprived of the right to make a charge for the increased value resulting from planning consent or some other trigger. Statute can override the overage bargain.

Business and farm business tenancies
Special rules apply in relation to redevelopment where the tenant is occupying for the purpose of a business whether that is a farming business or not where either the agricultural code or the business code applies.

Farm business tenancies
Where a lease is granted on or after 1 September 1995 and all or part of the land comprised in the tenancy is farmed for the purpose of a trade or business

---

1 This is common for farm business tenancies and is a hangover from the terms of agricultural tenancies which included such a break clause to take advantage of Agricultural Holdings Act 1986, s 25(2)(b) and Case B of Sch 3.

2 There are separate rules for agricultural tenancies under the Agricultural Holdings Act 1986, but new tenancies of that type cannot now be granted.

(whether or not the trade or business is agricultural) and since the beginning of the tenancy all or part of the land has been so farmed, then the lease is capable of being a farm business tenancy within s 1 of the Agricultural Tenancies Act 1995 (ATA 1995). The lease has to satisfy one of two other conditions. One condition is the 'agriculture condition' which is that, having regard to the terms of the tenancy, the use of the land, the nature of commercial activities and other relevant circumstances, the character of the tenancy is (and remains) primarily or wholly agricultural. The other 'notice condition' is that at the beginning of the tenancy, having regard to its terms and other relevant circumstances, the character of the tenancy was primarily or wholly agricultural and that on or before the beginning of the tenancy or the date of the lease the landlord and the tenant each gave to the other a written notice containing specified information. Then again, the tenancy will be treated as being a farm business tenancy, even if the greater part of the land has ceased to be used for commercial agriculture. Yet there must still be some commercial agricultural use, however small, for the lease to qualify as a farm business tenancy.

This is relevant to overage leases of farmland where the buyer/tenant/granter intends to continue farming until the trigger event occurs.

Where the ATA 1995 applies, the tenant has the right in certain circumstances to claim compensation for improvements. Improvements are very widely defined and include both tangible improvements such as the putting up of buildings and intangible ones such as the acquisition of rights (such as a planning consent or a right of way). Where the tenant intends to make an improvement and wishes to reserve the right to claim compensation for that improvement at the end of the tenancy, it will need the landlord's consent before the improvement has begun. If the improvement consists in the obtaining of planning consent, then only the landlord can give consent. In the case of any other improvement, however, if the landlord refuses consent or intends to give it on terms that are unacceptable to the tenant, then the tenant can apply to an arbitrator to give consent over the landlord's head. The tenant needs consent for obtaining planning permission only if he intends to claim compensation. If the lease does not prohibit an application for planning permission, the tenant can apply. (Even if the lease does, anyone else can apply for planning consent on any land.[1]) The physical construction of buildings pursuant to the permission will potentially be subject to the ATA 1995. The arbitrator has jurisdiction to give such consent. There is no decision as to whether an arbitrator can or should give consent in a case where the terms of the tenancy prohibit the making of improvements. Section 26 of the ATA 1995 provides that the tenant is entitled to compensation in accordance with

---

1   Except for Crown land, where there is no private interest. See Town and Country Planning Act 1990, s 299.

the provisions of the Act notwithstanding any agreement to the contrary. That relates specifically to compensation (to prevent a landlord depriving the tenant of the right to fair compensation for an improvement which the tenant is entitled to carry out). It is arguable that this section does not override the terms of the tenancy as to whether improvements can be made at all. The point remains to be decided. In any event, the matter is in the discretion of an arbitrator who might consider that where the parties freely entered into an agreement which for overage purposes restricted the making of improvements by the tenant then that agreement should be respected. Under s 19(4) of the LTA 1927 the provisions of that section do not apply to farm business tenancies.

Business tenancies

The LTA 1927 provides for compensation for improvements on business tenancies that are not farm business tenancies. Business tenancies for the purposes of the LTA 1927 are slightly different from those for the purposes of the LTA 1954 which confers rights of security. Part I of the LTA 1927 applies (under s 17) to 'premises held under a lease, other than a mining lease . . . used wholly or partly for carrying on thereat any trade or business and not being [agricultural holdings or farm business tenancies]'. The tenant of such a holding has the right under s 1 of the LTA 1927 to claim compensation for improvements carried out in accordance with the provisions of the Act. If the tenant wishes to make such an improvement, it must first serve notice on the landlord and the landlord has an opportunity to carry out the improvement at its own expense in return for an increase in rent. If the landlord refuses either to carry out the improvement or to consent to the tenant's doing so, then the tenant has the right to apply to the court[1] which can certify that the improvement is a proper one and in such case the tenant has the right under s 3(4) to carry out the improvement 'anything in any lease of the premises to the contrary notwithstanding'. The court 'may' certify the improvement and it is considered that this gives the court a discretion. Furthermore, the court may do so by imposing such conditions as it thinks fit. It is possible that if the lease is deliberately designed to protect an overage interest of the landlord, the court might feel it appropriate not to exercise its discretion or might do so on terms as to payment. However, as the object of the section is to give the tenant a right to compensation at the end of the tenancy, the payment of overage to the landlord may be thought inconsistent with that.

Termination

It should be noted that the procedures both for farm business tenancies under the ATA 1995 and for other business tenancies under the LTA 1927 give the tenant a right to compensation at the end of the tenancy. That includes

---

1   LTA 1954, s 63(2).

termination by re-entry but apart from that where a lease is granted for a term of several centuries it may be considered that this eventuality is too remote to be a matter of concern.

Landlord and Tenant Act 1927, s 19(2) and (3)

The specific provisions in relation to farm business tenancies and business tenancies apply whether or not there is an absolute prohibition against making alterations or improvements. Section 19 of the LTA 1927 contains provisions which apply to all tenancies except agricultural and farm business tenancies and mining leases. Under s 19(2), where there is a condition against making improvements without consent, then it is implied that consent shall not be unreasonably withheld. The person giving consent may require payment of a reasonable sum in respect of any damage to or diminution in the value of the premises themselves or in any neighbouring premises belonging to the landlord and other incidental expenses and there may be a requirement for reinstatement. Under s 19(3), where there is a condition against changing the use of the premises without licence or consent, then it is implied that, so long as that change does not involve a structural alteration, it is subject to a provision that no fine or sum of money in the nature of a fine (whether by way of increase of rent or otherwise) shall be payable for such consent, but again there can be compensation for damage or diminution in the value of premises or neighbouring premises and other incidental expenses. It should be noted that these apply only to qualified covenants where the thing may not be done without consent. They do not apply to absolute prohibitions where the thing may not be done at all.

Secure tenancies

In relation to secure tenancies, that is to say tenancies from certain public bodies such as local authorities, New Town Corporations, Housing Action Trusts, charitable housing trusts, housing co-operatives, urban development corporations and the Development Board for Rural Wales, then s 97 of the HA 1985 provides a substitute for s 19(2) of the LTA 1927. In such a case, the tenant may not make an improvement without the written consent of the landlord and such consent may not be unreasonably withheld. Section 97 of the HA 1985 applies in place of s 19(2) of the LTA 1927 and in certain cases the tenant has a right to compensation for improvements under HA 1985, s 99A. Under HA 1985, s 101, the rent may not be increased simply on account of improvements made by the tenant. These provisions apply irrespective of any express terms agreed between the parties.

General

It follows from the above that the scope for negative overage in relation to farm or other business tenancies or secure tenancies is limited. In the case of other tenancies, an absolute prohibition on improvements or change of use may be effective but a qualified provision will not be, although this may be used for positive overage as mentioned below.

7.2.2   Positive covenants in overage leases

The power of the Land Tribunal under s 84 of the LPA 1925 to modify or release restrictive covenants does not relate to positive covenants and a suitable covenant may be inserted to protect overage as mentioned above. Such a covenant may be difficult to enforce. The traditional view for many years was that while there was a power for the court to enforce restrictive covenants in leases by injunction and this was often done, the court had no power to enforce a positive covenant in that way. The problems relating to positive covenants affecting freehold land set out in Chapter 3 do not apply to leases, but there are other problems, particularly the difficulty for the court to supervise the performance of the positive covenant. In certain limited circumstances, the court has power to give a direction (eg keeping property in repair[1]) that a covenant designed to produce an ascertainable result should be performed because it will be possible for the court to know whether or not the actual physical result has been achieved. However, other covenants, such as the obligation to keep trading from a particular shop, will not be enforced because of the practical difficulties.[2] The landlord who has the benefit of a positive covenant will normally have the remedy of a right of re-entry if it is not performed[3] or the remedy of damages, but the exercise of a right of re-entry remains discretionary and equitable, even though the discretion must be exercised in accordance with legal rules, and damages will depend on establishing an ascertainable loss according to ordinary rules of breach of contract. The right of re-entry is generally regarded as a security for the interest of the landlord and while this should not be taken literally,[4] nevertheless the court will regard it in that light, particularly where it is intended to protect a financial interest of the landlord. Therefore, it seems possible that where a positive covenant has been inserted in a lease with the specific intention of protecting the landlord's right to overage, then the court might be prepared to give relief against the forfeiture of a lease which may perhaps have several centuries yet to run, on the provision of some form of substituted security. Indeed, if the value has already been triggered as a result of the breach of covenant, the court has jurisdiction to award damages instead of giving the injunction and that jurisdiction would no doubt be exercised

---

1   *Rainbow Estates v Tokenhold* [1998] 2 EGLR 34.
2   *Co-operative Insurance Society Ltd v Argyll Stores (Holdings) Ltd* [1998] AC 1.
3   The problem in *Rainbow Estates v Tokenhold* was that there was no re-entry clause.
4   *Exchange Travel Agency Ltd v Triton Property Trust plc* [1991] BCLC 396; *Re Olympia and York Canary Wharf Ltd* [1993] BCLC 453; *Re AGB Research Ltd* [1995] BCC 1091; *Razzaq v Pala* [1997] 38 EG 157; *Clarence Café Ltd v Comchester Properties Ltd* [1999] L&TR 303, ChD; *Essex Furniture plc v NPI* (unreported); *Re Lomax Leisure Ltd* [1999] EGCS 61; and *Christopher Moran Holdings v Bairstow* [1999] 2 WLR 396.

according to the principles laid down in *Wrotham Park Settled Estates v Parkside Homes Limited*[1] and *Jaggard v Sawyer*.[2]

7.2.3 Break clauses

An overage break clause in a lease operates in a very similar way to an option in relation to freehold land.[3] It is regarded by the courts as like an option and also like a notice to quit[4] and is subject to the normal rules that apply to such provisions. However, it would appear that a landlord's option to break a lease is not subject to the rule against perpetuities (on the basis that it is a contractual right and by analogy with a right of re-entry) and this corresponds to a tenant's right under s 9(1) of the Perpetuities and Accumulations Act 1964 to acquire the freehold.

In relation to business tenancies to which the LTA 1954 applies, it will be necessary to obtain a court order for the operation of the break under s 38(4)(b), but this is given as a matter of course if both parties are fully advised on their rights and consent.[5]

If title to the lease is unregistered and if the lease is capable of assignment or the premises can be sublet, then the break needs to be registered as a land charge,[6] but that will apply only to leases of less than 21 years.[7]

Instead of an option to break, a corresponding provision is sometimes inserted in the re-entry clause, but it is considered that this has the same consequences at least as far as business tenancies are concerned because it is a provision of the lease which would otherwise deprive the tenant of security under s 38(1).

7.3 LEASES AND POSITIVE OVERAGE

Leases are very commonly used to secure positive overage. Traditionally, this has been by way of a rent payable by reference to the increased value of land after an improvement is made or a beneficial change of use has been implemented, but since the passing of the LT(C)A 1995 attention has also been focused on the use of leases to secure capital payments.

---

1 [1974] 2 All ER 321.
2 [1995] 2 All ER 189.
3 See Chapter 8. Thus, preconditions must be strictly complied with. *Bass Holdings Ltd v Morton Music Ltd* [1988] Ch 493; *Stait v Fenner* [1912] 2 Ch 504; and *Bairstow Eves (Securities) Ltd v Ripley* [1992] 2 EGLR 47. See **8.3**.
4 *Pennel v Payne* [1995] QB 192.
5 See *Weinberg's Weatherproofs Ltd v Radcliffe Paper Mill Co Ltd* [1958] Ch 437; *Allnatt London Properties Ltd v Newton* [1981] 2 All ER 290; and *Bocardo SA v S and M Hotels Ltd* [1980] 1 WLR 17.
6 *Greene v Church Commissioners for England* [1974] Ch 467.
7 LRA 1925, s 123.

As positive covenants are binding by privity of estate, positive overage is more appropriate to leases than freeholds and in practice is widely used. The overage can be receivable either as a capital payment or more usually as an extra rent over and above the fixed or 'dead' rent.

7.3.1   Capital payment

The position at common law in relation to leases is in many ways similar to that relating to freeholds described at **3.2**. The rules in relation to leases were established in *Spencer's Case*[1] as modified by legislation between the Grantees of Reversions Act 1540 and the LPA 1925, s 141.[2] The broad effect of these rules was that a covenant to pay a capital sum was binding only as between the original parties to the lease and could not be enforced against a subsequent tenant because (unlike rent) such a covenant did not have 'reference to the subject-matter'[3] of the lease. Therefore, until 1996 it was unsafe for a landlord to take a covenant by way of positive overage on an assignable lease to pay a capital sum of money on the happening of an uncertain future event. The effect of s 3 of the LT(C)A 1995 is now that the benefit and burden of all landlord and tenant covenants of a tenancy pass to the successors in title to the landlord and the tenant. Section 28(1) provides that a 'tenant covenant' means a covenant falling to be complied with by the tenant. On the face of it, it is not made immediately obvious that this relates to payments of money, but s 28(3) (which applies to assignment of part of the premises and which excludes the operation of s 28(2) in certain circumstances) makes it clear that a tenant covenant can include a covenant to pay money. That must relate primarily to matters such as rent, rates, service charge and taxes but the wording is wide enough to cover any covenant to pay money. The problems mentioned above concerning the reluctance of the court to enforce a positive covenant[4] would not apply to a covenant to pay money because there is no difficulty in supervising such a payment.

7.3.2   Fines on assignment and renewal

There are a number of provisions still on the statute book which are capable of causing problems if the draftsman is not aware of them. They arise from an historic situation and the attempts to remedy this in the nineteenth century and in the 1925 legislation.

In past centuries, and in many parts of the country, the rent payable for land was a customary or 'usual' rent for the holding. In many cases that became fixed sometime in the Middle Ages or in the sixteenth and seventeenth

---

1   (1583) 5 Co Rep 16a.
2   *Hill v Booth* [1930] 1 KB 381. See **3.2** and the notes to it.
3   LPA 1925, ss 141 and 142.
4   See Chapter 3.

centuries and remained fixed for a great many years.[1] As the purchasing power of money reduced over the years and the productive capacity of land increased, this was dealt with not in the modern way by increasing the rent and having regular reviews but by having payments known as 'fines' from the tenant to the landlord. These were usually made on the start of the lease, although there might be fines payable at other intervals, for example when the child of the tenant succeeded on his parent's death. This was encouraged because a great many landlords only had a limited interest, either under settlements or under ecclesiastical or public law. They wished to exploit their position and in many cases had limited powers to grant leases typically for 31 years. In order to secure the maximum return to themselves they would grant leases at the usual rent and charge the tenant a premium for doing so. (Sometimes this was done at what was known as a candle auction, whereby the lease (at the fixed rent) was laid on the auction table and the auctioneer marked a line on a candle which he then lit. Prospective tenants had the right to bid until the candle had burned down to a particular mark when the last bidder was entitled to the lease in return for the premium.) The result of this was that tenants who had paid out a large outlay and had only a small rent were not inclined to improve the holding because they wished to exploit it for their own gain and landlords had no incentive to improve the holding either because they had only a limited interest and by the time the lease came to be renewed it would be a matter for their successor. The Victorians made various efforts to deal with this problem. They could not rule out leases for fines altogether, but where premiums were charged they required that the amount of the premium should not pass to the limited owner for the time being but should be set aside as capital and the owner should only be entitled to income earned on the premium. Other provisions required that leases could only be granted at the full market rent.

There were various ways around this for those who did not like the new rules. One was the device for a perpetually renewable lease. The tenant was granted (or had by custom) the right to renew the lease typically every 7 years (and such renewals could be repeated again and again for ever) and on each renewal would have to pay a premium to the landlord. Therefore, to counter such devices, LPA 1922, s 145 converts perpetually renewable leases into leases for 2,000 years and, if a fine is to be paid, decapitalises it.[2] Another avoidance device was to grant options to renew and this was dealt with[3] by providing that any provision for the renewal of a lease for a term exceeding 60 years from the termination of the original lease was void.

---

1   *Dyke v Bishop of Bath and Wells* (1715) 6 Bro PC 365.
2   LPA 1922, Sch 15, para 12.
3   LPA 1922, s 145 and Sch 15, para 7(2).

A further problem arose where the landlord claimed the right to make a charge for giving consent to the assignment of a lease. (This is much the same problem as was encountered prior to 1290 in relation to freeholds.[1]) That was remedied by s 144 of the LPA 1925, which provides that where a lease contains a condition against assigning or otherwise dealing without consent, then, unless the lease contains an express provision to the contrary, it is deemed to be subject to a proviso that no fine or sum of money in the nature of a fine should be payable for such licence or consent. It is noted that that could be contracted out of and 2 years later s 19(1) of the LTA 1927 provided that where a lease contained such a provision, notwithstanding any express provision to the contrary, it was deemed to be subject to a proviso that such licence or consent was not to be unreasonably withheld. Of course, it remained possible to exclude s 144, but that is only rarely done because most tenants will not accept such a provision when taking a lease. Where, however, the parties intend the landlord to have a share of any uplift in value on assignment then it is still possible to exclude s 144.

Section 19(1) goes on to provide that if the lease is for more than 40 years and is made in consideration wholly or partly of the erection, improvement, addition or alteration of buildings then, where the lease can be assigned with the landlord's consent, that consent is not in fact required more than 7 years before the end of a term, provided the landlord is notified within 6 months after the transaction. Therefore, where an improvement lease is granted which specifically contemplates the tenant putting up or improving buildings, and where the lease can be assigned with consent, then the landlord's control is materially diminished. Once again, however, s 144 can still be excluded so that a sum of money can be made automatically payable to the landlord in those circumstances and may be made chargeable on the lease. Furthermore, nothing in these provisions affects an absolute prohibition on assignment,[2] but a tenant is unlikely to be prepared to pay a substantial sum of money for an unassignable lease of any great length.

As a further consequence of the restriction on premiums on renewal or options, s 149(3) of the LPA 1925 provides that a term either at a rent or granted in consideration of a fine limited to take effect for more than 21 years from the date of the instrument which creates it is void, and any contract to create such a term is also void. There is an exception for a term taking effect in equity under a settlement, or created out of an equitable interest under a settlement, or under an equitable power for mortgage indemnity or other like purposes, but these exceptions do not seem to be wide enough to cover commercial overage arrangements where there is an occupation lease. Where the term is used for security, the exception may be available.[3]

---

1   See Chapter 3.
2   See also *Vaux Group plc v Lilley* [1990] 1 EGLR 60 as to the need for a guarantor.
3   See **7.5.2**.

As a result of the various provisions mentioned above, one method of securing overage which is entering into use is the lease for a long term, typically 100 years, with a covenant against changing the use or making alterations without the landlord's consent. There is further provision that during the first 25 years, if the tenant does change the use or make improvements, then the tenant for the time being will pay to the landlord a sum of money calculated by reference to any increase in value. The reason for the 25-year period is that, under s 84 of the LPA 1925, the Lands Tribunal may be able to vary the covenant after that date and, therefore, the right to the landlord would depend on the covenant as varied. Although s 19(2) and (3) of the LTA 1927 has the effect that the landlord cannot unreasonably withhold consent and if it is a business lease the landlord's refusal might in any event be overruled, there is nothing to stop a payment being made attributable to that event and by virtue of the LT(C)A 1995 that is now enforceable.

7.3.3 Overage receivable as income

A widespread form of investment lease used by local authorities, pension funds, insurance companies, charities and other institutions, is the development lease which involves an arrangement between a landlord and a development company or builder. The typical arrangement involves the institutional landlord granting a long lease, such as 120 years, to a property or development company on the basis that the rent receivable by the institution will be calculated by reference to (and is usually a proportion of) either the actual rents received by the head lessee or rents which might be received if the property were let fully. These arrangements are sometimes described as 'back-to-back' or 'side-by-side', but this is a misleading description. The developer is the active tenant who will be responsible for constructing or converting a building, finding occupational tenants and managing the building itself. Sometimes the building may be sub-let as a whole and the sub-tenant may sub-underlet further on this basis, and sometimes there is provision for the development company to surrender its intermediate lease to the institution once the building has been fully let, in return for a capital payment.

The rent is calculated by reference to the increased value and the normal rules that apply to standard rent review clauses will generally also apply to the development lease. The simplest method of calculating the rent due to the institution is to provide that it shall be a given proportion (such as 25 per cent) of the rents received by the property company on sub-letting. Provided the property is in fact sub-let at full rents, this does not present a problem, but cases have reached the courts where the head tenant has gone into occupation itself, as a result of which there have been no sub-lettings and therefore no rent under them. Where possible, the court will imply a term to give effect to the intentions of the parties or give a wide interpretation to the words used.[1]

This arrangement is suitable for long leases. The general rule in relation to contractual rent review clauses[2] is that, unless something is said to the contrary, the tenant is bound to pay rent on any improvement which it makes at its own expense. In the case of a development lease where the rent is only a proportion of the improved value, and that is the basis of the arrangement between the parties, that is obviously fair, but it is generally considered to be unfair in other contexts. Thus, under s 13(3) of the ATA 1995, the rent under a farm business tenancy must disregard the rental value of any tenant's improvements other than those provided under an obligation imposed on the tenant by the terms of his tenancy or any previous tenant or any tenant's improvement to the extent that allowance or benefit has been made or given by the landlord or to the extent that the tenant has received compensation from the landlord in respect of it. Similarly, where a business tenancy comes to be renewed under the LTA 1954, the rent determined by the court under s 34(1)(c) and (2) provides that there should be disregarded any effect on rent of an improvement carried out by the tenant otherwise than in pursuance of an obligation to his immediate landlord more than 21 years before the application for the new tenancy was made.[3] Under s 101 of the HA 1985, the rent of a dwelling let on a secure tenancy is not to be increased on account of a tenant's improvements. Under s 14(2)(b) of the HA 1988, where a rent assessment committee determines the rent of an assured tenancy, it has to disregard any increase in value of the dwelling-house attributable to a 'relevant improvement' carried out not more than 21 years before the review, otherwise than in pursuance of an obligation to the immediate landlord. Of course, it is true that the rent assessment committee will be involved only where the parties have not otherwise provided under s 13(1)(b) for a different mechanism for fixing the rent.[4]

These statutory provisions apply because it is generally considered unfair for tenants to have to pay rent to a landlord on the value of improvements made at their own expense. Nevertheless, the basic rule applies that this can be excluded in most cases and the landlord is entitled to secure a benefit from a tenant's improvement if this is fair.

For this purpose, an improvement normally constitutes a physical improvement, although the word is rarely defined. In the specific context of farm

---

1 *R&A Millett (Shops) Ltd v Leon Allan International Fashions Ltd* [1989] 1 EGLR 138; and *Ashworth Frazer Ltd v Gloucester City Council* (also *Fraser Pipestock Ltd v Gloucester City Council*) [1997] 26 EG 180, (1995) 71 P&CR 123.

2 *Ponsford v HMS Aerosols Ltd* [1979] AC 63.

3 This does not apply to a rent review clause in a negotiated lease where the parties are free to make what bargain they wish.

4 See also the Rent Act 1977, s 70(3)(b). No new Rent Act tenancies can now be granted.

business tenancies, it is provided that it can include an intangible improvement. Although the definition in s 15 of the ATA 1995 specifically applies to Part III which deals with compensation, s 13(5) applies that definition for the purposes of rent and, therefore, a holding made more valuable (eg by the provision of planning consent) will qualify as an improvement for the purposes of assessing a new rent.

7.3.4 Turnover rents

The traditional rent is a fixed sum (which may be subject to regular review) which takes into account all relevant factors including the earning capacity of the holding, but that will not always be suitable and often there will be no available market for holdings of a specific type. In relation to certain tenancies, therefore, methods have been evolved between landlords and tenants to enable a different form of rent to be secured. Although many of these would not be seen to constitute overage in the normal sense, the effect of them is that if the tenant does particularly well or if there is some special advantage in the holding then the landlord may secure an increase in income which would not be available if the premises were simply let at what might be considered to be a market rent.

Mining leases

There is a long-established practice of securing a special return to the landlord on a mining lease. This is largely because of the nature of the minerals which may be of unknown depth, whose quality and marketability may change and which are very often worked in a volatile market where prices can move rapidly. Thus, mineral landlords and tenants have long been used to charging payment by reference to the actual return from a mine or quarry and in recent years, as a result of new types of activity (particularly in worked-out quarries), this has been extended.

A typical mining lease may now contain a large number of different elements in its rent. A quarry will involve excavating a potentially large area of land, but very often the whole area will not be worked at the same time. Where, for example, it is opened in farm land the quarry operator may start excavation of one part of the site and the farmer will still be in occupation of the rest of it. The quarry will gradually move across the site and the hole be infilled as working is completed with the intention ultimately of restoring the whole surface to agriculture. The tenant will require land for storage heaps, grading and processing equipment and, possibly, for treatment of the mineral. There may also be a need for mine offices and accommodation for occupation by mine workers or security staff. There may be prospects of charging substantial sums for the deposit of waste to infill the quarry and there may be scope for treatment plants. Furthermore, the tenant may wish to import materials from other quarries to mix with the materials excavated in that particular quarry to improve their quality.

Typically, there will also be a tension between the landlord who wishes to have a regular income averaged out over the period of the lease and the tenant who will only wish to pay on materials as and when they are excavated, exported and sold. This is normally overcome by having a fixed dead rent either of a given cash amount (which will be varied from time to time) or of an amount related to a given quantity of minerals and the tenant will pay that sum every year. If in any year the tenant extracts less than the equivalent amount of material, then the shortfall may be carried forward to future years and set against any excess over the minimum amount that may occur. The tenant will then pay a royalty by reference to that excess, taking into account the previous year's shortfalls. Different royalties may also be payable for the different qualities and gradings of material. A typical payment structure will be as follows.

There will be an occupation rent for land actually taken and from which the farmer or other surface occupier is excluded, usually revised every 3 years by reference to current agricultural rents. There will also be a surface rent for plant, machinery, offices, occupied dwellings and other premises by reference to normal commercial rents in the locality typically reviewed every 5 years. The materials will be paid for primarily by reference to a royalty merging in a dead rent with a carry forward shortfall arrangement. There may be separate royalties for different qualities of materials. These will be subject to regular revision. It may be agreed that there should be a rate payable based on general market conditions and that may be revised every 5 years. Alternatively, the tenant may pay a proportion of what used to be called the 'ex-pit selling price'. In the past that was the price the operator charged to contractors who drove up to the quarry, loaded their lorries, paid by reference to a weigh-bridge and drove away. That practice is now rare and large-scale mineral operators will usually deliver material in their own lorries to the sites of purchasers so an allowance may be made for the cost of haulage.

If the quarry can be infilled at a profit, the landlord may also receive an infilling royalty, perhaps also with a dead rent. Different rates are normally payable for inert waste such as concrete from those for domestic or biologically active waste if the soil is suitable for tipping such materials. There may also be differences where the operator has a contract with a local authority which regularly delivers large quantities as distinct from the rate payable by private operators such as building contractors. If the operator imports materials to mix with those dug from the quarry, a royalty may be payable on those or a royalty may be payable instead by reference to the added value of materials manufactured on site and exported. Where waste material is imported, it may also be sorted and recycled, and the landlord may seek a royalty by reference to the recycled value of materials.

Each of these elements may be calculated separately and the resulting figure can vary considerably from year to year.

Other turnover rents

The standard form of turnover rent is that found in a shopping centre, where the performance of the centre (particularly if it has only recently been opened) is uncertain and where the landlord also wishes to be actively involved in the management and the prosperity of the units may depend on the number of visitors the landlord can attract to the centre as a whole. This is overage where the recipient plays an active part in earning it.

Another form of turnover rent is found in moorings for pleasure yachts, where the conditions for each estuary will be different and so there is virtually no comparable market. In this case, rents will normally be assessed either by reference to the number of moorings (with a fee revised every few years) or by a percentage of the receipts of the mooring operator.

Traditionally, in agriculture there have been a variety of turnover rents or corn rents typically based on the value of a given quantity of corn from year to year. Such rents are now very rare in this country (although in principle they could be used under the provisions of s 9(b) of the ATA 1995), but they are more common on the Continent.

Another form of turnover rent is rent by reference to barrelage charged on leases of public houses. A further one by reference to the number of looms installed is illustrated by *Walsh v Lonsdale*.[1]

There can also be overage rents by reference to the rent paid by undertenants. In *Crown Estate Commissioners v Possfund Custodian Trustee Ltd*,[2] the rent payable was 10 per cent of the tenant's rental income for an accounting year or a base rent of £135,000 per year – whichever was the greater. If in any year the rents exceeded £38.50 per square foot, then certain additional rents were payable. If the tenant failed to produce accounts, then the landlord was entitled to assume that the tenant's income represented the open market rent currently payable. Two issues arose. One related to a claimed penalty clause. The second related to the definition of 'net internal area' and involved the interpretation of the particular lease. There was no suggestion that the idea of an overage rent as such was not enforceable.[3]

---

1   (1882) 21 Ch D 9. See **7.5.2**.
2   [1996] EGCS 172.
3   For an example of a lease where the rent was a proportion of total receipts by the tenant, see *Standard Life Co Ltd v Greycoat Devonshire Square Ltd* (2000) *The Times*, 10 April.

7.4   JOINING LEASE TO FREEHOLD

The main purpose of overage by lease is to secure to the landlord the benefit of the overage payment. Once that has been paid, the landlord may no longer wish to have an interest in the land. Therefore, it may be appropriate for the tenant to be entitled to acquire the freehold and the overage may itself work on that basis.

In addition, the policy of the law over many years has been to allow tenants under long leases to acquire the freehold where the landlord does not himself perform a positive function and is merely in receipt of a money payment (or indeed does not even receive that). There are various rights of enlargement and enfranchisement conferred by statute, but in certain circumstances the landlord may retain rights over its former property or to terminate a lease for the purpose of redevelopment.

7.4.1   Enlargement

Section 153 of the LPA 1925 provides that where a term was originally created for at least 300 years and at least 200 years of that term are still unexpired, where there is either no rent or a peppercorn or the rent does not exceed £1 and has not been collected for 20 years, and where neither the lease itself nor any superior lease contains a provision for re-entry for condition broken, then the term can be enlarged into a fee simple. Such leases are rare in modern conditions, although there are many that qualify which were granted centuries ago. However, although a landlord under such a lease is liable to lose his freehold, this may not be of any practical importance because s 153(8) provides that the fee simple so acquired is:

> 'subject to all the same trusts, powers, executory limitations over, rights and equities, and to all the same covenants and provisions relating to user and enjoyment, and all the same obligations of every kind as the term would have been subject if it had not been so enlarged.'

Thus, where there are restrictions or other provisions designed to protect overage, they will continue in force, although only to the extent that they would have been enforceable under the lease. It would seem to follow that for this purpose s 84 of the LPA 1925 applies only after 25 years. Thus, even though a lease that qualifies[1] could be enlarged the day after it is granted, this will not relieve the tenant of any negative overage provisions. Where there is no rent initially and rent only becomes payable if the trigger event occurs, then the question must arise as to whether this is treated as being some 'other rent having no money value'. It would appear that if there is a prospect, however remote, of the trigger event occurring, then the rent must have some money value – even if that is very low and the contingency is remote. It would have to

---

1   There would have to be no rent, otherwise the tenant would have to wait 20 years.

be extremely remote to be valued at less than £1 in modern values. The law was enacted before the late twentieth-century inflation eroded the value of money.

7.4.2 Enfranchisement and first refusal

Parliament has intervened in long leases of residential property to allow leaseholders to acquire their freehold. This derives from the Leasehold Reform Act 1967 which itself was inspired by the coming to an end of some Victorian improvement leases, particularly in South Wales.

The practice which had developed by the 1850s and 1860s was for a landowner on the edge of an expanding town to grant to a builder a lease for 99 years. Normally, a price would be agreed for the value of the land itself in its undeveloped state (of course, this was long before the introduction of planning permission) and the landowner would then consider what income such a sum would produce if invested in government stocks. The lease would then be granted without a premium at a rent equal to that return and subject to an obligation on the builder to construct one or more houses. When they were built (or under construction), the builder would assign the whole or successive parts of the leasehold to residential occupiers who would then retain the lease and pay the ground rent. This was considered a very safe form of investment and it had the bonus that it was expected that at the end of the 99 years the lease would come to an end and the landowner's heirs would receive the value of the site with a house constructed on it which they would then be able to re-let at a full rent or sell for full value. When in the 1950s and 1960s the end of these leases began to approach, the owners of the houses were concerned at their future and made representations to their Members of Parliament. The first attempt to deal with this was in Part I of the LTA 1954 which conferred on such tenants the right to remain in occupation but subject to paying something approaching a market rent.[1] This was still considered unsatisfactory and in 1967 Parliament passed the Leasehold Reform Act. That gave tenants an option. If they could afford it, they could buy the freehold at a price which broadly represented site value.[2] If the tenant could not afford to pay even the modest purchase price, he was entitled to require a lease extension for a period expiring 50 years after the term date of the original tenancy. In such a case, the landlord retained the right under s 17 of the 1967 Act that no earlier than 12 months before the original term date of the tenancy he could apply to the court for an order to resume possession of the property for the purposes of

---

1   The rules have been changed from time to time, but normally a fair rent under the Rent Act 1968 will apply where the lease comes to an end before 15 January 1999 and a market rent under the HA 1988 if it comes to an end thereafter. See LTA 1954, s 3 and Local Government and Housing Act 1989, Sch 10, para 3.

2   For certain houses in a higher rent category, a greater proportion of the market value including sharing part of the marriage value will apply.

redevelopment and, if the court was satisfied that the landlord had established the ground, the court was obliged to order possession subject to the payment of compensation for the loss of the house to the tenant.

These provisions initially applied to leases of over 21 years at a low rent. Originally, this was defined as being for less than two-thirds of the rateable value and, subsequently, as a rent not exceeding £250.[1] Under the HA 1996,[2] the provisions of the Act apply to any lease over 35 years irrespective of the amount of the rent, although there are exemptions for example for certain existing leases in rural areas.[3]

There are parallel provisions for blocks of flats. Under the LTA 1987, tenants of blocks of flats were given a right of first refusal if the landlord wished to sell[4] and if the landlord was incompetent they would also have the right in certain circumstances to demand the freehold.[5] Under the Leasehold Reform Housing and Urban Development Act 1993,[6] a sufficient majority of tenants acting collectively in relation to certain blocks of flats were given the power to acquire the freehold of the block under a system of collective enfranchisement. In addition, the tenant of a flat was given an individual right to have a new lease expiring 90 years after the term date of the original lease,[7] although once again under s 61 of that Act a landlord had the right during the period of 12 months ending with the term date of the original lease to apply to the court for an order terminating that lease on the grounds of redevelopment, subject again to the payment of compensation.

The landlord is entitled to the benefit of certain covenants under s 10(4) of the Leasehold Reform Act 1967 restricting the use of the premises in such form as the landlord may require in a way that will not interfere with the reasonable enjoyment of the house and premises as they have been enjoyed during the tenancy but will materially enhance the value of other property in which the landlord has an interest. Although this has been interpreted[8] to allow the landlord to impose on the freehold disposal covenants similar to those contained in the previous lease the qualification in s 10(4)(c) would restrict the use of the covenants for overage. Similarly, under s 34(9)(a) and Sch 7, para 5 to the Leasehold Reform Housing and Urban Development Act 1993, the conveyance of a block of flats may include such provisions as the freeholder may require to restrict the use of the premises in a way which will not interfere

---

1   Leasehold Reform Act 1967, s 4, as amended by References to Rating (Housing) Regulations 1990, SI 1990/434.
2   Section 106 and Sch 9, para 1, inserting the Leasehold Reform Act 1967, s 1AA.
3   Leasehold Reform Act 1967, s 1AA(3) and the regulations made under it.
4   Part I.
5   Part III.
6   Part I, Chapter I.
7   Part I, Chapter II.
8   *Langevad v Chiswick Quay Freeholds Ltd* (1998) 77 P&CR D 39.

with the reasonable enjoyment of those premises as they have been enjoyed but which will materially enhance the value of other property in which the freeholder has an interest. It is an open question as to what extent the reservation of a covenant for overage will materially enhance the value of other property but it seems unlikely that the courts would interpret it in that way.

The Leasehold Reform Act 1967 does not apply to farm business tenancies and that exception extends to premises which were once part of an original farm and subsequently have been sold off.[1]

As a result of the provisions for enfranchisement, it is generally accepted that the old type of residential improvement lease with a reversion after 99 years is no longer a suitable form of overage. Furthermore, when coupled with the provisions mentioned above, overage has only a very limited scope in relation to residential leases at all. Thus, a long lease of bare land without any covenants restricting use or development would enable the tenant to build houses and assign or sub-let those houses to residential occupiers who would themselves be entitled to acquire the freehold. Even if there are restrictive covenants, they are potentially capable of release under s 84 of the LPA 1925 either after 25 years of the lease has run or immediately on acquisition of the freehold.

7.4.3 Option to acquire the freehold

There can be a deliberate agreement between the parties that the leaseholder will be entitled to acquire the freehold and this can be used as a form of overage. For example, an occupational lease of land may be granted for a premium that reflects its current use value and, if the trigger event occurs, the tenant will then have an option to acquire the freehold for a proportion of development value. Under s 9(1) of the Perpetuities and Accumulations Act 1964, such an option is not subject to the rule against perpetuities provided it is exercisable only by the lessee or his successors in title and ceases to be exercisable at or before the expiration of one year following the determination of the lease. There could also be a put option under which the landlord is entitled to require the tenant to purchase the freehold at such a price reflecting development value. Such an option would not appear to create an interest in land (rather the reverse) and, therefore, would not be subject to the rule against perpetuities. It may be that the lease could include a break clause exercisable at any time if the circumstances arise and the tenant does not perform its obligations to buy under the put option.

There should also be a mention here of the Right to Buy enjoyed by secure tenants under the provisions of Part V of the HA 1985. The housing authority

---

1   *Lester v Ridd* [1989] 1 All ER 1111.

is entitled to impose conditions, but an attempt to use these to secure overage was struck down in *R v Braintree District Council, ex parte Halls*.[1]

7.5 LEASEHOLD STRUCTURES TO SECURE OVERAGE

The foregoing discussion assumes a simple structure of a lease by a freeholder to an occupational tenant but the actual structure of leases, particularly commercial development leases, may be more complex. Such a structure can itself be used for overage.

7.5.1 Intermediate leases

In certain cases, the granter may require the freehold, but a leasehold structure can still be used. The imposer transfers the freehold to the granter who immediately grants back to the imposer a long lease containing minimal covenants and other provisions. The imposer then grants to the granter an underlease containing covenants and conditions designed to secure overage. Thus, the granter has both the freehold and the rights of occupation (or of sub-underletting) while the imposer retains a legal estate in the land sufficient to secure covenants. At common law such covenants can be enforced only where there is privity of estate, although under s 3(5) of the LT(C)A 1995 a covenant restrictive of the use of the land is capable of being enforced against any person who is the owner or occupier of any demised premises to which the covenant relates even though there is no express provision in the tenancy to that effect. Under the Contracts (Rights of Third Parties) Act 1999, a provision in a contract (including a lease) intended to benefit a third party may be enforceable by that third party. Therefore, it would be possible to include in a superior lease a provision that a sub-lease may not be granted unless it contains provisions intended to benefit the landlord to secure overage.

When the trigger event occurs, it may be appropriate for the recipient's intermediate head lease to be merged or surrendered.

7.5.2 Equitable leases

As overage is a contingent future interest and, therefore, is or is like an equitable interest, it can be appropriate for a lease securing overage to take effect as an equitable lease.

Leases normally subsist as legal estates comprising terms of years absolute, but it is possible to use equitable leases. An equitable lease can arise where what would otherwise be a legal lease is defective for lack of form but could in

---

1   (2000) 80 P&CR 266.

principle also arise where the substantial terms are not sufficient to satisfy the requirements for a legal estate comprising a term of years absolute.

The leading case is *Walsh v Lonsdale*,[1] which is one of the earliest reported overage cases in the books. There was a contract on 29 May 1879 whereby a landowner agreed to grant a lease of a weaving shed for 7 years from the date on which the shed should be put in working order by the landowner. The rent was stated to be £2 10s for each loom the tenant should decide to run. There was no maximum number, but he was bound to run at least 300 looms during the first year and at least 540 in subsequent years. The landlord retained the engine house, boiler house and other facilities for generating steam power, but if the tenant wished to and was able to find steam power, then those facilities were to be included in the demise. In that case, the rent reduced to £1 10s per loom per year. The other terms were to be by reference to such provisions 'as are usually inserted in leases of a similar nature' and particularly those in another lease of another property between other parties which reserved a fixed rent. Under that other lease, the rent was payable yearly in advance.

The tenant was let into possession on 1 July 1879. He began to pay rent quarterly 'and not in advance' (which suggests some irregularity in payment). He gave notice that as from 1 July 1880 he would provide his own steam. In March 1882 the landlord demanded one year's rent in advance and a few days later put in a distress.

Both sides conceded that relief could be given by specific performance. It suited neither to deny the lease. The landlord wanted rent and the tenant wanted occupation. Before the Judicature Act 1875, the tenant's right to specific performance of the contract would have been seen as giving rise to an equitable right in the land.

The court had to consider the effect of what, in his leading judgment, Jessel MR with judicial understatement called 'the present very peculiar agreement'. He held that following the Judicature Act 1875, there were no longer two estates (one at common law creating a tenancy from year to year by reason of payment of rent and one in equity under the agreement), but a single estate to which the equity rules applied. The court concluded that the landlord was entitled to claim and distrain for one year's rent at the minimum applicable, namely £1 10s for 540 looms which is £810. The landlord had actually claimed at the rate of £840 per year because there were 560 looms at the time. The court treated the £810 as comparable to a dead rent under a mining lease and, presumably, the excess payment for extra looms would be analogous to a royalty.

It is not clear that the concession (which the court was bound to accept) was properly made. There was no lease, merely an agreement, and the rent was

---

1   (1882) 21 Ch D 9.

uncertain, the commencement of the term was uncertain, the demise was uncertain and it was uncertain which of the terms of the other lease referred to ought to be incorporated. As Jessel MR said, 'The next question is, how ought the lease to be drawn? And that is a question of some nicety. I do not now wish to decide it'. He went on to confine his decision to the specific point at issue.

The court held that the arrangement in 1879 created an equitable lease. Since the LP(MP)A 1989, it is not so clear that it would create an enforceable contract, but there might nevertheless be an equitable lease based on the tenant going into occupation and paying rent by reference to the number of looms. The rent was ascertainable by a simple formula, even though it could not be predicted in advance, which is why the decision related to the contractual minimum number of looms. If there had been no minimum, presumably the landlord could not have distrained for anything. The case establishes that a lease of this nature can be an equitable lease. It does not necessarily follow that such a 'peculiar agreement' is capable of being converted to a legal term of years absolute.

Under the LP(MP)A 1989, a contract for the grant of a lease would now have to comply with the formalities in that Act, but if it does then specific performance should be available. It may also be possible for an equitable lease to arise where there is an actual assurance in equity, rather than simply an executory contract to create a legal lease.[1]

Although the doctrine of part performance no longer applies to contract under s 2 of the LP(MP)A 1989, where a tenant goes into occupation that may itself create rights under s 70(1)(g) of the LRA 1925 as an overriding interest of the person in actual occupation. Equitable leases can also arise where, for example, the tenant lacks capacity to take a legal estate.[2]

Equitable terms of years may also be created deliberately. In the eighteenth century, it was common practice to use a reservation of a term of years for the benefit of trustees to provide security for the payment of portions and annuities to widows, daughters and younger sons of the testator creating a settlement by will.[3] Similarly, where a beneficiary is entitled to the enjoyment of property under a will but all the inheritance tax has not been paid, the executors may transfer title to the beneficiary but protect themselves by the reservation of a term of years.[4] These equitable leases are intended for use as security rather than occupation, but of course security is the main function of overage. To the extent that overage is itself an equitable interest, it is appropriate for it to be protected in this way. The existence of such a term of

---

1   *Target Holdings v Priestley* [1999] Lloyd's Rep Bank 175.
2   *Kingston upon Thames Royal London Borough Council v Prince* [1999] 1 FLR 593, [1998] EGCS 179 (minority).
3   See **5.4**.
4   Inheritance Tax Act 1984, s 212, replacing earlier legislation.

years confers on the person having the benefit of it very considerable powers under s 3 of the LPA 1925. Under s 5 of that Act, where the purpose of a term of years created or limited out of freehold land becomes satisfied, then it merges in the reversion and ceases. Therefore, where a term of years is created simply for the purpose of protecting overage, then when the overage is paid the term will cease.

This should be distinguished from the provisions of s 85 of the LPA 1925 which allows a mortgage to be created by demise for a term of years absolute. That section is aimed at the specific creation of a mortgage and the type of interest considered under Chapter 6. Under s 149(3) of the LPA 1925, a term limited to take effect more than 21 years from the date of the instrument creating it is void, but the sub-section provides that it does not apply to any term taking effect in equity under a settlement or created out of an equitable interest under a settlement or under an equitable power for mortgage indemnity or other like purposes and therefore such a provision may be used. Clearly, an overage right does not arise under a settlement in the normal sense but, if this is considered to be an equitable power for a mortgage or like purpose, then it may be possible to provide that the mortgage term itself shall actually come into existence when the trigger event occurs even though that may be more than 21 years ahead. This should be distinguished from an occupational lease discussed at **7.3.2**.

7.6 CONCLUSION

Leases are a flexible and adaptable way of securing overage. A lease also has the advantage that it represents the reality of the situation where there is, in effect, a joint ownership of the overage land with the landlord and tenant owning different interests. The tenant has the immediate right of occupation for the purposes of current use, while the landlord as overage owner has some or all of the long-term development value. The courts are used to considering the interest of a landlord as owner of a deferred reversion and, while this concept may not always be easy to follow in other contexts such as freehold covenants or charges or even ransoms, it is well recognised that a leasehold structure can be used to secure two or more separate commercial interests in a single piece of property. To that extent, the courts are likely to be more sympathetic to leasehold overage than to other methods.

It is also common practice in leases to discount the effect of improvements on rent and, therefore, the courts are used to considering ground value as distinct from building (or development) value.

However, as indicated at **7.2.1** and **7.3.2**, Parliament has intervened on a much larger scale in relation to leases than it has for other types of property right used to protect overage. The consequences of that intervention (largely intended to protect the interests of business or residential tenants in occupation) has been to restrict in many ways the rights of landowners and in an extreme case to allow the tenant to acquire the freehold. That is not necessarily a bad thing and, indeed, an overage leasehold structure may be deliberately designed with s 153 of the LPA 1925 in mind to allow the landowner to have the freehold while at the same time reserving overage rights to the overage owner. Provided that the statutory rights are considered with care, the effect of the LT(C)A 1995 has been to make it easier to use leases for overage. There is also a wide experience of the use of development leases for overage. All these factors taken together mean that the lease will often be the most suitable approach.

Chapter 8

OPTIONS

8.1 WHEN OPTIONS ARE USED

Options are used in the context of other overage structures. The common form development option described below is used widely to secure development value for a landowner, but it involves the payment of a relatively small sum for the option and the landowner will not receive full current use value at the outset. Moreover, the imposer will retain the freehold of the potential development land until the trigger event occurs when he will receive a payment which comprises both current use value and a proportion of development value. Therefore, it is unsuitable for those who wish to part with ownership at an early stage and for those who wish to receive full current use value at the outset.

However, options can be used as an incidental device in the development agreement or as part of the method of securing extra payments.[1]

The most important use of options in overage is to convert a negative overage structure into a positive one. There may be a lease to the granter on terms that prohibit improvements, or a ransom strip which prevents access to a development site or a restrictive covenant against building. On their own, these prevent development and place the overage owner in a position to dictate terms, subject to what the market will bear. However, the granter may negotiate for an option that, if it obtains planning consent, it can acquire the freehold or the strip or take a release of the covenant on terms specified in advance.

Most options are 'take options', that is the person to whom the benefit of the option is granted has the right to require the landowner to transfer the land to it. The price will have been previously agreed or it will be determined in an agreed manner, such as a proportion of open market value, to be ascertained by an expert or arbitrator in case of disagreement. There can also be 'put options', where the landowner can require the other party to take and pay for the land at a time to be decided by the landowner.

---

1   *Briargate Developments Ltd v Newprop Co Ltd* [1990] 1 EGLR 283.

Rights of pre-emption (see **8.6**) are different again. They provide that the landowner cannot sell to a third party without first offering the land to the person to whom the pre-emption right has been granted.

8.2 STANDARD DEVELOPMENT OPTION AGREEMENT

This is in widespread use by many development companies around the country. The details vary from case to case and normally the major development companies wish to use their own form of agreement adapted to suit local circumstances.

8.2.1 Contents of the agreement

Certain provisions are becoming common and certain standard points are made on behalf of each side. The agreement will comprise:

(1) an initial option fee payable to the landowner who will remain in occupation or continue to receive rents from tenants;

(2) an obligation on the developer to promote the planning and, if the site is not already designated in the local plan, to seek to have it put in;

(3) an obligation to apply for planning consent, the form of which will have to be agreed with the landowner (this will provide for and protect any particular interests of the landowner such as architectural design, amenity, relocation of existing plant and any special issues, but it will normally be designed to maximise value);

(4) specific provisions to cover planning agreements under s 106 of the Town and Country Planning Act 1990 and other agreements relating to highways and services – the landowner will normally be consulted on these, but the terms tend to be standard and laid down by the relevant statutory authorities (the planning agreement will need to provide that it will not impose personal liabilities on the owner and will not impose any liabilities on the developer until commencement of development);

(5) on the grant of planning consent there will be a valuation procedure to determine the open market freehold value of the land with planning consent disregarding the costs of applying for it but having regard to any incidental features such as the cost of laying infrastructure and paying for any ransom strips of third parties. In the case of a large site which will need to be developed in phases there will need to be a provision for valuation of each part. Where there are several landowners involved in a consortium there may need to be provisions for equalisation between them to ensure each receives value – this is intended to secure that irrespective of whereabouts and on whose land the development begins or whose land is taken for public open space, schools, affordable housing and other purposes of no or low value, each landowner is treated fairly (not necessarily equally);

(6) a provision for arbitration in the event of the value not being agreed and the possibility of the developer withdrawing if he does not like the final package (there may also be possibilities for the owner to withdraw subject to compensating the developer);

(7) the price itself, which will normally be a proportion of the open market value and can be anywhere between 60 per cent and 95 per cent depending on the circumstances; and

(8) common form procedures for completion of the purchase (the form of transfer will need to grant to the developer rights for access and services over adjoining land and will need to reserve to the landowner similar rights over the land being sold, particularly if this is the first stage of a multiple development, or if the landowner retains back land).

The details will vary from case to case, depending on geographical situation, the likely requirements of the local planning authority, the relative bargaining position of the parties and the proposed use of the land when developed. There may also be special provisions to protect the tax position of the owner.

One feature frequently discussed, and which is referred to below, is the question of assignment. Normally, the landowner will seek to make the agreement incapable of assignment or at least permitting assignment only to another company of the group of which the development company forms part. Where the developer needs to raise finance on the basis of the development agreement, however, the agreement will have to be capable of being charged and the funder will need to be able to dispose of it to some other person. In some cases, the agreement will be made assignable so that the non-owning party can sell it to another developer.

8.2.2 Overage in development agreements

As indicated above, the sale price will be determined at the time planning consent is granted and therefore overage in its normal sense will not apply. However, there may be a place for it and it is frequently introduced as an addition.

The main issue relates to extra value if the developer, after completing the purchase, is then able to negotiate a more valuable planning consent, for example giving a higher density on a residential development. This may be covered in any of the normal overage methods such as a personal covenant (where the developer is a plc of standing) or a restrictive covenant for the benefit of defined land (eg limiting the number of houses to be built[1]) and often for a limited period such as 5 years from commencement of development, or a charge which can be released again after a limited period. Such arrangements work in the same way as those discussed in Chapters 2 to 7.

---

1   See *Surrey County Council v Bredero Homes*, discussed at **4.5.1**.

A more difficult issue may relate to the requirements of the planning authority that land be set aside for public open space (eg playing fields or landscape areas) or be designated for a limited purpose (eg a village hall). In such cases, there will be no value to be reflected in the price to be paid for the land, but the requirement to provide public facilities will be part of the overall costs of the development. It often happens in such cases that after a generation or so the land becomes surplus to the original requirement. Local authorities usually like to have this land conveyed to them freehold, then they are themselves in a position to capitalise on any future change in circumstances which can release value. For example, playing fields may become surplus and suitable for building. The normal method of dealing with that situation is for the landowner to retain the freehold of these communal areas and to grant a long lease at a peppercorn rent subject to suitable covenants. That is then subject to the same rules as landlord and tenant overage discussed in Chapter 7. However, some local authorities are not prepared to accept land on that basis and insist on a freehold. In that case, a restrictive covenant might be taken if the imposer has land in the vicinity capable of benefiting.

Options and pre-emptions can also be useful to protect back land. A developer may acquire more land than is needed for a road, perhaps because the exact position is unknown at the date of acquisition. In such a case, if the dedicated road does not extend to the limits of the seller's retained land, later the seller may wish to connect its back land to the new road. To avoid the developer ransoming the seller, the seller may take an option to reacquire surplus, undedicated land.

8.3   STRICT CONDITIONS

An option is seen in law as a privilege and, therefore, any conditions attached to the exercise of it must be strictly complied with.[1] In particular, if the option is exercisable within a specified time-limit, then time will be presumed to be of the essence of the power to exercise.[2] It can be easy for some condition to be overlooked and the person entitled to the benefit can thereby lose his rights.

8.4   REVERSE OVERAGE

A technique which is sometimes proposed, although it is not often used in practice, is for the developer immediately to acquire the freehold of the land at the outset paying full current use value. Often the imposer will remain in occupation under a farm business tenancy or under a business tenancy, either

---

1   *Hare v Nicoll* [1966] 2 QB 130.
2   *Benito di Luca v Juraise (Springs) Ltd* (1997) 79 P&CR 193, see *United Scientific Holdings Ltd v Burnley Borough Council* [1978] AC 904 at 928, 945, 962.

at a peppercorn rent or at a substantial rent. When the trigger event occurs, the imposer will have an option to re-acquire the land at a price ascertained by reference to current use value with an uplift to represent the sharing in development value. In practice, it is not intended that this option will be exercised, but instead the imposer will release it in return for a payment. The main problem with this is that the option period is limited to 21 years under s 9 of the Perpetuities and Accumulations Act 1964 and the normal rules about options apply that the right must be exercised strictly in accordance with its terms. A variation of this is a right of pre-emption if the granter wishes to dispose of the land whereupon the imposer will be entitled to acquire it at a price calculated in accordance with a formula but, as explained below, this is even more precarious.[1]

8.5   HOW FAR OPTIONS BIND THE LAND

An option creates an interest in land. This was established by the decision of the Court of Appeal in *London and South Western Railway Co v Gomm*.[2] In a passage that is quoted in virtually every case on options, Sir George Jessel MR considered that:

> 'If it is a mere personal contract it cannot be enforced against the assignee. Therefore the company must admit that it somehow binds the land. But if it binds the land it creates an equitable interest in the land. The right to call for a conveyance of the land is an equitable interest or equitable estate. In the ordinary case of a contract for purchase there is no doubt about this and an option for repurchase is not different in its nature. A person exercising the option has to do two things, he has to give notice of his intention to purchase, and to pay the purchase-money; but as far as the man who is liable to convey is concerned, his estate or interest is taken away from him without his consent and the right to take it away being vested in another, the covenant giving the option must give that other an interest in the land.'

That particular discussion took place in the context of the application of the rule against perpetuities, but it has been applied to other contexts.

This is particularly important in relation to conditional options where the option itself does not become exercisable until the trigger event occurs. To this extent, there is no doubt that a conditional option is in much the same position as a conditional contract, namely an agreement which is binding on both seller and buyer but only becomes enforceable if a specified event occurs.

The common form option, although its exercise may be made conditional on a trigger event for which a third party is responsible (eg the grant of planning

---

1   For an example of a reverse option and associated problems see *Smith v Royce Properties Ltd* [2000] EGCS 60, [2000] NPC 54.

2   (1882) 20 Ch D 562.

consent by the local planning authority), is itself instituted by the buyer exercising the option. A condition may not be in anyone's control, such as the death of the landowner. There may also be preconditions on the exercise in the control of the option holder. For example, a tenant's break clause in a lease is normally conditional on its having paid rent up to date and having performed its covenants. A condition in the control of the owner of the land is more likely to lead to a right of pre-emption,[1] although there may be cases such as a landlord's right to determine a quarry lease when the minerals have been worked out, where such control as there is can be exercised only by the person in possession.

In *Spiro v Glencrown Properties Limited*,[2] Hoffmann J had to consider the application of the LP(MP)A 1989 to options. Under s2 of that Act the document incorporating the terms of the contract or, where contracts are exchanged, one of the documents incorporating them (but not necessarily the same one) must be signed by or on behalf of each party to the contract. In the case of an option, there is an original agreement which is indeed signed by both parties, but the option itself is triggered by the unilateral action of the buyer who serves notice on the seller. The seller is not bound to sign another part.

Hoffmann J quoted the statement of Jenkins LJ in *Griffith v Pelton*,[3] where he said:

> 'An option in gross for the purchase of land is a conditional contract for such purchase by the grantee of the option from the grantor, which the grantee is entitled to convert into a concluded contract of purchase, and to have carried to completion by the grantor, upon giving the prescribed notice and otherwise complying with the conditions upon which the option is made exercisable in any particular case.'

However, in *Spiro v Glencrown Properties Ltd*[4] Hoffmann J went on to say that the analogy with a conditional contract is not a perfect one.

> 'An option is not strictly speaking either an offer or a conditional contract. It does not have to have *all* the incidence of the standard form of either of these concepts. To that extent it is a relationship sui generis. But there are ways which it resembles each of them.'

---

1   See **8.6**.
2   [1991] Ch 537.
3   [1958] Ch 205.
4   [1991] Ch 537.

8.6 RIGHTS OF PRE-EMPTION – HOW FAR THEY BIND THE LAND

An option must (although it is not always easy) be distinguished from a right of pre-emption or right of first refusal which is initiated by an action on the part of the seller. It would appear that such a right does not create an interest in land in favour of the buyer. This was established in *Pritchard v Briggs*.[1]

In that case, Major and Mrs Lockwood owned a hotel and an adjoining petrol filling station. In 1944 they sold the hotel to Mr Riddett and in the sale document they also granted Mr Riddett a right of first refusal over the petrol filling station, if they should ever wish to sell, at a fixed price of £3,000. Mr Riddett registered the right of first refusal as a class C(iv) land charge against Major and Mrs Lockwood. Before the end of 1944 he sold the hotel to Mr Mather and in 1954 Mr Mather resold the hotel to Mr and Mrs Briggs. Both on the sale by Mr Riddett to Mr Mather and again on the sale by Mr Mather to Mr and Mrs Briggs there was an express assignment of the right of first refusal.

In 1953 Major and Mrs Lockwood granted a tenancy of the petrol filling station to Mr Pritchard and that was renewed in 1958 when they gave him an option to buy the freehold of the petrol filling station following the death of both of them and that was renewed in 1964. Mrs Lockwood died in 1969.

In 1972 Major Lockwood's receiver, Mr Inman, negotiated with Mr and Mrs Briggs for the sale of the freehold of the petrol filling station to them at a price substantially over £3,000. It was suggested at the trial that they were exercising the right of pre-emption, but the court held that they were not in fact doing so. Nevertheless, the decision proceeded on the assumption that they might still have done so. Major Lockwood died in 1973 and Mr Pritchard immediately served notice exercising his option. The question for decision was whether he was entitled to enforce that against Mr and Mrs Briggs.

The Court of Appeal held that he could. It held that the right of pre-emption did not create an interest in land. This was a difficult conclusion to reach and, in particular, Goff LJ had to consider the wording of various provisions to the 1925 legislation and in particular s 186 of the LPA 1925, which strongly suggests that it does. Nevertheless, he concluded on the basis of the authorities and general principle that the draftsman of the 1925 legislation had been under a misapprehension and that all that a right of pre-emption created was an expectation that if the owner of the land took a decision to sell it then the holder of the right would be entitled to buy if he so wished. Until that

---

1 [1980] 1 Ch 338, following *Manchester Ship Canal Co v Manchester Racecourse Co* [1901] 2 Ch 37.

happened, there was no interest in land.[1] However, an option (and in this case the option to Mr Pritchard even though deferred until after the death of Major Lockwood was an option not a pre-emption) did create an immediate interest in land. Therefore, even though the right of pre-emption had been registered at the Land Charges Registry and even though it was itself capable of assignment and was assigned twice (and there was no question about that), nevertheless Mr Pritchard's option, which came into existence before Major Lockwood took the decision to sell the petrol filling station to Mr and Mrs Briggs, took precedence over it.

The case contains a detailed analysis of the law. It is possible that the court had regard to the conduct of the various parties, but it is quite clear that each of them knew about the other's rights all the way through and, indeed, Mr and Mrs Briggs went to considerable lengths, with the assistance of counsel, to devise what the judge called a scheme to get round the option.

The significance of this for overage is that where it is proposed to have a right of first refusal in the event of the granter disposing of the land, it has to be recognised that that right is not an interest in land and so is liable to be defeated by the later creation of an interest which obtains priority even though the right of first refusal may be protected, either by registration at the Land Charges Registry or on the Register of Title.

Therefore, there is a spectrum of situations which can arise.

(1) There is the immediate unqualified option, which is sometimes used in development sales where the potential developer has an option at a fixed price for a short limited period which in theory it can exercise whether planning consent is granted or not, although in practice it will not do so unless there is a consent.

(2) There is a conditional option which will arise only if the trigger event occurs and will be exercisable at a price determined by reference to value following the trigger event.

(3) There is a right of pre-emption which can be exercised in any circumstances if the owner for the time being of the land wishes to sell or create some other interest such as a lease or easement.

(4) There is a conditional right of pre-emption.

The matter is further confused by the fact that some of the conditions may or may not be under the control of the person exercising the right. Anyone is entitled to apply for planning consent on any land[2] without the consent of the landowner, but in practice only a person who has or is entitled to have an

---

1   As explained in *London and South Western Railway Co v Gomm* (1882) 20 Ch D 562, as until then there was no right to call for the land.
2   Other than Crown land. See Town and Country Planning Act 1990, s 299.

interest will do so because of the associated costs. However, the trigger might be something like an allocation of land for mineral extraction, which could be the unilateral act of the mineral planning authority.

However, certain triggers may depend on the action of one of the parties, for example a change of use within the Town and Country Planning (Use Classes) Order 1987,[1] or commencement of permitted development within the Town and Country Planning (General Permitted Development) Order 1995.[2] Thus, if the increase in value was not itself a trigger for the payment of overage, but payment was triggered by a sale which itself realised development value, then the pre-emption could be triggered by that.

If the imposer's option to repurchase is triggered by exercise of a consent given under the 1995 Order for permitted development and if that is itself instituted by the landowner for the time being, there is little difference between that and the normal right of first refusal, yet one is an interest in land and therefore a right of property and the other is not. Furthermore, the perpetuity period for an option is 21 years under s 9 of the Perpetuities and Accumulations Act 1964. The period for a pre-emption is not settled. *Pritchard v Briggs*[3] suggests that it is the normal perpetuity period. It is possible that it may be a purely contractual right with no period. The proviso to s 9(2) suggests that section covers pre-emption. The prudent course is to limit a pre-emption right to 21 years.

8.7 DERIVATIVES

Options are used in relation to financial interests and commodities in the context of derivatives. These include share options, namely an option to buy a share in the future, swaps which involve setting off one rate of interest, typically a variable one, against another, typically a fixed one, and forwards namely a promise to supply a particular commodity (such as wheat or coffee beans) at a set price on a set future date. These are not normally appropriate for interests in land.

There is a limited market in assignable land development options. As indicated above, development options are usually restricted to the developer itself or members of its group, but in certain cases the option holder has the right to assign and having secured the option it then goes into the market and seeks to find a developer. Although this is normally not to the advantage of the landowner, it can be in special circumstances where he does not wish to test the market himself or to get involved in the expense of dealing with a large

---

1   SI 1987/764.
2   SI 1995/418.
3   [1980] 1 Ch 338.

number of potential buyers, but is prepared to allow this to be done by an original option taker who will then go out and contact a developer of substance.

Derivatives in property are unusual in England, although they are used to some extent in the United States. They depend on very large funds normally held by banks and similar institutions with a widespread portfolio of let investments. Even there, they relate to developed properties yielding commercial rents. Rents may fluctuate, just as interest rates or the price of coffee. Pure development land not yielding an income is rarely suitable as the basis for a derivative. It follows that derivatives have little relevance to overage. Overage already has enough uncertainty, having regard to the chances of planning consent or other trigger event and to the fact that each piece of land is unique. Once a parade of shops has been constructed, it may be possible to compare the rents on that with some other parade elsewhere in the country and even more so for offices. But where land has not even been developed and there are all the associated development costs, including contamination, access problems, ransoms and other factors, the very great uncertainties associated with future values in the normal overage situation means that it is unsuitable for normal derivative treatment.

8.8   CONCLUSION

Options are not suitable as a primary means of securing overage and are not appropriate to the normal situation where the imposer needs to obtain full current use value. The reverse option, designed to overcome this, is cumbersome and there is a risk that if any conditions attached to its exercise are overlooked, the rights may be lost.

Options and pre-emptions do have a place in an overage scheme and can be useful as a subsidiary device. Furthermore, overage can be a useful adjunct to an arrangement primarily constituted as a development agreement.

Chapter 9

VEHICLES

9.1 HOW VEHICLES ARE USED

The legal devices which we have been considering in earlier chapters give direct rights to the overage owner. These can be enforced against the owner for the time being of the land or in some cases a credit-worthy person or body. Sometimes the land is put into a legal structure such as a company, a partnership, a limited liability partnership (LLP) or a trust.

Where a commercial vehicle such as a company or partnership is deliberately selected, it is usually for a short period (eg 5 years) while a specific development is being carried out. That can be done as a joint venture where the imposer may not receive much for the current use value and to that extent the arrangement is more like an option.

The deliberate use of trusts for overage purposes is rare but there may be cases where trusts have accidentally come into existence as a result of the arrangements that the parties have made. Trusts are often used in commercial contracts to share out an interest by way of securitisation. An interest (eg rights under a debenture or bond) is held by a trustee in trust for a number of investors, who can sell and buy their trust interests. In principle, such a structure can be used to take a share in overage rights, but in practice the uncertainties surrounding overage are such that this is unlikely to appeal as an investment to most of the pension and other funds which participate in such arrangements.

The result of putting the land into a vehicle is that the right of the overage owner to have overage no longer lies directly against the land itself or the person who has beneficial occupation of the land but indirectly. The overage owner has a right in its capacity as shareholder or partner or beneficiary. This may also be coupled with a degree of control over the vehicle when the overage owner becomes a director or partner or trustee but it would not normally be acceptable to the granter that the imposer should have any degree of control over day-to-day decisions.

As the overage owner will not normally have direct executive responsibility for the land and decisions will be taken by the landowner or persons appointed by it, the overage owner runs the risk that the land will be sold out of the vehicle. This risk can be minimised. The vehicle itself may contain provisions through its share structure and under the articles or under the partnership agreement or trust deed for the overage owner to have a say in any major decision such as a sale, but the law has developed in such a way that an innocent third party dealing with the vehicle will obtain a good title to the land free from the rights of a member of the company or a beneficiary of the trust. In certain trusts it is possible to have a restriction similar to that discussed at **3.4**, but even that can always be overridden by the court. If the overage owner wishes to overcome this risk by becoming part of the controlling structure of the vehicle, he will need sufficient power and influence to be able to control developments on the land which could prejudice his interests and this will probably be unacceptable to the granter who will have paid full value for the current use of the land. Where a trust is used, the trustees will have a duty both to the overage owner and to the landowner as beneficiaries. That could give rise to a conflict of interest between the beneficiaries, and if the landowner is a trustee then between trustee and beneficiary. For example, the best price on sale (for the landowner) could be obtained by selling undeveloped land free of overage rights. Unless the trust deed covers that situation, the trustees may have to apply to the court for directions as to their proper course of action.

However, a vehicle may be combined with some other means of overage to give the overage owner a proprietary interest in the land itself and so may be suitable in special circumstances.

I will continue to use the expressions 'granter', and 'landowner' to be consistent with the rest of the book, but it should be understood that the landowner in law will be the company or trustees even though a shareholder or beneficiary may have real control until the trigger event occurs.

9.2 COMPANY

9.2.1 How company overage works

The imposer sells the land to a company for current use value. The company finds the purchase price through the granter subscribing for shares. As the imposer is treated as having put in value (eg the possibility of future development value), then it will also be entitled to an allotment of shares. The shares will be divided into two classes: typically A shares held by the granter and B shares held by the imposer. The granter will be the managing director and the imposer may be a non-executive director possibly with a vote only in specified circumstances, such as on sale or development.

The Articles of Association will provide for the following.

(1) There will be no sale or long lease of any part of the overage land without the consent of the holder of the B shares. Possibly the B shareholder may also have to consent to any application for planning consent made by the company.

(2) Until a sale or until development occurs, it will be up to the holder of the A shares to decide whether or not a dividend is paid and only the A shares will qualify to receive a dividend.

(3) When the trigger event occurs, the B shares will become entitled to a dividend. The Articles may contain a formula to decide how development profits will be shared. If land is sold for development, and therefore the bulk of the proceeds of sale qualify as distributable profit, then the Articles might, for example, provide that two-thirds of that profit will go to the A shares and one-third to the B shares. The same may or may not apply if profits in the nature of income, for example from letting buildings erected on the land, should be divided in the same way.

(4) If the company is wound up, the net assets will again be split into specified proportions, but the holder of the B shares may have a veto on solvent liquidation or the Articles may govern what then happens.

(5) In addition to a restriction on sale or long leases, there may need to be other restrictions, for example on granting charges or guarantees of third party liabilities.

9.2.2 Powers of directors

When companies were first authorised by Parliament in the nineteenth century, it was quite common to include various types of restriction in the Articles, such as a restriction on a change in the nature of the business or on a sale. As the Articles of the company had to be registered with the Registrar of Companies and were open to inspection by any member of the public who wished to see them, any person dealing with the company was treated as bound by any provisions of the Articles whether that person actually knew about them or not.[1] During the twentieth century, this was found increasingly inconvenient commercially and in a number of provisions Parliament has provided that a person dealing with the company can assume that the company has the necessary powers irrespective of what the Articles may say. The current provision is s 35A of the CA 1985, which was inserted by the CA 1989, s 108(1). This provides:

---

1   The operation of this rule was modified in practice where an act was done within the ostensible authority of the directors. It is known as the Rule in *Turquand's Case, Royal British Bank v Turquand* (1856) 6 E&B 327.

'In favour of a person dealing with a company in good faith, the power of the Board of Directors to bind the company, or authorise others to do so, shall be deemed to be free of any limitation under the company's constitution.'

Furthermore, under s 35A(2)(b), a person is not to be regarded as acting in bad faith by reason only of his knowing that an act is beyond the powers of the directors under the company's constitution. Section 35A(3)(b) provides that the references to limitations on the directors' power under the company's constitution include limitations deriving from any agreement between the members of the company or of any class of shareholders.

The result of that is that even if there are clear provisions in the Articles of the company (or in a separate shareholders' agreement) for the benefit of B shareholders (representing a member interested in overage), or for the holders of class rights, the directors effectively have the power to override such a provision and it does not matter that the person dealing with the company knows that the act is beyond the powers of the directors. Thus, a sale in those circumstances would still be valid.

Section 35A(4) provides that s 35A(1) does not affect any right of a member of a company to bring proceedings to restrain the doing of an act which is beyond the powers of the directors, but that has to be done before the act is done and not afterwards. Of course, the directors may be liable to the shareholders, but that will not assist the B shareholder. Suppose that an imposer transfers farmland to a company and then takes B shares in the company and the Articles provide that no sale should be made without the imposer's consent. The granter which has provided the purchase money is unwilling to see the imposer as a director because it does not wish to have day-to-day fetters on freedom to determine farming policy. The directors appointed by the granter subsequently decide to sell the land when there is no prospect of development. They can do so. If the owner of the B shares learns about the action sufficiently well in advance of any legal commitment being made, he may be able to take out an injunction to restrain the action. However, if he acts later than that, he will not be able to do so. He will be left to a claim in damages against the directors which will be of little value and he will lose his main interest which relates to the value of the land itself.

9.2.3 Class rights

The B shares will be a class of shares and, therefore, under s 125 of the CA 1995, the rights cannot be changed without the consent of the members of that class. However, if the company incurs heavy liabilities and goes into insolvent liquidation, the liquidator can override the class rights and, indeed, has power to realise all the uncharged assets of the company for the purpose of an orderly payment of the company's debts. Thus, if the granter allows the company's farming debts to rise to such an extent that the bank takes action, again the result may be that the land passes out of the company. Thus, it does not matter what rights the overage owner may have in his capacity as a shareholder, they will not help him in the event of any future value deriving from the land.

If the landowner, namely the holder of the A shares, wishes to realise its investment by selling the land then, as indicated above, if there is a provision in the Articles to stop this, the holder of the B shares can do so provided he acts in time. In that case, however, the holder of the A shares will almost certainly wish to be in a position to have a put option to compel the owner of the B shares to take over the shares, otherwise there is a risk that the owner of the A shares may be locked into the company. The value of shares in the company where there are material restrictions in the Articles would normally be a great deal less than the equivalent value of land which was held directly.

Where the terms of the Articles are capable of giving rise to a stalemate situation, the courts may use a residual power to analyse the true position as being a virtual partnership and may order either a sale or liquidation of the company or a buy-out of the shares.[1] This can place the overage owner in a difficult position. Originally, he needed to realise the current use value of the land and, therefore, is unlikely to be willing to buy that value back. Equally, he does not wish to see the land itself sold for the reasons mentioned above.

It is largely for this reason that the companies are not often used as a long-term overage device. Sometimes they may be adopted for tax reasons, particularly where there is likely to be a relatively short-term profit which can sometimes be recycled within a group of companies, but where tax is not the overriding consideration a company will normally not be suitable.

Sometimes there may be a corporate structure coupled with a restriction on the Register, as described at **3.4**, but that operates on its own and because as a matter of law the company is separate from its shareholders, the two aspects of the transaction – the company shareholding and the restriction – need to be considered separately on their own merits.

9.3 PARTNERSHIP

A partnership is defined as 'the relation which subsists between persons carrying on a business in common with a view of profit'.[2] The normal type of unlimited partnership does not have a legal existence of its own, but consists of a number of individuals or companies acting together under the provisions of the Partnership Act 1890 as varied by any specific arrangements set out in a partnership deed or agreement. Any partner would be liable to the full extent of its individual assets for any partnership liabilities. There is a form of limited

---

1   See *Re Yenidje Tobacco Co Ltd* [1916] 2 Ch 426; and *Ebrahami v Westbourne Galleries Ltd* [1973] AC 360.
2   Partnership Act 1890, s 1(1).

partnership where some members of the partnership are allowed to restrict their liability to a given amount provided that they take no active part in the partnership business and such limited partnerships are sometimes used in development agreements.

In the context of land development, partnerships are often used through the medium of limited companies. If two or three substantial entities wish to develop a site jointly, each of them will form subsidiary companies specifically for that purpose and those subsidiaries will then enter into partnership. The subsidiaries themselves may have very little in the way of assets, but these can either be injected by their parent companies or the parent can give a guarantee up to a specified figure. In some cases, the contribution of one of the partners may well be in the form of land. One method is for the land itself to become a partnership asset which is then directly available for partnership creditors and which forms an asset of the partnership that is available for distribution among the partners when the partnership is dissolved, either at the end of the venture or earlier if disputes or insolvency or some other event occurs. In such cases, it is possible to provide that so long as the partnership liabilities are being met the land will go back to the partner that contributed it. An alternative approach is for the land to be kept outside the partnership, but for the landowning partner to make it available to the partnership on licence. This is common for certain types of commercial activity where the partnership simply makes use of land or buildings such as farming or shop keeping, but it is not normally suitable where the partnership money will be spent on improving the land as is the case of development. In that case, the landowning partner may retain the freehold but grant a lease to the partnership. Where the partnership holds assets, these will have to be retained in the names of trustees on behalf of the partnership as a partnership is not itself a legal entity capable of owning land.

Therefore, the partnership can be used easily and flexibly for a development project lasting only a few years. It is not normally suitable for a long-term overage arrangement. The very nature of partnership and the fact that a partner will be involved in the partnership activities by itself normally means that the original landowner (the imposer) would not be in a position to require a substantial payment from the other partners. By contributing the land to the partnership activity or by making it available, the original landowner may well expect to receive a substantial contribution possibly at no risk. This will normally be done by way of an option or a lease or one of the other methods previously discussed in Chapters 3 to 8.

9.4   JOINT VENTURE

A joint venture is a name given to an arrangement that can take many legal forms, again normally for a specified activity. It can be done by partnership or company or indeed in any legal form, but the term is most often used in the context of simple contractual arrangements where different entities such as a developer and a landowner make arrangements for the development of property and agree to share the proceeds. It is distinguished from a partnership because there is no activity carried on in common. However, so far as overage is concerned, many of the same arguments would apply as to partnership and joint ventures are usually unsuitable for long-term overage arrangements.

9.5   LIMITED LIABILITY PARTNERSHIP

The limited liability partnership (LLP) is a new form of entity established under the Limited Liability Partnerships Act 2000. It creates a new corporate body which will be modelled closely on a company, although it is intended for people who would otherwise be in partnership, and its main advantage is that it is taxed in much the same way as a partnership rather than having the tax disadvantages of a company. The LLP will have members as a company does and will need to be incorporated, although by a relatively simple form submitted to the Registrar of Companies instead of the elaborate details that are required for a company. Any member of an LLP is treated as its agent and has power to commit the LLP to a course of action or to a liability, subject to the proviso that the LLP is not bound by anything done by a member dealing with a third party if the member does in fact have no authority and the person with whom he is dealing knows or believe that to be the case.

The detailed provisions relating to LLPs will be set out in regulations, but if they follow company law (as is expected) then the same provisions will apply to them as to companies. They may prove to be suitable investment vehicles because of their tax benefits, but they would not appear to have any administrative advantages.

9.6   UNINCORPORATED ASSOCIATION

These are not normally deliberately used for overage purposes, but overage issues may well be relevant. It sometimes happens that land has been acquired by an association such as a member's club. A typical example would be a football club which needs to acquire a ground on which to play. The land will be put into the name of trustees who will hold it on behalf of the members for the time being. Many years later the club membership may have dwindled or the land may have become ripe for development and there is often a very substantial windfall gain arising from sale of the land for housing. That by itself does not present any particular overage issues, although there can be matters to consider in relation to the decision to sell and the way in which the proceeds of sale are divided. However, it sometimes happens that land is provided free of charge to the club on the basis that it will come back to the original landowner if the purposes of the club cease to apply. (For example, if the club comprises employees of a company and the employer provided the money for the sports ground.) This raises issues similar to those discussed under rights of re-entry in Chapter 3 and at **9.8.2**.

9.7 SITE REVERTERS

Similar issues can apply in relation to charities where a landowner may give land for a good cause such as a chapel or a village school on the basis that if the land ceases to be used for that purpose it will come back to him. Numerous problems of this sort arose under the School Sites Act 1841 and the Reverter of Sites Act 1977. Parliament established a procedure whereby if this happened the trustees of the land would hold it on behalf of the person entitled to the reverter. If (as very often happens) that person cannot be found, then the trustees have a power to sell the land and if after a period of time they fail to locate the successors of the original donor they may retain the proceeds for their own benefit. However, where the original donor or more likely his remote descendants can be traced (and this will commonly happen where land was given out of a traditional family estate for a village school for example), then it may be possible to reclaim the land. If the character of the neighbourhood has changed so that the land is now suitable for development, there may again be an element of gain. This would not be considered overage in the normal sense, but it has an overage element to it.

9.8 TRUST

A trust is an arrangement whereby the nominal title to property is held by one or more persons (the trustees) on behalf of themselves or other people (the beneficiaries), in such a way as to split the nominal titular ownership from the true beneficial enjoyment of either the property itself or the income from it.

Trusts are widely used in a commercial context including pension funds, securitised loans, partnership property, voting trusts and various nominee arrangements either to facilitate dealing in property or to conceal the true ownership. Therefore, they are well understood for commercial purposes and they are a flexible vehicle for a wide variety of arrangements.

The origins of trusts and of settlements lie in the rules that formerly applied to family property and many of the special provisions that are relevant to the use of trusts in overage depend on rules which were formulated in the context of family ownership, particularly that between successive generations. However, for most purposes it is not necessary to go back into the remote origins of the way the law has developed since the Middle Ages, as fundamental changes that were made first in the 1925 legislation and then in the TLATA 1996 have introduced a system of holding land in trusts which bears little resemblance to the earlier law.

9.8.1 Use of trusts in overage

Imposer Limited owns land which it wishes to sell but retain a share of value after a trigger event. A very simple form of transfer might provide for the land to be transferred to Granter Limited until planning consent is issued and then to Imposer Limited and Granter Limited in equal shares. This apparently simple form of arrangement, known as a limitation, raises a number of issues as to the nature and extent of the interest owned by each of the parties, the way the land is to be managed and the length of time the arrangement can continue.

9.8.2 Conditional and determinable interests

Rights of re-entry were considered at **3.3** in the context of a positive covenant to pay overage. The nature of the interest discussed there is known as a conditional interest or a conditional fee, as the person entitled to it may a obtain a fee simple. The terms on which the granter acquires the land are that it and its successors will continue to own the land, but if the trigger event occurs the imposer or his successors will have the right to re-enter on the land. As an alternative, the right of re-entry might be triggered by a refusal to pay the overage sum. The trigger (or failure to pay) is a condition, breach of which gives rise to the right of re-entry. Conditions are of two types: conditions precedent and conditions subsequent.[1] This is a condition subsequent because the granter will already have acquired the land and the subsequent effect of the condition is to terminate its rights and deprive it of its property. Traditionally, the courts have interpreted conditions subsequent restrictively (as being comparable to a forfeiture) and they are construed strictly, and the occurrence of the event has to be certain.

An alternative approach is to limit the interest of the granter by giving it a determinable interest (or determinable fee, although it will not normally have a legal fee simple because, as explained below, the determinable interest – which could be an equitable fee simple – will generally subsist under a trust). This operates by giving the granter an interest only until the trigger event occurs. At that point, its rights determine automatically and without any need for re-entry. Therefore, the nature and extent of the interest taken by the granter is itself limited to that period. In that case, the right that follows (eg for

---

1 See **1.6**.

Imposer Limited and Granter Limited in equal shares) comes into existence following a condition precedent, namely the grant of planning consent.

The distinction between conditional fees and determinable interests is important, but it depends on a matter of words and it can often be difficult to tell whether the words create a conditional or determinable interest. Words such as 'but if the trigger event shall occur' or 'on condition that the land is always used for agriculture' or 'provided that no buildings are erected' will create a conditional interest. On the other hand, words such as 'while the land is used for agriculture' or 'so long as no building occurs' or 'until planning consent is granted' will create a determinable interest.[1]

The distinction is brought out by s 7 of the LPA 1925. In broad terms, the scheme of the 1925 legislation (both the LPA 1925 and the SLA 1925) are that a single ascertainable person (a body of trustees or a tenant for life) would hold an unfettered fee simple and a person dealing with the nominal landowner would be able to do so safely without having to enquire into any interests that might lie behind that ownership. This was subject to certain provisions to protect those having beneficial interests, for example the need to have two trustees in certain cases, but as a general rule the policy of the legislation was to make interests freely marketable without requiring a prospective purchaser to undertake expensive investigations.

In particular, in the context of family arrangements, if one member of the family had an interest which was likely to terminate, for example on marriage, change of religion or the birth of a child, the policy of the legislation[2] was to give the legal title to an ascertainable individual (referred to as the 'tenant for life') and to set up machinery to provide that if the event occurred that individual would be bound to transfer title but a buyer would not be adversely affected if he failed to do so. Although the intention was that this should relate to individuals and family matters, the wording was wide enough to extend to companies.

Section 7 of the LPA 1925 provides some limited exceptions. In particular, s 7(1) (as amended by the Law of Property (Amendment) Act 1926) provides that a fee simple subject to a legal or equitable right of entry or re-entry is a fee simple absolute and therefore does not create a settlement within the SLA 1925. Section 7(2) provides that a fee simple vested in a corporation, which is liable to determine by reason of a dissolution of a corporation, is also a fee simple absolute. Thus, where land is transferred to a new owner, subject to a right of entry or re-entry, it is still a legal fee simple, but when the right of entry

---

1   Among the decisions on the distinction, see *Newis v Lark* (1571) 2 Plowd 408; *Mary Partington's Case* (1613) 10 Co Rep 35b; *Dean v Dean* [1891] 3 Ch 150; *Re Da Costa* [1912] 1 Ch 337; and *Sifton v Sifton* [1938] AC 656.
2   SLA 1925.

or re-entry becomes exercisable then the person entitled to it can re-enter and resume the land.

Apart from that exception, the policy of the legislation was that where there were successive or joint interests in land they should subsist under a trust. Initially this was a trust for sale, but by the TLATA 1996 this was converted into a trust of land. This did not apply where the machinery of the SLA 1925 conferred title on the tenant for life, but there were other protections in that case.

It followed that between 1925 and 1997 (when the TLATA 1996 came into force) if land was conveyed to Granter Limited until the trigger event occured and then for Granter Limited and Imposer Limited in equal shares, that would have created a settlement within the SLA 1925. Under s 13 of that Act, such a conveyance would not have passed the legal estate, but would have operated as a contract to enter into a vesting deed under which Granter Limited would have been entitled to be tenant for life with the powers and subject to the restrictions set out in the Act and there would have had to be trustees (normally at least two) in the event of any sale or other receipt of capital money. Since the TLATA 1996 came into force, it has not been possible to create new settlements and it follows that the effect of a transfer in those terms would now be to transfer the legal title to Granter Limited but in its capacity as sole trustee of the land. In particular, under s 27(2) of the LPA 1925 if the land is sold (or other capital money arises such as a premium on a lease), the proceeds of sale or other capital money are to be paid to at least two persons (individuals or companies) as trustees (or to a single trust corporation). Therefore, Granter Limited would hold the land as sole trustee on the terms of a trust which provide that it should have an equitable determinable interest until the trigger event occurs and when that happens if Granter Limited is still the landowner, it would hold the land on behalf of itself and Imposer Limited in equal shares.

An important distinction arises in the event of a sale. Where land is held on trust (whether the landowner knows it or not) by a single individual or a single company (not being a trust corporation) then if it sells, a buyer will not obtain a good receipt for his money. The money received by the sole owner (Granter Limited) from the buyer (New Landowner Limited) will of course be effective to satisfy its own beneficial interest, but it will not affect the rights of the other owner (Imposer Limited).[1]

However, the effect of such a sale would not overreach a beneficial interest under s 2 of the LPA 1925 because s 2(2) once again requires either two trustees or a trust corporation. Where the interests are not overreached, they

---

1   *First National Securities Ltd v Hegerty* [1985] 1 QB 850; and *Ahmed v Kendrick* (1987) 56 P&CR 120.

continue to attach to the land and, thus, New Landowner Limited (assuming it had paid full value to Granter Limited) would hold the land on its own behalf until the trigger event occurs and then as to one half for Imposer Limited and the other half for itself.

If, however, the sale was made by two estate owners, that would effectively overreach the equitable interest. Thus, if the original disposal by Imposer Limited was not to a single granter but to two individuals or two companies or an individual and a company either in partnership or by way of joint venture, then if those new landowners were to sell a buyer from them would get a good clear title.

9.8.3   Vested and contingent

As indicated above, an interest arising under a trust may be a present interest, which carries a present right either to possession of the land or to receipt of income from it, or a future interest. An interest limited to arise when planning consent is granted, where no application has even been submitted, is clearly a future interest. Although it is described as a future interest, it is an existing right of property so that the imposer and the overage owner can deal with that right even though there will be no immediate practical consequences at the time the dealing transaction takes place.

Most overage rights will also be contingent. The distinction between vested and contingent rights originally arose in the context of family property. There would initially be a grant of a limited interest (typically for a lifetime) to someone living and then what 'remained over' after that restricted grant was described as a remainder and might belong to someone else. The simplest course would be a limitation to A for life with remainder to B where both A and B are living people. For example, a house used by a pensioner might be given to the pensioner for the rest of his life and it would then go back to the employer. Nowadays that would normally be done by lease or licence, but in the past it could be done by a freehold. There could also be a limitation to A for life, with the remainder to his first-born son. If there was no son in existence at the time the original disposition was made but a son was born later, then that son would immediately on birth attain a right to the property – of course, that right could not be exercised until after his father's death. That right would exist even though the son might die during his father's lifetime, although in that case it would pass under the son's will or intestacy. Where such a right is an existing and permanent one, and is held by a definable person, it is considered to be vested.

An interest subject to termination on re-entry following the occurrence of a condition subsequent may result in land being taken away, but until that happens the interest in possession is vested. The right of re-entry is itself a legal right, but the owner of that right will have no interest in the land as such but normally a mere hope or *spes*.

Where the person in possession has a determinable right subject to possible termination on a contingency, then that right is again vested in possession. In that case, the right of the other person which can arise on that contingency is treated as an existing right of property, namely a (contingent) future interest.

The law evolved in a way that allowed contingent future interests to exist. This might be to A for life with the remainder to B if he survives A. It might be to A for life with the remainder to his eldest son living at his death. It might even go further so that the size of the share was unknown. Thus, if land was limited to A for life with remainder to his children contingent on their living at his death and (before or after his death) attaining the age of 21 years and if more than one in equal shares, then not only would the right to succeed be contingent but also the size of the share would be uncertain depending on how many children survived. The fact that the size of a share was uncertain would not necessarily prevent it being vested. There could be a vested interest such as to A for life, with remainder to his children in equal shares. In that case, a child on being born would attain a vested interest although the proportion of the value of the land that the child would take might be decreased if further children were born subsequently. Thus, there would be a vested interest subject to partial divesting.

Similarly, if an interest is held commercially by a trustee on behalf of investors, if the size of the class of investors changes as the result of sales and purchases of shares in the fund, and subdivision or amalgamation of shareholdings, the amount of the interest of each beneficiary will change correspondingly. However, in a commercial situation (other than on rare exceptions such as a tontine) the total of the interests will not change (in contrast to a family, where shares can decrease or increase as the result of the birth or death of beneficiaries), so that 'a share' will retain the same proportion of value in relation to other shares.

These principles can be applied to the commercial context of overage. An interest that is contingent on an event such as the grant of planning consent or the completion of a building is a contingent interest. A limitation to Granter Limited until planning consent is granted and then to Granter Limited and Imposer Limited in equal shares has the effect that the interest of Imposer Limited is contingent on the occurrence of planning consent. The size of the interest might also vary. Thus, there might be a formula which divides up the value of the land according to the type of development or, for example, the number of houses for which consent is given.

One important feature of the distinction between vested and contingent interests relates to the rule against perpetuities. Of course, the parties are free to choose a period of 80 years, although even that might not necessarily be long enough in certain contexts, but if they do not select such a period then they are thrown back on the basic rule and on the assumption that in the case of companies there is no 'life in being' then they are restricted to the fixed period of 21 years. Thus, a limitation to Granter Limited until planning consent is granted and then to Granter Limited and Imposer Limited in equal shares will have the result that Imposer Limited's interest would take effect only if planning consent is actually granted within 21 years.

9.9 USE OF EXPRESS TRUSTS IN OVERAGE

9.9.1 Documentation

Where the parties deliberately choose a trust as the appropriate vehicle for overage, the trust will need to be adequately documented. Although in theory it would be possible to have all the relevant provisions set out in the transfer, in practice this is undesirable, first because the transfer is retained in the Land Registry[1] and, secondly, because there will need to be provisions governing both the administration of the trust and the beneficial interests in the calculation of the respective shares which can more conveniently be set out in a separate document. In simple cases, particularly where the trust holds a leasehold interest (eg if the imposer retains the freehold and grants the lease to trustees for itself and the granter), it may be possible to set out the trusts in the lease itself. Normally, it is preferable even in that case to do it separately, so that provisions affecting the legal estate at nominal ownership are kept distinct from those affecting beneficial interests. This will apply in particular if the lease can be sold or surrendered.

9.9.2 The trustees

The first decision that needs to be taken is the identity of the trustees who will hold the land and administer the trust. As mentioned above, it is sufficient to have a single trustee and such a trustee can do anything except give a good receipt for capital money arising from a sale or mortgage or a premium on a lease or a similar transaction. Where the granter is to have beneficial use of the land until the trigger event occurs, it may even be sensible to have the granter as sole trustee. However, there is always a risk that the landowner might create an additional trustee in order to defeat the interest of the overage owner as beneficiary.

Normally, therefore, it would be more sensible to have at least two trustees. A possible procedure would be to have three of them: one always appointed by the overage owner and the other two always appointed by the landowner.

---

1   LRR 1925, r 306, although the parties could retain a duplicate.

If the trustees are companies, they may remain in place indefinitely, although if the overage owner or landowner sells his interests, his successors may want to appoint new trustees. If the trustees are individuals who die or wish to retire, the person who appointed them (or its successor) will appoint the replacement trustee.

It is not necessary to have individuals as trustees and, in practice, companies can be more suitable. If the landowner and overage owner could themselves be trustees, but if they do not wish to appear on the title then each of them could create subsidiary companies to act as trustees for this purpose.

9.9.3   Trustees procedure and relations with beneficiaries

The legislation governing trusts and the general law lay down certain rules relating to the manner in which trustees have to act. Some (but not all) of these rules can be displaced or modified by specific agreement between the parties or the inclusion of a provision in the trust deed.

Trustees normally have to act unanimously, but there is no reason why they should not be given power to act by a majority. Charitable trustees can always do this and private trustees may do it if the power is conferred on them. The trust deed could provide that that unanimity is required on certain issues, such as a sale or mortgage, but not on others, such as repairs or short-term tenancies.

In relation to land, s 11 of the TLATA 1996 requires trustees to consult beneficiaries, but the section specifically provides that the trust instrument can modify this. In the case of overage, the trustees will normally need to consult the landowner, even if the landowner does not manage the land under delegated powers. The trust deed could say that the trustees must consult the overage owner before performing certain functions such as sale or a long lease.

Section 9 of the TLATA 1996 contains very wide and flexible powers of delegation by trustees. Normally, it would be appropriate to delegate most management functions to the landowner subject to an indemnity. Under s 9(8), where a function has been delegated to a beneficiary, the trustees would only be liable if they did not exercise reasonable care in deciding to delegate a function. However, that appears to relate only to liability to any other beneficiaries and does not affect liability to third parties. Thus, the overage owner or any trustee appointed on his behalf may need additional protection in relation to any activities which give rise to liability to third parties, such as a specific indemnity in the trust deed from the landowner to other trustees.

In the absence of a specific charging clause, trustees must normally act gratuitously (they can claim out-of-pocket expenses), but it is very common to include a power to make charges and this is invariable in the case of professional trustees. If the landowner or a person appointed by him is a trustee, it will normally be desirable to give express power to recover any management costs incurred. The Trustee Act 2000 has clarified and extended charging powers. Professional trustees and trust corporations can charge fees either under the trust deed under s 28 or under general power in s 29. However, it would be sensible to include a specific power in the trust deed to avoid argument.

The rule against charging is an aspect of a wider rule that states that a trustee generally must not make a profit out of its trust. That rule normally goes further and, in most cases, prohibits any dealing between a trustee and the trust. Clearly, where a trustee is beneficially interested, that rule will need to be modified in the trust deed.

One advantage of using a trust as distinct from a company is that a trust tends to be transparent for tax purposes. This will not apply to a trust which is a collective investment scheme.[1] However, there may be liabilities, particularly where one of the participants is non-resident for tax purposes and trustees may need to be given power to meet tax liabilities in circumstances where this would not be implied.

9.9.4 Administrative powers

The general rule of law is that trustees like other limited owners have only the powers which the law confers on them. Thus, in the past it was necessary to include detailed provisions in the trust deed giving trustees extra powers. That is no longer necessary because s 6 of the TLATA 1996 provides that for the purpose of exercising their functions as trustees, the trustees of land have all the powers of an absolute owner in relation to the land subject to the trust. This is modified by s 6(6), which says that the power cannot be exercised in contravention of any rule of law and there are certain rules of law which are said to limit the powers of trustees, for example the power to grant options. The general view is that this is not a correct interpretation of the Act and that s 6(6) is limited to special provisions relating to particular trust or type of trust, such as restrictions on charity trustees. Nevertheless, it may be wise to include a provision stating that the trustees have wide powers. Then it will be necessary to cut those powers down to make sure that they are not exercised in a way that could prejudice the overage owner without its consent.

The main substantive power is a power of sale. Under s 8 of the TLATA 1996, any person (whether a beneficiary or not) may be given the power to consent (or withhold consent) to a sale. This will normally be protected by a restriction on the Register.[2] This is one of the main current exceptions to the general rule that a fee simple can be freely alienated, discussed in Chapter 3, but refusal to give consent can always be overridden by the court.

---

1   Financial Services Act 1968, s 75; Taxation of Chargeable Gains Act 1992, s 99.
2   LRR 1925, rr 235 and 236. See **3.4**.

Section 8 of the TLATA 1996 provides that the power of sale and indeed other powers of management including leasing, charging and partition can be excluded or restricted by the trust disposition. Section 8(2) provides that if the disposition creating the trust makes provision requiring any consent to be obtained for the exercise of any power, the power may not be exercised without that consent. However, s 8(4) provides that s 8(2) is subject to any enactment that prohibits or restricts the effect of provisions of such a description, and it would appear that *Quia Emptores* 1290 (which allows a fee simple to be freely alienated)[1] is such an enactment. That Act does not apply to leaseholds.

The overage owner will in his capacity as beneficiary wish to control a sale to make sure that his overage rights are protected if the land passes to a third party. As his beneficial interests arise under the trust, normally a sale by trustees would overreach his beneficial interest. Therefore, consent will be given on the terms that the buyer entered into a similar trust arrangement as the previous landowner had.

An overage owner will also be concerned by other dealings such as a lease (particularly a long lease granted for a premium), a mortgage or charge and other types of dealing (eg the grant of an easement) if that were to benefit adjoining development land.

Trust deeds normally cover a number of other administrative provisions, such as the power of the trustees to insure trust property[2] and recover the premiums from trust funds and the power to make improvements to trust property at the expense of the trust. It will be a matter to be considered in each case how far these provisions apply. It may be desirable to make the landowner responsible for insurance. Minor improvements, particularly where they relate only to the current use, should also be the responsibility of the landowner, but major improvements by way of development may themselves be carried out with a view to realising development value. In such a case, it may well be right for the initial cost of the improvements to be borne by the landowner but for that cost to be reflected in the ultimate division between the parties.

There is a wide power to act through agents under s 11 of the Trustee Act 2000. The overage owner will wish to control the act of any agent just as much as the powers of the trustees themselves are controlled.

9.9.5 Beneficial interest

The purpose of setting up an overage scheme by way of a trust is so that on the termination of the trust the overage owner receives a share of the trust fund. The trust deed will need to contain the normal provisions discussed in

---

1 See **3.1.5**.
2 See Trustee Act 1925, s 19, substituted by Trustee Act 2000, s 34.

Chapter 11 for the calculation of the division of any proceeds and the timing of payment.

The trust deed may also need to contain provisions for appropriation and partition. Section 7 of the TLATA 1996 confers a limited power of partition on the trustees, but it may be desirable to widen this where either or both parties wish to take land as such out of the trust arrangement. For example, where it becomes clear that particular land is not likely to be developable in the foreseeable future, there may be no objection to that land being released to the landowner outright for his own absolute beneficial ownership. Similarly, it may be desirable when planning consent is given for the land itself to be divided between the parties in appropriate proportions rather than selling the land and dividing the proceeds.

In the same way, the trustees may well wish to appropriate assets to beneficiaries as part of a division. In particular, this will be the case where instead of land being sold for cash what is received is value in another form such as a guarantee or shares in some third company or the right to take up a lease of a particular unit on completion of a development.

9.10 TENANCIES IN COMMON

The type of trust considered above involves successive interests, with an initial ownership for the granter, which is converted after the trigger event into a joint interest for granter and imposer. It is possible to have an immediate interest in common, for example for the granter to have a 99 per cent interest and the imposer a 1 per cent interest, with the shares varying after the trigger event. Indeed, if the share of the imposer specifically relates to the development value, that may be seen as an immediate interest.

Assume that immediately after the original sale by imposer to granter, the property were to be resold free of any overage incumbrance. It may well be that the price would reflect not only the current use value, but also a slight element of hope value. A valuer would be able to split the price achieved between the two. Normally, a court would disregard hope value as being a 'mere *spes*', and therefore not an item of property, but the parties are free to decide that any price achieved would be divided as they direct. The imposer would not want that to happen. The whole purpose of overage is to wait until added value materialises, not take the present value of a future prospect. However, this exercise shows that such a prospect does indeed have some value – however small.

Therefore, there is no difficulty in principle in agreeing that the land shall belong to granter and imposer as tenants in common in the proportions that, say, the current use value plus half the development value bears to the other half of the development value. Initially the imposer's interest will be very small, but it is a present interest, not a future one.

Section 1(6) of the LPA 1925 provides that a legal estate cannot subsist in an undivided share in land and s 34 provides that an attempt to create such an interest takes effect as a trust of land. Under the TLATA 1996, the trustees have powers of management and under s 2 of the LPA 1925 any sale by the trustees (where the purchase money is paid to at least two trustees, or a trust corporation) overreaches equitable interests. The issues mentioned above will still apply and, even though the legal estate may be vested in the granter and the imposer, it would be sensible for the imposer to have a restriction on the Register.

9.11 CONCLUSIONS

Vehicles such as companies, partnerships and trusts can be used in overage, but they are only suitable for special circumstances because of the way that both parties would be involved in the control and administration of the land and the extent to which trustees or directors owe duties to beneficiaries or shareholders. In some cases, these very features may make a vehicle suitable for use, but the circumstances will need to be special.

Chapter 10

GOVERNMENT CLAWBACK AND TAX

10.1 GOVERNMENT ATTITUDES TO DEVELOPMENT LAND DISPOSALS

This chapter deals with overage in relation to the public sector. It has two aspects. The first concerns disposals by government departments and other Crown bodies and local authorities, and the extent to which public bodies can realise additional value after disposal. The basic rules on this are the same as those that apply to overage imposed by private landowners, although there are some special rules. The second aspect relates to value that can be obtained for the government or local authorities when land increases in value, normally as a result of development. The major source of revenue here is taxation, but public bodies, particularly at present local authorities, can use the planning system to realise value for the community. This applies even where there may have been no Crown interest in the land for many centuries.

The government (including local government) has a great need for resources, particularly money, in order to carry out its functions. In general, all receipts by central government have to be paid into the Consolidated Fund and payments out of that Fund can be authorised only by Parliament. That is the basis of Parliamentary control over the government and, therefore, the basis of parliamentary democracy. Traditionally, the receipts were treated in different ways. In the Middle Ages, the king was expected to run the country from his own (substantial) resources or to 'live of his own'. The most important part of royal revenues, particularly regular ones which could be depended on or those which could be controlled by the king, were rents from land and proceeds of the sale of land, and these were known as 'Ordinary Revenues'. At special times of crisis, particularly in wartime, the king could ask Parliament to vote taxes and these were known as 'Extraordinary Revenues'. Since the seventeenth century, the government has largely been carried on out of Extraordinary Revenues and the Ordinary Revenues (most of which are under the management of the Crown Estate Commissioners) have played an increasingly marginal part, although in sum they are still substantial.

To some extent, it does not matter from the Crown's point of view whether revenues come from exploiting Crown land or from taxation. Indeed, where the government has to carry out a function, it may be possible to do this in some other way. For example, if a road is needed in a particular locality, it may be possible for the government (or local government) to enter into an arrangement, perhaps under the new Roads and Street Works Act 1991, or perhaps under an agreement under s 106 of the Town and Country Planning Act 1990 or s 278 of the Highways Act 1980 under which the road will be constructed by a private company, perhaps as part of a planning arrangement or perhaps with a return to the company from tolls on the road. So long as the government can achieve the correct result, it is not unduly concerned about the route followed.

The government has always been ready to exploit development value from land. In previous centuries, this involved converting waste land such as forest or moor to productive farmland. In the early seventeenth century, the Crown was making a last effort to carry on the ordinary administration without recourse to Extraordinary Revenue. The reclamation of waste land was an important source of revenue, either from outright sale or from lease or from a form of freehold grant in fee farm,[1] reserving a perpetual rent, similar to a private landowner selling for a rentcharge.

The Crown made arrangements with entrepreneurs to reclaim land. For example, there was an agreement with Sir Cornelius Vermuyden to drain large areas of East Anglian fenland on the terms that on completion he would receive one-quarter of the reclaimed land and the Crown could freely deal with the remainder.

These efforts by the Crown provoked considerable opposition, partly from smallholders who had rights of common over the wastes, but also from gentry and politicians who objected to this type of exploitation. Several paragraphs of the Grand Remonstrance of 1641, produced in the tense times leading up to the Civil War, concerned matters such as reclamation of foreshore, conversion of forest land and inclosure of grazing wastes by the Crown. Following the Restoration of 1660, it became accepted that government needed to depend on tax revenues to carry on its work and the pressure for Crown development receded. Private initiatives took its place.

In the twentieth century, the State reverted to some older attitudes. The efforts of successive Labour governments to obtain development value from land are in some ways reminiscent of medieval and early modern ideas of value directly from land rather than from taxation. In practice, nationalisation of land in general or specifically of development land or even of development value on its own (apart from the land it relates to) have not got far. As explained below, each new approach has been accompanied by a new tax, all of which have now been abolished, and it is from tax that the government derived whatever return it could.

---

1   The Crown, not being bound by *Quia Emptores*, could make such grants.

Where the State already owns land, it has accepted wholeheartedly the right to benefit from increased value. Following the Herstmonceux case discussed at **10.2.1**, the government has become ever more aware of the need to secure full value from land and is now one of the main users of overage. However, it is usually called 'clawback' rather than 'overage'.

This reflects a substantial difference in attitude between the public sector and the private sector. Overage, as the name suggests, refers to a payment over and above an initial price. It is treated by the private sector as getting something extra. It usually results from an event which is not under the control of the parties, such as the grant of planning consent by a district council (local government) or the Secretary of State.

The word 'clawback' is sometimes used to refer to the situation where the public body is legally entitled to a payment which has been remitted or has not been claimed in full. For example, it is sometimes used in tax law where a particular sum may be due by way of tax, but if the taxpayer observes certain conditions then the full amount of tax is not payable. If subsequently the condition is broken, the extra tax becomes due. Thus, under s 35A of and Sch 6A, para 1 to the Value Added Tax Act 1983, there may be a supply of land on development which would incur a charge to value added tax, but as the land is occupied for a qualifying charitable or residential purpose, the tax is not collected. If within 10 years the land is put to some other purpose, the tax becomes due and is said to be 'clawed back'. Similarly, under s 155 of the HA 1985, where a secure tenant of a house exercises the Right to Buy and claims a discount from the value of the property and subsequently re-sells within 3 years, then the discount is repaid. This is normally referred to as 'clawback'.

However, the phrase is applied, particularly by politicians and civil servants, to other situations which the private sector would call overage. As explained below,[1] there have been a number of attempts since 1947 by successive governments to claim for the State or the community the whole or a proportion of the development value of land. The justification for this is said to be that development value is in some sense created by the State (whether central or local government) by the grant of planning consent and, therefore, if a private landowner makes a profit by virtue of such a public act then the State is entitled to claw back the gain so realised. The private sector sees development value as created by the work of developers, who perceive opportunities, surveyors who can estimate its value, and funders who are prepared to risk capital. The government sees it as created by the resolution of a planning committee or the decision of an inspector and, therefore, as belonging to the State, which is entitled to the value the State has created. The private sector sees such impositions as a tax. As indicated above, from the government's

---

1 See **10.4**.

point of view, it does not matter whether it is a tax or not, it is simply revenue to enable the government to carry on its functions.

10.2   CLAWBACK POLICY

10.2.1   The Herstmonceux case

In 1986 it was decided that the former Royal Greenwich Observatory should move from its site at Herstmonceux Castle to Cambridge. The castle itself then became surplus to government requirements and was placed on the market for sale. The property was widely marketed, a number of tenders were received and one was accepted. Planning permission was not obtained and, therefore, the sale was presumably on a current use basis with some element of hope value. The planning brief approved by the local district council indicated clearly what consents might be forthcoming but, apart from that, development of the site was strictly limited by the local structure plan.

Higher bids were received at the time of the sale, but for various reasons they were not accepted. Subsequently, applications were made for planning consent and very substantial figures were placed on the value of the site and mentioned in the national press. Whether or not these figures were justified, they caught the attention of politicians. This was at a time of considerable sensitivity in relation to the sale of surplus government assets and it came after a time when various scientific and industrial companies had been sold by the government and the buyers had been able to realise a profit on their shares.

The resulting political discussions led to a formal report by the Comptroller and Auditor General,[1] which contained critical comments, although in general it exonerated those involved. The comments and the resulting policy reconsideration have had a considerable influence on those civil servants who are responsible for land sales and as a result clawback is now standard government policy.

10.2.2   Treasury guidelines

Even while the Herstmonceux sale was going through, the Treasury had issued guidance dated 29 April 1988 on the disposal of land by public bodies which was designed to ensure that the best possible price could be obtained. These guidelines provided amongst other things that land which had potential for development should normally be sold with the benefit of planning

---

1   National Audit Office Report 341, printed 4 April 1990.

permission.[1] The guidance went on to provide that where there are delays in resolving uncertainties over planning permission, it may be appropriate to dispose of the land before those uncertainties are resolved, but that in such cases 'it may well be appropriate to seek to secure from the purchaser any increase in value attributable to the grant of planning permission after the disposal terms have been agreed'.

Those guidelines have now been reissued several times and modified and the current ones are contained within Annex 32.1 of Government Accounting (Amendment No 8) dated March 1998. These guidelines stress the importance of disposing of surplus government property rather than retaining it, that land should be put up to tender and the highest bid should normally be accepted and the possibility that prices may rise in the future does not justify delay. Where there are sites with development potential then, where possible, planning consent should be obtained but there is then a specific section headed 'Clawback'. That section is set out below.

'Clawback

19. A department may decide that it should sell a property without the benefit of planning permission where:

   (a)   there are, or may be, delays in resolving uncertainties about the planning position of a property which is considered to have development potential;

   (b)   there is doubt as to the use which would generate the best price.

20. Where this is the case, departments should consider, in the interests of the taxpayer, whether they include a clawback clause in the terms of sale. The aim of such a clause is to enable the government to reclaim all, or at least a substantial part, of any increase in value attributable to the grant of planning permission after the disposal terms have been agreed. This can be achieved by various methods, depending on the particular circumstances, but may include selling the property subject to planning permission being obtained within a set period of time. Legal and surveying advice is likely to be required.

21. Professional advisers should be able to give an assessment of the likely effects of a clawback clause on the sale price. Departments will also wish to consider with the appropriate professional advice whether or not a clawback provision should be included to cover the eventuality of the purchaser significantly improving a planning consent to the purchaser's advantage, where this seems to be a possibility. The inclusion of a clawback

---

1   This had not been possible before the Town and Country Planning (Crown Land) Act 1984. Before that, planning consent could not be granted to the Crown (although it could to the owner of a 'private interest' in Crown Land) and the practice had been to obtain an informal assurance from the local planning authority as to what sort of consent a purchaser might expect to obtain. This practice became impossible after *R v Worthing Borough Council, ex parte Burch* [1984] JPL 261. See now Town and Country Planning Act 1990, s 299.

provision should also be considered where it is decided to sell the land subject to a planning brief rather than with outline or detailed planning consent. The Treasury Solicitor's Department can advise on the legal aspects in such cases.

22.   It can be difficult to gauge the commercial potential of property which has been used in the past for a purpose which is peculiar to the public sector. Changes in market demand can also lead to an unforeseen increase in the value of land after it has been sold. A department which has sold property for a price and on terms which were defensible at the time of sale may be criticised if the property is later resold for a higher price or used for a purpose which suggests that a higher price could have been obtained by the department. The proper response to such criticism is to be able to say that the department took all proper steps to secure the best price obtainable at the time and, in particular, took proper professional advice and marketed the property with due vigour.'

A footnote at the end of the passage refers to Part IV of the Land Compensation Act 1961. This provides that if a body which either used or could have used compulsory powers acquires land and within 10 years, planning permission is granted[1] then the former owner is entitled to claim additional compensation. Under s 23, this is equal to the difference between the compensation actually paid and the compensation which would have been paid if planning consent had been granted before the acquisition. If the land becomes surplus, it should normally be returned to the former owner,[2] but sometimes the acquiring authority can itself develop or resell. In that case, the former owner is entitled to extra compensation. That is a recognition by government that clawback can work both ways.

10.3   SPECIAL RULES

When government departments sell land and wish to reserve what a private landowner would call overage, the general rules governing the transaction are the same as those which govern transactions by private companies or individuals. The rule of law is a fundamental principle of the constitution of England and this applies particularly to rules relating to property. Apart from taxation, the effect of a transaction involving a government department or a local authority is the same as if no public body were involved.

However, this is subject to certain special rules which apply either from the nature of the legal entity or as a result of special intervention.

---

1   Under s 26, Crown development, which does not need planning permission, is treated as if it had permission. Section 26 is expressly mentioned in the footnote.
2   Under the Crichel Down Rules.

10.3.1 Crown re-entry

One exception applies as a result of the legal basis of landholding in England. The greatest interest that can be held by an owner other than the Crown is a fee simple absolute in possession free from incumbrances. As explained at **3.3**, fees simple are held from the Crown, normally directly, and the relationship between the Crown and the owner of the fee simple is in many ways similar to the relationship between a landlord and a tenant. The main difference is that a fee simple lasts for ever while a lease can last for only a limited period such as 3,000 years.

This is relevant to the exercise of rights of re-entry. As explained at **3.3**, these originally arose in 1290 when the rules that had previously applied to the grant by private landowners of inferior freeholds were applied when the landowner sold by substitution rather than subinfeudation. Experience has shown that it is necessary to place a restriction on the length of time this can work and, therefore, the perpetuity rules applied to freehold rights of re-entry. If the Law Commission proposals on perpetuities[1] are enacted, this will no longer be the case. However, it has never been the case in relation to Crown land and the law is declared in s 3(8) of the Crown Estate Act 1961 which applies to disposals by the Crown Estate Commissioners of land under their management. That subsection provides that when the Commissioners dispose of land subject to restrictions on the use of the land, those restrictions may be enforced at any distance of time. It is not clear how far the rule against perpetuities applies to Crown disposals in any event,[2] but the assumption must be that it does because of the general rule of law set out above. Nevertheless, as the relationship between the Crown and private landowners is one of (land)lord and tenant and so there is privity of estate, and because the statute *Quia Emptores* does not apply to Crown disposals,[3] then just as a re-entry clause in a lease is not limited to the perpetuity period so too a re-entry clause on a Crown freehold disposal is not so limited. The Crown Estate Commissioners and their predecessors in the nineteenth century used this provision on a wide scale. It applied in particular where land was given for some beneficial purpose or was sold at a low price in the public interest but it has been used even on commercial sales subject to a restriction on use.

10.3.2 Restrictions on transfer and rents

As *Quia Emptores* did not apply to grants by the Crown, it remains possible for the Crown to include a restraint on transfer of a freehold in circumstances where a private seller cannot do so. Therefore, whatever the doubts about the

---

1   *The Rule Against Perpetuities and Excessive Accumulations* Law Com No 251.
2   *Cooper v Stuart* (1889) 14 App Cas 286.
3   *In re Holliday* [1922] 2 Ch 698, citing *Magdalen College Case* (1616) 11 Co Rep 66b.

validity of a restriction on the Register in the case of a private imposer, the Crown can do this under English Law. However, it is possible that the effect of the Human Rights Act 1998 is to nullify any such restriction. Article 1 of the First Protocol to the European Convention on Human Rights allows every natural or legal person (thus including companies) the peaceful enjoyment of his possessions. One element in peaceful enjoyment of a freehold is the right to sell it. If a private imposer provides that a freehold may not be sold, or may be sold only on certain conditions, that is a matter for domestic law. If a public authority acts in a way which is incompatible with one or more of the Convention rights then under s 6 of the Act, such action is unlawful. The government is such a public authority and, therefore, although it is exempt from *Quia Emptores*, it will be bound by the 1998 Act.

For the same reason, it may still be possible for the Crown to make new grants in fee simple reserving a rent service. Where the Crown sells land out of its allodium, it involves the creation of a new freehold. Until 1977 there was no objection to the reservation of a substantial payment of rent, known as 'fee farm'.[1] The RA 1977 applies to the Crown under s 14 but under s 1(a) of RA 1977 does not apply to rent reserved by a tenancy, and this must include a tenancy in fee simple. The Human Rights Act 1998 would not seem relevant to this as there can be no objection to a long lease at a rent and, therefore, none to a freehold at a rent.

10.3.3 Privatised industries

Another special case is where the Crown is able to change the rules by legislation. This has been done in particular when industries that were previously in public ownership have been converted into commercial companies and their shares sold.

An example is s 156 of the Water Industry Act 1991, which provides that a water company must not dispose of 'protected land' (broadly speaking functional land and land in areas of special protection such as national parks) without the consent of the Secretary of State. Section 156(6) specifically provides for public access. This provision was included as a result of political pressure at the time of privatisation when there was concern that large areas of land held by water companies in connection with reservoirs and water abstraction might be sold and members of the public who had previously enjoyed free access might be restricted.

In fact, the section has been used for clawback. A statement issued by the Office of Water Services (OFWAT) outlines the basis of the clawback. This particularly applies when the original water holding company disposes of land to a property company under the same control. The statement says:

---

1   By the Tenures Abolition Act 1660, all such grants had to be in free and common socage, but it appears that tenure in fee farm was not separate. Co Inst 86a.

'OFWAT considers the likely profits, costs and risks involved in the proposal. If planning permission is virtually certain and little cost is involved in developing the site, the clawback percentage will be high. The appointed company should first obtain consent before disposing of the land, thus increasing its value. However, if the planning position is uncertain and decontamination or other site costs are high, the risks of the development are greater, so the clawback percentage will be lower. The regulation system attempts to reflect the free market system.'

The note goes on to say that clawback is not imposed on every such transaction and the appointed companies are encouraged in many cases to impose their own clawback conditions by means of options or conditional contracts.

10.3.4   Local authorities

Local councils, as creatures of statute, are subject to the *ultra vires* rule and, therefore, cannot do anything without clear statutory authority.[1] As a matter of policy, they are encouraged to dispose of surplus land[2] and that may be in an undeveloped state or ahead of development. Thus, they may wish to reserve clawback. Disposals are made under s 123 of the Local Government Act 1972. Section 123(1) provides in broad terms that:

'Subject to the following provisions of this section, a principal council may dispose of land held by them in any manner they wish.'

One of the provisions is that under s 123(2) a council cannot charge less consideration than the best that can reasonably be obtained unless it obtains the consent of the Secretary of State. If clawback is reserved and, therefore, the price received is less than what could be obtained on a sale free of overage, is that within the section? It may be argued that the value of the price plus the overage rights together amount to the best consideration, but the point cannot be taken for granted. In practice no doubt, having regard to the Treasury Guidelines, the Secretary of State would normally give consent, but the need to obtain it could delay or prevent a sale, especially if the sale was politically controversial.

10.4   GOVERNMENT CLAIMS TO SHARE IN DEVELOPMENT VALUE

As explained above, both national and local government considers it proper to take a share in development value, normally when it is realised in cash but

---

1   The point does not need authority, but in this context see *Trustees of the Chippenham Golf Club v North Wiltshire District Council* (1991) 64 P&CR 527.

2   And may be directed to do so under the Local Government, Planning and Land Act 1980, s 98.

sometimes simply when it accrues in value. In part this is justified simply on the general ground of taxation that anyone who has the means to pay tax should contribute to government expenses. It is further justified by the view that development value is in some sense created by the community, particularly where planning consent has been given and especially in the case of planning gain agreements with local authorities where the value is often linked directly to the grant of planning consent. This was also the justification that underlay the community land schemes described below which were operated by central government.

This book is primarily concerned with arrangements between a private seller and buyer for the sharing of development value but it is important to take account of government intervention for two reasons. The first is that the government normally takes a first share of any development value by way of tax or planning gain. This will then leave a balance to be divided between the imposer and the granter. It may not be expressed in that way. Typically, planning gain agreements are to be performed by the developer after it has acquired land frequently at full market value, but the developer will take the cost of the planning gain into account in considering the price it would bid to buy the land from the original landowner, therefore the cost of performing the planning gain agreement has to be taken off the land value. Similarly, most forms of taxation are charged on one party or another. Capital gains tax is charged on the seller of land. Stamp duty is charged on the buyer. Nevertheless, both parties will take this into account – the seller in determining what price it will accept and the buyer in considering what price it will pay.

The second reason for considering these impositions is that they can often be adapted for use by private parties. The concepts and techniques developed particularly in relation to sophisticated taxes such as development land tax can be applied to the situation that prevails between the parties to a private transaction. These arrangements were worked out in great detail by academics and civil servants and the drafting of the legislation was carried out by government Parliamentary draftsmen, and there is no reason why those advising private parties should not take advantage of the skills applied to that work. Therefore, it very often happens that when a practitioner needs to draft an overage provision it will be found that the work has already been done and incorporated in one or other of the relevant statutes.

Similarly, there has been a good deal of litigation in relation to planning gain agreements and, once again, many of the concepts that have been developed by the courts can be applied between private parties.

10.5 PLANNING GAIN

This is an imposition normally made by the local planning authority, although it can be extended more widely to cover arrangements made with other bodies such as the highway authority, the education authority and statutory undertakers responsible for supplying water, gas, electricity and other services. Most attention is focused on agreements or unilateral obligations under s 106 of the Town and Country Planning Act 1990 reinforced by s 33 of the Local Government (Miscellaneous Provisions) Act 1982, but other provisions (eg s 278 of the Highways Act 1980) can also be relevant.

The most widespread form of planning gain arises where a developer applies for planning consent. The planning authority resolves to give consent subject to the completion of a s 106 agreement (or, if the matter is dealt with on appeal, the inspector may give consent conditional on such an agreement or a unilateral obligation may be tabled by the developer, often in a form negotiated with the planning authority).

The primary legal purpose of both s 106 agreements and other similar planning agreements is for planning and other purposes such as highways. Nevertheless, they have been used by local authorities in the past to secure very wide benefits. In the 1970s, it was common for local authorities under the predecessor of s 106 (s 52 of the Town and Country Planning Act 1971[1]) to require payments of money perhaps to a charity totally unconnected with the land in question and developers were prepared to pay this in order to purchase planning consents. This type of activity attracted criticism. Government guidance on proper requirements is now given in Department of the Environment Circular 1 of 1997 following certain decisions of the courts. The courts have laid down that whilst it is legitimate for a developer to offer a wide variety of benefits as part of a planning bargain,[2] they must be related to the proposed development. In *Tesco Stores Ltd v Secretary of State for the Environment,*[3] Tesco offered as part of a proposed planning agreement to pay for the construction of a by-pass. The Secretary of State considered that was only tenuously related to the development and whilst the construction of a proposed supermarket would have involved some extra use of local highways, it would not (in this particular case) have been sufficient to justify the construction of a totally new by-pass. Consent for the supermarket was refused. On Tesco's appeal, the House of Lords held that, as the Secretary of State had properly taken all relevant factors into account, the court should uphold his decision in this case. On different facts (eg if a development was

---

1   Which replaced the Town and Country Planning Act 1962, s 37, which replaced the Town and Country Planning Act 1947, s 25.
2   *R v Plymouth City Council, ex parte Plymouth and South Devon Co-operative Society* (1993) 67 P&CR 78.
3   [1995] 1 WLR 759.

likely to involve major traffic movements), such a bargain might be justifiable on planning grounds. Thus, the courts have imposed limits on the extent to which these agreements can be used in order to obtain for the local authority a share of the development value over and above what is legitimate in planning terms.

Although the ability to use s 106 agreements to secure this has been restrained, it may still be helpful for private parties wishing to use overage to consider some of the provisions which relate to these agreements. For example, they normally provide that the obligations will not come into force until planning consent is granted and they contain provisions to cover the transmission of the property and to release landowners if they are no longer holding an interest in the land. The agreements can by statute be both positive and restrictive, and by reason of their very nature the restrictive covenants do not have to benefit other land of the local authority.[1] These powers are conferred on the local authority by statute (and, therefore, must be used for a proper public purpose) and to that extent are not a good parallel for private landowners, but nevertheless the wide experience in dealing with s 106 agreements means that very often suitable provisions for arrangements between private landowners can be adapted from them.

10.6   NATIONALISATION OF BETTERMENT FOR THE COMMUNITY

There is a close link between the imposition of planning controls and successive attempts to secure all or part of development value for the benefit of the State either by way of taxation or under a system of nationalisation.

The planning system has developed in this country through most of the twentieth century, but it was put on a formal and general basis by the Town and Country Planning Act 1947, which came into force in 1948. That Act was introduced by a Labour government which was strongly influenced by socialist ideas and had a major programme of nationalisation relating to many national assets including coal, railways and hospitals. One of the main aims of many socialists had been the nationalisation of land. Land was seen as a natural asset capable of generating wealth, but not created by the efforts of any person. Therefore, it was argued that it rightfully belonged to the community. For many centuries, the power of the aristocracy had been based on control of land and, as a result, those involved in the labour movement were very keen to secure this benefit for the State.

---

1   Town and Country Planning Act 1990, s 106, reinforced by Local Government (Miscellaneous Provisions) Act 1982, s 33.

In communist countries, it was possible simply to nationalise all land, but that was not practicable in Western Europe. However, in the UK, a serious attempt was made to nationalise development value from land. The opportunity was given by the introduction of the planning laws.

The government recognised that at the time of nationalisation certain landowners already had the prospect of developing their land profitably. Before planning controls were introduced, landowners could develop their own land without permission of central or local government and those who were in a position to do that at the time the new law came in were to be compensated out of money set aside for that purpose by Parliament. This compensation was paid for by Part VI of the Act and, therefore, these claims are known as Part VI claims. The basis of compensation was assessed under s 61 of the Town and Country Planning Act 1947 by providing that an interest in land was treated as being depreciated in value by virtue of the provisions of the Act if the restricted value of that interest was less than the unrestricted value. The unrestricted value was the value immediately before the Act was passed. The restricted value was the value on the assumption that planning permission would be given for permitted development but no other. That concept formed the subsequent basis of all future attempts either to nationalise or tax development value and it represents the underlying concept of development value itself.

Therefore, in practice, the concept of development value is defined by reference to planning consent.

10.6.1 Planning

Therefore, it is helpful to consider the way in which planning restrictions worked. In 1947 and for many years thereafter the basic assumption was that a landowner was free to do whatever he wished with his land subject only to controls imposed either in the national interest (for planning or security or other reasons) or in the interests of neighbours (eg the ordinary law of nuisance and negligence).[1] The planning laws did not initially make any development unlawful. What they did was to say that if a landowner carried out development on land without planning consent, then the local planning authority could decide to issue an enforcement notice. Failure to comply with that notice can become a criminal offence. In principle, planning consent is needed for anything that is development and that is defined as the carrying out of building, engineering, mining or other operations in, on, over or under land or a material change in the use of the land.[2] This needs to be subject to qualifications.

---

1   It is now generally considered that this presumption has been displaced by s 54A of the Town and Country Planning Act 1990.
2   Town and Country Planning Act 1990, s 55.

The first is that certain types of change of use are specifically provided as not being material. These are now set out in the Town and Country Planning (Use Classes) Order 1987 and change of use within a class, and in certain cases from one class to another, is treated as not being material and, therefore, not requiring planning consent unless there is a special condition or other requirement which negatives that.

More important for the purposes of planning consent and overage is permitted development. The Town and Country Planning (General Permitted Development) Order 1995 gives a general consent for specified types of development (subject to various conditions). This is development in every sense of the word, but there is no need to obtain specific consent unless there is in force a direction known as an Art 4 direction. In the absence of such a direction, an owner or occupier of land can carry out permitted development not without planning consent but without express planning consent because the 1995 Order itself gives consent.

10.6.2   Development charge in 1947

Section 69 of the Town and Country Planning Act 1947 imposed a development charge payable to a new body called the Central Land Board of 'Such amount (if any) as the Board may determine'. However, this remarkable freedom for a government body to decide the amount of tax was restricted to some degree. First, s 69(2)(a) provides that the sums assessed do not apply to operations specified in Sch 3 to the Act which, broadly speaking, covered permitted development. Secondly, s 70(2) specifies how the Board was to determine the development charge and that is having regard to the amount by which the value of land with the benefit of planning permission exceeds the value without the benefit of such permission.

The approach to ascertaining development value in the 1947 Act is by later standards extremely simple and experience showed that a much more detailed analysis was required. The attempt simply to nationalise development value straight out did not last very long and, on the change of government in 1951, although the planning system itself and the need to obtain planning consent was retained (and still remains) virtually intact, provisions for nationalising development value were repealed.

10.6.3   Betterment levy in 1967

The Conservatives remained in power from 1951 to 1964, then a new Labour Government was elected which determined to have another attempt at securing for the State the benefit of development value. This was done through the Land Commission Act 1967, which introduced an elaborate procedure to secure that interests in land should belong to the Crown. Most of that procedure was not in fact brought into force and relates to compulsory acquisition rather than to securing development value itself, but it is worth noting the introduction of Betterment Levy in s 27 of the Land Commission Act 1967. That was charged by reference to five main cases known as cases A to E with an additional case F as a miscellaneous provision. Each of the cases had its own separate set of rules. Case A related to a sale of the fee simple or an assignment on sale of a tenancy of not less than 7 years. Case B was the grant of a tenancy for a term of not less than 7 years. Case C was the carrying out of a project of material development. Case D was the entitlement of the landowner to compensation (normally on compulsory purchase). Case E was the grant of an easement or the release or variation of an easement or restrictive covenant. The outline rules are set out in ss 27–35 of the Act, but the detail was contained in Schs 4, 5 and 6.

Levy was assessed by reference to the amount of betterment. In case A, the sale of a freehold or a long lease, the calculation was relatively straightforward and comprised the difference between (first) the market value of the land disposed of and (secondly) the value of the land on the assumption that planning permission would not be granted for material development. Case B involved the exercise of capitalising the value of the rent and any other consideration, but the period of the lease had to be taken into account. Case C, the start of operations, involved a much more complex calculation. It had to be considered what rent might be charged for the land on a letting in the open market and that was then capitalised on the assumption that the land was let for a lease for 99 years which included a covenant on the part of the tenant to carry out the development in question. Numerous assumptions had to be made as to the sort of planning consent that might be granted and the effect of that on rent and adjustments had to be made for reversionary leases and other matters. Further assumption had to be made in relation to cases D and E, and there were then a number of general assumptions in relation to all the cases.

10.6.4 Development gains tax in 1974

The Labour Government in its turn lost office and the betterment levy was repealed by the following Conservative Government. At the time, however, there was a strong national feeling that developers were making large sums of money from what was seen as the grant of planning consent issued in the public interest and, therefore, it was not possible to dispense altogether with some form of tax on development. Furthermore, the Treasury took the view that this was an attractive source from which to raise tax revenue at the expense of a small number of developers without imposing a general tax on the majority of tax payers.

The Finance Act 1974, s 38, introduced a special tax on development gains from land. That in turn reflected back to para 23 of Sch 6 to the Finance Act 1965. The 1965 Act introduced a general tax on capital gains (there had previously been a short-term tax on such gains) and para 23 contained some provisions which were subsequently overtaken by the Land Commission Act 1967, which applied where the consideration for the land exceeded what its market value would be if immediately before the disposal it had become unlawful to carry out any development in, on or over the land other than permitted development as defined in Sch 3 to the Town and Country Planning Act 1962.

10.6.5   Development land tax in 1976

There was a further change of government in 1975 and the Development Land Tax Act 1976 introduced the third major attempt by a Labour Government to secure development value for the State. This was accompanied by the Community Land Act 1975 passed at the same time which was intended to give local authorities the power to acquire land at low value for the purposes of development, but that aspect was never fully implemented. The tax aspect was implemented and the tax remained in place until 1985.

Section 1 of the 1976 Act charged tax in respect of the realisation of the development value of land in the UK. The charge was levied principally by reference to an actual disposal of land, but there was also a deemed disposal at the start of any material development. The computation of tax operated by taking the disposal proceeds (or the deemed proceeds if there was no actual disposal) and deducted from that a base value assessed in accordance with a number of different formulas laid down in the Act. Indeed, the Act contains several mathematical calculations and fractions. Again, the broad approach was to distinguish between development value and current use value and s 7(2) provides that the current use value of an interest in land at any time is the market value of that interest calculated on the assumption that planning permission would be granted for certain types of permitted development, but that it was and would continue to be unlawful to carry out any other form of material development.

10.6.6   Vehicles

Most of the legislation described above deals with straightforward disposals of land, irrespective of the identity of the person making the disposal. This is because taxes such as the development charge under the Town and Country Planning Act 1947, betterment levy under the Land Commission Act 1967 and Development Land Tax were independent charges and related only indirectly to other taxes. The different approach to taxing development gains in the Finance Act 1974, however, operated by reference to existing taxes and in particular by treating as income for tax purposes receipts which would otherwise be chargeable to capital gains tax. These taxes varied according to the status of the tax payer and, in particular, special rules were needed to deal with companies and trusts. Therefore, it was necessary for the Finance Act 1974 to deal with disposals of interests in land affected indirectly and this was done under s 41 in relation to companies and s 42 in relation to trusts. Section 41 covered the position where a person disposed of shares in a close company (broadly speaking, a company controlled by five or fewer persons or their relatives) or in a company he controlled, and the company itself either was or controlled a 'land-owning company' (three-quarters of its net assets comprised land held otherwise than as trading stock). The provisions of s 42 related to disposal of a beneficial interest in a 'land settlement', that is a trust where land amounted to three-quarters of the value of the trust fund.

10.6.7 The present position on development charges

Following the repeal of the Development Land Tax Act 1976, development value is now taxed in the same way as any other increase in value in land by reference to the gain accruing to the landowner, as mentioned at **10.7.2**.

Experience has shown that special taxes on development value suffer from two main disadvantages.

The first is that in order to be fair and to cover every possible type of realisation of development value, they have to be drawn in a very complex way. The simple approach of the Town and Country Planning Act 1947 is not adequate and even that depended on a discretion given to the Central Land Board of a type which would now be politically unacceptable. Therefore, there have to be elaborate and detailed rules to specify exactly when the charge to tax arises (distinguishing between the case where a landowner realises value in cash or in kind from the situation where the landowner itself carries out the development) and computation of the value on which the tax or levy is to be charged (and various different cases specified in relation to betterment levy indicate the complications there). Indeed, experience showed that the development land tax itself was a relatively crude tax to start with. It had to be elaborated over the period of its short existence and the terms of the tax were so complex that there was great scope for avoidance. For example, many large sites were divided up among a number of different landowning companies, each of which was then taxed separately.

The second problem is that the tax was generally seen as unfair. Although at one time it was politically attractive to attack those seen to be generating large profits out of the sale of land, in practice experience showed that it was not that simple. If a charge to tax was too heavy, a landowner would simply refuse to sell. This was appreciated both in relation to betterment levy and to development land tax which were accompanied by separate provisions allowing the local authority to take the initiative in taking over land that was ripe for development but that itself had problems in increased bureaucracy and in extension of compulsory powers of the State. Furthermore, experience showed that in the great majority of cases profits were not as large as they had originally been thought to be. While there were a few relatively simple cases of farmers selling land for housing estates for large sums, in practice a great many cases involved the redevelopment of existing sites, often contaminated, and hit small developers who were seeking to carry out normal development in the course of business. This had an adverse effect on the amount of land coming forward for housing.

As a result, the tax was very expensive to collect and produced a relatively small return. It became much easier to deal with it as part of the general range of disposals which were subject to capital gains tax, and special issues could be dealt with by way of planning agreements.

10.7 CURRENT TAXATION

Following the abolition of development land tax, there are no separate taxes aimed specifically at overage or development value. Instead, it is taxed under the general rules of taxation. However, there are a number of specific rules, both in statute and developed out of the decided cases, which need to be considered.

The circumstances of each overage case will be different. The rate of tax and the basis on which the tax is calculated varies not only from one tax to another, but also by reference to many other circumstances. Large companies are taxed at different rates from small companies. Trading companies are treated differently from investment companies. Individuals may pay at a different rate depending on the amount of their taxable income. Trusts are taxed differently depending on whether one or more individuals has an interest in possession in the income of the trust or not. There are special rules relating to charities, pension funds, local government and other special bodies.

The past use and occupation of the land may also be relevant. It can affect the amount and timing of tax, depending on whether it has been used as a business asset in the past and whether or not it has been occupied by the tax payer. This relates particularly to capital gains tax and 'rollover relief'. In the case of individuals, it may be relevant that he or she has used it as a principal residence, and that could relieve a sale of part of a garden from tax. The length of ownership, the nature of occupation and, in particular, whether or not it has been occupied for trade will all be relevant for the rate of capital gains tax. The motive for the original acquisition of the land can also be relevant under s 776 of the Income and Corporation Taxes Act 1988.

The manner of disposal is relevant not only to whether or not tax is payable but also possibly to the treatment of the tax. The way in which land and its disposals are treated in the accounts of the tax payer can be relevant.[1] The

---

1   *Herbert Smith v Honour* [1999] STC 173.

identity of the person to whom the land is disposed may also affect the tax payer's liability, for example whether it is an individual putting land into a company controlled by him or one company parting with the land to another company in the same group.

The taxes are charged by reference to a number of objective factors. Thus, stamp duty is charged on documents. Individuals pay capital gains tax on disposals and income tax on income and companies pay corporation tax on both, but the rules are similar. Value added tax is payable on a supply and inheritance tax is payable normally on death. Therefore, it will be easier to deal with the separate taxes rather than considering the distinct methods of overage individually.

The following account is not intended to be a full analysis of the relevant tax rules. Such an account would need a book to itself and many of the issues would be of marginal interest to some buyers and sellers because of the way the different taxes impact. Furthermore, tax rules change frequently. This outline can refer only to some of the tax issues which are most frequently discussed in the context of overage. Taxpayers will need to consider their own particular situations, needs, timing and values. The longer time aspect is also important for another reason. The government may change the tax rules, perhaps several times during the 20 or more years while an overage right is running. Sometimes when changes are introduced, the rules provide that they will not affect existing bargains, or contracts made or even options granted before the new rules came in. Sometimes this depends on rights being exercised by a particular date. Sometimes the new rules affect all transactions. Different rules may apply to one tax (eg stamp duty) from another (eg capital gains tax). The impact of tax can be important and as overage arrangements can run for a long time, the parties may have to take a view on this.

10.7.1 Stamp duty

Stamp duty is a tax on documents, and responsibility for payment falls to the buyer or tenant of land. Unlike the other taxes where failure to pay creates a criminal offence, the sanction for non-payment of stamp duty is that a document cannot be produced in evidence in legal proceedings. It cannot be relied on for any official purpose such as registration of title at the Land Registry or deduction of payments for tax purposes. In practice, it is so designed that it is difficult to avoid. It is payable at 4 per cent, although where the value is less than £500,000 a lower rate may apply. Special rates also apply to the taxation of rent and such matters as exchanges.

For overage purposes, the most important issue for stamp duty depends on the contingency principle. If land is sold for £1m, the buyer will have to pay stamp duty by reference to that payment. If the sale is for £1m immediately and a further instalment if planning consent is granted, the stamp duty treatment depends on the way the document is drawn. If there is either a maximum further payment or a minimum one, then the total amount of the additional contingent payment will be included as part of the proceeds of sale for the purpose of calculating duty. However, if there is no express maximum or minimum limit and the further payment is simply stated to be, say, a proportion of the uplift in value, then stamp duty will simply be payable on the fixed sum. This approach has been developed in the context of leases which contain rent review clauses where stamp duty is assessed by reference to the amount of the rent originally payable even though it is liable to be increased subsequently.

If the price is ascertainable by reference to events occurring after the date of the document, for example by reference to the value of government stock on a later date, then stamp duty will be payable by reference to the value as at the date of the document.[1] It would follow logically that if land was sold for a price to be ascertained after completion by reference to a formula, then the same principle would apply if the formula had any realistic application at the completion date. This cannot relate to circumstances which may not occur for several years, for example the grant of planning permission where there has not even been an application at the date of sale.

10.7.2 Capital gains tax

This is the main tax in relation to overage so far as sellers of land are concerned. In very broad terms, the tax is payable as a proportion of the difference between the cost of an asset and the value for which it was disposed of. This relatively simple rule with some minor modifications was indeed the basis of the tax when it was first introduced in 1965, but since then the rules have developed considerable complications. If the asset was owned prior to 1998, then the base value is either the acquisition cost or the value in 1982 if acquired earlier plus a figure for indexation from 1982 to 1998. The gain over that figure and the price for which the land is sold will then be taken and that gain will be reduced by reference to the length of ownership since 1998 and the rate of tax payable by the tax payer in order to ascertain the tax bill. As well as the original costs, certain other items can be taken into account, including costs associated with the acquisition, costs associated with enhancing value (with the cost of improvements and the cost of perfecting title) and the costs of disposal. There are various reliefs, for example for traders who reinvest (or roll over) the proceeds of sale in buying a new asset.

Where land is disposed of for an immediate price and the possibility of an additional payment, then the value of the additional payment at the time of disposal is taken into account in the calculation of the original gain. That right

---

1   *LM Tenancies 1 plc v Inland Revenue Commissioners* [1998] 1 WLR 1269.

is then treated as a separate asset which in turn is treated as being disposed of when it matures. The leading case is *Marren v Ingles*,[1] which did not itself relate to land but to shares. The tax payer agreed to sell some shares in a private company which was to be floated on the Stock Exchange. The price was (first) an immediate payment per share and (secondly) a right to a future cash payment to be calculated by reference to the sale price quoted for those shares on the first day on which they were dealt on the Stock Exchange following flotation. The point at issue in the case was the question as to whether there was a disposal of assets at the time of the second payment following the flotation; the House of Lords held that there was. It was treated as intangible property and not as a debt (debts being exempt under the capital gains tax legislation) and was not to be treated simply as part of the price of the shareholdings.

The case was concerned with the tax bill (if any) on the flotation. The House of Lords held that the value was part of the disposal proceeds. Lord Fraser of Tullybelton said:

> 'It is therefore apt to include the incorporeal right to money's worth which was part of the consideration given for the shareholdings in 1970. The vendors could have disposed of the right at any time after 15th September 1970 by selling it or giving it away and assigning it. If they had done so, there would have been an actual disposal of an asset and the vendors would have been liable for capital gains tax on the amount, if any, by which the price or value of the asset at the date of disposal exceeded its value on 15th September 1970. Of course, if the price or value had been less than the value on 15th September 1970, they would have made a chargeable loss...'

The tax payer claimed that the further payment was exempt as a debt, but that argument was rejected. It follows that if overage is secured by a mortgage, the overage would be treated as a separate asset from the mortgage and, therefore, would be taxable, even though a mortgage by itself is not.

The case did not concern the extent to which the value of the right should be taken into account at the date of the original sale in 1970. That raises a separate issue. The issue of consideration for the initial disposal was considered in a case whose circumstances are closer to overage. In *Chaloner v Pellipar Investments Limited*,[2] a landowner owned three areas of land. He granted a lease of two of them to a developer and there was no doubt that that was a disposal for capital gains tax purposes. In relation to the third site, the developer agreed to construct a building for the benefit of the owner. In that case, it was decided that the value of the expenditure on constructing the building was to be taken into account as part of the consideration for the disposal of the other two plots.

---

1   [1980] STC 500.
2   [1996] STC 234.

It follows from these cases that in the ordinary circumstances of overage where land is sold for full current use value plus a contingent obligation to pay overage, capital gains tax will be charged by reference to the total of the money received for the current use value and the value at the time of that sale of the right to receive further value. That right itself may be of negligible value at the time of the original sale depending on the prospects of further value accruing. When subsequently the trigger event occurs and the further value accrues and becomes payable, there will be a further disposal of the separate asset of the right to the additional payment at that time, with an acquisition cost of the value of that right as at the time of the original disposal.

In *Marson v Marriage*,[1] the tax payer agreed in 1965 to sell 47 acres of agricultural land to a development company for £47,000. The company agreed to pay a further £7,500 for each acre for which it obtained planning permission and, if the land was compulsorily purchased by a local authority, one half of the compensation money. Eleven years later, before planning permission was given, the tax payer agreed to release his right to further money in return for a single payment and that was paid in 1976. The court held that at the time of the original disposal in 1965 the further consideration was uncertain (both as to whether it would occur and as to the amount if it did). Accordingly, the full value did not have to be taken into account, but the payment made in 1976 was a capital sum derived from the right to a further payment and taxable accordingly.

However, a mere hope that a payment might be received is not a separate asset.[2] This may be relevant in relation to negative overage, where there is no specific bargain for a further payment. In *Davenport v Chilver*,[3] the tax payer became entitled under the terms of her mother's will to the benefit of whatever interest her mother had in some land which had been confiscated by the USSR before the mother's death. At the date of the mother's death, there was simply a hope that there might at some time be something, but no legal entitlement. Such a hope did not constitute an asset for capital gains tax purposes. Subsequently, under the Foreign Compensation (Union of Soviet Socialist Republics) Order 1969,[4] the tax payer as heir to her mother became entitled to a legal right to compensation. It was held that the Order itself gave the tax payer a statutory right to share in the fund and that was held to be an independent right which constituted an asset for the purposes of capital gains tax. As a general rule, where land is sold subject to a covenant prohibiting development and perhaps many years later the recipient (as being entitled to the benefit of the covenant) releases it in return for a cash payment, that later transaction will be treated as the disposal of an asset usually with a nil base

---

1   [1980] STC 177.
2   See **2.5.5**.
3   [1983] STC 426.
4   SI 1969/735.

value. In *Kirby v Thorne EMI plc*,[1] the company sold the shares of three subsidiary companies and, in addition, entered into a covenant that no other company in its group would engage in business of the same sort as the three subsidiaries. It was argued that the payment in respect of the covenant was not subject to capital gains tax, but it was held that it was taxable so far as it derived from an agreement not to exploit its goodwill and to that extent it was treated as a disposal of an asset. The same logic would apply to any other form of covenant, including one relating to land (whether positive or restrictive).

Overage can arise on a part disposal of land. This can occur if a physical part of a large unit (eg a farm) is sold or where only part of an interest is sold, as on the grant of a lease at a premium, or the grant of an easement. The legislation includes a formula to calculate the base or acquisition value of the part sold in such a case. The interest retained will have a base value equal to the rest of the base value of the asset. However, if a new asset is acquired on the disposal, that may not have any base value, and the whole gain will be taxable.

The grant of an option also has special rules, in that the sum payable for the grant is taxed as a separate asset but if the option is exercised the tax calculation of the disposal of the land takes account of the tax paid in respect of the option payment.[2]

10.7.3 Income tax

If the proceeds of overage are received in the form of revenue, they will be subject to income tax. This applies to rent, however calculated, but it may be extended further. Thus, if a capital sum is received by payments over a period of time, these may have the quality of income. Furthermore, if the recipient is treated as carrying on a trade, such as the business of dealing in land, then its receipts will be taxed accordingly.

Of course, the recipient may be specifically involved in a land dealing business, but the tax laws extend this further. The best-known example is the provision now found in s 776 of the Income and Corporation Taxes Act 1988. This was originally passed before the introduction of capital gains tax, and long before the rates of income and corporation tax were harmonised, and it subjected to income tax certain gains from the disposal of land. Of these, the most important arises under s 776(2). This applies in three situations:

'wherever −

    (a)   land, or any property deriving its value from land, is acquired with the sole or main object of realising a gain from disposing of the land; or

    (b)   land is held as trading stock; or

---

1   [1987] STC 621.
2   See *Garner v Pounds Shipowners and Shipbreakers Ltd* [2000] 1 WLR 1107.

(c) land is developed as the sole or main object of realising a gain from disposing of the land when developed;

and any gain of a capital nature is obtained from the disposal of the land –

(i) by the person acquiring, holding or developing the land, or by any connected person, or

(ii) where any arrangement or scheme is effected as respects the land which enables a gain to be realised by any indirect method, or by any series of transactions, by any person who is a party to, or concerned in, the arrangement or scheme.'

The leading case on this section is *Page v Lowther*,[1] which concerned the development of the Holland Park Estate in West London. The trustees of the estate entered into an arrangement with a property development company, under which they agreed that the company would build houses and the trustees would then sell long leases for premiums. The premiums were then divisible between the trustees and the developer. The court held that the premiums were chargeable to income tax in the hands of the trustees because the trustees, under s 776(2)(c), realised a gain from disposing of the land when developed.

In rare cases, a single transaction may be treated as an 'adventure in the nature of a trade'[2] and the receipts taxed as income, but such cases affecting land are likely to come within s 776(2)(a).

Another circumstance in which a premium on a lease may be taxed as income arises under s 34 of the Income and Corporation Taxes Act 1988, where there is a lease not exceeding 50 years. In that case, part of the premium (whether in cash or in kind, eg the value of an obligation on the part of the tenant to construct a building) will be subject to income tax according to a formula by which for each year of the term less than 50 years the term is to last, 2 per cent of the premium is subject to income tax.

10.7.4 Value added tax

This is a European tax based on a supply of goods or services. Land is treated as goods for this purpose, but most land is exempt unless the owner has opted to pay tax.[3] This might be done where the land owner incurs substantial expense in repairs and wishes to off-set the value added tax which it pays on the repairs against the value added tax it is entitled to receive from the tenants under leases. Where an election has been made, any disposal of the land will also attract tax. If no election has been made, normally tax is not payable. Where a covenant has been taken for the benefit of land, the VAT status of a payment for release of the covenant depends on the status of the land which benefits from the covenant, not the land which is bound by it.

---

1   [1983] STC 799.

2   *Pearn v Miller* (1927) 11 TC 610; and *Leeming v Jones* (1930) 15 TC 333.

3   Under para 2 of Sch 10 to the Value Added Tax Act 1994.

The Capital Goods Scheme[1] applies where there has been expenditure on construction of a dwelling or for certain charitable purposes or conversion to a dwelling. If this is done otherwise than in the course of a business and VAT is payable on a supply, then the person incurring the expenditure can claim a refund of VAT. If there is a change of use, the refunded tax is clawed back.[2]

10.7.5 Inheritance tax

This tax is normally not relevant to commercial overage, but certain tax payers may be subject to it in respect of development value. Inheritance tax normally arises on the death of an individual, although it can arise under other circumstances such as a gift into or payment out of a discretionary trust or, occasionally, in relation to transactions by close companies.

In general, tax is calculated by reference to the value of the asset transferred or treated as being transferred on death. If land has potential development value or if the chargeable estate includes some interest reflecting development value then that will be subject to tax by reference to its value at the relevant date, such as death or termination of a discretionary trust.

Certain assets are exempt or relieved. Of these, the most important are business assets and agricultural assets. Under s 116 of the Inheritance Tax Act 1984, the agricultural value of agricultural property is normally exempt from tax. This exemption does not apply to non-agricultural value such as development value. The agricultural value of agricultural property is:[3]

> 'The value which would be the value of the property if the property were subject to a perpetual covenant prohibiting its use otherwise than as agricultural property.'

However, under Inheritance Tax Act 1984, s 104, relevant business property may also be exempt and that extends to property consisting of a business or interest in a business and to any land or building which immediately before the transfer of value was used wholly or mainly for the purpose of the business. The exemption relates to the value of the land or building irrespective of the fact that that value may reflect development potential.

10.8 CONCLUSIONS

It will be seen that public authorities, both central and local government and bodies associated with them have a variety of methods of tapping development value. These vary from using the same methods as those which are available to private imposers to using the power of the State to take some of

---

1   Value Added Tax Act 1994, s 35.
2   Value Added Tax Act 1994, Sch 10, para 1.
3   Inheritance Tax Act 1984, s 15(3).

the development value from land in the form of planning gain or taxation. These issues need to be borne in mind when preparing any overage documents so that it can be clear what burden falls on the different parties and their successors as far as this can be ascertained at the time the documents are drawn up.

Furthermore, the concepts that have been used, particularly in relation to the special taxes devised for development gains, can be employed (with suitable modification) by those responsible for preparing documents for use by the private sector.

Chapter 11

NEGOTIATION AND DRAFTING

11.1 WHAT NEEDS TO BE CONSIDERED

This book has considered overage as a main purpose of the parties. In practice, overage provisions are often included as a 'bolt on', particularly where the prospect of planning consent is remote. The main purpose which the parties have in mind is an immediate sale for a price representing current use value, but sometimes during the discussions a provision is added to cover the possibility of future development. At the time of the original sale, this may be a distant prospect and, therefore, the parties may not think it worth paying much attention to or worth going into overage issues in detail.

The preceding chapters of this book have shown that overage must be taken seriously and all aspects of it considered with care. Even where from the outset the overage provisions have been included as part of the terms of sale, the professional advisers will need to point out to the principals some of the implications. This is especially important where the overage rights may not come into effect for a great many years, perhaps when different people have succeeded to the land and to the overage. When that happens, the relationship between the parties, particularly in the context of positive overage, will be governed by the terms laid down at the time of the original sale. They may negotiate new terms, but they will do so against that background. Thus, the parties need to consider the details of what may happen many years ahead.

The first issues to look at are the definition of the trigger event on which overage will become payable and the way in which the development value will be divided between the parties. Apart from those two issues, there are a number of others that need to be considered.

11.2 THE TRIGGER EVENT

This is normally most relevant to positive overage. In the case of negative overage, such as an unqualified restrictive covenant or a ransom strip, the overage owner will be in a position to veto any development and, therefore, can impose whatever terms are appropriate and those terms can be negotiated at the time the development is carried out. Where, however, the parties have decided ahead of time that a particular event such as planning consent will lead to a payment, then the event will need to be specified.

There are two main approaches. The first is that overage becomes payable when an increase in value occurs. If the land becomes more valuable by the grant of planning consent, then that itself will be the trigger for payment. In some cases, this is modified to provide that it will not be the grant of planning consent itself, but the implementation of it when the landowner begins to do something such as the construction of roads or buildings which is authorised by the planning consent. This can be important where a third party unconnected with the landowner may obtain consent, in which case it may not be appropriate for such a third party's action to trigger a liability on the landowner.

The alternative is that overage should be triggered by an event that realises the increase in value. This will apply typically to a transaction (eg a sale or the grant of a lease) which itself involves a payment reflecting development value. The advantage from the landowner's point of view is that it will have cash with which to pay the overage.

Of course, uplift in value can derive from events other than planning consent. For example there may be restrictive covenants in favour of some third party which if released increase market value. Similarly, the property may need to have rights of way granted over the land of the third party (which may itself be seeking overage) and the position as between the landowner and the overage owner whose interests we are looking at may itself depend on the transaction of the third party. There may be increases in value which simply result from activities on the land without necessarily obtaining planning consent, for example the growth of a business or a commercial sub-letting at an additional rent. Alternatively, an existing asset, such as land with minerals in it, may become valuable if the minerals become workable. However, overage is normally linked to a major and specific increase in value as a result of a radical change in the use of the property. It is generally considered that simply exploiting a property for its existing use will not itself be suitable for overage and, indeed, the potential for such exploitation may well be reflected in the current use value.

11.2.1 Uplift in value

The most typical uplift is the grant of a planning consent. The main advantage of this approach is certainty in that it is an ascertainable event the knowledge of which is publicly available and the terms of which are ascertainable to anyone who enquires of the local authority. The main disadvantage from the landowner's point of view is that the grant of consent does not itself give the landowner cash. It gives it the means of obtaining cash, for example by borrowing on the security of the increased value. From the overage owner's point of view, it is possible that a future consent may produce greater value so that linking overage to a specific planning consent or perhaps the first planning consent to be granted may not necessarily secure the best value for the overage owner.

A number of other matters need to be considered at this point. A major development will normally go ahead by initially obtaining outline consent subject to subsequent approval of a number of reserved matters by the local authority. When these have been approved, a detailed consent is granted. A detailed consent is often easier to value than an outline consent and it may be preferable to link the overage to that.

As indicated at **10.6.1**, certain types of development or changes of use do not require specific planning consent. These mainly comprise permitted development within the Town and Country Planning (General Permitted Development) Order 1995 or changes of use within the Town and Country Planning (Use Classes) Order 1987. A decision needs to be made as to whether these will trigger overage. In most cases it will not be appropriate, but there may be special circumstances where overage may be linked to them.

Certain types of development may be exempt from planning consent. Thus, under s 55(2) of the Town and Country Planning Act 1990, certain internal works, the use of land for agriculture, forestry and certain types of demolition do not constitute development at all. Some types of landowner, most importantly the Crown, do not need to obtain planning consent for their own development, although in practice they either do so or follow a similar procedure[1] and it is possible to define development as referring to that. There can also be special arrangements, for example for Simplified Planning Zones under s 82 of the Town and Country Planning Act 1990 and there could be comparable provisions introduced in the future.

Quite apart from this there is unauthorised development where an occupier of land carries out development without obtaining consent. If operational development is started, it is exempt from an enforcement notice after 4 years and, if there is a change of use, it is exempt after 10 years.[2] In such cases there will be no formal grant of planning consent, but it may still be possible for the landowner to realise the value if the local authority decides not to serve an enforcement notice or is simply not aware that the development has taken place.

If overage is payable by reference to the grant of consent, the payer may be concerned at a consent granted on the application of some totally unconnected

---

1 Town and Country Planning Act 1990, s 299 and Department of the Environment Circular 18/84.
2 Town and Country Planning Act 1990, s 171B.

third party. Therefore, it may seek to link the payment to development carried out by itself. However, the recipient will be concerned to cover this in case the consent is granted to (or implemented by) a person associated with the landowner such as a connected company or a tenant.

Another issue relating to the uplift in value is that the value of the overage land may accrue because it is part of a larger assembly of land. The land itself may provide access to some other plot perhaps as a ransom strip or it may need to be taken into account for example for the provision of public open space without itself being used for valuable development.

11.2.2 Start of development

For these reasons, overage is sometimes linked to the implementation of any planning consent. If the land becomes available for or involved in any larger development or if development is commenced with the authority or approval of the landowner for the time being, then overage becomes payable.

One problem is that a consent may be obtained and implemented by a squatter. Normally the owner of valuable land can be relied on to protect its interests, but particularly where the overage percentage is high the landowner may not have any particular incentive to do so if a large proportion of the development value is going off to the recipient. Sometimes, therefore, a squatter may move in, particularly if the land has been left vacant for some time while waiting for a consent. The overage may need to be drafted so that it is binding on anyone having an interest in the land whether derived from the granter or not. For example, restrictive covenants remain binding on the land even in the hands of a squatter.[1]

11.2.3 Realisation of value

The alternative approach is to provide that when cash accrues to the landowner, that will trigger the payment of overage. Normally, it will not be any sale because the parties usually do not intend that a simple increase in current use value will by itself trigger overage. That is not invariably the case and sometimes the parties may agree that a straightforward resale at an increased price for whatever reason will trigger a payment to the recipient.[2]

Where, however, the intention is that only a sale reflecting development value is to trigger the payment of overage, this will need to be defined, and there may

---

1   *Re Nisbet & Potts Contract* [1906] 1 Ch 386.
2   *Briargate Developments Ltd v Newprop Co Ltd* [1990] 1 EGLR 283. That case related to the price under an option. A similar arrangement could apply where a landlord of an agricultural holding or a dwelling subject to the Rent Act 1977 sells to the sitting tenant at a price reflecting the tenant's statutory security on the basis that if the tenant resells the landlord will share in the uplift.

need to be a formula under which any added value provided at the expense of the payer should be taken into account in calculating overage.[1] The provisions here are very similar to those which applied to development land tax and which continue to apply to capital gains tax, and regard may be had to those provisions.[2]

The trigger event could either be a sale of the interest of the payer or the grant of a lease or (if the payer is itself a tenant) of a sublease. If the property is capable of being sold or let in parts, then overage may be payable either in respect of the whole site on the grant of the first letting (eg units constructed on a new industrial estate) or separate payments may be triggered by each separate sale or letting. There may need to be a distinction between short lettings and long ones.

This distinction is particularly important where the landowner wishes to retain the overage land as an investment producing income. Where this happens in relation to commercial development, the imposer will prefer to retain the freehold and give a lease to the granter so that if value does arise from a sub-letting, the rent under the head lease can be varied to reflect that. If the landowner uses the land for his own occupation, there may need to be a notional rent.[3] Where the land is to be occupied for residential purposes, this will normally not be appropriate because the tenant or tenants may have the right to acquire the freehold under the Leasehold Reform Act 1967, the Leasehold Reform Housing and Urban Development Act 1993 or indeed the LTA 1987.

The overage payment will be linked to the cash received and the formula should be the subject of careful negotiation between the parties. It will need to distinguish between current use value and development value. It may allow for expenditure by the landowner or it may simply be decided that the recipient will receive a proportion of the gross value that the payer itself receives.

Where there is a series of dealings, overage may be cumulative, so that expenses are set against the first proceeds. The provisions will need to be drafted carefully because the payer may wish only to realise value to the extent that it covers his expenditure. Once that has been done, the overage land will have an effective nil cost and the landowner can 'land bank' the land without cost and without the need to make any payment to the recipient. This risk is inherent in much overage and may be acceptable to an imposer who initially wants only to receive current use value with a share of development value seen as a bonus.

---

1 The landowner might incur expense in obtaining planning consent or a release of incumbrances.
2 See **10.6.5** and **10.7.2**.
3 See **7.3.3**.

Cash receipts are normally a good basis, provided that the payer himself is obtaining the best possible price, but regard must be had to circumstances where this need not arise. There are many of these, but the following may be relevant:

(1) the payer may sell at an undervalue – this could arise where he is an individual who wishes to benefit a member of his family or it is a company which is selling to another company in the same group;

(2) there can be a part exchange in which case the value of the property acquired in exchange has to be taken into account;

(3) there may be a sale on tight terms, for example a restrictive covenant which can affect the value received;

(4) the sale may be part of a deal where the seller obtains some other asset, such as shares in the acquiring company;

(5) in special cases, such as heritage properties, part of the terms may reflect the provision of an endowment fund for the future maintenance of the building;

(6) there can be side deals – the payer may accept a relatively low price in return for some totally different benefit as part of another transaction; and

(7) where the property is a housing development, there may be various special terms such as equipped kitchens or even a 'free' holiday thrown in as part of the bargain.

For these reasons, it may be decided that if either there is a disposal for less than the best price obtainable on the open market or where the disposal reflects other terms or where the landowner takes occupation for his own use or the use of an associated person then either party will have the right to have market value substituted for the actual realisation price. Indeed, it may be preferable to state that overage will be calculated by reference to market value but that any actual proceeds of disposal will be treated as evidence of what that market value should be unless there are good reasons to discount it.

Where the disposal is the grant of a lease and the recipient requires a capital sum, it may be possible to capitalise the rent, but once again regard needs to be had to any special conditions. For example, property may initially be let at a concessionary rent or even a rent holiday may be granted in order to encourage initial occupation of some units so that other occupiers may be attracted to a commercial site. This type of arrangement is especially common in developments such as shopping centres to first occupiers, but it can be used on freehold sites with encouragement for, say, the first industrial occupier. Some landlords also allow an initial rent-free period with a greater rent in later periods. The purpose of this is that if the landlord wishes to sell the property in a later period, the apparent income, and therefore value, will be higher.

11.2.4 Choice of trigger

The choice will depend on what the parties wish to achieve and also on the financial needs and positions that they either have at the time of the original negotiation or expect to have at the time when the trigger event occurs. They may want to link the trigger to the first occurence of the grant of planning consent, the carrying out of works of construction or alteration or the sale or letting reflecting development value. Where there is a possibility of further value arising in the future, for example by the grant of a better planning consent later, the parties will need to consider whether to have a further imposition, perhaps of a new overage device on the occasion of the first payment. In most cases, however, this refinement is considered to be too complex, particularly where at the time of the original bargain the prospect of any development may be a long way off.

11.3 DIVISION OF EXTRA VALUE

A positive overage arrangement will need to provide not only when the overage is paid, but also how it will be calculated. The payment will normally involve the division of any additional value between the payer and the recipient. The amount of that division will depend on the relative strengths of the negotiating position of each party and their respective needs. If they are able to agree on a split (even if it is as simple as 50:50), they will still need to agree the basis on which the split is made and what is to be split.

11.3.1 Fixed price

In relation to short-term overage, the parties may be prepared to agree specific figures. For example, the sale of land for a housing development with consent for 100 houses where the developer is to start work straightaway could provide that if the developer obtains a consent for more dwellings,[1] there will be a given sum payable for each extra plot for which consent is granted. In the case of commercial developments, it may be possible to agree a figure by reference to the area of any factory or shop to be constructed and provide for this to be indexed by reference to one of the commercial property indices that are published by some of the larger firms of surveyors. This is suitable only where payment is likely to be made within a short period of time because many issues such as changes in the market, in taxation and in building costs as well as unforeseen matters such as new burdens arising from environmental needs will make any figures out of date after only a few years.

---

1   This may have been the intention of the covenant on *Surrey County Council v Bredero Homes Ltd* [1993] 1 WLR 1361 but it seems no figure was agreed.

11.3.2   Gross or net?

Overage can be payable by reference to the total value or the total sum received without deduction of expenses or even of current use value and this can be the simplest way of dividing value. In practice, the parties are more usually seeking to distinguish between current use value for which the granter is paying at the outset, and which is treated as remaining in the granter's ownership, and development value, part of which is reserved to the imposer. Therefore, it is necessary to have a clearly defined distinction between development value and current use value.

Normally, market value will comprise the total of current use value plus development value, but this will not always be the case. There may be an element of marriage value. This is often encountered in the context of tenanted property, where the value to an owner/occupier of the entire interest in a piece of land may be greater than the total of the separate values of the freehold and the tenancy. This marriage value is recognised for example under para 4 of Sch 6 to the Leasehold Reform Housing and Urban Development Act 1993. That arrangement will not normally apply to overage, although in some cases where the imposer is an existing tenant he may sell his interest to a granter on the terms that if the landowner manages to acquire some other interest in the same property (eg by buying in the freehold), a proportion of the marriage value will become payable as overage.

Similarly, there may be marriage value in combining adjoining properties.[1] This is especially important where a developer is assembling a site from a number of sellers.

A further element in the price which is sometimes relevant to overage is hope value. Where there is a medium-term prospect of development, the market value may be made up largely of current use value, but having regard to the possibility of development there may also be an element of hope value that planning permission may be available in the foreseeable future. One of the justifications for overage is sometimes said to be that it allows purchasers to acquire land at current use value where apart from overage they would have to pay for hope value as well. It has to be said that such cases are rare in practice, but there may be some situations particularly in regard to contaminated sites or sites which are suitable for assembly with adjoining properties where hope value as well as marriage value may be relevant and by reserving that to the original seller it may make a deal go through more easily.

---

1   This aspect of marriage value reflected in rent was upheld in a leasehold context in the case of *Childers Trustees v Anker* (1995) 73 P&CR 458.

11.3.3 Ascertaining development value

The most common approach is to adopt one of the methods used by the government in relation to development taxation discussed at **10.6**. In broad terms, this assesses current use value by assuming that the property can be used for any purpose that is lawful at the time of sale or to which the property could lawfully be put by virtue of permitted development. An alternative approach is to assume that the property is subject to a perpetual covenant against using it for any purpose other than its current use.[1] The market value is then ascertained and current use value deducted to determine development value.

11.4 THE RELEVANT PERCENTAGE

Just how the development value should be split between payer and recipient can be a difficult issue. As discussed at **6.10**, the courts have normally had to consider this either in the context of compulsory purchase or where a payment is being awarded instead of an injunction.

Examples of the former are *Stokes v Cambridge Corporation*[2] and *Hertford-shire County Council v Ozanne*.[3] In that type of case, if the matter came before the court, it has simply confirmed the decision taken by the Lands Tribunal, provided the Lands Tribunal has taken into account the relevant matters and has disregarded irrelevant matters. Where the Tribunal itself has had to consider issues, it has either simply adopted the view of one party (because no counter argument was put forward) or has taken its own view as to what the appropriate division should be on a valuation assessment of the sort of figure that it would expect parties to reach by agreement.

In the latter type of case, for example *Wrotham Park Estate Co v Parkside Homes Ltd*[4] and *Jaggard v Sawyer*,[5] the court has awarded the sum that it considers that a person having benefit of a covenant or ransom strip might charge as consideration for granting the rights to enable development to proceed. Again, therefore, it has been based on what the courts consider the parties might have expected to negotiate. This is an award of equitable damages instead of an injunction under s 50 of the Supreme Court Act 1981.

In neither the compulsory purchase cases nor the equitable damages cases have the courts been prepared to lay down as a matter of law the issues which

---

1   As in the Inheritance Tax Act 1984, s 15(3). See **10.7.5**.
2   (1961) 13 P&CR 77.
3   (1991) 62 P&CR 1. See also **6.10**.
4   [1974] 1 WLR 798.
5   [1995] 1 WLR 269. See also **6.3**.

the parties should have taken into account in deciding the split. Nor have the courts laid down guidelines as to how that split should be calculated.

11.4.1 General approach

Therefore, the matter must rest on wider issues. The proportions that might be expected to be negotiated between parties in positive overage will depend on what one might expect in negative overage.

The minimum payment will be the sum the recipient would be prepared to accept in return for giving up the veto over development. In most cases, this minimum is likely to be small because any payment will be better than none and, if the overage owner exercises his veto, he will receive nothing. Where overage is secured by something such as a ransom strip which may have its own value, then that of course will be a basic figure. Similarly, where a restrictive covenant serves an amenity purpose, for example by preserving a view, then the minimum will equal the difference in value between the benefited property with the view over open country and the value of the same property with a view over a housing estate or whatever the development might be.

Particularly in relation to ransom cases, compulsory purchase cases can be a guide to some extent. This is because under the compulsory purchase code[1] the sum payable is made up of the total of (first) the value of the land taken and (secondly) compensation for severance and injurious affection, namely the amount by which the value of the seller's retained land is diminished by reason of the acquisition.[2]

The maximum overage payment will reflect the minimum sum that a landowner would be prepared to keep for himself as part of his return for developing the land or allowing a development to go ahead. This figure will vary according to the different situations of different landowners. A commercial developer would normally expect a return on investment put into the development. A private landowner such as a farmer who was intending to sell on to a developer might relate to the minimum he would wish to retain having regard to the current use he is making of the land in agriculture and the possibility that at some future date he might be able to drive a better bargain. There may also be an emotional content in the minimum that a landowner is prepared to retain for himself because of the strong feeling that 'this is my land and I own it'.

---

1   Compulsory Purchase Act 1965, ss 7 and 10.
2   In actual compulsory acquisitions, injurious affection covers damage but not loss of a ransom element: *Wrotham Park Settled Estates v Hertsmere Borough Council* [1993] 2 EGLR 15. But see *Brown v Heathlands Mental Health NHS Trust* [1996] 1 All ER 133.

The division in the case of negative overage will also depend on the likely attitude of the courts and the Lands Tribunal. If overage is protected by a restrictive covenant or ransom strip, the parties will have to assess whether the court is likely to give an injunction. If it is a lease, then there may be various means for overcoming the opposition of a landlord to building, for example under Part I of the LTA 1927, and the prospect of doing this will be reflected in the bargain struck.

Taking account of all these factors, the normal rule is that the overage payment will lie somewhere between one half and one-third of the development value, but it has to be said that this depends very much on who is in the market and the attitude taken by the valuers to the parties.

11.4.2 Illustrations from decided cases

The decided cases illustrate a variety of approaches and a wide range of awards ranging from 90 per cent of the proceeds[1] to 5 per cent of the development profits. Some are awarded by the courts and may represent what the judge thinks is fair in all the circumstances. Some are awarded by the Lands Tribunal, where the basis may be more scientific, or may again depend on the Tribunal's feeling of what is right.

To some extent, the award reflects the basis of jurisdiction. Where there is a ransom strip, there is a greater readiness to respect the value of the interest of the recipient on the basis that in the absence of compulsory powers he would normally be in a position to exercise a veto. Apart from that, most of the cases relate to restrictive covenants which were originally imposed for amenity purposes. There is a statutory jurisdiction to vary them and compensation is calculated under s 84(1) of the LPA 1925. The compensation may be on either but not both of two heads, namely (i) a sum to make up for any loss or disadvantage as a result of the relaxation or (ii) a sum to represent the difference in value at the time the covenant was imposed between the land with and without a covenant.

An example of (i) is *Re Kennet Properties*,[2] where there was a paddock subject to a restrictive covenant preventing building. A number of houses benefited and the Tribunal awarded varying sums for loss of amenity between £5,000 and £10,000.

An example of (ii) is *Re Cornick*,[3] where Cornick bought a part of a garden subject to a covenant not to use it except for a jam factory. The Tribunal considered that the seller would have asked for a higher price if no restriction had been imposed because he believed that the imposition of the covenant

---

1   *R v Braintree DC, ex parte Halls* at first instance [1999] EGCS 96, overruled on other grounds at (2000) 80 P&CR 266.
2   (1996) 72 P&CR 353.
3   (1994) 68 P&CR 372.

gave him the chance to share in the enhanced development value and, therefore, would have demanded an extra £5,000. In *SJC Construction Co Ltd v Sutton London Borough Council*,[1] the Tribunal took the view that on the original sale the property would have fetched £54,000 free of the restriction and £35,000 subject to it, therefore the development value was £19,000 and they awarded a percentage of this amounting to £9,500. The Court of Appeal decided that the Tribunal had adopted a fair and reasonable approach and would not interfere with it.

The share of profit basis is used more openly in compulsory purchase cases. Thus, in *Hertfordshire County Council v Ozanne*,[2] the Lands Tribunal awarded £1.24m for ransom strip. The matter reached the House of Lords, which was not directly concerned with the merits but only whether the Tribunal was able reasonably to reach its view. It held that it could. It is understood that this represented half the development value of the adjoining land. Similarly, in *Batchelor v Kent County Council*,[3] the Tribunal awarded compensation of £500,000 apparently on that basis. The court quashed the actual decision of the Tribunal on the basis that the reasons given could not be understood, but considered that in principle the Tribunal might well have taken the right approach if its reasons could have been followed.

This basis can also be applied to restrictive covenants. In *Re Fisher & Gimson (Builders) Ltd*,[4] a house was built in breach of covenant and three properties had the benefit. Two adjoining owners agreed to be paid out for £12,500 and £10,000 respectively. A third owner objected and began an action for an order that the house be demolished. This was stayed pending an application to the Tribunal which awarded £6,000 on the basis of an unspecified development value having regard to the sums paid to the other owners. In *Wrotham Park Estate Company v Parkside Homes Ltd*,[5] the court awarded damages of such a sum as a covenantee might reasonably have demanded for relaxation of the covenant. Counsel argued on the basis of expert evidence that one half or one-third of the development value was right, but the Court of Appeal considered that the covenant was not designed to be turned to account and awarded 5 per cent of the profit to the building.

Certain cases are difficult to follow, but are illustrations of what the parties themselves put forward. In *R v Braintree District Council, ex parte Halls*,[6] the judge at first instance was prepared not to interfere with the demand by the Council of 90 per cent of the proceeds of sale. The decision itself was overturned on appeal on the grounds that the council could not demand

---

1 (1975) 29 P&CR 322.
2 (1991) 62 P&CR 1.
3 (1989) 59 P&CR 357.
4 (1992) 65 P&CR 312.
5 [1974] 1 WLR 798.
6 [1999] EGCS 96, overruled (2000) 80 P&CR 266.

anything at all. In *Re New Ideal Homes Ltd*,[1] a local council conveyed land to the company for £801,000 subject to a covenant restricting the use to 75 houses. Later the council gave consent for a further four houses and then the Secretary of State gave consent for an additional 77. The council sought to object on the grounds that a high density development would reduce its chance of selling its adjoining land for a profitable low-density high-value development. The Tribunal did not accept the argument, but in this case the amount of the compensation had been agreed between the parties at £51,000.

The courts may award what the judge considers to be a fair sum. In *Jaggard v Sawyer*,[2] which involved both a covenant and extra use of a right of way, the court held that the payment should not be valued on the basis of a ransom but at the price which might reasonably be demanded for relaxing the covenant and for granting the right of way. On *Wrotham Park* principles, the court considered a reasonable price for all the houses having benefit together would be £6,250 and, as there were nine of them, payment was £694.44. In *Bracewell v Appleby*,[3] the judge awarded what he considered to be a fair sum for loss of amenity and increased use of a private road, but not so great a sum that the defendant would have been deterred from building a house. Once again, there were several houses and the judge considered a total figure would be £2,000 and one-fifth amounted to £400. Again, *Wrotham Park* principles were applied. In *Amec Developments Ltd v Jury's Hotel Management Ltd*,[4] the judge awarded the sum of money he considered likely to have been agreed in all the circumstances and did not use the mathematical approach suggested by the expert.

In one case, Parliament has provided for a scale of charges. These are to be laid down in regulations under s 68 of the Countryside and Rights of Way Act 2000 which provide for the compulsory acquisition of a right of way across common land. The charge is to be whichever is less of 3 per cent[5] of the value of the property benefiting from the right and one-third of the increase in the value of the property resulting from the existence of the statutory right. This gives some statutory support to the one-third figure in *Stokes v Cambridge Corporation*[6] but there is a special situation here because the right is given by Parliament in recognition of the fact that a vehicular right of way cannot be acquired by prescription over common land.

---

1   (1978) 36 P&CR 476.
2   [1995] 1 WLR 269.
3   [1975] 1 Ch 408.
4   [2000] NPC 125.
5   One per cent for houses built before 1 December 1930.
6   (1961) 13 P&CR 77.

11.4.3 Successive tranches

Another approach is to split the price in slices. This may be appropriate to relatively short-term overage, but it is more flexible than using straightforward figures. The parties will agree that the first element of value (normally related to current use value, but may be a given figure possibly indexed by reference to the price of comparable land) will belong to the landowner. It might, for instance, have a first take equal to double current use value. The next slice of value may be treated as belonging to the overage owner. For example, this might be a further sum equal to current use value. If the land is then sold for more than the total of the two foregoing figures, there may be a further slice or the parties may agree to split the surplus value in some given proportion.

11.4.4 Development costs and expenditure

Where the landowner has spent money on the land, it is right that that expenditure should be reimbursed before any surplus value is divided. Often this will be reflected in the current use value, but the parties may wish to take specific account of major expenditure, for example on defending or strengthening the title to land. This might include buying in third party rights such as tenancies and easements. There would also be major expenditure in relation to any development sale. These can include the costs of obtaining planning consent, the costs associated with a s 106 agreement, the costs of providing infrastructure particularly if these are to be taken as a retention out of any sale price to a developer, such as the provision of gas and electricity, and there may be associated costs of acquiring extra land as a means of access or to straighten a boundary. There may be professional fees such as architects' fees. Sale expenses for a major site may themselves be substantial. Particularly in short-term overage agreements, it will often be provided for these costs to be credited to the person who has borne them before the division of the proceeds between the parties.

11.5   DRAFTING ISSUES

Once the outlines of the arrangement have been agreed, the parties' advisers will need to look at a number of other aspects of the transaction beyond the amount and timing of the overage. All the normal provisions which apply to any commercial documents will apply here, but there are a number of additional issues which the advisers to the parties need to take into account.

11.5.1   Expression of overage intention

The attitude of the courts to overage provisions is discussed at **12.3**, but it is sufficient to say that in the past it appears that the courts have not fully accepted that overage is a legitimate purpose. Sometimes this seems to have arisen because the parties have not made this intention clear and, indeed, may have been confused about the need to do so. In other cases one party, usually the one claiming a financial benefit, has tried to take advantage of a situation that was not designed for overage. Where a restrictive covenant was imposed for amenity purposes or a right of way granted or reserved for normal access, parties have tried to take commercial advantage of a right that was not designed for that purpose.

Apart from the relatively simple situation in *Briargate Developments Ltd v Newprop Co Ltd*,[1] where the intention of the parties was quite clear, the courts were not formerly sympathetic to overage claims, even where as in *Surrey County Council v Bredero Homes Ltd*[2] there was some justification for doing so. However, this may have changed as a result of *Attorney-General v Blake*.[3]

If the parties expressly make it clear that they intend the arrangements to apply for overage, then it is likely that the courts would wherever possible give effect to that intention. This may not always be possible. *Bredero* itself was an example of an attempt to impose a restrictive covenant which did not benefit retained land. Even leaving aside the fact that Surrey County Council was not in a position to claim an injunction (because it had no land capable of benefiting), it would appear that the court would not have awarded one and was not prepared to make a substantial award of damages. (However, in *Attorney-General v Blake*, this was treated as an issue of drafting not of substance.) Even where there was land to benefit, as in *Stockport Metropolitan Borough Council v Alwiyah Developments*,[4] the court deliberately chose not to do so. In ransom cases, the court has proved itself readier to give an injunction, but that appears to have been more out of respect for the property rights of a property owner. Those situations have not normally arisen from previous common ownership or any intention to impose overage and the courts therefore have simply had to balance the opposing interests of adjoining landowners.

The drafter of the document may consider that if overage can be disguised as something else, such as a right of a more traditional nature, then it stands a better chance of being supported in court. This is unlikely. The disclosure procedure before any hearing is likely to reveal the intentions of the parties and if overage was intended at the outset, this will readily become apparent to most judges. This attitude may have more force in the case of restrictive covenants which are designed to benefit the amenities of nearby land, but they will then be vulnerable to removal under s 84 of the LPA 1925.

---

1 [1990] 1 EGLR 283.
2 [1993] 1 WLR 1361.
3 [2000] 3 WLR 625.
4 (1983) 52 P&CR 278.

In the case of positive overage, if there is a clear intention to do a deal, then even though the parties may not have provided fully for the necessary adequate machinery to agree a split and valuations, the court will if necessary supply the defect.[1]

The situation is otherwise where there is no specific intention to do a deal. This will normally be the case for negative overage where the overage owner wishes to have a veto. Even though his intention may be to sell that veto for a proportion of the development value, if it is not expressed then there is no deal for the court to complete. In that case, there is a risk that the overage may be disallowed altogether on the grounds that the overage owner is being unreasonable. If he offers to do a deal, then particularly in the context of a restrictive covenant that may be taken as evidence that the covenant itself is of no amenity value.[2] Thus, it may be wise when reserving even negative overage to make it clear that that is the intention and particularly that the imposer intends to reserve the development value. It would appear from the remarks *Rhone v Stevens*[3] that this is seen as a perfectly legitimate thing to do.

11.5.2   Future changes in circumstances

Long-term overage arrangements are intended to last for many years and during that time circumstances can change radically. This is not always appreciated by those responsible for drafting documents. Far too often there is an implicit assumption that any individuals involved will live for ever, that companies will remain in existence and under the same control, the title to land will not change, that the local environment will not alter and that the law will remain the same. All of these are very far from the truth. Land once in open country may become built up. Land that is contaminated may be reclaimed. Tax rules in particular are likely to alter considerably. Land may be subject to a compulsory purchase order. Development may be prevented by the land being designated as being in a green belt or perhaps in a green lung between two expanding settlements and a small area of potential development land may become designated as part of a larger site, for example as public open space within it. The needs, intentions and wishes of parties will change radically and this is particularly likely to apply where individuals die and their estates are inherited by successors with very different views and needs, or where companies are taken over or their assets are disposed of.

It is not normally possible for the parties to foresee these, but their advisers should be aware of the possibilities. For example, where a particular action needs the consent of one party (as in the case of a restriction on the Register),

---

1   *Sudbrook Trading Estate Ltd v Eggleton* [1983] 1 AC 444, and see **12.5.3**.
2   *Gafford v Graham* (1998) 77 P&CR 73.
3   [1994] 2 AC 310. See also *Attorney-General v Blake* [2000] 3 WLR 625.

provision needs to be made for the rights of that party to be transmitted to others.

In practice, an overage structure, however carefully designed, is unlikely to meet all the circumstances at the time that the payment is expected to mature. This is true of normal development agreements, few of which are implemented as originally intended, and overage is more speculative than that. However, an overage structure can create a situation against which future negotiations can take place. For that reason, it is often more important to give both parties veto rights so that each can prevent development by the other. If that happens, there may be a lockout situation. The courts have difficulty in dealing with such a situation. To some extent, procedures have been developed in the context of private companies[1] and partnerships. Often they will not be found to be satisfactory for overage because the solutions tend to involve either a compulsory acquisition of one party's interest by the other or a sale of the whole of the property (perhaps on liquidation or winding up) with the proceeds being shared. In overage, that is normally what neither party wants.

It follows, therefore, that wherever possible the overage arrangement should be designed to be workable on its own terms despite a change in circumstances, but with the knowledge that it may in fact be used as a basis for further negotiation once the actual circumstances are known.

The documents need to have regard to the commercial needs of the parties. The landowner will wish to mortgage the land in order to raise funds or if he does not wish to occupy himself, he will wish to grant a tenancy. If the landowner is an individual, he may die and his personal representatives will need to pass the property to a beneficiary. If it is a company, its assets may need to be distributed to its shareholders or to another company on reconstruction.

Equally, the terms have to have regard to the physical realities of the situation. Sometimes these will be obvious. There is no point in taking a ransom strip on one side of the property if there is adequate access from a different direction. This may not be evident at the time of the original deal, but it is always possible for a completely new road to be constructed as an addition to the motorway or trunk road network and experience has shown that such roads have often unlocked development value. The physical design, particularly of a commercial development, can also be relevant to the method of disposal. Parades of shops have been replaced by shopping centres and they in turn may give way to new structures suitable for e-commerce. Similarly, the capacity and layout of warehouses have changed substantially in recent years. A site

---

1   See *Re Yenidje Tobacco Co Ltd* [1916] 2 Ch 426; and *Ebrahami v Westbourne Galleries Ltd* [1973] AC 360.

that at one stage was thought to be suitable for occupation as a single industrial unit may in the course of time become more appropriate for sub-division into large numbers of small units and vice versa, and this needs to be taken into account.

11.5.3   Maximising value

The overage return to the recipient will depend on the extent to which the value of the overage land has been increased and, therefore, it will have an interest in seeing that value maximised. Normally, the landowner's interest will be the same, but the landowner will have other matters to take into account as well. It will itself be occupying the overage land or letting it and presumably obtaining revenue from that occupation or from rent.

Either the overage owner or the landowner may have adjoining land which might be adversely affected by development on the overage land. Equally, either may have back land which can benefit from the use of some of the land as an access while the other would prefer that land to be used to build a house on. Indeed, either as an individual may wish to preserve the amenities. In a few unusual cases, either the overage owner or the landowner may actually be opposed to development (or at least development of a particular type, such as residential rather than industrial). An imposer who wishes to preserve the amenities, appearance and ecology of a piece of land might well sell it on the terms that the whole of the development value was reserved. Although this would be done by way of overage, it would not be the imposer's intention to profit from that, but to stop the landowner profiting by changing the character of the land. On the other hand, it is entirely possible that a body such as an environmental charity might acquire overage land for nature conservation or landscape purposes and be unwilling to see any development even though the overage owner might wish to see the value exploited. However, such cases are rare.

In the more normal case where both parties wish to benefit from an increase in value, their interests will in this respect be the same and, therefore, the overage owner may consider that it can rely on the landowner to maximise value. Where their interests may diverge, for example because the landowner has other land that might be capable of development and so might be ready to see the overage land simply go as public open space, the overage owner will have an interest in maximising the value of the overage land as distinct from others. Thus, he may want to have some control over the planning process.

The consent of the landowner is not needed for anyone applying for planning consent over any land[1] and, therefore, an application can be made by or on

---

1   With the exception of Crown land under s 299 of the Town and Country Planning Act 1990.

behalf of the landowner or the overage owner or an unconnected third party. Fees are payable and a good deal of other expenses are normally incurred in connection with the planning application. Under s 65 of the Town and Country Planning Act 1990, notice has to be given to the owner of the land and to an agricultural tenant. Therefore, even under the general law, there is provision for the parties to be aware of what is happening and a major development is likely to involve publicity in the press. Nevertheless, the parties may wish to include their own provisions.

These could include covenants not to submit an application without the consent of the other party, or at the minimum without consulting the other, or the provisions might go into more detail. The extent to which such provisions are enforceable will depend on the particular device being used. There is some doubt as to whether a restrictive covenant not to apply for planning consent (and equally not to object to another's application) is enforceable, because there is a view that this is a right conferred by public law on every citizen and cannot be the subject of a private contract not to exercise it. If the structure is the leasehold, then such a provision is probably enforceable as protecting the interest of the landowner or the tenant. However, the practicalities of enforcement need to be taken into account. If the party having the benefit of such a covenant is aware of a breach before it happens, then it may be entitled to take out an injunction. Yet the court will allow an injunction only if it considers that it will serve some useful purpose and is not contrary to public policy. As a result of the ease with which such a provision can be got round (eg by allowing a nominally unconnected third party to make an application), the courts in practice may well decline to enforce it. If a breach of covenant had occurred (and an injunction is not granted), it might be difficult for the party having the benefit of a covenant to show that it has suffered damage sufficient to enable it to claim damages in court.

Perhaps of more relevance would be an obligation to supply information, for example in connection with any sale as to the bids received and as to the terms of sale such as restrictive covenants and other provisions. This is connected rather more to the questions of valuation discussed above. There could also be an obligation to supply information as to what is happening on the land, for example as to the terms of any tenancies.

It may in any event be necessary for the parties to co-operate in any planning application. If a s 106 agreement is required, the local authority may need 'any person interested' in the land to enter into a planning obligation. In practice, local authorities normally require as many persons as possible to do so. They will require the freeholder and any mortgagee and certain types of tenant to join him. This is because a s 106 agreement is enforceable only against the persons who entered into it or any successor in title of such person. If, for example, a freeholder whose interests were subject to mortgage made an obligation and the mortgagee did not join in and subsequently the mortgagee sold under its power of sale, the agreement would not be binding against the buyer even though the planning consent issued following the s 106 agreement would exist for the benefit of the land. This will apply where the overage is by charge. The same would be true if the overage owner had a power of re-entry.

In this context, it should be noted that following the TLATA 1996 the interests of beneficiaries under a trust are interests in land even though they can normally be over-reached under s 2 of the LPA 1925. However, as the right of a future owner would be derived from the trustees, planning authorities do not require beneficiaries to join in the planning agreement.

11.6 ASSIGNMENT

Thought needs to be given to the assignment both of the benefit and of the burden of overage. For this purpose, it is convenient to distinguish between overage itself and the means by which it is secured. If overage is an equitable interest (see **12.5.1**) then under s 4 of the LPA 1925 it can be assigned and under s 53 that assignment must be in writing. If it takes effect as an incorporeal hereditament, then under s 52 it must be by deed.

The assignment of a promise was considered in Chapter 2 and simple writing is required, although if it is to be an absolute assignment then the provisions of s 136 of the LPA 1925 must be complied with. The same applies to the assignment of a simple positive covenant but a rentcharge and a right of re-entry are both legal interests which need to be assigned by a deed. A rent-charge will normally be supported by a Land Certificate and that will need to be transferred by registered land transfer. A restriction on the Register will be assigned by an application to the Land Registry to alter the restriction so that it names a different person.

Restrictive covenants cannot be assigned separately from the land which they benefit. Mortgages are transferred by Land Registry form. Ransoms again are part of the land or rights affecting land and will be transferred in the normal way. A ransom strip as such will be transferred by the normal form of transfer. An easement can be transferred only with the land that it benefits. Where overage is by lease, the superior interest of the landlord will need to be transferred by deed. In principle, options can be transferred in writing alone, but in practice a deed is more usual. Shares in an overage company will be transferred by a normal share transfer. Beneficial interests under a trust can be transferred in writing.

As discussed at **2.4**, the general rule is that the burden of an obligation cannot be transferred as such and that, in principle, applies as much to the obligation to pay overage as any other but some consideration does need to be given to the means of transfer of land subject to overage rights. In general, the land can be transferred freely subject to any specific restrictions such as a restriction on assignment of a leasehold property.

(1) Where there is a restriction on the Register, the Land Registry will not register a transfer without the consent of the named person having the benefit of the restriction. Some consideration needs to be given to the precise form and procedure for obtaining that consent and it may be preferable to set out a form of Deed of Covenant in a schedule to the original overage document.

(2) Where land is subject to restrictive covenants, the land itself can still be transferred freely. However, if the covenant is drawn in a form that is binding on the original covenantor even after he ceases to own the burdened land, he will normally be entitled to the benefit of an indemnity covenant. It may therefore be desired to draft the covenant in a form which is not binding against the original covenantor after he has parted with all interest in the land.

(3) Land subject to an overage charge can be transferred in the normal way, but the estate owner will not be in possession of the Land Certificate. The Land Certificate itself is retained in the Land Registry and the Charge Certificate may be issued to the overage owner. Under s 28 of the LRA 1925 there is an implied covenant on the part of any person who is the registered proprietor of the land at the time of creation of the charge to pay the sum charged. If the intention is that the original granter is not to remain liable after parting with interest in the land, then s 28 will need to be negatived and there will need to be an entry on the Register under s 28(2) to that effect.

(4) Where overage is by lease, the lease itself will need to be looked at to see if any special provisions (eg an express Deed of Covenant) are required on the assignment. Under the LT(C)A 1995, any covenant in a lease is in principle not binding on a lessee after parting with the freehold.[1]

(5) In the case of options, there is often an obligation in the option (protected by a restriction on the Register) not to transfer the land subject to the option without the new owner entering into a deed of covenant with the holder of the option. This applies particularly where there are positive obligations on the part of the landowner, for example to join in a s 106 agreement.

---

1   Except under an authorised guarantee agreement under s 16, which complies with the Act, or in a few other cases such as an unlawful assignment or by operation of law under s 11.

11.7 ARRANGEMENTS FOR PAYMENT

If the result of the overage is to produce a sum due to the recipient, then that payment will need to be documented and, where the recipient has a right over the overage land, the payer will wish to have that right released or modified.

When the arrangements are originally being negotiated, the parties will probably be prepared to accept in very broad terms that the sum will be payable on the trigger event without being too concerned as to details which may not be relevant for 20 years. When payment time comes, however, the precise arrangements for payment can be important.

If payment is to be made by reference to a receipt of money by the payer, then it will be possible to require payment to be made at the same time as, for example, the payer itself sells its interest in the land. Indeed, if there is a restrictive covenant, the buyer will want to be sure that the covenant is released before parting with its money. Where the overage sum is a proportion of the sum received by the payer on its own sale, then if there is a delay in completing that sale the payer may become entitled to interest from its buyer. Where that happens, the recipient should be entitled to an appropriate share of that interest.

It is normally sensible to agree the form of release or receipt at the outset. If there is a simple promise to pay, the payer should be content with a receipt. If there is a rentcharge, a right of re-entry, a restriction on the Register or a restrictive covenant, those will need to be released. A charge should be discharged. A ransom will normally be released by a conveyance of the ransom strip or perhaps by the grant of an unfettered right of way over it and, if the ransom is a right of way across the overage land, then that right of way will need to be released or the route of it varied. Where there is a leasehold structure, the formalities will depend on the details of the arrangement, but if that is for the freehold to be transferred to the tenant then the transfer of title will normally be in return for the overage payment.

11.8 REMEDIES

During the overage period, it is quite possible that there may be disputes or failures to comply with obligations. The parties may wish to consider a disputes procedure whether arbitration or decision by an expert, but they may feel that the type of dispute is going to be unforeseeable and it would be preferable to have the matter referred to court. When a dispute arises, the parties are of course free at that time to agree on their own disputes procedure.

If any default occurs on the part of the landowner, the overage owner's remedies will depend again on the form the overage takes. Where there is a continuing obligation such as a restrictive covenant not to develop, then the overage owner's remedy will normally be for an injunction against breach. Similarly, if there is a ransom strip, the remedy will be for an injunction against trespass. If there is a right of way with a limited use, then the remedy will be an injunction for nuisance. By the nature of things, damages will normally not be a sufficient remedy.

Where there is positive overage, the main breach is likely to be failure to pay when the sum is due. In this case, the recipient will normally not want an injunction, but would prefer the money.

(1) There could be an action in debt for money due if the amount is known or can easily be ascertained.

(2) A simple action in damages at common law is unlikely to be sufficient because the recipient will not have suffered damage in the normal way.

(3) If a claim for an injunction is made then either:
   (a) the recipient can enforce it (or threaten to) and use that as a basis for negotiation; or
   (b) equitable damages may be awarded instead of the injunction.[1]

Where there is a breach on the part of the overage owner, the remedy of the landowner will most likely be for a declaration that the overage owner cannot enforce his rights. Where, for example, the overage owner refuses to consent to a transfer to a buyer, the remedy will be for a declaration either that that consent is not necessary or for the court (or the Chief Land Registrar) to consent on its behalf.

Where there is a dispute as to the payment of any overage sum, it may need to be paid into court coupled with an application for a declaration that, for example, a covenant is not enforceable or that some restriction on a right of way no longer applies. In an appropriate case, there may also be an application to the Lands Tribunal on the grounds that a covenant has become obsolete.

---

1   Supreme Court Act 1981, s 50; and *Wrotham Park Estate Co v Parkside Homes Ltd* [1974] 1 WLR 798.

Chapter 12

THE FUTURE

12.1 HOW WILL OVERAGE DEVELOP?

The discussion in this book has focused on the particular rules applying to transactions now recognised as constituting overage. In the past, there has been no separate law of overage and the rules have been assembled from different aspects of property law. The rules do not always fit together and sometimes contradictory results can be reached by applying rules derived from different approaches.

However, there are certain general principles that we can recognise emerging in response to commercial needs. These principles can be combined to form the basis of a set of legal rules which can be used by owners of property, developers, investors and funders to achieve their needs.

The law could be developed either by Parliament or by the courts. For the reasons discussed below, the present law has many inconsistencies and rules which obstruct its development. Whilst it is not too late for the courts to overcome these problems, decisions of the courts can be based only on the resolution of problems coming before them. The smooth development of the law does not need to depend on the chances of litigation and Parliament may want to provide a set of legal rules to govern the matter. This might be referred to the Law Commission. Alternatively, as explained in Chapter 10, there is a strong interest on the part of the Treasury in securing clawback for the State. It would need only two or three cases where a government department had sold land reserving what it thought to be effective clawback but found that that had been struck down as a result of some legal rule for the Treasury to want to initiate reform.

The Law Commission has already been very active in the area in its recommendations on restrictive covenants and perpetuities and limitation and the law of landlord and tenant, and no doubt its involvement in such an active area of the law will continue.

Legislation needs Parliamentary time and that is scarce and, therefore, it is more likely that the immediate development of the law will be through the courts. So far there have been very few genuine overage schemes that have come before judges. One was *Briargate Developments Ltd v Newprop Co Ltd*.[1] It is possible that a restrictive covenant case, *Surrey County Council v Bredero Homes Limited*,[2] was an overage case although it was not decided on that basis. *Re Cornick*[3] before the Lands Tribunal was decided on overage lines. Such examples are few.

This is partly because overage schemes began to be used on a wide scale only in the late 1960s. By now many of these will be ripe for development and the sums at stake will be large enough to make it economically worthwhile fighting a major case.

12.2   INFLUENCES ON THE LAW

Like any other dispute between commercial organisations, the development of overage will depend on the needs of the market and of landowners, developers and investors. Of course, this is materially affected by the planning system as the grant of planning consent normally triggers an increase in value.

In the future, it is likely that controls on the use and development of land will tighten. There are pressures for development to be restricted to brownfield sites, many of which need large sums to be spent on them before they are capable of redevelopment. The sequential development rule[4] encourages development in or on the edges of existing settlements. The priority of the development plan[5] again constrains where development can take place. There are also growing environmental controls, and the influence of European planning laws[6] is already making itself felt. All of this means that as development land becomes more scarce and more controlled than land which has a long-term prospect of development, it is still worth taking trouble over because so much other land will be protected.

12.3   THE ATTITUDE OF THE COURTS

In general, the courts will take the view that if there is a clear commercial deal, they will give effect to that, subject obviously to the overriding rules law. However, if there is a deliberate attempt to use something devised for another

---

1   [1990] 1 EGLR 283.
2   [1993] 1 WLR 1361. See *Attorney-General v Blake* [2000] 3 WLR 625.
3   (1994) 68 P&CR 372.
4   Department of the Environment Planning Policy Guidance Note 6 dated 6 June 1996 (Town Centres and Retail Development), para 1.10.
5   Town and Country Planning Act 1990, s 54A.
6   Council Directive No 85/337 on Environmental Impact Assessment implemented by Town and Country Planning (Environmental Impact Assessment) Regulations 1999, SI 1999/293.

purpose in order to obtain overage, there is a difference of view. The traditional view, established in relation to restrictive covenants, is the one expressed by Denning LJ in *Driscoll v Church Commissioners*[1] quoted at **4.6**. Against that there is the view, established in relation to ransoms, that protects the interests of landowners. There the standard position was stated by Sir George Jessel MR in *Eardley v Granville*[2] and is more recently exemplified in the oversailing cases referred to at **6.3**.

The tendency of the courts is to try to strike a middle way and cases such as *Bracewell v Appleby*[3] and *Jaggard v Sawyer*,[4] which apply the principles in *Shelfer v City of London Electric Lighting Co*,[5] show the judges as trying to strike a balance between the needs of developers and the rights of landowners. However, these have arisen in the context of unforeseen situations. It is more likely where the intentions of the parties to have an overage arrangement are made clear at the outset that the courts would have regard to those and a judge would not try and impose a new bargain on the parties.

12.4 APPLICATION OF STATUTES

The use of overage provisions can sometimes run up against statutory provisions and these may need to be interpreted in the light of it. The most important is s 58 of the LRA 1925 and the provisions of the LRR 1925 relating to restrictions on the Register as discussed at **3.4**. The Court of Appeal has already indicated that para 5 of Sch 6 to the HA 1985 cannot be used for overage.[6] Section 156 of the Water Industry Act 1981[7] is currently being used for overage, although it was designed for environmental purposes. Most of the litigation has taken place in relation to s 84 of the LPA 1925 on the release of restrictive covenants and in general the courts have upheld the clear power of the Tribunal to remove covenants on the grounds that they are obsolete or impede practical use of the land. The jurisdiction under s 84 itself should not be used to override an overage arrangement,[8] but the courts might conclude that the whole underlying purpose of restrictive covenants since *Tulk v Moxhay*[9] has been for amenity and not for financial purposes. The conse-

---

1   [1957] 1 QB 330.
2   (1876) 3 Ch D 826. See **6.3**.
3   [1975] 1 Ch 408.
4   [1995] 1 WLR 269.
5   [1895] 1 Ch 287.
6   By reason of para 6: *R v Braintree District Council, ex parte Halls* (2000) 80 P&CR 266.
7   See **10.3.3**.
8   *Re Cornick* (1994) 68 P&CR 372.
9   (1848) 2 Ph 774.

quences of the rules allowing leaseholders to make improvements are discussed at **7.2.1**.

For many years it has been possible for the value of bare land to be held by one person and the added value by another. The lease at a ground rent discussed in Chapter 7 is one method and this principle is recognised by statute in s 15(2) of the Leasehold Reform Act 1967. Others are the profits of timber and minerals where, even though the trees or minerals are in law part of the land, their value (and the right to take that value) may belong to a different person from the landowner and that is recognised in ss 47 and 66 of the SLA 1925.

12.5   THE NATURE OF OVERAGE

The rules applied by the court in interpreting bargains between parties will depend on how the judges see the situation and, in particular, whether they consider that achieving overage is a legitimate commercial purpose or an illegitimate attempt to take advantage of an uncovenanted benefit.

This has most clearly been developed in the restrictive covenant cases. Thus, in *Ridley v Taylor*[1] Harman LJ said:

> 'it seems to me that it should be more difficult to persuade the court to exercise its discretion in leasehold than in freehold cases. In the latter the court is relaxing in favour of a freeholder's own land restrictions entered into for the benefit of the persons owning other land. In the former the land in question is the property of the covenantee who is prima facie entitled to preserve the character of his reversion.'

That suggests that a restrictive covenant is a fetter on the full ownership of the landowner. However, in *Rhone v Stephens*[2] the court considered that the correct interpretation was that the landowner had never acquired certain rights in the first place.

Overage may be seen either as security or as a property right or sometimes as a mere hope (or *spes*). In the case of security, it is seen as an infringement (legitimate or not) on the rights of a landowner and the natural tendency of the court to protect the rights of landowners will prevail. If, on the other hand, it is seen as a form of joint ownership (particularly ownership of development value), the same tendency of the court will work to uphold overage rights.

In this context, the idea of 'property' is one that is developing rapidly at present.[3] It appears from this that anything that has commercial value, and

---

1   [1965] 1 WLR 611 at 617.
2   [1994] 2 AC 310. See **4.1**.
3   *Swift v Dairywise Farms Ltd* [2000] 1 All ER 320; *Official Receiver v Environment Agency* [1999] 46 EG 187; *Bater v Greenwich London Borough Council* [2000] L&TR 1; and *Melville v Inland Revenue Commissioners* [2000] STC 628.

particularly anything that is capable of being transferred, can be property. In the words of Lord Wilberforce in *National Provincial Bank Limited v Ainsworth*:[1]

> 'it must be definable, identifiable by third parties, capable in its nature of assumption by third parties, and have some degree of permanence or stability.'

12.5.1 Equitable nature of overage

At **9.8.3** it was suggested that overage could be a contingent future interest. Such an interest is a well-recognised type of property of an intangible nature. Overage is contingent because it depends on a contingency such as the grant of planning consent. It is future because that has not yet occurred. It is an interest because it is not an estate in land. Prior to 1925, certain types of contingent future interest could exist as legal interests or future estates although they were subject to very tight restrictions developed in the Middle Ages. Since 1925, they have only been capable of subsisting as equitable interests. That does mean that in certain cases they are capable of being overreached on a sale, but apart from that it does not affect their subsistence as rights of property.[2]

In *Marren v Ingles*,[3] the House of Lords had to consider a similar type of right in relation to shares. Lord Fraser of Tullybelton said:

> 'The first question is whether the right to half of the profit is properly to be regarded as a separate asset, or simply as a deferred part of the price of the shareholdings. In my opinion the former view is correct. "Asset" is defined in s 22(1)[4] in the widest terms to mean all forms of property and it has been construed accordingly – see *O'Brien v Bensons Hosiery (Holdings) Limited*[5] – by my noble and learned friend Lord Russell of Killowen. It is therefore apt to include the incorporeal right to money's worth which was part of the consideration given for the shareholdings in 1970. The vendors could have disposed of the right at any time after 15 September 1970 by selling it or giving it away and assigning it.'

Going on from there, in relation to land it may not only be an incorporeal right but also an incorporeal hereditament. In s 205(1)(ix) of the LPA 1925, 'hereditament' means any real property which on an intestacy occurring before the commencement of the Act might have devolved on an heir. Certain types of overage are clearly hereditaments, for example easements, ransom strips and (possibly) freehold mortgages. The significance of that is that an incorporeal hereditament is land for the purposes of the LPA 1925 and under s 52 a conveyance of land has to be by deed.

---

1   [1965] AC 1175.
2   See the words of Jessel MR in *London and South Western Railway Co v Gomm* (1882) 20 Ch D 562, quoted at **8.5**.
3   [1980] 1 WLR 983.
4   Of the Finance Act 1965, now s 21(1) of the Taxation of Chargeable Gains Act 1992.
5   [1980] AC 562.

12.5.2 Equitable nature of security

Whether or not overage itself considered as a separate right is legal or equitable, the means of security taken to protect it will either be equitable in its nature or governed by equitable principles.

(1) A promise to pay is a contractual right enforceable at common law but, to the extent that it may create an equitable chose in action and therefore s 136 of the LPA 1925 does not apply, equitable rules will govern it. In particular, this may well apply to negative overage where there is a contract in the form that 'if I obtain value from the release of a restrictive covenant benefiting my retained land, then I will share part of that value with you'. Furthermore, the issues relating to penalties would be governed by equitable rules.

(2) A positive covenant (simply considered as such and without special rules) is also enforceable at common law, but covenants by themselves are of little more value than promises and may be less so than contractual arrangements:
   (a) a rentcharge creates a legal interest, but as explained at **3.2**, it is not suitable for overage,
   (b) a right of re-entry again exists at common law, but is subject to the equitable jurisdiction relieving from forfeiture,[1] and
   (c) a restriction on the Register is largely a creature of statute, but the examples given in the LRR 1925[2] are designed to protect either directly equitable interests arising under trusts or the administration of an estate or rights governed by the Chancery jurisdiction such as charities.

(3) To the extent that an arrangement associated with a positive covenant creates a conditional fee then the interest of the landowner is legal, but to the extent that it creates a determinable fee then the interests of both landowner and overage owner are equitable.

(4) A restrictive covenant is entirely equitable in nature.

(5) A legal charge by itself is a legal interest, but as an agreement to grant a mortgage in the future must always be equitable,[3] it is likely that an existing charge to cover a future liability will also be governed by equitable rules. In any event, equity has played a large part in relation to mortgages, for example the rules relating to clogs, but further than that the interest of the landowner was until 1925 an equitable one and is still normally described as an equity of redemption.

---

1 *Shiloh Spinners v Harding* [1973] AC 691.
2 Forms 9–12D in Sch 2.
3 *Swiss Bank Corporation v Lloyds Bank Limited* [1982] AC 584.

(6) A ransom strip is a legal right and other interests such as easements exist at common law. However, infringements of those rights would normally only give rise to a claim for nominal damages and the importance of them depends on being able to claim an injunction. The injunctive jurisdiction is entirely equitable.

(7) A company is the creature of statute and the structure itself exists at common law, but the court has a wide equitable jurisdiction to decide disputes between shareholders.

(8) The trust is entirely a matter of equity.

(9) A lease is capable of existing as a legal estate except in the case of equitable leases. However, here again the equitable jurisdiction is involved, for example in giving relief against forfeiture, and the power to enforce covenants will again depend on the equitable injunctive jurisdiction.

Therefore, it will be seen that the equitable jurisdiction is involved closely in all types of security for overage. In consequence, the rules of equity will apply so that, for example, a person seeking the support of a court of equitable jurisdiction will himself need to demonstrate that he has acted in an equitable manner. The court has a considerable discretion and, although that discretion has to be exercised in accordance with rules of law, it is available to an extent that would not apply in relation to strict common law rights.

12.5.3 Completion of incomplete overage

If overage is recognised as a right distinct from its means of security, then equity would be able to complete a transaction for value (but not a gift) where the formalities are incomplete. If there is an assignment of overage rights (eg as part of the transfer of the assets of a company on sale of its business or by a liquidator) it may happen that the particular security is overlooked. If that is by positive covenant or charge, a court of equitable jurisdiction can compel an assignment subsequently. If the security is linked to land, such as a restrictive covenant or an easement, and the land itself is not transferred, then transfer of overage can be more difficult. Equity may still compel the owner of the retained land to hold any overage proceeds in trust for the buyer. If, however, the land is later transferred to a bona fide purchaser of the legal estate without notice of the overage, then the overage will be overreached. The solution (if the omission is noted in time) may be a caution on the Register or, if the land is unregistered, against first registration, assuming that a caution against first registration can constitute notice.

Equity looks at the substance not the form of a transaction, and if the substance is the transfer of overage, equity is able to protect the rights and ensure a wrong does not go without remedy.

Equitable estoppel

This is demonstrated by the cases on equitable estoppel. These complement overage. In overage, the imposer transfers title to the land to the granter and then agrees for a payment if the land later increases in value. In equitable estoppel cases the original owner retains title but the other party is entitled to value or a right of occupation or some other claim as the result of an increase in value.

The classic statement is by Lord Kingsdown in *Ramsden v Dyson*:[1]

> 'The rule of law applicable to the case appears to me to be this: If a man, under a verbal agreement with a landlord for a certain interest in land, or, what amounts to the same thing, under an expectation, created or encouraged by the landlord, that he shall have a certain interest, takes possession of the land, with the consent of the landlord, and upon the faith of such promise or expectation, with the knowledge of the landlord, and without objection by him, lays out money upon the land, a Court of equity will compel the landlord to give effect to such promise or expectation.'

That principle has been widened to a number of other situations.[2] The court may order a conveyance of the land.[3] Where appropriate, the court may order a sale of the land at its unimproved value.[4] It may order that to give effect to a joint development venture the land be held on trust and the non-owning party be given a share in the equity to participate in profits.[5] The court can order the grant of a lease[6] or an easement[7] or various types of licence[8] or order the purchase of land.[9]

In those cases, the court grants a remedy where one person, having no existing rights, improves the land of another or in some other way acts in such a way that it is equitable that the other should grant or take an interest in land. The typical situation is of adding value by doing works. The same principle could apply to other increases in value, for example by obtaining planning consent,

---

1   (1866) LR 1HL 129 in a dissenting speech which is taken to state the law.
2   See *Plimmer v Mayor of Wellington* (1884) 9 App Cas 699; *Dillwyn v Llewellyn* (1862) 4 De GF&J 517; and *Burrows & Burrows v Sharp* (1991) 23 HLR 82.
3   *Pascoe v Turner* [1979] 1 WLR 431; *Voyce v Voyce* (1991) 62 P&CR 290; and *Lim Teng Huan v Ang Swee Chuan* [1992] 1 WLR 113, (1992) 64 P&CR 233.
4   *Duke of Beaufort v Patrick* (1853) 17 Beav 60, where owners of land were required to convey land developed as a canal. The price was to be ascertained at agricultural value, disregarding income from canal tolls. The judge considered that if the parties did not agree he could fix a price.
5   *Holiday Inns Inc v Broadhead* (1974) 232 EG 951. See below.
6   *Stilles v Cowper* (1748) 3 Atk 692; and *Yaxley v Gotts* [2000] All ER 711.
7   *Ward v Kirkland* [1967] Ch 194; *ER Ives Investment Ltd v High* [1967] 2 QB 379; and *Crabb v Arun DC* [1976] Ch 179.
8   *Plimmer v Mayor of Wellington* (1884) 9 App Cas 699; *Inwards v Baker* [1965] 2 QB 29; and *Re Sharpe* [1980] 1 WLR 219.
9   *Salvation Army Trustee Co Ltd v West Yorkshire Metropolitan County Council* (1981) 41 P&CR 179.

and Parliament has moved some way to recognising this in s 21 of the ATA 1995. Such cases can give rise to a charge on the land.[1]

These principles as applied to overage cover the situation where the imposer retains title and the granter does not get it, but the converse should also be true. If the bargain is that the granter obtains title on the basis that it will give the imposer a share of the proceeds, that should give the court power to complete any incomplete aspect by awarding overage security.[2]

Constructive (or resulting) trusts

The issues have also been explored in cases concerning constructive trusts. In the context of overage, it may be better to refer to resulting trusts because title is originally provided by the imposer and equity may impose a trust for its benefit.

In *Gissing v Gissing*:[3]

> 'A resulting, implied or constructive trust – and it is unnecessary for present purposes to distinguish between these three classes of trust – is created by a transaction between the trustee and the cestui que trust in connection with the acquisition by the trustee of a legal estate in land, whenever the trustee has so conducted himself that it would be inequitable to allow him to deny to the cestui que trust a beneficial interest in the land acquired. And he will be held so to have conducted himself if by his words or conduct he has induced the cestui que trust to act to his own detriment in the reasonable belief that by so acting he was acquiring a beneficial interest in the land.'

In *Yaxley v Gotts*,[4] Robert Walker LJ cited the words of Millett LJ in *Paragon Finance v Thackerar*[5] on the distinction between constructive trusts and proprietary estoppel:

> 'Plainly there are large areas where the two concepts do not overlap ... But in the area of a joint enterprise for the acquisition of land (which may be, but is not necessarily, the matrimonial home) the two concepts coincide.'

Those words were cited in *Banner Homes plc v Luff Developments Ltd*,[6] which concerned the acquisition of land for a joint venture where the party which took title then tried to deny any share in development value to the other party. The case was decided by reference to a number of cases going back to 1878[7]

---

1   *Unity Joint Stock Mutual Banking Association v King* (1858) 25 Beav 72; and *Raffaele v Raffaele* [1962] WAR 238.

2   See *Holiday Inns Inc v Broadhead* (1974) 232 EG 951.

3   [1971] AC 886 at 905.

4   [2000] All ER 711.

5   [1999] 1 All ER 400.

6   [2000] 2 WLR 772.

7   *Chattock v Muller* (1878) 8 Ch D 177; *Pallant v Morgan* [1953] Ch 43; *Holiday Inns v Broadhead* (1974) 232 EG 951; *Time Products Ltd v Combined English Stores Ltd* (1974) unreported, 2 December; and *Island Holdings v Birchington Engineering Ltd* (1981), unreported, 7 July.

and the claimant was awarded a share in the property. Chadwick LJ cited the words of Megarry J in *Holiday Inns v Broadhead*:[1]

> 'It seems to me that if A and B agree that A shall acquire some specific property for the joint benefit of A and B on terms yet to be agreed, and B, in reliance on A's agreement, is thereby induced to refrain from attempting to acquire the property, equity ought not to permit A, when he acquires the property, to insist on retaining the whole benefit for himself to the exclusion of B. If on the facts it would be inequitable for the quantum of B's interest to be a moiety, I do not doubt that equity could determine what justice required the quantum to be; but where the facts suggest no other basis, then there should be equality.'

In principle, this could apply where A acquires the land from B rather than from a stranger.

However, in *Banner Homes plc v Luff Developments Ltd*, Chadwick LJ went on to say:

> 'The *Pallant v Morgan* equity does not seek to give effect to the parties' bargain, still less to make for them some bargain which they have not themselves made, as the cases to which I have referred make clear. The equity is invoked where the defendant has acquired property in circumstances where it would be inequitable to allow him to treat it as his own; and where, because it would be inequitable to allow him to treat the property as his own, it is necessary to impose on him the obligations of a trustee in relation to it. It is invoked because there is no bargain which is capable of being enforced; if there were an enforceable bargain there would have been no need for equity to intervene in the way that it has done in the cases to which I have referred.'

Machinery

Where there is a bargain, equity can give effect to it under other principles. The normal remedies of specific performance, injunction and damages are available where there is a concluded agreement. But what of the situation where the parties have agreed that overage should exist, have agreed the trigger event and the calculation of the payment but have not agreed the mechanism, such as charge, positive covenant or other method? If, as has been argued, the true nature of overage is a contingent future interest, and as since 1925 such interests can subsist only behind a trust, the court has a jurisdiction to perfect the trust where the party claiming the court's assistance is not a volunteer but has given value.

Simply seen as a commercial bargain, the transaction may be completed by the court. In *Sudbrook Trading Estate v Eggleton*,[2] a landlord had granted a tenant an option to purchase the freehold (the primary obligation) at a price to be determined by valuation and, as the court found, the parties were obliged to appoint valuers to agree the value (the secondary obligation). The landlord

---

1   In the preliminary interlocutory application (1969) unreported, 19 December.
2   [1983] 1 AC 444.

refused to appoint a valuer and claimed that the performance of the contract was thereby impossible.

The House of Lords found for the tenant. Lord Diplock said:[1]

> 'The real issue is whether the court has jurisdiction to enforce the lessors' primary obligation under the contract to convey the fee simple by decreeing specific performance of that primary obligation, or whether its jurisdiction is limited to enforcing the secondary obligation arising on failure to fulfil that primary obligation, by awarding the lessees damages to an amount equivalent to the monetary loss they have sustained by their inability to acquire the fee simple at a fair and reasonable price, ie for what the fee simple was worth. Since if they do not acquire the fee simple they will not have to pay that price, the damages for loss of such a bargain would be negligible and, as in most cases of breach of contract for the sale of land at a market price by refusal to convey it, would constitute a wholly inadequate and unjust remedy for the breach.'

The House went on to find that the procedure for the appointment of valuers was merely machinery to carry out the primary obligation and held that the court could determine the price.

In *Attorney-General v Blake*,[2] the House of Lords took the law a step further. The case itself concerned a claim by the Crown for royalties due from a publisher to Blake for a book which he had written contrary both to the Official Secrets Act 1911 and to the terms of his employment contract as a member of the security services. The House held that the Crown was not limited to the ordinary measure of damages in tort or contract (which reflect the loss of the claimant) but could claim the whole proceeds generated by a breach of contract. The case was decided on general principles of law and was not restricted to the special position of the Crown.

It must follow that in an overage case the court would be able to award a proper proportion of the proceeds or profit received by the landowner. The House discussed *Wrotham Park*,[3] *Jaggard*[4] and *Bracewell*[5] (which were approved) and *Bredero*[6] (which was criticised). The award of 5 per cent of the developers' profit in *Wrotham Park* was specifically approved.

It is a substantial further step from that to the court imposing a specific method of overage, but having regard to the wide discretion available in cases of equitable estoppel, the court must have the power to grant such an interest as would enable overage to be secured.

---

1   At p 478.
2   [2000] 3 WLR 625.
3   *Wrotham Park Settled Estates v Hertsmere Borough Council* [1993] 2 EGLR 15.
4   *Jaggard v Sawyer* [1995] 1 WLR 269.
5   *Bracewell v Appleby* [1975] 1 Ch 408.
6   *Surrey County Council v Bredero Homes Limited* [1993] 1 WLR 1361.

12.6　TREATMENT OF OVERAGE RIGHTS

As mentioned above, overage can be seen either in the light of security or in the light of joint ownership. In broad terms, arrangements such as a secured promise (eg by a guarantee), a covenant (either positive or restrictive) or a charge are seen as security. Arrangements such as a ransom strip or a landlord and tenant structure are seen as conferring on the overage owner a right of property and, therefore, the land is owned partly by it and partly by the landowner. In a company structure, the shareholder owns the shares, although he has no direct interest in the land of the company. Since the coming into force of the TLATA 1996, a beneficiary under a trust has a proprietary interest in land, although one liable to be overreached.

The object of the parties is usually that current use value will belong to the landowner completely and the development value will either belong entirely to the overage owner or, more usually, will be divided between them.

The overage owner has a present interest in the development value and a contingent future interest is seen as an existing right of property, not as something that could arise in the future. Its present *value* may be negligible if the prospect of development is remote and uncertain, but that does not affect the fact that it is a present *right* of property. The law regards such a right as an existing right of property. Its enjoyment may be in the future, or may never occur, but the right itself is a present one. When property lawyers refer to the future, they refer not to the time a right comes into existence but to the time that right will confer possession of land or receipt of capital or income derived from it.

Valuing such a right can be a difficult exercise. If someone has a definite right to receive a definite sum in a definite period of time, then that right can be valued by reference to expected rates of interest and (sometimes) to the burden of taxation in the meantime. Commercially published valuation tables and programs are available to help professional valuers and actuaries.

More difficulties arise in allowing for the uncertainties in overage. The time of payment will depend on a number of factors, most notably the date of the trigger event and the likelihood of its occurring. There will also be uncertainty as to the actual receipts if these represent a proportion of sale proceeds or valuation at a future date. Nevertheless, it is normally possible for a valuer to allow for these uncertainties in estimating the current value of the overage rights.

There is limited experience in this type of valuation, but 'hope value' often has to be taken into account when property is sold on the market and it can be a relevant factor in other types of valuation, for example for inheritance tax if an individual dies.[1] For example, the Inland Revenue may take the view that the

1　*Re Sutherland* [1963] AC 235.

owner of a house with a large garden could obtain planning consent for an additional house and may require that to be reflected in the current valuation for tax.

There is also experience of valuation in relation to derivative rights in other areas of the law. The calculation of the price to take account of currency fluctuation, the supply and price of commodities and future movements in interest rates is a well-established area and, although the very considerable uncertainties relating to planning consent make overage in development land unsuitable as a derivative itself, the approach is still there.

In all of these cases, therefore, it is well recognised that there can be a present valuation of future uncertainties. In principle, this is no different from the valuation adopted by insurance companies and reversionary companies when advancing money on contingent future interests in family arrangements which was very common in the nineteenth century. For example, if there are two brothers, the younger brother might have the possibility of inheriting a life estate in the family property if he survived his older brother (and perhaps if that older brother had no children). It was quite common for money to be lent on the security of such interests even though they might never come into possession and some investors were even prepared to buy them up, although at a considerable discount from asset value.

12.7 SOURCES OF DIFFICULTIES

In view of what I have said above, it is not immediately obvious why overage should present the complications which I discussed earlier in this book. The ideas are familiar and the intentions of the parties are clear. Nevertheless, the law seems to place a great many obstacles in the way of parties.

None of the methods of securing overage is free of complications. In general, promises and covenants can be enforced only against the party who gives them. Although there are devices to make positive covenants binding on future owners, these are subject to numerous restrictions and qualifications. A restrictive covenant is designed for amenity and is subject to variation by the Lands Tribunal. A mortgage suffers from problems of priority and possibly a clog on the equity. Ransom strips are vulnerable to the court refusing to grant an injunction. In general, landlord and tenant arrangements work well (they are a recognised form of divided ownership), but there is wide scope for any landlord's veto over improvements to be overridden under statutory provisions and Parliament has extended the rights of tenants (seen as the 'real owners') to buy out their landlords.[1] Vehicles are unsatisfactory because they

---

1   See Chapter 7 generally.

do not give the overage owner a direct interest in the land itself and in the case of both companies and trusts those rights can be overridden on liquidation or sale.

Why should these problems have occurred in the law? On the face of it, it looks like a coincidence. Each separate method of securing overage has problems, but those problems are specific to that method. Nevertheless, the issues do raise wider questions of policy which will have been present in the minds of judges who decided specific cases.

The law in general protects what is described as 'freedom of disposition', but this has two contrasting meanings. Sometimes it is taken to mean freedom of contract under which parties are free to make any bargain they wish and to bind their successors, provided the bargain does not infringe against the general law and it does not cause unlawful injury to any third party. On the other hand, the expression can also apply to freedom of the present landowner to dispose of its land without control by any previous owner. In this case, it is more correctly seen as freedom from incumbrances.

In previous centuries the courts' experience with these conflicting aims was worked out through family arrangements including wills and entails. On the one hand, there was the freedom of the present landowner to deal with his property as he wished and control the extent to which it could be passed down among his descendants for generations to come. On the other hand, there was the policy of the law in protecting the rights of the landowner for the time being from being ruled by an ancestor from the grave. Although policy fluctuated over the centuries, the general development of the law was to favour the landowner for the time being. It can be very difficult for someone making arrangements under his will to foresee all that might happen over the next century and there can be good compelling reasons for his descendants to wish to act inconsistently with the terms of that will. That policy has been recognised both by the courts and by Parliament and in general represents the law.

To the extent that overage rights are an infringement on the freedom of the current landowner to deal with property, they will run up against that principle. At the present time, commercial considerations are given the importance that previous generations gave to family arrangements, but the basic policy of the law must always be to protect the freedom of the market and the freedom of parties to deal with their property. To the extent that a person unconnected with the present owner can interfere with that freedom by controlling it through an overage mechanism, the courts will discourage such control. In general, it is considered that the person who owns the land itself is best placed to decide what is to be done with that land. It is for this reason that the law has not only controlled family arrangements such as entails and strict settlements, but also has put limits on clogs and other restrictions by means of mortgage, has tightly controlled the operation of options and has prohibited perpetually renewable leases. This policy of the law goes back at least to *Quia Emptores* 1290 and has been reinforced frequently since that time.

This could be understood by considering the position of a landowner perhaps 20 or 30 years after the original overage arrangements were made. It owns some land which has now become ripe for development. It applies for planning consent and spends money on realising that value only to find that at the relevant point the owner of the overage (who may be a person who has had no connection with the land for 20 years and may possibly even be a successor of that person) appears and claims a substantial proportion of the value of the land. Such an approach would always be unwelcome to a present landowner and, therefore, it can be expected that any overage arrangements will be carefully scrutinised and be subject to challenge by successive landowners.

12.8 CONTROLLING OVERAGE

Despite that consideration, it is likely that landowners will continue on sale or lease to seek to reserve overage where the payment that has been made for the land does not reflect development value to arise in the future. This then raises the question as to whether such freedom should be unfettered. The law has experience of controlling contingent future interests. This experience was developed out of the sixteenth and seventeenth centuries, when a wide variety of contingent future interests were attempted to such an extent that they were liable to cause serious problems in relation to the ownership of land. The solution reached by the court in the *Duke of Norfolk's Case*[1] was the rule against perpetuities. There had been a number of earlier examples of the rule (known as the 'old rule') developed in the Middle Ages, but which went on being refined up to the nineteenth century based on principles such as no abeyance of seisin and the rule against double possibilities, but these rules often appeared arbitrary and their scope could be uncertain and difficult to follow. Although to some extent they remained in force up until 1925, they were of little practical significance after the seventeenth century. The rule laid down in the *Duke of Norfolk's Case* as subsequently modified was that virtually any arrangement could be made provided that it must vest (either in interest or in possession or both) by a period no later than a life in being at the time of the disposition plus 21 years plus any actual pregnancy at the end of that time. Although sometimes arbitrary and substantially modified in the Perpetuities and Accumulations Act 1964, this rule was workable and gave a certainty which was acceptable to landowners.

The Law Commission has now[2] proposed the virtual abolition of the rule against perpetuities, except in relation to trusts where it is to be a fixed period

---

1 (1681) 2 Swans 454.
2 (1998) Law Com No 251.

of 150 years. That is entirely to be welcomed because the existing rule in its various forms can be arbitrary and illogical and is not suited to commercial realities. If it is not to apply to commercial overage, however, there must be some other rule or set of rules which can control the unrestrained operation of overage, otherwise there is a risk that all sorts of interests might be capable of arising at any time in the remote future.

The rule against perpetuities applies only to a limited extent to overage at present. It does not apply at all to straightforward contracts.[1] It does not apply to rent charges or to restrictions on the Register, although it does apply to rights of re-entry.[2] It does not apply to restrictive covenants.[3] It does not apply to mortgages.[4] By its nature, it does not apply to ransom strips nor does it apply where the ransom is by way of easement such as a right of way or profit such as sporting rights. In general, it does not apply to landlord and tenant arrangements although it does apply in a modified form to future leases and certain options.[5] It does apply to options in relation to freehold land and some leases,[6] but not where the option is in favour of the tenant and can be exercisable no later than the end of the term. It does not apply to companies. It does apply to trusts.

12.9 REFORM

The present law of overage is in need of reform, indeed it needs to be given a coherent form in the first place.

The law needs to apply to a situation where there is an arrangement for one person to receive extra value from land in the circumstances that have been discussed. First, the arrangement should make it clear that that is the intention and, secondly, it should satisfy certain specified legal conditions. If so, then the arrangement should be upheld by the courts. Thus, the court would not refuse an injunction even where there is a small infringement of airspace or breach of a restrictive covenant. The Lands Tribunal should not vary or release a restrictive covenant. A disposal by trustees will not overreach overage rights. A restriction on the Register will not be treated as an unlawful fetter on the right of a freeholder to sell.

It is suggested that certain principles need to be applied and these will be modified in relation to the application to both positive and negative overage:

---

1 *Walsh v Secretary of State for India* (1863) 10 HL Cas 367.
2 *Re Trustees of Hollis Hospital and Hague's Contract* [1899] 2 Ch 540.
3 *London and South Western Railway v Gomm* (1882) 20 Ch D 562 at 583, per Jessel MR.
4 *Knightsbridge Estates Trust Ltd v Byrne* [1939] 1 Ch 441.
5 Section 149 of the LPA 1925 and Sch 15, para 7(2) to the LPA 1922.
6 Section 9 of the Perpetuities and Accumulations Act 1964.

(1) there should be a clear commercial benefit even though at the time that overage is imposed it may be of negligible value on its own;

(2) the parties should be clear about their intention to create overage;

(3) the identity of the overage owner and the prospective payer should at all times be ascertainable; and

(4) in the case of positive overage, the time of the payment and the amount to be paid should be readily ascertainable at the outset by reference to a formula or the decision of an arbitrator working on clear instructions; in the case of negative overage, this is not appropriate, but it should be made clear that the maximum liability of the landowner will be ascertainable even if this is only because the development process can only be triggered by the landowner.

12.10 SOCIAL FUNCTION

Overage will only work and be acceptable to landowners, developers, investors and funders as well as to Parliament and the courts if it is seen to be fair and to perform an important and useful social and commercial function. Government policy as exemplified by the Treasury Guidelines is strongly in favour of reserving clawback.

In certain cases, overage can undoubtedly assist the sale and development of land. If there is an effective overage arrangement, it can encourage landowners to put surplus land on the market and realise current use value so that they do not have to retain the land indefinitely, perhaps in an undeveloped and unoccupied form, pending the possibility of uncertain future development.

Even within a landowning structure there can be good reason for a separation between current use value and development value and these can be linked to commercial reasons for distinguishing between a company carrying on a trade and an investment company. They attract different sources of finance and owners with different attitudes. They can also be taxed differently. For that reason, owners of land may wish to separate the ownership of current value of a piece of land and put that into one company while putting the development value in another.

Overage itself may in due course become a suitable vehicle for investment. Although at present it is not appropriate to be used as a traded derivative, particularly as each separate piece of land is unique, it may be possible for an investor to put money into overage rights. This is only likely to be worth doing where there is more than a simple contribution of cash, particularly as at the time of the initial investment the overage is unlikely to be worth very much. Where, however, it can encourage a partnership between a landowner and an overage owner to lead to the future development of land, allowing a developer more flexibility than applies under existing options, then it may be a useful economic tool.

In the end, overage will flourish only if it is seen to be important and valuable and worth developing as an effective system of law with coherent and well understood rules. That is not the position at the present time, but there are good prospects that it will be in the future.

Appendix 1

WORKED EXAMPLES

A SURPLUS FACTORY

Northern Commercial plc owns the freehold of a factory site. Technical developments and changes in the market allow it to produce its products more easily in a different place in smaller buildings. The factory is in a run-down industrial area. In the long term there are prospects for a major redevelopment, but the planning process could take 15 years. In the meantime, the company does not wish its capital to be tied up in these premises.

The property could be sold on a lease of 250 years at a premium and then a peppercorn rent. The lease should not contain an obligation to repair so that it cannot be forfeited if the buyer fails to repair, but in that case the lessee should demolish the buildings and maintain the land as an open landscaped area. As the planning process is likely to be less than 25 years, the lease can include restrictive covenants against making alterations or putting up new buildings or controlling the use. If planning consent is granted, there could be a break clause allowing the landlord to take the land back in return for a payment calculated by reference to development value or an option for the tenant to buy the freehold on a similar basis.

If the factory is unlikely to be worth mortgaging, then the freehold could be sold reserving a charge for a proportion of development value.

B CONTAMINATED INDUSTRIAL SITE

Chemical & Industrial Estates Ltd is the freeholder of an industrial estate on which various polluting activities including a chemical works and a gas works were carried on. The industry has moved away and the land needs substantial reclamation which will take many years and be very expensive, but in the long term the reclamation is likely to produce a valuable site.

The current value of the polluted site is likely to be small or even negative. Therefore, the owner will want to part with the freehold to minimise environmental liability. It could take back a charge to cover any development value, but any buyer is likely to need to raise finance on the prospect of redevelopment and so a charge is commercially unacceptable. The best solution is to take a positive covenant to pay a proportion of any uplift with a restriction on the register so that any buyer acquires the land subject to taking on the positive covenant.

An alternative might be to have the property put into the names of two specially created £100 companies, which together would hold the land as trustees. One company would belong to Chemical & Industrial Estates Ltd and the other to the buyer. The buyer would have an interest until redevelopment. If the trustees had no assets of their own, they would not be vulnerable to claims on the basis of pollution.

As Chemical & Industrial Estates Ltd itself would have been responsible for the pollution (in its capacity as landlord of the chemical works), it may not be possible for it to avoid liability altogether under the Environmental Protection Act 1990.

C FARMLAND NEAR A VILLAGE

Mr Giles is a farmer who needs to raise money to pay off the bank, to put up a new cow shed and to buy a combine harvester. He owns some fields near the local village which are detached and difficult to farm. At present the land is not allocated for building, but it could become suitable in the future.

Mr Giles will continue to own nearby land and, therefore, he could take a restrictive covenant limiting development. If the physical situation of the land allows, he could retain a ransom strip and he should either let that to the buyer, perhaps on a farm business tenancy, or ensure that he continues to occupy it himself. He might sell the surface of the land and a sufficient amount of air space to allow it to be adequately farmed, but retain ownership of all air space above that. The ransoms might be coupled with an option for the buyer to purchase the ransom land if planning consent is granted.

D LARGE GARDEN

Mrs Harris is a widow whose children have grown up. The family home is a substantial house with a large garden. A number of gardens in the area have been built on but the local authority is at present opposed to further building. She needs to move to a bungalow with a small garden.

Mrs Harris should sell the freehold of the house. She could grant a long lease of the garden at a premium with a peppercorn rent. The lease should contain covenants to cultivate and maintain the land as a garden and might even contain specific provisions as to where the lawns and flowerbeds could be. If there is likely to be only one means of access, Mrs Harris could retain ownership of the entrance, but as other gardens in the area have been developed it is possible that access might be obtained from adjoining land so that a ransom might not be suitable. If development is likely in less than 21 years then it may be preferred to sell the freehold of the garden but have an option to re-purchase the garden if planning consent is granted. The re-purchase price could be at a fraction of development value.

E   FAMILY LANDED ESTATE

Augustus Greenfield is the owner of a substantial country estate. There are death duties to pay on the death of his father and he has a divorce settlement to finance. The estate is near a motorway junction and the regional plan suggests that a new settlement could be located on his land, but the planning process is likely to take many years.

As Mr Greenfield will retain adjoining land, he could take a restrictive covenant. He may wish to take covenants in the event that development takes place to protect the amenities of his adjoining land and make sure that whatever houses are put up are suitable to the locality. However, care must be taken that all the covenants are consistent, so that he does not at the same time have a covenant that prohibits any building and then goes on to control the appearance of buildings if they are put up.

He could consider granting an option to a development company in return for an option payment if that payment is substantial enough to meet his liabilities.

If access is likely to come from the motorway junction, he could retain land immediately around the junction as a ransom strip. However, on any development a public highway will have to be built to connect to the junction and, therefore, this ransom can only be used once so that he has to be sure that the whole of the land he is selling is likely to go for development in one go.

He could consider a positive covenant and a right of re-entry. He might also wish to reserve the sporting and mineral rights, although these by themselves are unlikely to prevent development. If the land he retains is likely to be developable in the longer term, he may wish also to reserve rights of access to construct or connect to roads and services for the benefit of his retained back land.

F   SURPLUS CHARITY LAND

The Foundation of William Scholar has been established as a school for many centuries. It is the owner of some substantial Victorian school buildings which are no longer practical for modern educational needs. The building is listed, but it has potential for conversion to other uses. The Foundation needs to raise money to put up new school buildings and to form an endowment fund.

The charity should retain the freehold and grant a long lease at a premium. It will need to comply with the formalities under s 36 of the Charities Act 1993. If the existence of any overage rights means that it is granting the lease for a consideration which is less than the best it could possibly obtain, then (unless it can establish that the terms, as distinct from the price, are the best) it will need Charity Commission consent, but that should be available if a sufficient explanation is given. An alternative could be to grant a lease reserving a full market rent and then to borrow from a bank on the security of the property (and again the Charities Act formalities must be complied with or Charity Commission consent obtained) and use the rental income to service the bank loan so that there will be no net cost to the charity. The occupier will need to spend money on converting the buildings to its own use and, therefore, it will need to recover the investment so that the lease will have to be sufficiently long for it to do so. Thus, if there is development potential, the charity will need to include a break clause subject to the payment of compensation for a proportion of the value added by the tenant. Alternatively, there could be an equity sharing lease under which if the building was converted and sub-let that would be reflected in the rent under the headlease.

G   SHORT-TERM LEISURE DEVELOPMENT

The North Barset District Council is proposing to make an arrangement for a short-term sports arena with a local charity. The buildings are designed to last for 15 years after which it is likely that other land will become available for permanent sports facilities. The Council is under a duty to realise the best value. The body intending to erect the arena is a local charity which needs to be sure of recouping its investment, but has no objection to the Council retaining additional value.

As the buildings have only a short life, they should be kept safe and in good order during that time but there should be no obligation to repair them after that. The solution, therefore, would be a lease with a limited repairing clause. Once the buildings are no longer fit for practical use, the charity lessee should be allowed to demolish them, but that should not involve termination of the lease. There should be a restricted use clause so that the Council can control any alternative use and there might be a break clause for the Council subject to paying compensation to the charity which might be sufficient to enable it to continue its activities elsewhere.

H   GOVERNMENT LAND

The Ministry of Agriculture owns an experimental farm which it has decided is surplus to government requirements. The farm is intended to continue in use for research purposes, but the Ministry considers that there are long-term prospects that if the research ceases the land might be suitable for housing development.

The most likely form is a sale of the freehold with a positive covenant to pay a proportion of any uplift in value. The government normally requires this to be paid when the value accrues on the grant of planning consent although it may sometimes be persuaded to accept that the uplift should only be paid when the owner realises that either on sale or implementation of the consent.

As an alternative, the land might be put into a company which is then privatised by selling its shares. The government might retain a golden share in the company which enables it to a special payment if development materialises.

I PERSONAL PLANNING CONSENT

Mr Green owns a site on the edge of an industrial estate. A local company, Dale Furniture Ltd, has obtained planning consent limited to that company with very tight conditions. It is prepared to buy the site from Mr Green, but only at a price that reflects its very tight use. Mr Green considers that there is a long-term chance that the planning restrictions will be relaxed and the value increased.

If Mr Green continues to own land and, particularly, if he owns the roads in the industrial estate, he could use this as a ransom and grant a right of way limited to the use. As the planning consent is personal, the site has a very limited market value because a buyer could not itself occupy the site but could only let it back to Dale Furniture Ltd. Therefore, Mr Green might take a charge over the land to protect development value which would automatically secure any increase if the planning restriction is released. Another possibility could be to set up a jointly owned company, giving Dale Furniture Ltd the right to occupy but giving Mr Green a right to a special dividend if the value increases.

J SALE AND LEASEBACK

Retail Sports Ltd owns and occupies a shop in Oldborough town centre. It needs to sell the freehold to finance expansion and it will take a lease back to stay in occupation. Oldborough District Council has started discussions on a major town centre redevelopment likely to take 15 years to carry out. The shop will be an important element in that and unlock access to a new shopping centre.

The lease should be a long one, perhaps for 125 years or more. The buyer will need to protect its investment in the buildings by including repairing obligations but there should be a provision allowing redevelopment with the consent of the buyer/freeholder, such consent not to be unreasonably withheld. The resulting development value should be reflected in some increase in the rent, but allowing Retail Sports Ltd to retain part of the benefit and the lease should be freely assignable. There could be an option for Retail Sports Ltd to re-purchase the freehold for a price equal to the total of the current use value at the time the option is exercised, plus a proportion of the development value.

K   FUTURE VARIATION OF PLANNING CONSENT

Mr Brown has obtained planning consent for a site for 15 houses. He has agreed terms with Smallscale Homes Ltd, which expects to sell them for £90,000 each. Mr Brown thinks Smallscale may be able to redesign the layout and get consent for another two or three houses and he thinks prices will go up in the 18 months the development will take.

As this is a very short-term arrangement, Mr Brown may be prepared to take a personal promise from Smallscale Homes Ltd if he can be satisfied that it will remain solvent. As there is a risk that it might not, Mr Brown could ask that the solicitor acting for Smallscale Homes Ltd (provided the solicitor is duly authorised by any bank or other lender) give an undertaking to pay out of the proceeds of sale of any houses for more than £90,000 a proportion of the extra value. The number of houses could be limited by restrictive covenant, but again as this would have to be released, it may be better to cover this by an undertaking or perhaps by a charge. If the amount of the extra payment is fixed or cannot exceed a certain maximum, then it may be possible to obtain a guarantee from the bank (particularly if the bank is lending in any event and therefore will be secured on the land) provided that Smallscale Homes is prepared to pay the fee for the guarantee. If lending comes from some other body, it might be possible for Mr Brown to take a sub-charge on the charge for any overage.

L   SECTION 106 CONTROL

The Rural Estate Company has arranged a sale of land with consent for 30 houses. The local planning authority will require an area of 2 acres to be set apart for a park under a s 106 agreement and handed over free of charge to the parish council to manage. The Company considers that in 20 years' time other land (some of which may be provided by it) will become available for building and other provision for public open space will be available. If so the park will become surplus and available for building.

The best option for the Rural Estate Company is to retain the freehold and grant a long lease to the parish council for, say, 150 years, subject to tight covenants with a provision to terminate if the land is used for any purpose other than a park. If the change of use were to occur more than 25 years in the future, there is a risk of the Lands Tribunal releasing the covenant under s 84 of the LPA 1925 but the Tribunal may not give a release if that would undermine a bargain. If the Rural Estate Company has retained land, it could take a restrictive covenant. In theory, it could take a charge for development value as the parish council is unlikely to wish to sell but the council may be unwilling to accept land subject to a charge. However, there could be a right of re-entry if the covenant is broken.

M POSSIBLE SKYSCRAPER

Financial Estates Ltd owns two adjoining buildings in a city centre. One is surplus to its needs and it wishes to sell for the best price. It is possible that in a few years consent might be given for a tall building, which would therefore need deep piled foundations. Financial Estates Ltd would like to share in any uplift in value from the redevelopment.

The simplest course would be for Financial Estates Ltd to sell the surplus building and to retain the air space above the building and the subsoil beneath the existing foundations. There might be an option for the buyer to purchase the air space and subsoil if necessary, although such an option can only exist for 21 years. As Financial Estates Ltd retains an adjoining building, it could take a restrictive covenant, but if it then needed to sell the retained building, it would need to have a special arrangement with the buyer of that building so that Financial Estates Ltd would get the benefit of the covenant on the first building to go and that may be unduly complex. Having regard to *Shiloh Spinners v Harding* [1973] AC 691, it may be possible to reserve a right of re-entry in this case, but if there were genuine independent redevelopment as distinct from a deliberate breach of any covenant, the court might give relief against re-entry on terms unacceptable to Financial Estates Ltd.

N LANDSCAPING

Green Farms Ltd has a small farm on the edge of an expanding business park. Over the years it has sold off plots for offices and it is now negotiating with Intercom Bank for a new regional centre. The office is high prestige and is to be surrounded by a wide landscaped area. Green Farms Ltd expects that in the medium term the bank may need additional office space.

If Intercom Bank is likely to be in existence for many years, it may be sufficient for the bank to promise to pay any uplift in value if it builds additional space on the landscape area. As Green Farms Ltd has adjoining land, it could take a restrictive covenant, but as it has clearly been selling off plots it might eventually find it had no land left to benefit. Possibly, Intercom Bank would purchase the freehold of the new office but simply have a lease (with landscaping obligations) on the landscaped area.

O FAMILY DIVISION

Mr Jones died aged 95 leaving his farm to his five great grandchildren in equal shares. One of them is a competent farmer and wishes to farm and is prepared to pay a rent to his cousins. Two of them wish to keep ownership of their shares as an investment in return for rent, but the other two wish to realise the value of their inheritance. They consider that part of the farm on the edge of the village could obtain planning consent in 10 or 15 years. The rest of the farm is further away in an area of outstanding natural beauty and planning consent is extremely unlikely. They would like any value from development to come to them or their children.

The family could establish a trust of land under which the two who want to realise value have a small interest which would mature into a significant interest only if planning consent is granted and the value increases.

The immediate occupation could be dealt with by way of a lease from the trust to the farmer, but an alternative is to use s 13 of the TLATA 1996, which allows provision for payment by way of compensation to a beneficiary who is not in occupation. In the case of those who realise their value, that payment could be triggered only if planning consent is granted or if the land is sold. At present, the trust could last for 80 years or in this context it might be preferable to limit it to the lifetime of all the existing beneficiaries with an additional period of 21 years on top.

Appendix 2

PRECEDENTS AND DRAFTING

1	PROMISE TO PAY AND POSITIVE COVENANT	244
Form 1.1	Positive covenant triggered by planning consent	244
Form 1.2(1)	Positive covenant by reference to disposal	249
Form 1.2(2)	Modification for allowable expenditure	255
Form 1.3	Restriction on the Register	257
Form 1.4	Deed of Covenant	257
Form 1.5	Valuation	259
Form 1.6	Re-entry	260
2	RESTRICTIVE COVENANT	260
Form 2	Restrictive covenant	261
3	CHARGE	261
Form 3	Deed of Charge	262
4	RANSOMS	263
Form 4.1	Airspace	263
Form 4.2	Top floor of office block	263
Form 4.3	Right of way	263
5	LEASEHOLD	264
Form 5.1	Negative overage lease at a premium	264
Form 5.2	Payment under lease	269
6	OPTIONS	270
Form 6.1	Option to acquire ransom, or freehold of lease or take release of right of way	270
Form 6.2	Reverse option	271
7	EXCESS PAYMENT ON SALE	272
Form 7.1	Excess payment	272
Form 7.2	Security	273
Form 7.2(1)	Equitable charge	274
Form 7.2(2)	Restriction on Register	274
Form 7.2(3)	Solicitor's undertaking	274
Form 7.2(4)	Costs	· 275

All precedents need to be treated with care and that is particularly true of those that follow. Although they are based on some that have been in use for some years, they are untested in court and challenges should be made both to the underlying principles and to the details of drafting. Each overage situation is unique and therefore any form must be adapted to the particular situation, parties and circumstances. The forms cannot cover all possible eventualities and the drafter will need to look out for potential problems and adapt the forms to allow for them. Therefore, the forms should not simply be used as they stand. The drafter of an overage structure should start with a blank sheet of paper or screen; however, parts of some of the forms may be helpful.

1　PROMISE TO PAY AND POSITIVE COVENANT

These can be taken together for drafting purposes. The form of covenant set out below can be converted to a simple contractual promise without security.

The precedents comprise:

(a)　a positive covenant incorporating a set of definitions, which will need to be adapted to particular circumstances and bargains and are designed for overage to accrue on the grant of planning consent (Form 1.1) with an alternative for a disposal (Form 1.2(1)) and a modification for allowable expenditure (Form 1.2(2));

(b)　a restriction on the Register (Form 1.3) with the deed of covenant on change of ownership (Form 1.4);

(c)　a charge to secure the payment (which can be adapted from Form 3);

(d)　a valuation clause (Form 1.5);

(e)　a re-entry clause (Form 1.6).

Form 1.1(1)　Positive covenant triggered by planning consent

This form is suitable where the trigger is to be the uplift in value of the overage land by the commencement of development or disposal following grant of planning consent. The overage payment is determined by valuation at that time and the valuer will take into account issues such as the costs associated with planning agreements, ransoms of third parties, costs of decontamination and construction, and the timing and nature of any eventual return, including changes in the market between the planning consent and the ultimate disposal. Such a valuation is likely to be cautious and the imposer may prefer to seek a payment by reference to cash realisation, but that has its own issues as indicated in the notes to Form 1.2. Using actual disposals and expenditure can in practice be more complicated than using a valuation basis.

This form can be adapted to apply on grant of planning consent unaccompanied by any disposal.

Definitions and interpretation

In this Deed the following expressions have the following meanings:

Current use value
in relation to a given **trigger date** means the **open market value** of the **relevant land** at that date on the basis that
(i) it is not lawful to change the state or use of the **relevant land** by carrying out on it any **material development** from that existing immediately before the **trigger date**, and
(ii) that any unlawful **development** of the **relevant land** that has occurred is ignored, and
(iii) on the assumption (whether or not such be the case) that the **relevant land** is free from encumbrances (save for any easements or covenants affecting the same at the date of this Deed [or granted under this Transfer]) and the **relevant land** is to be sold with vacant possession.

Development
has the meaning given to it by section 55 of of the Town and Country Planning Act 1990.

Development value
means the difference between the **enhanced value** and the **current use value** of any land in question.

Disposal
is construed widely and includes a lease or grant of easement.

Enhanced value
of the **relevant land** at a given time means:
(i) if **planning permission** has been granted for the **material development** in question the **open market value** of the **relevant land** with the benefit of that **planning permission**.
(ii) If **planning permission** for the **material development** in question is required but has not been obtained the **open market value** of the **relevant land** on the assumption that **planning permission** for the **material development** in question had been granted.

(iii) In both cases the **relevant land** being valued on the assumption (whether or not such be the case) that it is free from encumbrances (save for any easements or covenants affecting the same at the date hereof [or granted under this Transfer]) and the **relevant land** is to be sold with vacant possession.

Excepted disposal   means one or more of the following:

(a) any mortgage or charge of the **overage land** or any part of it;

(b) the granting of a licence or a tenancy in respect of the **overage land** or any part of it on terms which (under the law prevailing at the time) would entitle the owner of the **overage land** without obtaining any court order and without taking any steps save for service of notice on the occupant to vacant possession not later than 23 months from the date of such grant;

(c) the granting of an easement over or the giving of a covenant affecting any part of the **overage land** which in either case does not materially affect the value of it.

Material development   means any **development** of the **relevant land** for which **planning permission** is required (other than **development** for which at the relevant time **planning permission** has been granted by means of a **development** order which comes within the scope of section 59(2)(a) of the Town and Country Planning Act 1990) which would when implemented increase the value of the **relevant land** by more than 5 per cent of its **current use value** but does not include any **development** consisting solely of the laying of pipes cables or other media for the purposes of meeting statutory obligations in relation to the supply of gas, water, electricity or other services to the general public.[1]

Open market value
means the best price at which the sale of the land in question might reasonably be expected to have been completed unconditionally for cash consideration on the date in question assuming:
(a) a willing vendor and a willing purchaser;
(b) that prior to the date of valuation there had been a reasonable period (having regard to the nature of the land in question and the state of the market) for the proper marketing of the **overage land** for the agreement of price and terms for the completion of the sale;
(c) that the state of the market level of values and other circumstances are on any earlier assumed date of exchange of contracts the same as on the date of valuation; and
(d) that no account is taken of the possibility that there may be a willing purchaser who by reason of ownership of adjoining land or otherwise may be regarded as a special purchaser.[2]

Overage land
means the land shown for the purpose of identification only edged red on the plan annexed to this deed.

The Planning Acts
include the Town and Country Planning Act 1990, the Planning (Listed Buildings and Conservation Areas) Act 1990, the Planning (Hazardous Substances) Act 1990, the Planning (Consequential Provisions) Act 1990 and any subsequent legislation of a similar nature and any regulation or direction in pursuance of any of them.

Planning permission
means a permission for **development** required by reason of [section 57 of the Town and Country Planning Act 1990 or legislation from time to time replacing the same or legislation of a like nature from time to time in force] *or* [**the Planning Acts**].

Qualifying disposal   means a **relevant disposal** with the benefit of a **planning permission** for a **material development**.

Relevant disposal   means any **disposal** of any part of the **overage land** or any interest in it whether by sale or lease gift or otherwise other than an **excepted disposal**.

Relevant percentage   is [   ] per cent.

Relevant land   means the **overage land** or a part of the **overage land** for which **planning permission** has been granted or on which any **material development is begun**.

Trigger date   means:

(i)   if **planning permission** has been obtained for a **material development** the date on which **development** is commenced or if earlier the date on which any **disposal** of any part of the **relevant land** or any interest in it whether by sale or lease or otherwise takes place;

(ii)   if **planning permission** is required for a **material development** but no **planning permission** has been obtained therefor the date on which the **material development** in question is commenced.

PROVIDED that no date more than [   ] years after the date hereof will be a **trigger date**.

For the purposes of ascertaining when **material development** commenced any work operation or action carried out on the **relevant land** which would be treated as implementation of a **planning permission** for the **material development** in question on the assumption (if not a fact) that **planning permission** had been granted therefor will be deemed to be a commencement of that **material development**.[3]

The **Granter** COVENANTS with the **Imposer** that it will:

(a) not later than 20 working days after any **trigger date** pay to the **Imposer** a sum equal to the **relevant percentage** of the **development value** of the **overage land** as at the **trigger date**; and

(b) in the event and to the extent that any moneys to be paid by the **Granter** pursuant to this Agreement are not paid within the said 20 working days following the **trigger date** in question to pay to the **Imposer** interest at the rate of [   ] per cent per annum above [Bank plc] base rate from time to time in force on such amounts as are from time to time due to the **Imposer** until payment is made in full such interest to be compounded with quarterly rests.

---

1   The above excludes permitted development under the Town and Country Planning (General Permitted Development) Order 1995 and changes of use under the Town and Country Planning (Use Classes) Order 1987 which are not material changes. The form can be adapted to include them.

2   Alternatively, the drafter may prefer to incorporate a statement of recommended practice used by one of the Institutions such as the RICS.

3   This may need to be modified if a different definition of 'material development' is used or in special cases. In particular, the Crown does not need planning consent as such so that a reference to Department of the Environment Circular 18/84 could be inserted.

Form 1.2(1)   Positive covenant by reference to disposal

It might appear that it would be easier to provide for overage to be paid on a sale out of the proceeds. A formula such as

The **Granter** covenants with the **Imposer** that on any sale of the **overage land** it will pay to the **Imposer** a sum equal to half of the difference between the **current use value** (defined as the value of the land at that time as if it were subject to a perpetual covenant limiting its use to the use at the time of the original overage deed) and the proceeds of sale (or the net proceeds after expenses of sale)

might appear attractive. In a simple case it might work but there are other factors to consider.

(a) The landowner might obtain planning consent for its own occupation and not sell.

(b) The landowner might grant short leases or longer ones at rent rather than a capital premium.

(c) The value might be obtained from the grant of an easement for adjoining land.

(d) The land might be used as part of a larger development as an access (perhaps dedicated as a highway) or a public open space and therefore have no separate value of its own (or even a negative value).

(e) The 'sale' could be by an intra-group transfer followed by a sale of the transferee company.

(f) The 'sale' could be a disposal within a family, perhaps at an undervalue.

(g) There could be other terms such as part exchange, grant of rights, or building works.

(h) A sale of a residential property can include a fitted kitchen or other benefits such as a 'free' holiday.

(i) The sale could be of the shares in a single asset company owning the overage land.

Therefore, both parties need a fallback to substitute a valuation. The trigger event could then be either a sale or the first letting or first beneficial occupation after a change of use but in that case the transaction would represent the value with new or converted buildings.

(a) The percentage of the overage could be set low enough to compensate for the construction costs, or the construction or conversion costs should be deducted from the proceeds before they are divided. Those costs need to be monitored so that unnecessarily expensive materials are not used or other costs, such as an uneconomic workforce (which might otherwise have to be made redundant) or the developer's head office overheads are not loaded into the overage calculation. See notes to the alternative definition of allowable expenditure in Form 1.2(2).

(b) It may be possible to take a ground value of the overage land in an undeveloped state as at the date of sale as the basis for calculation, but again that involves a valuation.

(c) Where the trigger is first letting, the rent (either passing rent or ground rent) can be capitalised but the parties need to consider:

   (i) letting of part, especially if different parts can command different rent levels;

   (ii) letting on special terms, such as a rent free period, or a reverse premium with a high initial rent;

   (iii) change of plan to beneficial occupation by the head tenant/developer.

The solution will normally be to have the overage payment based on valuation, but to provide that the 'disposal' will be first letting or beneficial occupation. The actual circumstances of sale or letting will be primary evidence of the value and the onus is put on the party challenging that to have an independent valuation substituted. There need to be provisions for the landowner to supply full details of development costs (if relevant) and of the marketing of the property and the terms of sale and any related transactions. The key is therefore the definition of 'accountable value' and the valuation clause Form 1.5 provides for the valuer to take into account actual figures. In practice, if the figures are clear there will be no need to refer to a valuer and the parties can agree them.

If the land forms part of a larger site then it may have its own ransom value, which it would have had if in separate ownership from the other land so that in principle a valuer would be able to place a distinct value on the overage land. In that case, the trigger may have to be the first use of the road or open space or similar purpose.

If it is wished to charge overage on a disposal of shares in a single asset company, it is better to use company law methods designed for that company. The government draftsman tried to cover this in the Finance Act 1974, ss 41 and 42 (see **10.6.6**) and the draftsman in *Briargate Developments Ltd v Newprop Co Ltd* [1990] 1 EGLR 283 tried the same but property law approaches are rarely helpful in this context.

The following precedent as it stands is unlikely to fit precisely any actual commercial deal. It involves an elaborate procedure and also seeks to consider issues arising out of successive accruals of value. In practice, the parties will want a simplified version adapted to suit their requirements. The form uses ideas adapted from tax law, particularly capital gains tax, but I have suggested a base value of current use value. The base value could be fixed at a given event and then indexed according to a suitable index.

The form includes a brief deduction for allowable expenditure to cover the possibility that a developer might spend money on the site before sale. In practice, this provision will need to be adapted, for example to allow for a developer's profit and other expenses. Two approaches are possible, to retain a high percentage of development value, but allow full deduction of development costs, or to calculate overage by reference to gross proceeds, and have a low percentage. The simplified wording for allowable expenditure in Form 1.2(1) can be replaced as in Form 1.2(2).

Where the disposal is by lease the rent will have to be capitalised, unless the imposer retains the freehold when it can be by a geared rent. If the lease is a short one then a special formula will be needed, also if there is a premium and a rent.

Because of the complications of overage by reference to disposal proceeds, this approach is normally best avoided. If the granter is unable to agree to overage on uplift in value, it may be preferred to have the overage calculated on that occasion and then secured by a charge which will be paid off on first disposal, letting or occupation, perhaps with the sum secured being adjusted by reference to a suitable index.

Definitions

Accountable profit   means **accountable value** less **allowable expenditure**.

Accountable value   (a) in relation to a **relevant disposal** means a single capital sum equal to the greater of:

    (i) the amount by which the value of the **relevant interest** of the **disponee** in the **relevant land** immediately after the **relevant disposal** exceeds the value (if any) of the **relevant interest** of the **disponee** in the **relevant land** immediately before the **disposal** (or if the **disponee** had no **relevant interest** of value) the full amount of such value; and

    (ii) the amount by which the value of the **relevant interest** of the **disponor** of or out of the **relevant land** immediately before the **relevant disposal** exceeds the value (if any) of the **relevant interest** of the **disponor** in the **relevant land** immediately after the **disposal** or (if the **disponor** retained no **relevant interest**) the full amount of such value.

(b) In relation to **relevant occupation** means the amount that would be ascertained under paragraph (a) of this definition on the assumption that the **relevant occupation** had been made by a **relevant disposal** comprising the whole **relevant interest** which the person permitting the **relevant occupation** to take place (whether by itself or another person) had been able to assure or grant.

Allowable expenditure   means any expenditure reflected in the **accountable value** (including costs of acquiring, defending, improving or disposing of the **relevant interest** or in improving the **relevant land** and but for which the **accountable value** could reasonably be expected to be lower than it is or is deemed to be for the purposes of this deed).[1]

Current use value	(a) on any **trigger event** relating to any **relevant land** after the date of this deed but before any payment has been made to the Imposer under the provisions of this deed means the value of the **relevant interest** assuming the **relevant land** is subject to a perpetual covenant restricting its use to the **initial current use**;
	(b) on any subsequent **trigger event** relating to any land which has been both the subject of a previous **disposal** after the date of this deed and also in respect of which a payment has been made to the Imposer under the provisions of this deed means the value of the **relevant interest** assuming the **relevant land** is subject to a perpetual covenant restricting its use to the use by reference to which the last preceding payment was ascertained under the provisions of this deed.[2]
Development value	means the difference between the **accountable value** and the **current use value**.
Disponee	means a person to whom or in whose favour a **trigger event** is made or deemed to be made.
Disponor	means a person by whom or at whose cost a **trigger event** is made or deemed to be made.
Disposal	is widely construed and includes:
	(a) any grant or assurance release or surrender of a **relevant interest**;
	(b) a gift or exercise of a right of re-entry or break clause whether or not value or compensation is given in return;
	(c) the grant of a right to occupy (but not a licence merely to carry out works).
Excepted disposal	means one or more of the following:
	(d) any mortgage or charge of the **overage land** or any part of it;

(e) the granting of a licence or a tenancy in respect of the **overage land** or any part of it on terms which (under the law prevailing at the time) would entitle the owner of the **overage land** without obtaining any court order and without taking any steps save for service of notice on the occupant to vacant possession not later than 23 months from the date of such grant;

(f) the granting of an easement over or the giving of a covenant affecting any part of the **overage land** which in either case does not materially affect the value of it;

(g) a licence to carry out works on the **relevant land** which does not carry the right to occupy.[3]

Initial current use	[*specify, eg agriculture, hospital*]
Overage land	[*define*]
Relevant disposal	means any **disposal** of a **relevant interest** in the **relevant land** except an **excepted disposal**.
Relevant interest	means an estate or interest in the **relevant land** (including where the context allows estates or interests existing or not existing at the date of this Deed).
Relevant land	means the **overage land** or part of it being the subject of a **trigger event**.
Relevant occupation	means the first taking of beneficial occupation on or after any change in the use of the **relevant land**.
Relevant percentage	[ ] per cent.
Trigger event	means a **relevant disposal** or taking of **relevant occupation**.

(a) The **Granter** COVENANTS with the **Imposer** that if [and so often as] there is a **trigger event** in relation to the **overage land** or any part of it and at the date of that **trigger event** the **accountable value** is [*more than 5 per cent*] greater than the **current use value** then the **Granter** will pay to the **Imposer** a sum equal to the **relevant percentage** of the **accountable profit**.

(b) In the event and to the extent that any moneys to be paid by the **Granter** pursuant to this Agreement are not paid within the said 20 working days following the **trigger event** in question to pay to the **Imposer** interest at the rate of [   ] per cent per annum above [Bank plc] base rate from time to time in force on such amounts as are from time to time due to the **Imposer** until payment is made in full such interest to be compound with quarterly rests.

(c) The **Granter** covenants with the **Imposer** to supply [on demand] *or* [within   days of the **trigger event**] such evidence as the **Imposer** reasonably requires to support the calculation of **accountable profits**.

---

1   See also modification and notes in Form 1.2(2).
2   If there is only one overage payment, para (b) will be deleted and para (a) modified.
3   This may be needed to cover a building licence.

Form 1.2(2)   Modification for allowable expenditure

Instead of the general reference above, the parties may wish to define what they intend. This can be risky because the more detailed the list the more likely it is that something will be left out. Over the long period of many overage arrangements there is a good chance of some new head of expenditure appearing. The general approach used in Form 1.2(1) is based on that of the tax laws. It does, however, give scope for argument as to what is allowable.

If the parties wish to specify heads, it is better to include a separate schedule and incorporate that in the definitions by reference.

An approach could be to refer to all costs reasonably and properly incurred by the Granter or by persons deriving rights or acting under its authority exclusively incurred in connection with the development of the overage land which were not caused by the neglect or default of the Granter or such persons including:

–   the purchase price of the overage land (or the latest price paid if it has changed hands);
–   the cost of getting in other interests including the surrender of leases and the release of easements and perhaps the acquisition costs of rights over ransom land;
–   site investigation costs and the cost of investigation and where applicable remediation of:
    –   pollution and contamination;
    –   archaeological sites;
    –   environmentally sensitive sites (eg badgers);
–   environmental assessments;
–   preparation and submission of planning applications;

- laying or relaying of services;
- provision or alteration or improvement of access;
- payments to statutory undertakers and costs relating to adoption;
- statutory agreements, such as section 106 obligations;
- compliance with statutory requirements;
- costs of disposal including premiums payable to or rent free periods allowed to tenants, cost of credit on deferred payment for freehold;
- insurance premiums;
- third party claims including damages (to the extent they are not the fault of the Imposer);
- professional fees of lawyers, surveyors, architects, planners, experts of various sorts relating to:
  - acquisition (or the latest acquisition of any specified area);
  - surveys;
  - planning applications and appeals;
  - possession, including sitting tenants, trespassers and demonstrators;
  - disposal;
- stamp duty and land registry fees;
- holding costs including cost of interest on money borrowed;
- developer's profit.

The parties may also wish to bring into the equation costs incurred by the Imposer. It will also have expenses and perhaps monitoring costs. If it retains an interest such as a ransom strip or a freehold or charge, it may also be involved in planning agreements.

The parties may wish to allow for the time that expenses were incurred such as indexing them from the date of expenditure or allowing a notional rate of interest from that date. If the developer is relying on borrowed money and finance costs are allowed, there should be a provision to prevent double counting.

There may also be factors to be brought in against these expenses such as grants for remedying polluted land, premiums received from tenants, sales of small areas of land such as for road widening, and sales of materials such as gravel excavated for water balancing ponds.

Where the developer is a large concern, it may also wish to allow a part of its central office overheads as part of the cost of development.

One approach is to provide that any costs which can be justified on an audit basis as properly incurred may be allowed but that simply shifts the burden on to the auditor.

Form 1.3   Restriction on the Register

This can be used with a variety of overage methods. It is put here for use with a positive covenant and is subject to the caveats in **3.4.1**, but if it is correct that overage is an equitable contingent future interest and thus by definition involves a trust of land, a restriction is available. Restrictions are commonly imposed by commercial lenders and may be used with a charge. A restriction can of course be used with an express trust, and it can also be used with a company structure. It is not suitable for leases as it would in that case simply reinforce the normal controls on alienation and in view of privity of estate is not necessary.

1   The **Granter** COVENANTS with the **Imposer** that on any **relevant disposal** (other than any **qualifying disposal**) or on the granting of any mortgage or charge of the **overage land** or any part of it to procure that the person in whose favour the **relevant disposal** mortgage or charge (as the case may be) is made enters into a new deed of covenant with the **Imposer** to pay any sums due under this Deed (other than sums which have before such **relevant disposal** mortgage or charge been paid to the **Imposer**) at the same time and in the same manner as the **Granter** is bound by this Deed to pay and the new deed will contain such provisions as are necessary to take account of the particular extent of the **overage land** or the nature of the interest in it that is the subject of the disposition in question.

2   The parties apply to the Chief Land Registrar to enter in the title to the **overage land** a restriction that except under an Order of the Registrar of the Court no disposition of the **overage land** or any part of it or of any interest in it shall be registered without the consent of the **Imposer** [or such other person or persons entitled to the benefit of the restriction by reason of Clause 3.3 of this Deed].

3   The benefit of the said covenants contained in Clauses 2 and 3 and of the said restriction may be freely assigned by the **Imposer**.

4   The **Imposer** or other person or persons entitled to the benefit of this restriction will consent to the registration of a disposition of the **overage land** or any part of it or of any interest in it either if the disponee of it has entered into a deed with the **Imposer** in accordance with subclause 3 of this clause and the **Imposer** has received the new deed from the **disponee** duly stamped with the appropriate stamp duty [if any] or if by reason of the nature of the disposition in question no such deed is required.

Form 1.4   Deed of Covenant

This Deed of Covenant is made the   day of   between (1) (person to whom the **land** is conveyed or transferred) (or Interest granted) [of (*address*) or whose registered office is at (*address*)] ('the **New Owner**') and (2) (**Overage Owner**) [of (*address*) or whose registered office is at (*address*)] ('**the Grantee**').

NOW THIS DEED WITNESSES as follows:

1   Definitions

the Overage Deed	a deed dated [*Date*] and made between **Imposer** (1) and **Granter** (2)
the Land	[*Describe*]
the Interest	[*Describe eg a lease for 50 years from date*]
the Imposer	includes the person originally entitled to the benefit of the Covenant in clause 3.

2   Recitals

2.1   This Deed is entered into pursuant to the obligations contained in the **Overage Deed**.

2.2   The **New Owner** has become the owner of the **Land** [the **Interest**].

2.3   The **Grantee** is the successor in title to the **Imposer** to the benefit of the **Overage Deed**.

3   Covenants

The **New Owner** [jointly and severally] covenants with the **Grantee** in respect of [the **Land**] [the **Interest**] that the **New Owner** will at all times after the date of this Deed observe and perform all of the covenants conditions and obligations on the part of the **Granter** contained in the **Overage Deed** whether running with the land or of a personal or collateral nature and will do and perform all acts and things as will be necessary or appropriate to enable the **Grantee** to exercise its right to [receive the payments referred to in the **Overall Deed**] *or* [purchase the **Land** in accordance with the terms and conditions of the **Overage Deed**].

4   Restriction

4.1   The parties apply to the Chief Land Registrar to enter in the title to the **Land** [**Interest**] a restriction that except under an Order of the Registrar or of the Court no disposition of the **Land** [**Interest**] or any part of it or of any interest in it shall be registered without the consent of the **Imposer**.

4.2   The **Granter** will consent to the registration of the **Land** [**Interest**] or any part of it or of any interest in it either if the disponee of the same has entered into a deed with the **Granter** in the form of this Deed (things being changed which ought to be changed) and the **Granter** has received the same from the disponee duly stamped with the appropriate stamp duty (if any) or if by reason of the nature of the disposition in question no such deed is required.

IN WITNESS etc

Form 1.5 Valuation

The valuation clause contains a formal part governing the appointment and procedure of the valuer and a substantial part whose function is to set out the matters the valuer must take into account, the assumptions on which the valuation is made, and the basis of valuation. In overage the valuer will normally have to make at least two valuations, one of current use value and the other of open market value. The difference is the development value on which overage is paid. The parties may wish to exclude hope value, for example of a possible future planning consent, so that may also have to be ascertained and deducted from the open market value.

1   Any dispute concerning matters of valuation arising by reason of the provisions of this deed may be referred by either party to an independent valuer (acting as an expert and not an arbitrator).
2   The independent valuer will be appointed by agreement between the parties or failing agreement then on application by either party to the President for the time being of the Royal Institution of Chartered Surveyors.
3   The fees and expenses of the independent valuer and the costs (if any) of his or her appointment will be borne equally by the parties who will otherwise bear their own costs and expenses.
4   The parties will be entitled to make representations to the independent valuer.

In the case of overage by reference to actual or deemed (as on letting or occupation) disposal add:

5   Where any payment under this deed is triggered by an actual **disposal** between unconnected parties at the best price reasonably obtainable in the open market then there will be a rebuttable presumption that the actual price obtained is the **accountable value**.
6   Where the **Granter** can demonstrate that actual sums have been incurred in **allowable expenditure** then there will be a rebuttable presumption that those sums have been reasonably incurred and the **Imposer** will be entitled to bring evidence or argument to rebut it.
7   Where the **trigger event** in relation to the **relevant land** is part of a larger transaction or scheme of development the **accountable value** will be equal to the value that could have been achieved by an owner of the **relevant interest** who is independent of the owner of any other interest (whether part of the **overage land** or not) involved in the transaction or scheme if the owner of the **relevant interest** took full advantage of its bargaining position in relation to any increase in the value of any interest of the other land.

Form 1.6   Re-entry

1   If during the period of *seventy-nine* years from the date of this deed (which is the applicable perpetuity period) in relation to any **relevant land**:

1.1 the **trigger date** occurs; and

1.2 the **Granter** does not pay the **overage sum** within *forty* days of its becoming due (whether formally demanded or not),

then the **Imposer** may (without prejudice to any other right or remedy and notwithstanding any actual or constructive waiver of any previous right or remedy) enter upon the **land** [*or* **relevant land**] (or any part of it in the name of the whole) and hold and enjoy it in fee simple in possession free from incumbrances (except those subsisting at the date of this deed or created with the consent of the **Imposer** or created under any statutory power by a body having compulsory powers).

2   In such case the **Imposer** will become entitled to any land or charge certificate affecting the **overage land** [*or* **relevant land**] and the **Granter** appoints the **Imposer** its attorney for the purpose of doing all things necessary to vest the **overage land** [*or* **relevant land**] in the **Imposer**.

3   This clause will not prejudice the right of the **Granter** to relief against the consequences of re-entry on paying the **overage sum** and any interest and costs or restrict the power of the court to order relief on such terms as the court thinks fit.

2   RESTRICTIVE COVENANT

This is designed as a normal restrictive covenant but the normal rules will not necessarily apply. In particular, a decision is needed on subclause 6. Restrictive covenants are designed to protect amenity and there is an argument that in law they must be kept to that. If it appears that a covenant was intended for overage but is disguised as an amenity covenant this is unlikely to attract the sympathy of the Lands Tribunal or the court and it is better to be open about the purpose from the outset. An overage covenant was upheld in *Re Cornick*.[1]

---

1   (1994) 68 P&CR 372.

Form 2 Restrictive covenant

1 The **Granter** covenants with the **Imposer** in the terms of this clause.

2 The **Granter** intends to bind each part of the **overage land** (into whomever's hands it may come).

3 The **Granter** intends to benefit each part of the land comprised in [the part retained by the **Imposer** of] [*Title Number ABC123*] capable of benefiting (into whomever's hands it may come) except for any part that may be transferred on sale unless the benefit of all or part of this covenant is expressly assigned (either wholly or to benefit the land sold in common with land retained by the assignor).

4 The terms of this clause were taken into account in negotiating the sale effected by this Transfer and the sale price reflects this clause.

5 The **Imposer** reserves to the person having the benefit of this covenant the right (on application by the person subject to the burden or if different parts of the **overage land** come into separate ownerships then on application by the owner of part (in relation only to that part)) to vary or release any covenant in whole or part on such terms as the **Imposer** thinks fit (including payment of a sum of money).

6 This clause is intended to reserve to the **Imposer** part of any future increase in value of the **overage land** arising from the opportunity to develop it or put it to a more valuable use.

7 The covenants are:

7.1 Not to use the **overage land** for any purpose other than [agriculture].

7.2 Not to erect on the **overage land** any building or structure (other than garden sheds or greenhouses) nor to construct any road.

7.3 Not to make any external alteration or extension to any existing building or structure on the **overage land**.

7.4 Not to apply for planning permission for **development** or change of use of the **overage land** or authorise or consent to any application.

3 CHARGE

The land charged will usually be the overage land but does not need to be. This will be used with a promise to pay or positive covenant in Form 1.1 or 1.2. If there is to be no personal recourse then clause 1 can be adapted and section 28 of the Land Registration Act 1925 will be excluded with an application for an appropriate entry on the Register.

Form 3   Deed of Charge

THIS DEED OF CHARGE is made [*date*]
BETWEEN

(1) **[GRANTER]**
(2) **[IMPOSER]**

WHEREAS

(A) By a Transfer ('the Transfer') dated [*date*] and made [*date*] the property described in the Schedule ('the **Property**') was transferred] by the **Imposer** to the **Granter**.

(B) In the [Transfer] [In a deed ('the Overage Deed')] dated [*date*] and made [*date*] the **Granter** covenanted with the **Imposer** to pay to the **Imposer** in certain circumstances as provided in the [Transfer] [Overage Deed] Further Sums ('the **Further Sums**').

(C) It was agreed that this Deed of Charge should be executed by the **Granter** in order to secure payment to the **Imposer** of all the **Further Sums**.

(D) Since the calculation of the **Further Sums** payment of which is to be secured by this Deed depends on events and acts to take place at some future uncertain occasion [*or* occasions] there is doubt whether such payments can be secured by a charge by way of legal mortgage.

(E) The parties intend that in so far as such payment can be secured by charge by way of legal mortgage it will so be secured under this Deed of Charge but that in so far as it cannot so be secured then it will be secured by the equitable charge provided in this Deed but not further or otherwise.

NOW THIS DEED WITNESSES as follows:

1   In pursuance and in consideration of the agreement mentioned above the **Granter** HEREBY COVENANTS with the **Imposer** to pay to the **Imposer** ALL the **Further Sums** to which the **Imposer** will be entitled under the terms of the [Transfer] [Overage Deed].

2   In further pursuance and in consideration of the agreement the **Granter** with full title guarantee HEREBY CHARGES BY WAY OF LEGAL MORTGAGE ALL THAT the **Property** with the payment to the **Imposer** of all the **Further Sums** [covenanted to be paid in] [intended to be secured by] the terms of the [Transfer] [Overage Deed].

3   In further pursuance and in consideration of the agreement but to the intent recited above the **Granter** [with full title guarantee] HEREBY CHARGES IN EQUITY ALL THAT the **Property** with the payment to the **Imposer** of the **Further Sums**.

4   So far as the **Property** is hereby charged in equity and not by way of legal mortgage but not further or otherwise the **Granter** HEREBY DECLARES that it holds the **Property** on trust for the **Imposer** to

have such powers of sale as the **Imposer** would have under the charge by way of legal mortgage if it were valid and effective and the **Imposer** has full power to appoint itself and any other person or persons trustee or trustees in place of the **Granter** in respect of that said trust but subject thereto the **Granter** will hold the **Property** in trust for itself absolutely and beneficially.

IN WITNESS *etc*

THE SCHEDULE
(Description of the Property)

4   RANSOMS

Form 4.1   Airspace

This will be done by a definition of the property transferred such as:

The land whose horizontal dimensions are shown (with measurements) on the attached plan and which lies between a lower limit of [   ] metres above Ordnance Datum Newlyn and an upper limit of [   ] metres above Ordnance Datum Newlyn TOGETHER WITH the right for machinery and equipment to pass through the volume of airspace [three metres] above the upper limit for the purpose of [*specify eg repairs, maintenance, agricultural machinery or as applicable*].

Form 4.2   Top floor of office block

The wording can be adapted from any lease of a flat or suite of offices on long lease, including rights of access, support and shelter. There may be a covenant by the landlord not to build above (or beside) the top floor unit. The result will be that the building cannot be redeveloped without the consent of the owner of the top floor.

Form 4.3   Right of way

Except and reserving for the benefit of the adjoining land shown edged green on the plan
and granting for the benefit of [*specify land not owned*] so that the benefit may pass to the owner of it under the Law of Property Act 1925, s 56 and the Contracts (Rights of Third Parties) Act 1999 PROVIDED that the right of way will not be exercisable by any person who is not authorised by the **Imposer** or its successors to whom this power to authorise has been expressly assigned (and such assignment may be at the same time as any transfer of the land edged green or any part of it or at some other time before or after such transfer)
the right at all times and for all purposes to pass over the land coloured brown on the plan right to enter on the land coloured brown to make up and repair and maintain it.

5 LEASEHOLD

Form 5.1 Negative overage lease at a premium

The following form assumes a lease of less than 300 years and contains a right of re-entry. If the term is longer, consideration should be given to reserving a rent of say £10 per year but it must be regularly collected as failure to do so for 12 years could allow the tenant to obtain a possessory title. It could be combined with an option to purchase the freehold on a trigger event. It may be possible to enlarge a lease over 300 years into a freehold on the same terms as the lease under the Law of Property Act 1925, s 153 and this may be wished by the parties in which case the clause for re-entry on forfeiture should be omitted.

THIS LEASE is made the [*date*]

BETWEEN

(1) **Imposer** ('the Landlord') and

(2) **Granter** ('the Tenant')

NOW THIS DEED WITNESSES as follows:

1   Demise
In consideration of the payment of [   ] pounds (the receipt of which the Landlord acknowledges) and the covenants by the Tenant reserved and contained in this Lease the Landlord with full title guarantee demises to the Tenant all that field situated at [   ] and edged red on the plan annexed to this Lease ('the demised premises') [together with a right of way in common with the Landlord and others so authorised on foot or with motor and other vehicles for the purpose of the use of the said field as a [*specify limited purpose*] and not for any other purpose whatsoever over and along the private road delineated on the said plan and thereon coloured brown ('the accessway')] to hold the same unto the Tenant for the term of two hundred and fifty years ('the term') from [   ] excepting and reserving out of the demised premises the rights set out in Clause 2 of this Lease yielding and paying therefor during the term the yearly rent of a peppercorn if demanded on the anniversary of the date of this Lease.

2   Exceptions and reservations
There will be excepted and reserved out of this demise to the Landlord for the benefit of its retained land and estate known as [   ] and each and every part capable of so benefiting the rights and privileges as follows:
2.1 The free and uninterrupted passage of water and soil through the water pipes and drains and of electricity and other services (if any) through the electric wires, pipes, conduits, supply equip-

ment and meters which now are or may hereafter be in, on or passing through the demised premises and which serve or which will or may be capable of serving other property of the Landlord and the full right and liberty [within the perpetuity period of seventy-nine years from the date of this deed] to enter upon the demised premises with all necessary equipment and machinery for the purpose of [constructing or laying and at all times after laying or construction for the purpose of] inspecting, maintaining, repairing and renewing all such water pipes, drains, electric wires, pipes, conduits and supply equipment and meters Provided that the Landlord or other person or persons exercising such right will make good all damage caused to the demised premises.

2.2 Full right and liberty to use and build upon or alter any property now or hereafter belonging to the Landlord or the Landlord's tenants not hereby demised at any time or for any reason and in any manner whatsoever notwithstanding that the access of light and air to the demised premises may be obstructed or interfered with and notwithstanding that the carrying out of such works in a reasonable and proper manner may cause annoyance or inconvenience to the Tenant or its occupation or use of the demised premises.

2.3 Full right and liberty for the Landlord and its licensees and invitees at all times during the term to pass and repass by foot over the demised premises subject nevertheless to the uninterrupted right of the Tenant to the use of the demised premises in accordance with permitted use as defined in this Lease.

[2.4 There will also be excepted and reserved to the Landlord all rights of development in the demised premises including the value derived from any building work and any change of use Provided that this exception and reservation does not authorise any entry on the demised premises without the consent of the Tenant.]

3 Tenant's covenant

The Tenant hereby covenants with the Landlord as follows:

3.1 Outgoings
To discharge all existing and future rates, taxes, assessments and outgoings whatsoever imposed on or payable by the owner or occupier of the demised premises in respect of it.

3.2 Repair
To keep all building erections, fences and gates upon the demised premises always in good repair and condition [and the gates to the accessway always locked when the demised premises are not in use] and to cleanse all drains and ditches upon the demised premises [and further to maintain the accessway in good repair and condition as aforesaid during the term].

3.3　Condition

[Include any positive covenants which are applicable, such as landscaping or painting.]

3.4　Insurance and indemnity

3.4.1　To effect or secure and maintain insurance against liability to the public and to third parties in such sum as may be prudent and which from time to time will not be less than that sum (if any) designated by the Landlord.

3.4.2　To indemnify the Landlord against any claims, proceedings or demands and the costs and expenses incurred thereby which may be brought against the Landlord by any person on the demised premises with the consent of the Tenant and any visitors and any trespassers in circumstances where the occupier has a liability for injury in respect of any accident, loss or damage whatsoever to person or property howsoever caused occurring in or upon the demised premises.

3.5　Works

Not to erect or allow to be placed on the demised premises any building or structure and not to make any alterations, additions or improvements to any existing buildings for the time being upon the demised premises nor to alter in any way the character and general arrangement of the demised premises.

3.6　Register alienation

Within one month after any transfer or other devolution of the demised premises including any underlease or transfer or devolution of it to give notice to the Landlord and to pay a reasonable fee for registration in the Landlord's records.

3.7　Use

To use the demised premises and such buildings (if any) as may be situate for the time being thereon as a *[specify]* ('the permitted use').

3.8　Planning

3.8.1　Not to apply for or authorise any other person to apply for planning consent under the Town and Country Planning Act 1990 in relation to the demised premises nor to carry out on the demised premises any development as defined in section 55 of that Act [except for permitted development].

3.8.2　Not to do or omit or permit or suffer to be done or omitted any act, matter or thing in, on or respecting the demised premises required to be omitted or done (as the case may be) by the Town and Country Planning Act 1990 or any statutory re-enactment of them or any regulation made under that Act or which contravene the provisions of that Act and at all times hereafter to indemnify and keep indemnified the Landlord against all actions, proceedings, costs, expenses, claims and demands in respect of any such matter, act or thing contravening those provisions.

3.9 Notices

To comply forthwith at the Tenant's own expense with any nuisance, sanitary or other statutory notice lawfully served by any local or public authority upon either the Landlord or the Tenant with respect to the demised premises and to keep the Landlord fully and effectually indemnified against all proceedings costs, expenses, claims and demands in respect of it.

3.10 Notice to Landlord

Within seven days of the receipt of notice to give full particulars to the Landlord of any permission, notice, order or proposal for a notice or order made, given or issued to the Tenant by any government department or local or public authority under or by virtue of any statutory powers and if so required by the Landlord to produce such permission, notice, order or proposal for a notice or order to the Landlord and also without delay to take all reasonable or necessary steps to comply with any such notice or order [and also in case of any proposal for compulsory acquisition of part or all of the demised premises or rights over them at the request of the Landlord to make or join with the Landlord in making such objections or representations against or in respect of such notice, order or proposal as aforesaid as the Landlord considers expedient].

3.11 Entry

To permit the Landlord and its duly authorised agents at reasonable times to enter upon the demised premises:

3.11.1 to inspect the condition of them and for all other reasonable purposes;

3.11.2 to demolish and remove any works carried out contrary to the provisions of this Lease and to pay to the Landlord on demand the cost incurred by the Landlord in such demolition and removal.

3.12 Yield up

To deliver up the demised premises at the determination of the term in a condition consistent with the foregoing provisions.

4 Landlord's covenant

The Landlord covenants with the Tenant that the Tenant observing and performing the provisions and stipulations on its part shall peaceably hold and enjoy the demised premises during the term without interruption by the Landlord or any person rightfully claiming under or in trust for it.

5 Provisos

Provided always as follows:

5.1 Re-entry on forfeiture

If the Tenant at any time fails or neglects to perform or observe any of the covenants, conditions or agreements contained in this Lease and on the Tenant's part to be performed and observed then and in any such case it will be lawful for the Landlord or any person or persons duly authorised by it in that behalf into or upon the demised premises or any part of them in the name of the whole to re-enter and the said premises peaceably to hold and enjoy thenceforth as if these presents had not been made but without prejudice to any right of action or remedy of the Landlord in respect of any antecedent breach of any of the covenants by the Tenant contained in this Lease.[1]

5.2   Reinstatement

At the end or sooner determination of the term the Tenant will carry out to the reasonable satisfaction of the Landlord all or any such works of restoration or reinstatement as will then properly be required to be carried out either by virtue of the provisions of this Lease [or alternatively by the terms of any licence or licences granted by or on behalf of the Landlord to the Tenant at any time during the term] and in the case of any default by the Tenant occurring (or continuing in the case of any such works which were due to have been carried out prior to the determination of the term) the Landlord may carry out or complete the carrying out of the said works and the cost incurred by the Landlord in so doing will be paid or reimbursed by the Tenant to the Landlord on demand.

5.3   VAT

All sums payable by the Tenant hereunder which may be subject to Value Added Tax will be considered to be tax exclusive sums and the Value Added Tax at the appropriate rate for the time being will be payable by the Tenant in addition thereto.

5.4   Notices

Any notice under this Lease is to be in writing and will be sufficiently served:

5.4.1   in the case of a notice to the Tenant if sent to the registered office of the Tenant by registered post or the recorded delivery service or normal address if the Tenant is an individual;

5.4.2   in the case of a notice to the Landlord if sent by registered post or the recorded delivery service to the registered office Landlord or normal address if the Landlord is an individual.

[6   **Stamp duty**

It is certified that there is no agreement for Lease to which the Lease gives effect.]

IN WITNESS etc

---

1   This clause should be omitted if enlargement is intended under the Law of Property Act 1925, s 153.

Form 5.2   Payment under lease

This is a relatively simple provision to be inserted in a schedule to a normal commercial occupation lease to cover an anticipated but uncertain planning consent.

1   In this Schedule:

'additional space'	means the **gross internal area** authorised to be constructed by a **relevant planning permission** of building or buildings in addition to or in substitution for those to be constructed pursuant to the **existing planning permission** whereby building or buildings having a **gross internal area** exceeding [XX] sq ft or if it be greater the area authorised by the **existing planning permission** may be constructed upon the **demised premises**.
'gross internal area'	means the floor area of any building or buildings to be constructed pursuant to a **relevant planning permission** measured between the inside faces of the external fabric of such buildings (assuming the walls to be unplastered) excluding open sided covered areas but otherwise measured in accordance with the current edition of the Code of Measuring Practice published by the Royal Institution of Chartered Surveyors and the Incorporated Society of Valuers and Auctioneers.
'existing planning permission'	means [*define*].
'date of commencement'	means the date upon which the Lessee or any person with the authority of the Lessee first carries out any work or demolition construction or work of preparation therefor or for the provision of services.

'relevant planning
permission'   means permission [other than a
                               renewal of the **existing planning
                               permission** on [substantially] the
                               same terms] granted at any time
                               before the expiration of   years
                               from the date of this Lease
                               pursuant to the **planning Acts**
                               authorising the construction upon
                               the demised premises of **additional
                               space**.

'relevant period'   means a period of Y years from the
                               date of this Lease.

2   In the event that during the **relevant period** the Lessee begins to
     carry out **development** pursuant to a **relevant planning per-
     mission** then the Lessee will within 14 days of the **date of
     commencement** pay to the Landlord a sum equal to the number
     of square feet comprising the **additional space** multiplied by the sum
     of £[Z].

Insert an interest provision if not contained elsewhere in lease.

6   OPTIONS

Form 6.1   Option to acquire ransom or freehold of lease; or take release of right of way

This will need to incorporate suitable definitions.

1   If the **trigger event** occurs then the **Granter** will have the option to
     purchase the [fee simple estate in possession in the] **land/demised
     premises** or part of it (*or take a release of the right of way*) for a sum
     equal to [one half of] the difference between the **open market value**
     and the **current use value** at the date of exercise ('**the purchase
     price**').
2   The Option will be exercisable by service by the **Granter** on the
     Imposer of an **option notice** at any time after a **trigger event** occurs
     during the **option period** and if it is exercised the **Imposer** will sell
     the **land/demised premises** (release the Right of Way) to the
     Granter at the **purchase price**.
3   The date for completion of the sale (release) pursuant to the exercise
     of the Option will unless otherwise agreed in writing be the first
     Working Day after the expiration of 30 working days from the date the
     purchase price is agreed or determined in accordance with the
     provisions of Schedule 2.

4 [Normal provisions for capacity of transferor, vacant possession, title, deposit if required, existing rights, incorporation of conditions of sale.]

5 [Provision for ascertaining purchase price by valuation of open market value and current use value.]

Form 6.2   Reverse option

This is a form of negative overage allowing the imposer to take back the land at current use value.

1 If the **trigger event** occurs then the **Imposer** will have the option to purchase the **land** or part of it (as the case may be) for an estate in fee simple in possession at the **current use value** [plus one half of the difference between **open market value** and **current use value**][1] at the date of exercise ('**the purchase price**') and on the terms contained in this Deed on exercising the Option.

2 The Option will be exercisable by service by the **Imposer** on the **Granter** of an **option notice** at any time after a **trigger event** occurs during the option period and if it is exercised the **Granter** will sell the land to the **Imposer** for the said estate at the **purchase price**.

3 The date for completion of the sale pursuant to the exercise of the Option will unless otherwise agreed in writing be the first working day after the expiration of 30 working days from the date the **purchase price** is agreed or determined in accordance with the provisions of Schedule 2.

4 [Normal provisions for capacity of transferor, vacant possession, title, deposit if required, existing rights, incorporation of conditions of sale.]

5 [Provision for ascertaining purchase price by valuation of open market value and current use value.]

6 If the **purchase price** is to be determined by a surveyor in accordance with the provisions of Schedule 2 then within the period of 20 working days from the date that such determination is made the **Imposer** will have the right by serving written notice upon the **Granter** to determine the contract then subsisting for the sale of the **land** by reason of the exercise of the Option whereupon such contract will cease and determine but without prejudice to the rights of the parties pursuant to this Deed which shall continue in full force and effect.[2]

---

1 The words in square brackets or some other formula convert negative overage to positive.

2 In the case of a lease the corresponding provision is a landlord's break. If the lease is a business tenancy protected under Part II of the Landlord and Tenant Act 1954 there will need to be a court approval under the Landlord and Tenant Act 1954, s 38(4)(b).

7   EXCESS PAYMENT ON SALE

This form is for use when the terms of sale provide for a basic purchase price payable on transfer of title and a further payment dependent on the actual market at the time the developer resells. It may be used on a residential development where the developer sells in plots. This form is designed for the situation where the developer lays out the plots and provides roads and services up to the plot boundary but does not actually build the houses. (It may do so under another contract with the house buyer.) A different form would be used for sales by a house builder of completed houses in which case there may need to be an estimate of the anticipated threshold selling price of each plot and the overage could be triggered by reference to each plot, or to the total sale proceeds or a combination.

Form 7.1   Excess payment

1   **Overage**

If the **gross revenues** from disposals of the **land** or parts of it exceed pounds (£   ) ('the **threshold sum**') the **Granter** will pay the **Imposer** a further sum equal to [   ]% of the excess receivable on the disposal ('the **overage**').

2   **Gross revenues**

Gross revenues shall subject as below comprise the total of the purchase prices receivable on the disposal of each part of the **land** (or all of it if sold as a whole) to a person who acquires for valuable consideration ('the **buyer**') and so that:

2.1   it is acknowledged that the **Imposer** intends to sell areas laid out as plots ('**plots**') having constructed an accommodation road up to the boundary of each plot and having provided drainage water and electricity up to the boundary of each plot but without having begun the erection of any new buildings or the conversion of existing buildings and the **Granter** agrees with the **Imposer** not to sell the **land** or any part of it or any **plot** without doing so and this agreement is intended to reflect that expenditure but no expenditure on constructing any dwellings.

2.2   In the calculation of the **overage** no deduction will be taken for costs and expenses of sale or taxation or additional expenditure relating to the development of the **land** or any part of it for any other reason save as expressly mentioned below.

2.3   If the price is payable by instalments or part of the price is left outstanding for a period or there are other similar concessions the **overage** will be calculated by reference to the nominal purchase price and no allowance will be made for time of payment being deferred.

2.4   If the **Granter** allows to any **buyer** any special benefit or inducement not related to the disposal of any plot (for example a 'free' holiday) of part of the terms of sale then to the extent that it benefits the **buyer** the cost to the **Granter** of such inducement will be taken into account as shall be appropriate.

3   Connected persons

3.1 If **the buyer** of the **land** or any part of it is connected to the **Granter** then the **Imposer** may require there to be substituted for any actual price the price that could reasonably be expected to be received on a transaction with an unconnected willing buyer by a willing seller in the open market.

3.2 For this purpose a person is connected if he is an associated company or is a shareholder or investor or funder in or of the **Granter** or is a member of the family of such a person or is a company connected with such a person or company or if he (or some connected person) has contractual arrangements with the **Granter** which have given rise to concessionary terms.[1]

4   Payment

4.1 At any time when contracts for the disposal of parts of the **land** have been exchanged for such consideration that on completion the **gross revenues** would exceed the **threshold sum** the **Granter** will give notice in writing to the **Imposer** and the **Granter** will pay the **overage** within 10 days of completion of the sale of any plot whose proceeds are such that when added to the proceeds of previous **plots** the **gross revenues** exceed the **threshold sum** (credit being given for any previous payments).

4.2 When the contract for the last plot is exchanged the **Granter** will give notice in writing to the **Imposer** with the date of completion and proceeds of all sales whether or not the total proceeds will exceed the **threshold sum**.

4.3 Any sum due under this clause will carry interest at a rate equal to 2% above [Bank plc] base rate from time to time from the date 10 days after completion of any relevant sale until payment.

---

1   The parties may wish to include a disputes clause in the event of a difference of view as to whether a person is connected and if so the amount of the open market value. If there is no such provision disputes will be referred to the court or alternative dispute resolution.

Form 7.2   Security

The imposer will want security but this may not be readily available. If the granter is not charging the whole of the land to a bank or other funder then part of it may be available for an equitable charge, which will normally be sufficient, even apart from the doubts about a legal charge securing a future uncertain sum (see **5.4**). There could be such a charge ranking behind a first lender as follows.

Form 7.2(1)   Equitable charge

The **Granter** will provide an equitable charge over one or more **plots** to be approved by the **Imposer** (such approval not to be unreasonably withheld) to secure the **overage** sum and such a charge shall rank behind any sum due to any third party up to the **threshold sum** but in priority to any sum in excess of that.

Form 7.2(2)   Restriction on Register

Alternatively, a restriction may be appropriate, without in this case the need for a deed of covenant.

1   The parties apply to the Chief Land Registrar to enter on the title to the **land** a restriction that except under an order of the Registrar or the Court no disposition of the defined area of the land is to be registered without the consent of the **Imposer**.

2   The defined area will be such one or more **plots** as the **Imposer** from time to time reasonably approves.

3   The **Imposer** will consent to the disposition if either:

3.1 the defined area represents the last **plot** to be sold and the **overage** has been paid; or

3.2 another area reasonably approved by the **Imposer** is substituted for the area released and a like restriction is entered on the Register in relation to that area in which case the **Imposer** will consent on the like terms.

Form 7.2(3)   Solicitor's undertaking

The granter may be prepared to give an instruction to its solicitors to give an undertaking to the imposer's solicitors. The granter's solicitors will need to check that other security documents (including floating charges) permit this and may wish to put a time-limit on it. The solicitors will also need irrevocable confirmation from the granter and all secured funders that they will be instructed on all sales or that if they are replaced the new solicitors will only be instructed on the terms that they give the imposer's solicitors an undertaking in the same terms. As the undertaking may take effect as an appropriation out of a fund comprising the proceeds of sale of a plot it may in law constitute a charge and therefore if the granter is a company the charge will need to be registered at Companies House.

The **Granter** will give an irrevocable instruction to its solicitors to give an irrevocable undertaking to the **Imposer**'s solicitors to hold in their client account a sum from time to time (or a sum derived out of the proceeds of parts of the **land**) to be reasonably approved by the **Imposer**'s solicitors as security for the payment of **overage** and to retain such sum until the **overage** is fully paid.

Form 7.2(4) Costs

The imposer may wish any costs incurred by its solicitors to be covered.

> The **Granter** will in addition to the **overage** pay the reasonable costs of the **Imposer**'s solicitors in relation to any matters under this [*clause*] as they are incurred from time to time.

Index

References are to paragraph numbers and Appendices.

Abandonment of right   6.2.2, 6.8
Access
  see also Airspace; Ransom; Right of way
  common land, public right   6.2.2, 6.9
Adverse possession   6.2.2
Agricultural property
  inheritance tax exemption   10.7.5
Agricultural tenancy   7.2.1
  turnover or corn rent   7.3.4
Airspace   6.1, 6.3, 6.5
  advertising sign, case   6.3
  crane oversail using   6.3
  injunction or damages for invasion
    6.3
  retention of rights over   6.5
Alienation, *see* Freehold land
Assignment of rights   2.1, 2.5, 2.9
  agreement against   2.5.2
  agreement to assign   2.5.6, 2.5.7
  contingent future interest, of   2.5.4
  deed, by   2.5.4, 2.5.7, 11.6
  development agreement   8.2.1, 8.7
  equitable   2.5.3, 2.5.5, 2.5.7, 2.9, 11.6
    formalities   2.5.5
  incomplete, completion of   12.5.3
  legal   2.5.3, 2.5.4
    formalities   2.5.4, 11.6
    non-assignable rights   2.5.2
  present, of future rights (expectancy)
    2.5.6
  promise   2.5.2
Attorney, power of
  equitable mortgage, in   5.10

Back land
  protection of   8.2.2
Bank
  see also Mortgagee/funder
  guarantee   2.3
Bankruptcy, *see* Insolvency
Beneficiary, *see* Trust
Benefit and burden principle   2.4.3,
    3.1.2

Betterment levy   10.6.3
Breach   11.8
Break clause, *see* Lease
Business tenancy
  break clause   7.2.3
  improvements by tenant
    compensation   7.2.1
    rent, effect on   7.3.3
Buyer, *see* Granter

Cable
  right of way for   6.4
Capital gains tax   10.6.7, 10.7, 10.7.2
  base value   10.7.2
  companies   10.7
  disposal method, relevance   10.7
  overage, on   10.7.2
  past use, and   10.7
Case-law
  overage law developing through   12.1
Charge   5.1 *et seq*
  see also Mortgage
  court equitable remedy   12.5.3
  enforceability   2.4.1
  equitable mortgage, treated as   5.10
  legal and equitable distinguished   5.3
  order for sale   5.1
  precedent   App 2
  re-entry right   5.9
  registration
    equitable charge, of, effect   5.4
    priority   5.6
  release   11.7
  transfer of benefit and burden   2.4.1,
    11.6
  use for overage   5.1, 5.4, 5.9, *see also*
    Mortgage
Charity
  gift to, with reverter provision   9.7
  land, alienation restrictions   3.4.2(*C*)
  overage charge   5.11
Chose in action
  assignment   2.5, 2.5.3–2.5.5, 3.1.2

Chose in action – *cont*
  contractual right as   2.5.6
  legal or equitable, overage as   2.5.9
  legal right to overage payment as   2.5,
    2.5.3, 2.5.4
Clawback
  see also Public sector overage
  meaning   1.3, 10.1
Club   9.6
Commercial vehicle   9.1 *et seq*
  see also Company; Partnership; Trust
  result of putting land into   9.1
Common land   6.2.2, 6.9
Common law   4.5, 4.10
Common rights   6.9
Company
  dissolution   2.2, 9.8.2
  liquidation   2.2
  subsidiary   2.3, 9.9.2
    partnership of subsidiaries   9.3
  taxation   10.7
  trustee as   9.9.2
  use for overage   9.1, 9.2, 11.5.2
    articles of association   9.2.1
    class rights   9.2.3
    directors' powers   9.2.2
    imposer and granter as
      shareholders   9.2.1–9.2.3
    method   9.2.1
    restriction on register, use with
      9.2.3
    stalemate situation   9.2.3
    suitability   9.2.3
Compensation
  see also Damages
  compulsory acquisition of rights   6.4
  improvements (lease), for   7.2.1, 7.3.3
  modification or discharge of restriction,
    on   4.9, 11.4.2
  Part VI claims   10.6
  percentage of development profits,
    cases   11.4.2
  ransom right infringement, for   6.10
Compulsory acquisition
  compensation   6.4, 6.12, 10.2.2,
    11.4.2
  code for   11.4.1
  relevant percentage   11.4, 11.4.1
  right of way over common land, *see*
    Right of way
Conditional contract   1.4, 2.5.10, 8.5
Conditional fee/interest   3.3.1, 9.8.2
  condition or trigger event   9.8.2

condition precedent or subsequent
  9.8.2
  determinable interest distinguished
    9.8.2
Conflicting interests in land   1.9, *see
    also* Mortgagee/funder
Constructive or resulting trust   12.5.3
Contingent future interest
  assignment of   2.5.4
  overage is   2.5.4, 3.4.7, 5.4, 9.8.3,
    12.5.1
    control by law   12.8, *see also*
      Perpetuities rule
    present right of property   12.6
    valuation   12.6
Contingent interest
  vested interest contrasted   9.8.3
Contract   2.1 *et seq*
  benefit and burden principle   2.4.3,
    3.1.2
  conditional, *see* Conditional contract
  forms, *see* Positive covenant; Promise to
    pay
  new, *see* Novation
  obligation transfer   2.4
  third party benefit   2.5.3, 2.5.8, 2.5.9
    contractual right as 'property'   2.5.8
    enforcement of contract   2.5.9
  void for remoteness   2.6
  wager, as   2.7
Costs   11.4.4
Court attitude   4.6, 11.5.1, 12.3, 12.5
Court jurisdiction
  damages, *see* Damages
  equitable   12.5.2, *see also* Equity
Covenant
  construction of   4.7
  control of planning process, for
    11.5.3
  indemnity   11.6
  lease, in, *see* Lease
  payment in respect of, tax on   10.7.2
  personal   8.2.2
  positive, *see* Positive covenant
  restrictive, *see* Restrictive covenant
  rules for   3.1.2
  successive owners, whether binds,
    general rule   3.1.2
  tenure, by reason of   3.1.2
  'touching and concerning the land'
    3.1.2, 3.2.4

Crown   10.1
    see also Public sector overage
    fee simple held from   3.3, 10.3.1
    planning consent exemption   11.2.1
    reclaiming land, historical   10.1
Current use value   11.2.3, 11.3.2, 12.6,
    12.10

Damages
    court power   4.10, 6.3, 6.9, 7.2.2,
    12.5.3
        amount   12.5.3
        insufficient   11.7, *see also* Injunction
    obstruction of right of way   6.8
    ransom infringement, amount for
        6.10
    relevant percentage   11.4
    sporting rights, loss of   6.9
Death
    granter, of   2.2
    inheritance tax   10.7.5
    transfer of rights on   2.5.1
Debt, contract
    legal right to overage as   2.5.4
    promise to pay as   2.1
Deed
    assignment by   2.5.4, 2.5.7, 11.6
    conveyance by   12.5.1
Default   11.8
Definitions   1.3, App 2
Delay
    effect of   4.10, 4.12
    injunction grant, and   6.3
Derivatives   8.7, 12.6
Determinable interest   3.3.2, 9.8.2
    conditional interest distinguished
        9.8.2
    trigger event, effect of   9.8.2
    vested interest   9.8.3
Development
    costs   11.4.4
    covenant against, *see* Restrictive
        covenant
    lease   7.3.3, 7.5
    option, *see* Option
    parties opposed to   11.5.3
    restrictions, *see* Planning permission;
        Restrictive covenant
    value, *see* Development value   11.2,
        11.3.3
Development gains tax   10.6.4, 10.6.6

Development land tax   10.6.5, 10.6.7
Development value   11.2, 11.3.3
    current use value distinguished
        11.2.3, 11.3.2, 11.3.3, 12.10
    'relevant percentage'   11.4
        approach to, general   11.4.1
        case examples   11.4.2
        successive tranches approach
            11.4.3
    splitting between payer and recipient
        11.4, 12.6
        proportion as overage payment
            11.4.1, 11.4.2
    taxation   10.6, 10.6.2, 10.6.7
Director, *see* Company
Disposal
    overage as, for CGT   10.7.2
Disputes procedure   11.8
Document(s)
    see also Drafting issues
    payment arrangements   11.7
    trust, for   9.9.1
Drafting issues   11.5–11.8
    commercial needs of party   11.5.2
    cumulative overage   11.2.3
    disguising overage   11.5.1
    intention to provide for overage
        11.5.1, 12.9
    long-term arrangements and unforeseen
        change   11.5.2
    payment arrangements   11.6
    physical realities   11.5.2
    precedents   App 2
    squatter, binding   11.2.2
    trigger event, *see* Trigger event
    veto rights, importance of   11.5.2

Easement
    constraints   6.8
    transfer   11.6
Electricity
    services   6.4
        pylons   6.5
Enfranchisement   7.4, 7.4.2
Enlargement   7.4, 7.4.1
Equitable assignment, *see* Assignment of
    rights
Equitable estoppel   12.5.3
Equitable interest
    overage as   2.6, 12.5.1
    security protecting overage   12.5.2

Equitable jurisdiction of court   12.5.2
Equitable lease   7.5.2
Equity   12.5–12.5.3
    incomplete overage, completion of
        12.5.3
    restrictive covenant operates in   4.10
Estate rentcharge   3.2
    equitable charge   3.2.4
    methods   3.2.1
    no interest in land required   3.2.2
    property right, as   3.2.2
    rent, as type of   3.2.2
    rent service contrasted   3.2.2
    use   3.2.3
        overage, for   3.2.4
        positive covenant, for   3.2.3
Estovers, right of   6.9
Examples   App 1
Expectancy
    assignment   2.5.6
Expenditure
    reimbursement of   11.4.4

Farm business tenancy
    improvements by tenant
        compensation for   7.2.1, 7.3.3
        rent, effect on   7.3.3
Fee farm   10.3.2
Fee simple, *see* Freehold
Fees
    reimbursement for   11.4.4
First refusal   7.4.2, 8.6
    not interest in land   8.6
Forfeiture   3.3.2
Forms of overage   1.6, 1.7, 2.1, App 2
    see also Negative overage; Positive
        overage
    no unified set of rules   1.7
Freedom of disposition
    conflicting interpretations   12.7
Freehold
    'conditional fee'   3.3.1
    Crown, fee simple held from   3.3,
        10.3.1
    freely alienable rule   3.1.2, 3.4.2,
        10.3.2
        exceptions, *see* Restriction (Land
            Register); Unregistered land
    origins   3.1.4, 3.1.5
    laws, background   3.1.3, 3.1.4
        Medieval 'infeudation'   3.1.3
        Quia Emptores 1290   3.1.4, 3.1.5

movable   6.2
peaceful enjoyment   10.3.2
positive covenants, and successive
    owners   3.1.1, 3.1.2
rent, at   10.3.2
tenant acquiring   7.4
Future interest, *see* Contingent future
    interest

Government department   2.2, 10.1, *see
    also* Public sector overage
Granter   1.3
    company   2.2
    creditworthiness   2.2, 2.3
    death   2.2
    individual   2.2
    promise to pay, liability on   2.2
Grazing, right of   6.9
Guarantee   2.3
    variations, effect on   2.3

Hereditament   12.5.1
Highway
    see also Subsoil
    road construction, financing   10.1
Human rights
    Crown restraint on transfer, effect on
        10.3.2

Imposer   1.3
Improvement lease   7.1, 7.3.2, 7.4.2
Improvements
    leasehold property   7.2.1, 7.3.3
        meaning   7.2.1, 7.3.3
        rent, and, *see* Rent
    trust land   9.9.4
Income tax   10.7, 10.7.3
Incorporeal hereditament   12.5.1
Incorporeal right   12.5.1
Indemnity   2.3
Inheritance tax   10.7, 10.7.5
    outline   10.7.5
Injunction
    damages instead   4.10, 6.3, 6.9, 7.2.2
    discretion of court   6.3
    jurisdiction, nature of   12.5.2, 12.5.3
    likelihood of, and development value
        split   11.4.1
    ransom case   11.5.1
    remedy   11.8

Injunction – *cont*
  restrictive covenant in lease, to
    enforce   7.2.2
  right of way, to preserve   6.8
Insolvency
  granter, of   2.2
Intention of overage arrangement
  documents to make clear   11.5.1, 12.9
Intermediate lease   7.5.1
Investment
  overage as vehicle for   12.10
  overage land as   11.2.3
Investment lease   7.3.3

Joint ownership
  overage viewed as   12.5, 12.6
Joint venture   9.1, 9.4, 12.5.3

Laches doctrine   4.10, 6.3
Land
  enforcement of rights against   2.4
  interest in   2.5.2, 2.5.7
Land charge, *see* Unregistered land
Landlord, *see* Lease
Lands Tribunal
  awards   6.10
  modification or discharge of
    covenant   11.8
  compensation   4.9
  lease, in   7.2
  scope   4.8
Law
  see also Case law; Legal background
  development of   12.1, 12.7
  influences   12.2
  obstacles for overage   12.7
  reform, need for   12.9
  statutory provisions, interpretation for
    overage   12.4
Law Commission   3.1.5, 12.1, 12.8
Lease   7.1 *et seq*
  assignment   11.6
    consent   7.3.2
    enforcement of terms after   2.4.1
  block of flats   7.4.2
  break clause   7.2, 7.2.3
    registration   7.2.3
  consent for improvements   7.2.1
  covenants   3.1.1, 3.1.2, 7.1 *et seq*
    enforcement   7.2.2, 7.3.1, 7.5.1
    enlargement into freehold   3.1.2

money payment   7.3.1
  release   7.4.2
  rent or premium payments   3.1.2
  see also 'positive covenant' and
    'restrictive covenant' below
development lease   7.3.3, 7.5
enfranchisement   7.4, 7.4.2
  effect on overage   7.4.2
  first refusal rights   7.4.2
  flats   7.4.2
  origins and workings of   7.4.2
enlargement   7.4, 7.4.1
  overage protections   7.4.1
equitable lease   7.5.2, 12.5.2
  leading case (*Walsh v Lonsdale*)
    7.5.2
farmland   7.2.1
fines   7.3.2
flexibility of   7.6
forfeiture and relief of court   3.3.2
freehold acquisition by tenant   7.4–
  7.4.3, 7.6, 11.7
  agreement, by   7.4.3
  statutory, *see* 'enfranchisement' and
    enlargement' *above*
grant as trigger event   11.2.3
improvement lease   7.1, 7.3.2, 7.4.2
improvements   7.3.2, 7.3.3, 7.6
  compensation   7.2.1
intermediate lease, use of   7.5.1
  covenants securing overage   7.5.1
  trigger event, provision for merger
    on   7.5.1
investment lease   7.3.3
legal nature   3.1.2
long lease   7.3.2, 7.4
  institutional landlord, from   7.3.3
mining   7.3.4
negative overage, for   7.1, 7.2, 7.2.1
occupation lease   7.3.2
positive covenant   7.2, 7.2.2
positive overage, for   7.1, 7.2.2, 7.3
  capital payment   7.3.1
  extra rent   7.3
  'tenant covenant'   7.3.1
  uses   7.3
precedent   App 2
premium   3.1.2, 7.3.2
  income tax   10.7.3
re-entry right   7.2.2
  leave of court   7.2
  relief of court   7.2

Lease – *cont*
  rent, *see* Rent
  repairing covenant   7.2
  restrictive covenant   4.6, 7.2
  secure tenancy, *see* Secure tenancy
  trust, under   9.9.1, 9.9.4
  use for overage   7.1, 7.3, 7.5, 7.6
Legal background
  ancient   1.5
  fast development of present law   1.10
  long leases   1.5
  not legally mature   1.7
  recent   1.4, 12.7
Levy, betterment   10.6.3
Light, right of   6.7
Limitation
  effect   2.6
  mortgage money   5.8
Limited liability partnership
  use for overage   9.5
Liquidation
  granter, of   2.2
Local authority
  see also Public sector overage
  development agreement, and   8.2.2
  human rights restrictions   10.3.2
  positive covenant imposition   3.1.2
Local planning authority, *see* Planning gain
  agreement; Planning permission
Long-term   11.5.2

Manorial waste   6.2.2
Market value
  meaning   1.3, 11.3.2
  sale price less than   11.2.3
Marketability   1.9
Mineral rights
  airspace created by excavation,
    ownership of   6.6
  natural support of surface   6.6
  reservation of   6.6
    scope of grant   6.6
  termination of lease   8.5
Mining lease   7.3.4
  rent and royalties   7.3.4
Mortgage   5.1 *et seq*
  agreement to grant in future   5.3,
    12.5.2
  'all monies due'   5.4
  charge distinguished   5.2
  contingent future liability   5.4
    present value of   5.4, 5.12

  deed   5.2, 5.8, 5.10
  definition   5.2
  discharge, court discretionary power
    5.5
  equitable   5.3, 5.4, 5.10
    conversion to legal   5.4
    power of attorney with   5.10
  equitable lease distinguished   7.5.2
  'irredeemable'   5.5
  legal   5.2, 5.3, 5.10
  limitation   5.8
  mortgagee's powers, *see* Mortgagee/
    funder
  perpetuities rule   5.8
  priority   5.3, 5.6, 5.12
    deed of priority   5.6
    general rule   5.6
    restriction to protect   5.6
  redemption   5.5
    legal redemption date   5.5, 5.8
  relief from foreclosure   5.5, 5.9
    double overage   5.9
  remedies of mortgagee, *see* Mortgagee/
    funder
  transfer   11.6
  uncertain future liability   5.4
  use for overage   5.1, 5.4, 5.5, 5.10
    involvement of mortgagee   5.7
    modification of leasing power   5.7
    trigger event   5.5, 5.8
Mortgagee/funder
  attitude to overage devices   3.3.3,
    3.4.6, 5.6, 5.12
  leasing, power   5.7
  sale, power of   5.1, 5.3, 5.8, 5.10

Nationalisation of betterment   10.6
  betterment levy   10.6.3
  development gains tax   10.6.4, 10.6.6
  development land tax   10.6.5, 10.6.7
  development value   10.6, 10.6.2,
    10.6.7
Negative overage
  assignment of fruits of   2.5.6
  lease for, *see* Lease
  meaning   1.3, 1.6
  no specific intention to deal   11.5.1
  ransom as   6.1, *see also* Ransom
  re-entry rights   3.3.1, 3.3.3
  relevant percentage in cases of   11.4.1
  situations for use   1.6

Negotiable instrument
  use of   2.5.10
Negotiation, *see* Drafting issues
Non-party, *see* Third party
Notice
  restrictive covenant, of   4.11
Novation   2.4.2

Option   8.1 *et seq*
  CGT on payment for   10.7.2
  common form   8.5
  conditional   8.3, 8.5, 8.6
    conditional contract compared   8.5
  derivatives   8.7
  development agreement   1.4, 8.1, 8.2,
    8.6
    agreement contents   8.2.1
    assignment   8.2.1, 8.7
    back land   8.2.2
    obligations   8.2.1
    overage, place in   8.2.2, 8.8
    planning authority requirements
      8.2.2
    planning consent   8.2.1, 8.2.2
    sale price   8.2.1, 8.2.2
  fee   8.2.1
  formalities   8.5
  freehold acquisition   7.4.3
  legal nature of   8.5
  perpetuity period   8.4, 8.6
  precedent   App 2
  pre-emption distinguished, *see* Pre-
    emption right
  repurchase   3.1.5
  reverse option   1.6, 8.4, 8.8
  share option   8.7
  'take' option   8.1
  time-limit   8.3
  transfer   11.6
    deed of covenant on   11.6
  use for overage   8.1, 8.8
  wager, as   2.7
Overage
  meaning   1.1, 1.3
  nature of   12.5
Overage owner
  breach by   11.8
Overreaching
  beneficial interest, of   11.5.3
  overage of, by purchaser   12.5.3
Oversail   6.3

Partnership
  corporate form, *see* Limited liability
    partnership
  definition   9.3
  limited   9.3
  subsidiary companies in, overage
    arrangements   9.3
  use for overage   9.1, 9.3, 11.5.2
  suitability   9.3
Payment   11.2.3, 11.4.1
  arrangements   11.7
  dispute   11.8
  fixed price   11.3.1
  gross or net   11.3.2
  positive overage, considerations for
    11.3, 12.9
  release or receipt on   11.7
  tax on, *see* Tax
Penalty
  contract void for unreasonable   2.8,
    3.2.4
Perpetuities rule   2.6, 3.1.5, 4.10, 12.8
  break clause in lease, not subject to
    7.2.3
  contingent and vested interests,
    distinction   9.8.3
  fee simple   3.3.1, 10.3.1
  mortgage, not subject to   5.8
  option to reacquire land, period of
    8.4, 8.6
  overage, application to   12.8
  pre-emption right   8.6
  reform of rule proposed   3.1.5, 12.8
Personal overage   2.5.2
Pipe
  right of way for   6.4
Planning agreement
  development option agreement
    provision   8.2.1
Planning control, *see* Planning permission
Planning gain agreement   10.4, 10.5
  's 106 agreement'   10.5, 11.4.4,
    11.5.3
    enforceability   11.5.3
    parties   11.5.3
Planning permission
  applicant   7.2.1, 8.6, 11.5.3
  attaches to land   2.4.3
  background   10.6.1, 10.6.2
    betterment levy   10.6.3
    development value   10.6, 10.6.2
  brownfield sites   12.2

Planning permission – *cont*
  control over process, provision in
    agreement for   11.5.3
  costs of obtaining   11.4.4, 11.5.3
  detailed   11.2.1
  development or material change in use,
    for   10.6.1
  effect on land value   1.4, 11.2, 11.2.1
    development option, valuation for
      8.2.1, 8.2.2
    grant or implementation
      distinguished   11.2, 11.2.2
  enforcement period where failure to
    obtain   11.2.1
  exemptions   11.2.1
  further value from later consent
    11.2.4
  imposition on, *see* Planning gain
    agreement
  interest contingent on grant of   9.8.3,
    see also Contingent future interest
  leases
    improvement, as   7.2.1, 7.3.3
    restrictions in   7.2
  more dwellings than agreement states,
    effect of   11.3.1
  outline   11.2.1
  overage payment, and   11.2, 11.2.1
  permitted development   10.6.1, 11.2.1
Positive covenant   3.1 *et seq*, 12.5.2
  binding successive owners   3.1.2, 4.1
  burden of   2.4.3, 3.1.2
  lease, in, *see* Lease
  nature and use of   3.1.1, 3.5
  overage obligation   3.1.2, 3.2.4, 4.7
  precedent   App 2
  re-entry right, use for performance
    3.3.3, 3.5
  rentcharge, use for performance
    3.2.3, 3.5
  restriction, use for, *see* Restriction (Land
    Register)
  restrictive contrasted   4.7
  'touching and concerning the land'
    3.1.2, 3.2.4
Positive overage
  assignment of fruits of   2.5.6
  breach, remedy   11.8
  lease for, *see* Lease
  meaning   1.3, 1.6
  payment method and calculation
    11.3, 11.5.1

  situations for use   1.6
  trigger event, *see* Trigger event
Powers
  checking limits and restrictions   1.9
Pre-emption right   8.1, 8.6
  assignment   8.6
  conditional   8.6
    whether condition in control of
      owner   8.5, 8.6
  legal nature of   8.6
  option distinguished   8.2.2, 8.4, 8.6
    case, option taking precedence   8.6
  perpetuity period   8.6
  registration   8.6
  trigger event   8.6
Premium (lease)   3.1.2, 7.3.2
  income tax   10.7.3
Prescriptive rights   6.2.2, 6.2.3
Price of land
  effect on   1.9
  factors   11.3.2
  local authority sale   10.3.4
  market value, less than   11.2.3
  'relevant percentage', *see* Development
    value
  stamp duty, and contingency
    principle   10.7.1
Principles   12.1, 12.9
Privatisation   10.3.3
Promise to pay
  see also Assignment of rights; Contract;
    Positive covenant
  assignment   11.6
  drafting   App 2
  equitable rules govern   12.5.2
  form of overage   2.1, 2.5.7
  perpetuity period   2.6
  promisor's liability   2.2
  release   11.7
  suitability and limitations   2.2, 2.9
Property
  overage as right of   12.6
  scope   12.5
Public house
  barrelage, rent by reference to   7.3.4
Public sector overage   10.1 *et seq*
  'clawback', use in   1.3, 10.2.2, 10.3.3
  Crown disposal and re-entry   3.3.1,
    10.3.1
    restraint on transfer   10.3.2
  development value, methods for share
    in   10.4

Public sector overage – *cont*
  development value, methods for share in
    – *cont*
    nationalisation, *see* Nationalisation of
      betterment
    planning gain agreement 10.4,
      10.5
    taxation 10.1, 10.4
  disposal by public body 10.1 *et seq*
    guidance 10.2.2
    rules for 10.3
  Herstmonceux case and report
    following 10.2.1
  privatisation 10.3.3
  special rules 1.8, 10.3
  taxation, *see* Tax
  ultra vires rule, and local councils
    10.3.4
  price 10.3.4
Public sector tenancy 7.2.1

Quarry 7.3.4, 8.5

Ransom 6.1 *et seq*
  access for repairs etc 6.3
  airspace, *see* Airspace
  compensation for infringement,
    calculation of 6.10
  dominant overage land 6.2–6.7
  forms 6.1
  injunction, grant of 11.5.1
  licence or lease of 6.2.2, 6.2.3
  light 6.7
  meaning and nature of 6.1
  pipes and cables 6.4
  prescriptive rights 6.2.2, 6.2.3
  release 11.7
  right of way 6.1, 6.2.3, 6.8
    cases on use of 6.2.3
    express, wording for 6.2.3
    implied 6.2.3
    obstruction of, basis of damages
      6.8
    overage land, over 6.8
    statutory provision, under 6.2.3
  rights of owner 6.1 *et seq*
    injunction or damages 6.3, 6.4
    level of compensation 6.10
  servient overage land 6.8
  sporting rights 6.1, 6.9
    development prevented by 6.9

strip 1.6, 4.5.3, 6.1, 6.2
  active management or occupation
    required 6.2.2
  common land 6.2.2
  position of 6.2.1
  'ransoming the ransom' 6.2
  squatter taking over 6.2.2
  transfer 11.6
  use of 6.2
  value of 11.4.1, 11.4.2
subsoil, *see* Subsoil
use for overage, overview 6.1, 6.11
value uplift from 11.2.1
Re-entry right 3.1.2, 3.3
  assignment 11.6
  chargee's right 5.9
  conditional or determinable interest,
    with 9.8.2
  Crown 3.3.1, 10.3.1
  forfeiture
    distinguished 3.3.2
    relief 12.5.2
  freehold subject to 3.3.1–3.3.3, 9.8.2
  exercise of right, period for 3.3.3
    funders, attitude of 3.3.3
    perpetuity period 3.3.1, 10.3.1
    vested interest 9.8.3
  lease, in 7.2, 7.2.2
  origins for freehold land 3.1.5
  refusal to pay overage, on 9.8.2
  release 11.7
  relief of court 3.3.2, 3.3.3
    leasehold, for 7.2
    overage, application to 3.3.3
  rentcharge, annexed to 3.3.3
  when arises 3.3.1, 3.3.2
Registered land
  see also Restriction (Land Register)
  notice on Register 4.11
Release
  see also Restrictive covenant
  payment, on 11.7
Relevant percentage, *see* Development
  value
Remedy 11.8, 12.5.3
  equitable 12.5.3
Rent
  capitalising 11.2.3
  development lease, in 7.3.3
  'fines', historical background 7.3.2
  improvements, effect on 7.6
    assured tenancy 7.3.3

Rent – *cont*
  improvements, effect on – *cont*
    farm business tenancy   7.3.3
    secure tenancy   7.2.1, 7.3.3
    overage payment, as   7.3–7.3.4
    enforceability   7.3.4
    review   7.3.2, 7.3.3
    turnover   7.3.4
    'usual'   7.3.2
Rentcharge   3.1.2
  see also Estate rentcharge
  assignment   11.6
  legal interest   12.5.2
  origins   3.1.5
  prohibition on new   3.1.5
  release   11.7
  unsuitable for overage   3.1.5, 3.2.4
Rent service   3.2.2, 10.3.2
Repairing covenant (lease)   7.2
Repurchase option   3.1.5
Restriction (Land Register)   2.4.2, 3.1.2,
    3.4
  alienation fetter, as   3.4.2(*A*)
  assignment, and consent to   11.6
  charity land   3.4.2(*C*)
  equitable interest, protection of
    12.5.2
  overage, application to   3.4.2–3.4.7,
    3.5
    court approach   3.4.7
    expense, practicalities of   3.4.5
    Land Registry Practice leaflet
      3.4.2(*F*)
    mortgagee, position of   3.4.6
    name of overage owner on register
      3.4.4
  priority of charge, use to protect   5.6
  release   11.7
  restrictive covenant, for   4.2
  statutory provision   3.4.2(*A*), 3.4.4
  trusts and settlements, relates to
    3.4.2(*E*)
  trust land   3.4.2(*D*), (*E*), 3.4.7, 9.9.4,
    9.10
  use of   3.4.1
Restrictions on use of overage   1.5, 1.9,
    2.2
  examples   1.9
Restrictive covenant   1.6, 2.4.1, 4.1 *et*
    seq
  advantages   4.3
  assignment   11.6, *see also*
      Assignment of rights

  background   4.4
  benefiting land, significance   4.4, 4.5,
      4.6, 4.12
    enforcement where no land to
        benefit   4.5.1
    Highway Authority taking over land,
        cases   4.5.3
    land to benefit   4.5.2, 4.5.3
    ransom strip, combined with   4.5.3
    road, whether satisfactory support
        4.5.3
  breach by later owner, restraining   4.1
  cash benefit   4.6, 4.8
    settling for, effect of   4.6
  common law   4.5, 4.10
  damages instead of specific
      performance   4.10
  delay, effect of   4.10, 4.12
  development, against, re-entry relief on
      breach   3.3.3
  discharge or variation, *see* 'release or
      variation' *below*
  discretion of court   4.6, 4.10
  equitable nature of   4.10
  fetter on ownership, whether is   12.5
  form less important than substance
      4.7
  impedes reasonable use   4.8
  injunction, enforcement by   4.4, 4.5.1,
      4.6
  lease, in, *see* Lease
  not to apply for planning permission
      11.5.3
  obsolete, ground for discharge   4.8
  overage, use for   4.1 *et seq*, 4.12
    form of covenant   4.2
    legal analysis   4.1
    sale of part   4.5.2
    wording to annexe benefit   4.5.2
  payment on release, contract to pay share
      from   2.5.6
  positive, construed as   4.7
  precedent   App 2
  protection   4.11
  re-entry rights   3.3.1, 3.3.3
  release or relaxation   4.2, 4.6, 4.7,
      4.11
    compensation   4.9, 11.4.2
    court approach   12.4
    discretion   4.12
    effect on value   11.2
    grounds   4.8

Restrictive covenant – *cont*
   restriction on Register, supported by
      4.2
   'restrictive', must be   4.7
   variation, *see* 'release or relaxation'
      above
Reverse option   8.4, 8.8
Reverse overage   1.6, 4.11
Reverter   9.7
Right of way
   compulsory acquisition over common
      land   6.2.2
     scale of charges   11.4.2
   conditional on acceptance of
      obligation   2.4.3, 3.1.2
   express, drafting of   6.2.3
   interference as nuisance   6.8
   overage land, to protect   6.8
   ransom, as   6.1, 6.2.3

Sale
   see also Price of land
   developer, by, excess payment on
      App 2
Secure tenancy   7.2.1
   improvements   7.2.1
   right to buy, and overage   7.4.3
Security
   legal nature of   12.5.2
   overage as   12.5.2, 12.6
   priorities and problems, outline   1.9
   types   12.6
Seller, *see* Imposer
Services
   compulsory procedure for statutory
      undertakers   6.4
   right of way for   6.4, 6.6
Settlement   3.4.2(*A*), (*D*), 9.8.2
Shares
   close company   10.6.6
   company used for overage   9.2.1
   transfer   11.6
Sharing arrangement
   uplift, in   2.3
Shopping centre
   rent holiday at start   11.2.3
   turnover rents   7.3.4
Short-term   11.3.1, 11.4.3
Site reverter   9.7
Solicitor
   undertaking   2.3
Specific performance   12.5.3

Sporting rights   6.1, 6.9
   injunction or damages for loss   6.9
   overage, reservation for   6.9
Squatter   11.2.2
Stamp duty   10.7, 10.7.1
   overage, and contingency principle
      10.7.1
State, *see* Public sector overage
Striking off of company   2.2
Sublease
   grant as trigger event   11.2.3
Subsoil
   injunction for owner   6.4
   ownership retained   6.6
Successive owners, *see* Third party

Tax   10.1 *et seq*
   advantages from use of trust   9.9.3
   'clawback'   10.1
   companies   10.7
   development land, on   10.1, 10.4,
      10.6, 10.7
     betterment levy   10.6.3
     current tax on   10.7, *see also*
      Capital gains tax
     development gains tax   10.6.4,
      10.6.6
     development land tax   10.6.5,
      10.6.7
     development value   10.6, 10.6.2,
      10.6.7, 10.7
     disadvantages of special taxes
      10.6.7
   income tax   10.7, 10.7.3
   inheritance tax   10.7, 10.7.5
   stamp duty   10.7.1
   VAT   10.7
Telephone line   6.4
Tenancy in common   9.10
Tenant, *see* Lease
Third party
   contract benefit, *see* Contract
   guarantor, *see* Guarantee
   indemnifier, *see* Indemnity
   obligation, imposition on   2.4, *see*
     also Novation
   positive covenant binds   3.1.1, *see*
     also Positive covenant
Trade, adventure in nature of
   income tax   10.7.3

Transfer of rights
  see also Assignment of rights
  benefit   2.5, 11.6
    automatic   2.5.1
  burden   2.4, 11.6
  untransferable overage   2.5.2
Trespass
  airspace, in   6.3
Trigger event
  see also Planning permission
  choice   11.2.4
  meaning   1.3, 11.2
  sale or lease grant as   11.2.3
Trust
  see also Trust of land
  alienation restrictions for land
    3.4.2(*D*), 3.4.3
  appropriation and partition, provision
    for   9.9.5
  beneficiary
    consultation with   9.9.3
    interest of   3.4.2(*A*), 9.9.5, 9.10,
      12.6
    land released to   9.9.5
    overage owner as   9.9.4, 9.9.5
    planning agreement, not parties to
      11.5.3
    transfer of interest   11.6
  charge on land   5.11
  collective investment scheme   9.9.3
  constructive   12.5.3
    proprietary estoppel distinguished
      12.5.3
  declaration of   2.5.5
  equitable nature of   12.5.2
  implied   12.5.3
  present or future interests   9.8.3
  purchaser, position of   9.8.2
  resulting   12.5.3
  sale of land under   9.8.2, 9.9.4
  successive or joint interests   9.8.2,
    9.8.3, 9.10
    imposer and granter shares   9.10
  tenancy in common   9.10
  use for overage purposes   9.1, 9.8, 9.9
    documentation   9.9.1
    limitation arrangement   9.8.1
    tax advantages   9.9.3
    trustees, *see* Trustee
  vested and contingent interests
    distinguished   9.8.3
Trust corporation   9.8.3, *see also*
  Trustee

Trust of land   3.4.2(*D*), 3.4.7, 9.8.2
  conversion of trust for sale into   9.8.2
  determinable interest, land held on
    9.8.2
  equitable interest, overreaching of
    9.10
  family charge   5.4, 5.11
  restriction of Register, need for
    3.4.2(*A*), (*D*), 9.9.4, 9.10
  sale or other dealing under   9.9.4,
    9.10
  trustee powers   9.9.4, 9.9.5, 9.10
Trustee
  administrative powers   9.9.4
  agent, acting through   9.9.4
  charging trust land   5.11
  company as   9.9.2
  delegation by   9.9.3
  granter, as   2.2, 9.9.2
  identity and number of   9.9.2
  imposer holding overage payment as
    2.5.5, 5.11
  management   9.9.3, 9.9.4
  powers   9.9.4, 9.9.5
  procedure   9.9.3
  remuneration   9.9.3
  restrictions on   1.9, 5.11
  sole   9.8.2, 9.9.2
  unanimity, circumstances for   9.9.3
Turnover rent   7.3.4

Undertaking   2.3
Unincorporated association   9.6
Unregistered land
  caution against first registration   3.4.3
  land charge, registration of   4.11
  overage, no restriction possible for
    3.4.3
Use, change of
  material, for planning consent   10.6.1
  overage linked to   11.2

Value
  additional   12.4, 12.5.3
    division of   11.3
  development value, *see* Development
    value
  market, *see* Market value
  marriage, adjoining properties   11.3.2
  maximising   11.5.3
  overage right, of   12.6

Value – *cont*
   realisation   11.2.3
   terms, various   1.3
   uplift in   11.2
     planning consent, *see* Planning
      permission
Value added tax   10.7, 10.7.4
   Capital Goods Scheme   10.7.4
   outline   10.7.4
Variation
   restrictive covenant, of, *see* Restrictive
     covenant
Vested interest   9.8.3
Veto rights   11.5.2

Void contract
   penalty, *see* Penalty
   remoteness   2.6

Wager
   circumstances of   2.7
Wastes   10.1
   manorial   6.2.2

Yacht moorings
   turnover rent   7.3.4